THE LAST CHOPPER

OTHER BOOKS BY WELDON A. BROWN

Empire or Independence: A Study in the Failure of Reconciliation (1941)

The Common Cause: Collectivism Menace or Challenge (1949)

Democracy: Man's Great Opportunity (1949)

Prelude to Disaster: The American Role in Vietnam, 1940-1963 (1975)

THE
LAST
CHOPPER

The Denouement of the
American Role in Vietnam,
1963–1975

by

Weldon A. Brown

Author of
Prelude to Disaster: The American Role
in Vietnam 1940–1963

National University Publications
KENNIKAT PRESS / 1976
Port Washington, N. Y. / London

Manufactured in the United States of America

Published by
Kennikat Press Corp.
Port Washington, N.Y./London

Library of Congress Cataloging in Publication Data

Brown, Weldon Amzy.
    The last chopper.

    (National university publications)
    Bibliography: p.
    Includes index.
    1. Vietnamese Conflict, 1961–1975–United States.
I. Title.
DS558.B76   959.704'3373   76-000001
ISBN 0-8046-9121-5

To El Rita Wachs Brown,
whose high sense of honor, integrity,
and enduring affection have always
spurred my noblest efforts

CONTENTS

PREFACE

Alas, "A policeman's lot is not a happy one."

In behalf of freedom, justice, and humanity, "the momentum of our good intentions," wrote one student, carried us from Eisenhower to Johnson into a bog that no one seemed to want us to enter, but no one appeared able to avoid. By our often instant reaction to specific events, such as the attacks on the destroyer *Maddox* in Tonkin Gulf, we found ourselves dragged deeper into the quicksand of a land war in Asia. In spite of presidential promises—"We are not about to send American boys nine or ten thousand miles away from home to do what Asian boys ought to be doing for themselves"—events pushed us along. Shortly after the election of 1964, it was painfully obvious that Saigon was losing the war, that the Communists would achieve an open military victory within six months, as General Westmoreland repeated in early 1965, unless mighty reinforcements of combat troops and material assistance came from America. Facing the only two real choices he had—withdrawal or warfare—the president decided to fight. Johnson's objective was not conquest, occupation, or the destruction of North Vietnam. He meant only to invest enough force against the enemy to persuade him to cease his effort to conquer South Vietnam and to leave its people alone to govern themselves. *That was our war aim.*

Once that hard decision was made, the Pentagon and the generals in the field immediately pressed for the men and material needed to check Ho Chi Minh. Between the hawks and the doves thus began a struggle. One group, by increased force, the other, by negotiation, sought to persuade the enemy to abandon his effort to conquer the South. The stony responses of Hanoi, Moscow, Peking, and the Vietcong made easier the cause of the hawks. However, Johnson did not wish to risk a third world war and went far to reassure China, Russia, and others that he meant to limit our military response to Indochina alone. Limited warfare was not popular with extreme hawks, for it barred quick victory, allowed the enemy time to adjust and prepare and perhaps prolong the war, and cost us more in lives and money. As our involvement grew, the administration sought with little success to silence partisan opposition to the war by declaring to one and all: "Those aren't Republican or Democratic boys over there fighting. Those are American boys and this is an American war."

As the rhetoric of the war rose in intensity, objectivity vanished. Passionate defense or vicious denunciation polarized the debate about the war. In Congress, the press, the forum, the classroom, and on the campus, as well as on the street, people gathered mainly to denounce it, and as time passed few could defend it. Within a few decades it will not be easy, if at all possible, for our children to appreciate this war and the objectives of those very sincere men who decided it was necessary. Equally important also is it that we should understand those dedicated spirits who denounced our intervention in this war, resisted the draft, and sought finally with success our withdrawal.

Once the decision was made for war, there seemed no way to turn back. Yet Johnson's administration was never able to justify fully its war policy. There was no formal declaration of war, no dramatic call up of the reserves, and nothing was done to mobilize public opinion behind the war. No nation, no people, and especially no men should be asked to fight for a cause when its own government has failed to justify it wholly and completely. Neither we nor our ally South Vietnam fully accepted the defense of the war. Without such popular support, the drive, the total effort, and the persistence essential to win were absent. A mighty effort would have been required to persuade the nation that a war in this faraway land—small, economically backward, badly divided—was truly vital to our national security. In this war nothing we ever did was enough.

Blacksburg, Virginia

THE LAST CHOPPER

CHAPTER ONE

OUR WAR, 1963-1966

In the 1954 debate over an air strike to relieve Dien Bien Phu, Senator Lyndon B. Johnson had favored caution and restraint and strongly urged Eisenhower, Dulles, Radford, and Nixon to secure French pledges of independence, British endorsement, and the support of Asian nations before asking Congress to approve direct action in Indochina. In 1964, with only the support of Congress, a doubtful interpretation of SEATO, and a questionable reading of recent history, President Johnson launched air attacks upon North Vietnam and in early 1965 ordered our ground forces to enter the war. Thus began an expansion of our military operations that grew by 1968 to a half million men and nearly $30 billion a year.

The Johnson administration failed to sell its war policy to the people of America and Europe. Intellectual circles fell victim to Communist propaganda, ignored or excused the terror of the Vietcong, failed to sense the vital danger of revolutionary warfare, mistook minority subversion for socialistic and progressive utopianism, and grew impatient with the shortcomings of democracy and its failure to solve the many cancerous problems of modern society. From classroom to ghetto, from soapbox to riot, from dropout to sniper, deep frustration erupted against a man who did more than any president in all our history to advance internal reform in the United States. In time most of our national troubles were blamed upon the Vietnam War, and the administration was alone held responsible for getting us into the quagmire of a land war in Asia.

The Johnson decision to enlarge the war in 1965 merits a full review. He rejected the implications, generally accepted by scholars, that the conflict in South Vietnam was merely a civil war, fought by groups indigenous to South Vietnam; rather he stressed solely that it was a war inspired, financed, and reinforced from North Vietnam, China, and Russia. Although the governments of Saigon were not democratic or free, even less so were those of the Vietcong and Hanoi. In spite of the fact that the Communist global monolithic conspiracy had been shattered by polycentrism, a fact then much debated, few could believe that Ho's victory in the North or a possible Vietcong victory over the

3

South would be a great liberal achievement. Even national communism was still communism. Dictatorial and autocratic systems might work through nationalist patterns, but they were still a menace to freedom. The brutal overthrow of the Dubcek regime in Czechoslovakia in August 1968 revealed that aggressive or imperial communism was still very much alive.

President Johnson declared that his three predecessors had left him no choice. In truth, these administrations had offered South Vietnam only limited economic assistance and military advice. Neither example nor binding commitment required the United States unilaterally to enter the war to save South Vietnam. Truman had offered material and financial aid, but no ground forces, to help the French and Indochinese defeat Ho Chi Minh. He intervened in Korea without first securing the approval or support of any other nation, but under specific obligations inherited from the settlement ending World War II. Eisenhower made any direct military aid to South Vietnam and France in the crisis of 1954 strictly conditional upon the definite grounds of French request, French grant of independence to Vietnam, English and Asian approval and assistance, plus official congressional consent. There would be no approval by him of unilateral intervention with our full ground or air forces. He well understood that a mighty nation, once its honor and aid were committed, could not launch just one air strike to save Dien Bien Phu but would have to stay in the war until final victory. In 1954 Eisenhower had a healthier idea of the consequences of his decision than either Kennedy or Johnson did later. Arthur Larson, speech writer and adviser in the Eisenhower administration, believed Eisenhower would have handled Vietnam in the 1960s as he handled the Congo crisis, by denying the aid of our troops, avoiding any challenge to Russia, and insisting that the United Nations settle the whole problem—certainly without involving us in a land war.[1]

As early as December 31, 1963, President Johnson wrote to General Minh, Chairman of the Revolutionary Council in South Vietnam, pledging

on behalf of the American Government and people a renewed partnership with your government and people in your brave struggle for freedom. The United States will continue to furnish you and your people with the fullest measure of support in this bitter fight. We shall maintain in Vietnam American personnel and material as needed to assist you in achieving victory.

He said their common aims were to protect the people of South Vietnam from acts of terror caused by Hanoi insurgents and prevent the "neutralization" of South Vietnam. Finally, he wrote: "Your government and mine are in complete agreement on the political aspects of your war against the forces of enslavement, brutality and material misery. Within this framework of political agreement we can confidently continue and improve our cooperation."[2] The president would have accepted the neutralization of both North and South Vietnam, but not the southern half of the country alone.[3]

In a television and radio interview of March 15, 1964, when reminded that

Kennedy believed in the domino theory and felt we could not risk the loss of South Vietnam, Johnson declared:

I think it would be a very dangerous thing, and I share President Kennedy's view, and I think the whole of Southeast Asia would be involved and that would involve hundreds of millions of people, and I think it's—it cannot be ignored, we must do everything that we can, we must be responsible, we must stay there and help them, and that is what we are going to do.[4]

Kennedy had avoided a crisis over Laos by observing its neutrality as agreed upon by China, Russia, the United States, and others. A similar suggestion by General de Gaulle to solve the Vietnam problem was brushed aside by the Johnson administration. Nor did Johnson pressure Saigon for the political and economic reforms absolutely essential to any possible military victory. Talk was incessant about rural pacification, land reform, and strategic hamlets. However, enemy ambush, destruction and terror, and Saigon-condoned corruption and rule by the generals and their cronies among the landlords doomed to failure all hopes of winning the support or the security of the countryside. By 1968 even the cities, which the famous Tet offensive then made the prime targets, were unsafe.

In spite of the ever more obvious fact that the Vietcong were composed overwhelmingly of native South Vietnamese—Communists and non-Communists led or inspired, but not always dominated, by North Vietnam—Washington refused to admit the existence of a full-scale civil war in the South, proclaimed the fact of aggression from the North aided and inspired by the world Communist conspiracy, and denounced all opposition to its increasingly solely military response as ignorance, appeasement, and near treason. The domino theory of Eisenhower remained the official policy, and the cold war continued. Few thought of the long-range consequences of daily decisions, when seldom had the need for such thought been greater. Hence our involvement grew insidiously, in slow stages, with each step hard to fault. Philip L. Geyelin concluded: "Essential, immediate needs would be looked after. But nobody, not least the American Government, ever seemed quite capable of looking ahead to the long haul. . . ."[5]

In a brilliant interpretation of the roots of our intervention in Vietnam, Townsend Hoopes, an insider among Johnson's advisers, recorded his impression of "no central guiding philosophy in foreign policy, as well as of slackness in coordinating the disparate elements." Of limited intellectual background and "much uncertainty in foreign affairs," Johnson inherited an organization "made deliberately loose and flexible by President Kennedy." While Kennedy had a "broad knowledge, intuitive grasp, and determined initiative" in the field of foreign policy, Johnson did not. Thus the quality of Johnson's decisions after 1964 suffered from "inadequate attention to long-range policy planning," and the results were "fragmented debate, loose coordination, and an excessive concentration on problems of the moment."[6] Out of World War II had come the necessity to unify the armed forces of the nation under a central leader, the secretary of defense, and then to bring the Defense and State departments "into close and continuous relations" in order to plan foreign policy, weigh its military risks, judge the demands on our resources, and coordinate daily operations. Thus was established the National Security Council. But there had still occurred a serious decline of the long-range views, so much so that

our large-scale military entry into the Vietnam War in early 1965 reflected the piecemeal consideration of interrelated issues, and that this was the natural consequence of a fragmented NSC and a general inattention to long-range policy planning. Consultation, even knowledge of the basic facts, was confined to a tight circle of presidential advisers, and there appears to have been little systematic debate outside that group.[7]

Geyelin termed the war in Indochina the "orphan war," the one no one wanted. When he came to understand its complexity, Kennedy expressed his astonishment that Eisenhower had left him such a problem "without so much as an explanatory note." In listing the problems left for his successor, Eisenhower apparently thought Vietnam not worth a mention. One month after he was in office Kennedy told his advisers: "This is the worst one yet. . . . You know, . . . Ike never briefed me about Vietnam."[8] However, Hoopes observed, in December 1960 Kennedy and Eisenhower discussed Southeast Asia, and Eisenhower declared the United States had a vital interest in keeping the region free of "Communist domination." Although "Eisenhower attached special importance to Laos" in these talks, more than to Vietnam, he expressed concern for the whole region. According to Clark Clifford, Kennedy's coordinator of the succession arrangements between the outgoing and incoming administrations, "Eisenhower felt a political settlement of the conflict in Laos would be the best solution"; but if that was not possible, then he favored an "allied military intervention." In the final analysis, however, he deemed Laos important enough to warrant our "military intervention alone." Surely our concern for Vietnam would equal that for Laos. Certainly any military intervention in Laos would pose far greater difficulties and dangers than in Vietnam. Eisenhower's warning for Laos would seem to apply equally to Vietnam in the event of attempts, already evident, by Communists to grab the country. Certainly Hoopes supported this view when he wrote: "It was this appraisal that had formed the basis of Clifford's general support for the Johnson Administration's policy in Southeast Asia."[9]

Precisely when did the United States enter the war? The time, the place, and the cause, not to mention the justification, it seems safe to say, will be long debated. Franklin Roosevelt gave limited aid to Ho Chi Minh during World War II, Truman advanced great sums for military and economic assistance, and by 1954 Eisenhower was paying approximately 80 percent of the cost of the French effort to crush the Communist Vietminh. Thereafter, Eisenhower sent additional millions of dollars and close to seven hundred military advisers. Kennedy continued vast aid programs and sent over fifteen thousand military advisers with orders to defend themselves when attacked. American pilots of helicopters and planes flew combat missions and suffered casualties in the Kennedy years. This significant action changed sharply our national policy from a minor to a major risk and involvement. One explanation, given by James Reston of the *New York Times,* suggested that Kennedy, after his Vienna meeting with Khrushchev in June 1961, expressed the belief that the Russian had decided that anybody stupid enough to get into such a mess as the Bay of Pigs and then fail to see it through was immature and timid. Hence such a man could be bullied. To prove him wrong, recoup his losses, and improve his image, without much thought of the ultimate consequences, Kennedy sent twelve thousand troops to Vietnam. *Newsweek* reporters Edward Weintal and Charles Bartlett observed, "Had he followed a long-range policy plan rather than an understandable concern for his image, as a result of the Bay of Pigs fiasco, he might have reduced rather than increased his Vietnam commitment."[10] The Kennedy decision was directly opposed by Undersecretary of State George Ball, who believed it would seriously change the character of the war and, most likely, soon require three hundred thousand United States soldiers in Southeast Asia. Rusk and McNamara agreed with Ball but were willing to risk the proposed action. This decision was certainly a critical step toward our larger involvement, but at the time its tragic significance was not fully realized.[11]

Alfred Steinberg wrote that even before the Vienna meeting Kennedy had sent Vice-President Johnson to Saigon on a special investigative mission. Presidential aides spread the story that Johnson, fearing he would be killed, had argued for two weeks against the journey: "I don't want to embarrass you by getting my head blown off in Saigon." The young president supposedly answered: "That's all right, Lyndon. If anything happens to you out there, Sam Rayburn and I will give you the biggest funeral in the history of Austin, Texas." Kennedy's aides, not the greatest admirers of Johnson, then noted that the vice-president agreed to go only if Kennedy's sister, Mrs. Stephen Smith, went along to prove there was little danger.[12]

On this journey Johnson praised Diem as the Churchill of Asia. Back in Washington, he proposed a major commitment to Saigon, only to have Chester Bowles, then undersecretary of state, oppose it. Bowles favored neutralization of the whole region as preferable to a wider war. According to Steinberg, "It was following his slap in the face by Khrushchev that Kennedy adopted the Johnson approach," backed Diem's government with larger military support, and ordered our men to fire back when fired upon and our pilots to continue and expand their missions. Pacification, reform, political stability, and much else would simply have to wait until the country could be made secure against Communist terror.[13] That was what both Kennedy and Johnson sought. That was what they meant by victory. Certainly Kennedy and Johnson never sought the conquest of North Vietnam. The most crucial decision to send in combat ground forces was left to Johnson and his advisers. This would seem to be the greater responsibility; this was the act long feared and denounced by military and civilian leaders. Kennedy and his advisers, especially General Maxwell Taylor and Walt Rostow, had anticipated the need for ground troops and air strikes, even reprisals against Hanoi, but Kennedy had shied away from direct combat involvement.

Hoopes declared that as president, Johnson wished to preserve the appearance of continuity and argued forcefully that the acts and policies of his predecessors left him no alternative but to meet whatever challenges the Communists raised for him. Although he could not initiate direct action or ask Congress to declare war "without shattering the posture" of continuity and risking exceedingly dangerous responses from China and Russia, he could take strong defensive reactions against Communist actions. Such actions and excuses soon followed, and in short order our air strikes were "almost transformed into a systematic program of bombing the North, but without formal acknowledgment of the shift until long after it was established fact." By June 1965, the fifty thousand American troops then in Vietnam were "authorized" to engage in direct action under limited conditions, but the public was told that such actions were nothing new.[14]

The war critics then and especially later sought with too much success to make these steps appear as a diabolical conspiracy on the part of the president and his advisers deceptively to maneuver the nation into open war but without the full knowledge, debate, and support of either the American people or the Congress. While Johnson contended he was merely following his predecessors, his critics charged him with trying "to pretend the war was not happening."[15]

Hoopes wrote that just after the Pleiku attack and before the order for our retaliation, Vice-President Humphrey urged no further expansion of the war. Bombing the North would not solve the problems in the South, he told the president, but would rather require our ground forces in the South to protect airfields and aircraft and bring a wider war and deeper involvement. Also any real effort to win a military solution in Vietnam would require years—far beyond 1967, when presumably he would have to "position himself for reelection." Humphrey felt that negotiation, political reform, and pacification offered the major means to achieve any solution, but his views for months seemed unwelcome to the inner councils of the White House, until he too decided to "get back on the team."[16]

Hoopes bluntly, and erroneously,* declared in 1969 that:

By moving with secret purpose behind a screen of bland assurances designed to minimize or mislead, by admitting nothing until pressed by the facts and then no more than was absolutely necessary, by stretching to the limit (and perhaps beyond) the intent of the Tonkin Gulf Resolution, the President carried a bemused and half-aware nation far beyond the Eisenhower and Kennedy positions to a radically different involvement in the intractable Vietnam conflict. It would have to be conceded that the performance was a piece of artful, even masterful, political craftsmanship. Unfortunately for Lyndon Johnson and the American people, it could be vindicated only by a quick and decisive military victory. But when the mists of summer confusion lifted, there were 170,000 U.S. troops in Vietnam, U.S. air forces were bombing the North with mounting intensity, and the enemy showed no sign of surrender or defeat. There was the President and there was the country—waist-deep in the Big Muddy. And the integrity, the trust, the credibility without which the leadership of great democratic nations cannot govern were all gravely strained by a pattern of actions that seemed an inextricable blend of high-mindedness, inadvertence, and either massive self-delusion or calculated deceit.[17]

By the end of 1963 our military personnel in Vietnam exceeded twenty-five thousand and use of the word *advisory* to describe our role was no longer accurate. Some reporters more aptly began to speak of our participation as war. The spadework, the plans, and the theories had been developed in the Kennedy years, but, as with so many other unfinished tasks of the assassinated president, it was left to Johnson to execute them. A major mistake of Johnson's was his failure to impress sufficiently upon the American people the important fact that we were at war, that sacrifices were essential, and that a clever and insidious enemy by a new strategy of unconventional warfare was nibbling away at the edges of the free and would-be free world. It was a very dangerous and costly war, hard to stop and extremely frustrating. No one said strongly enough that we could not simultaneously afford all the "guns and butter" we wished plus the continuation of vast programs of global aid and domestic welfare. A war of little sacrifice, one that disturbed only a few people and used but a small part of our total power, preserved too long the illusion of peace. A war it was, however, and in time became ever more troublesome, costly, and dangerous.

The phantom of peace and prosperity in the midst of the cold reality of war—once truly realized by the public—helped to develop the famous charge against the administration of a credibility gap. Especially when the initial steps expanding the war were so widely accompanied by repeated assurances of victory, early withdrawal of our armed forces, Saigon's ability to assume shortly a greater share of the fighting, and Vietcong collapse. Naturally when such rosy promises failed of fulfillment rising numbers lost faith in official statements about the war. Newspaper reporters earned and deserved more trust than did officials of the United States government. Far better would it have been to give the people the hard facts and the full case for a wider commitment. Nowhere, at home, in Europe, or in Asia, with all our vast communication media and techniques of publicity, did we convincingly—even to our friends—justify the war. It was Johnson's tragic fate to lead a great nation into the most truly unpopular and the least justified war in its history. Whatever the case for the war, its critics appeared to have more influence and a wider audience than its advocates in powerful circles around the globe.

History may reveal ironically that the most unpopular war a great nation ever fought was simultaneously the most unselfish war. In response to a 1961 Vietnamese request for assistance, Kennedy declared that "our primary purpose is to help your people maintain their independence. If the Communist authorities in North Viet-Nam will stop their campaign to destroy the Republic of Viet-Nam, the measures we are taking to assist your defense efforts will no longer be necessary."[18] Rusk added a year later that no threat to the peace of Southeast Asia came "from the south or from across the Pacific Ocean"; it came only from the North—from Hanoi, China, and Moscow, from those who have declared their intention to force the rest of the world into their pattern—despite the fact that no people has yet chosen that pattern in a genuinely free election. There can be peace overnight in Viet-Nam if those responsible for the aggression wish peace. The situation is just as simple as that.[19]

Aggression by indirection, conquest by externally inspired and supplied control, takeover by deception, subversion, and terror were still aggression and conquest.
  Antiwar forces refused to accept this major thesis of the hawks, and the issue may never be finally decided. They insisted the crisis was purely local, a civil war, and the Geneva settlement of 1954, which we did not sign but pledged to respect, did not provide for a permanent division of the country; hence all non-Vietnamese forces present in the country were the aggressors. No invasion could be charged against Hanoi, because the whole region of North and South Vietnam was but one country. The official Washington position opposed this with the contention that for whatever time necessary prior to reunification, as in Korea and Germany, two sovereign and independent countries existed and were entitled to the respect of their positions. Therefore, when South Vietnam, an independent and sovereign nation, asked our help, we gave it; consequently our role was solely defensive in nature, designed to contain Communist aggression from North Vietnam, supported by China and Russia. Nothing infuriated the doves more than this interpretation of the situation. And nothing more angered the hawks than the refusal of many doves to understand and admit the strategy of indirect aggression. Doves noted our intervention, but not that of the Communists. It was a central issue in the debate, which will no doubt endure for ages to come. Although the South Vietnamese, under Diem and the generals who followed him, were not free, they did not wish to live under communism. They also wanted something freer than the personalism and despotism Diem offered. Corrupt, inefficient, landlord- and military-oriented as the Saigon governments were, it was better to have them on our side, to help them to work for changes toward a richer freedom, and trust that time and effort might direct them down more liberal paths than would ever be possible under such Communist despotism as was launched initially in North Vietnam between 1953 and 1956, when a great Communist purge murdered in cold blood unknown thousands.
  The Truman doctrine of aid to peoples seeking to establish the strength to defend their freedom against Communist subversion was a major source of defense for Johnson's wider war. However, the love of freedom predated anticommunism by ages. United States national security was not immediately endangered by whatever happened to South Vietnam. Pacifism, resurgent isolationism, appeasement, even cowardice could save our nationalism for a while longer. The whole land of South Vietnam was scarcely worth the nearly $30 billion one year of the war cost in 1968. Nevertheless, our dedication to individual and national freedom, an expanding humanism, and cherished concepts of progress did not permit us to stand idly by while despotism overran faraway areas. Freedom was not an island unto itself. It had to have its defenders, its advocates, its strength, and its unity. There was either collective

security or there was no security. The cause of one was the cause of all.

American aid since 1950 was generally offered on the condition of necessary political and economic reforms, deemed essential to enlist a widespread popular support for the government in Saigon and to justify it before the American people on grounds of humanity, freedom, and justice. No United States official ever tried fully to pressure Saigon to execute the necessary reforms, but Vietcong harassment, Saigon corruption, intransigence, and governments composed of militarists and landlords most apt to suffer from reform checked whatever efforts we made. Saigon made promises, even token gestures toward rural pacification and repressing corruption, but by no means enough to unite the people behind any regime in Saigon. Since Eisenhower's initial support of Diem in 1954, virtually every government in Saigon was regarded by most Vietnamese, North and South, as a puppet of the United States, just as once Bao Dai and others were deemed puppets of France. Somehow we could never explain to them and much of the world the vital difference of purpose between the French and American roles there.

The truth was that France regarded Indochina as a French colony which she struggled to preserve, while the United States tried to establish an independent and free national state. There is a difference between a colony and an independent free state. In one, the individual is a subject, in the other a citizen, equal in rights and duties. Yet, talk as we did of proposed reforms, strategic hamlets, drafting constitutions, and establishing representative governments, both Kennedy and Johnson realized no solution was possible until security could be obtained—and that required increased force. According to Hoopes, although Johnson exercised extreme care in the supervision of the air attacks to avoid all possible complications with China and Russia, he allowed General Westmoreland "the broadest discretion in devising U.S. ground strategy in South Vietnam." Neither Johnson nor McNamara ever employed the sharp control over the ground warfare they did over the bombing. Thus ground warfare expanded to ever larger proportions "subordinating by its sheer weight (and undermining by its sheer destructiveness) the political efforts aimed at pacification, reform, and nation-building." This made it impossible to relate our military effort to our political objectives for South Vietnam. As it was, Hoopes declared too strongly: "The preferred military doctrine dictated the strategy and the strategy determined the policy. Though not officially acknowledged, nor even planned that way, military victory became an end in itself."[20]

This suggested falsely that Johnson sought a conventional military victory, when his objective was to prevent a victory by Hanoi over South Vietnam. His concept of victory in this struggle was just that—to save South Vietnam from total defeat and enslavement. Hoopes would leave the impression that Johnson sought the total defeat of Hanoi. Many antiwar groups never realized that physical security had to precede pacification. The enemy saw the point and sought to perpetuate turbulence and insecurity everywhere possible. Hence the failure of other methods, plus the increase of Vietcong terror, raids, and attacks, helped advance the wider war. Kennedy appeared to realize before his assassination, said one of his aides, "that Vietnam was his great failure in foreign policy."[21] Pouring in men and material aid did not really improve the situation, wrote Steinberg, "because the emphasis had been on treating the struggle as a military rather than a political problem." He believed finally that the only successful way to defeat the guerrillas "was to win over the peasants," to arm and enable them to defend themselves.[22]

The question arose: How could anyone achieve reforms in the midst of a civil war when the enemy knew also that victory would be impossible without reforms and had the will and the means to frustrate them? The endless attacks and harassment made difficult any correction of abuses or political solutions before military victory over the guerrillas could make secure the whole country. Johnson's strategy was to keep raising the pressure upon the enemy bit by bit until they would simply quit the effort to seize South Vietnam. Faced with the manpower surplus of North and South Vietnam, not to mention the potential source of China, such an expansion could not be accepted indefinitely by the United States and its allies. The birthrate of North Vietnam plus the Vietcong tactics of intimidating the young men of South Vietnam could ensure endlessly sufficient manpower to supply the Vietcong forces at the rate of 1965-1968 requirements. In any case, would China and Russia have stood idly by and allowed the United States to increase its numbers and strength required to defeat Hanoi and the Vietcong? Most likely they would have entered the war.

The United States would be most apt to run out of will and men before the enemy did. Only its technical superiority would offset its shortage of manpower. Man for man we could not match the potential enemy with conventional methods. Nor would our own and world opinion support the use of nuclear weapons. No easy escape was available. An enlarged war would bring only greater devastation, and retreat or noninvolvement would leave the field to the Communists. Before 1968 Johnson would withdraw only after Saigon was secure from Communist conquest; Hanoi only after the Vietcong had conquered all South Vietnam and laid the basis for a reunited country under Ho. Thus followed the deadlock of peace negotiations between 1963 and 1968. Both sides intensified their war efforts in behalf of their objectives. Each step up the ladder toward a bigger war was blamed on the other side. Johnson frequently declared that we sought "no wider war," but as it expanded he explained it was necessary because the enemy's escalation left him no other choice. The failure of many peace efforts left Johnson with no apparent alternative but to try for enough success from military efforts to pressure Ho and the Vietcong to the conference table. Hence occurred a growing "Americanization" of the war.[23] This trend had been feared by Kennedy, who often expressed his desire to avoid turning the war into "our war."

With Johnson in power, the Kennedy advisers felt unsure. Except for Rusk, they had ignored Johnson during the Kennedy years. At his first foreign policy meeting on Vietnam, November 24, 1963, the Kennedy crowd present felt great doubts.

From Truman, Eisenhower, and Kennedy, Johnson felt he inherited a set of assumptions, a reading of history, and a belief in the lessons it taught which justified our expanding involvement around the globe, including Southeast Asia. However, inside and outside his administration many able scholars and statesmen challenged these assumptions. Townsend Hoopes, an insider, declared:

What seemed in retrospect to have made large-scale military intervention all but inevitable in 1965 was a fateful combination of the President's uncertainty and sense of insecurity in handling foreign policy, and a prevailing set of assumptions among his close advisers that reinforced his own tendency to think about the external world in the simplistic terms of appeasement versus military resolve.[24]

In this critical and antiwar view Johnson was "out of his depth in dealing with foreign policy." His long experience in Congress had given him little direct knowledge of this broad field, and for reasons peculiar to himself he lacked faith in his own judgments. Whereas Truman, Eisenhower, and Kennedy had confidently overruled their advisers, Johnson was more subject to persuasion and variation. According to Hoopes, Johnson lacked "Truman's practical horse sense, Eisenhower's experienced caution, Kennedy's cool grasp of reality." A study of his record revealed no "solid core of philosophical principle or considered approach to foreign policy—indeed no indication that he gave the subject much serious attention before 1964."[25]

With his predecessors, however, he did believe the cold war legacy still remained. The generation that fought and won World War II strongly believed: that the cold war had not ended; that the Communist bloc remained a solid and cohesive global conspiracy determined to bury the non-Communist world; that any increase of Communist strength anywhere would benefit Moscow and Peking at the expense of the free world and must therefore be resisted, whatever the cost, lest the very delicate balance of power between the two great forces, reflected in an extensive series of alliances, be overturned in favor of communism, and that the lesson of Munich—aggression must be resisted everywhere to prevent eventual global war—still applied. This view admitted that native South Vietnamese may have supported the war against the Saigon regime, but it more strongly stressed its belief that the major cause of the trouble was aggression by North Vietnam supported by Russia and China. In South Vietnam guerrilla warfare presented to us aggression by internal and external subversion. The war was just one example of a global challenge already successfully launched in Central Europe, China, Cuba, and Africa; if victorious here, it would spread indefinitely to other regions, especially whenever it met no resistance. Out of World War II, wrote Hoopes, came "a bitter bipolar enmity stretching around the globe, and apparently restrained from the plunge into final holocaust only by a delicate balance of terror."[26]

Inside and outside the Johnson administration and among the most powerful intellectual circles of the United States and the Western world a contrary view prevailed. This revisionist outlook maintained that these dominant conceptions, initially justified or not, were no longer valid in 1965. Johnson's case for the war was obsolete because it rested on a set of "misperceived assessments."[27] The truth, according to Townsend Hoopes, was that the existence of "an effective military balance in the center of Europe," the product of NATO counterpower and enduring with a measure of stability for twenty years, made unlikely any deliberate Soviet attack. Also under this nuclear shield Western Europe was no longer weak, but was strong and prosperous. Further, behind the iron curtain, time revealed that the aging process, dissensions, territorial disputes, and even vested interests of ruling elites had undermined Russian orthodoxy. National deviationism and ancient jealousies and fears revealed that a people could be Communist and yet give first concern to national interests. The monolithic pattern was broken, and many-centered national Communist states replaced it.[28]

The Sino-Soviet split was a most significant factor that shattered both the global conspiracy and the domino theories. This separation assured the free and uncommitted nations that the danger of a combined attack upon them was receding. As NATO and the nuclear shield checked Russia in Europe, Chinese ineptness, "ideological ferocity," and the deeply ingrained historical fears of many nations of Chinese imperial aspirations dampened any hopes of an easy extension of Chinese Communist hegemony in Asia. Events in Central Europe marked by a spirit of rebellion against Russian intervention revealed that Russian hopes for a peaceful acceptance of her ideology and her dream of a world proletarian revolution were virtually dead. That dream of peaceful Communist internationalism died in East Europe when Czechs faced the Russian tanks in Wenceslaus Square and referred to the Russian troops as masters, not comrades. This revealed to the world that peaceful partnership with Russia was possible only on Russian terms. Naked force and ruthless subjugation fixed the fate of all who accepted the Russian embrace. Areas beyond the grasp of Russian military power now found the Russian system most unwelcome. However long it might take to overthrow Russian control of Central Europe, these events showed Russia had failed to build a stable integrated empire in Central Europe. Hoopes concluded: "Nationalism had proved stronger than imposed ideology. What Stalin with total power could not do was no longer a serious possibility for his successors."[29]

In Europe and elsewhere, outside of Russia's reach, Soviet control was weakened, and her ideological appeal "to some sixty small and fragile ex-colonies" was sharply reduced. Many new centers of political initiative were forming, and the dream of a unified empire of the proletariat was fragmented into separate nationalist patterns. Behind the Soviet facade of leadership of the global poor lay a most powerful industrial nation beginning to revive ancient imperial aspirations long "in hibernation." The accent was shifting from ideology to power, from partnership to domination, subjugation, and exploitation. The result of these events was, said Hoopes:

The world was no longer neatly divided between Free World and Communist Bloc and while these new realities did not greatly diminish the dangers of an inherently precarious century, they did alter the shape and character of problems in ways that strongly suggested the need for new analysis and new responses.[30]

Hoopes went on to say that such a response Johnson and his advisers, products of the long cold war, could not understand or adopt, because the tenets of the cold war were "bred in the bone." It was virtually impossible for them to abandon or outgrow ideas so long deemed valid and basic reference points for national policy, even when they "no longer fully square with the facts." Thus a major cause of the escalation of the war in Vietnam sprang from the tragic fact that

as the President's advisers appraised the world situation in 1965, the Russians and the Chinese still seemed to them in full pursuit of bellicose, expansionist policies across the globe, and still quite ready and able to join in the support and manipulation of proxies for purposes inimical to our own.[31]

The critics, noticing that the cold war syndrome still prevailed in Washington in 1965, asserted that while there was an excuse for Kennedy to frame policies in the light of its validity, there was no justification for Johnson to continue the policy in his day. Yet, Johnson retained Kennedy's principal foreign policy advisers and followed their advice. Even Hoopes declared:

All carried in their veins the implicitly unlimited commitment to global struggle against Revolutionary Communism which had grown out of our total immersion in World War II, and which had been specifically enunciated in the Truman Doctrine of March 1947. None as yet perceived the necessity—or the possibility—of redefining U.S. interests or the U.S. role in the world in ways that would permit the drawing of more careful distinctions between those commitments and interventions that are in fact *vital* to our national security, and those that spring more or less from our deeply held view of what the world "ought" to be and of how it "ought" to be organized—that is, from our reforming zeal and our desire for wish fulfillment. To the President's men in early 1965, there seemed no logical stopping point between isolationism and globalism.[32]

A summary by Hoopes of the counsel of these advisers in the fateful decisions of 1965 reveals their state of mind. Right or wrong, they argued that Communist China and Russia were actively promoting and abetting hostile conduct against South Vietnam; it was aggression by the method of guerrilla warfare and political subversion, in the false guise of national liberation as earlier proclaimed by Khrushchev. This action was precisely along the same lines as Hitler's in Europe, and appeasement in Southeast Asia would have the same tragic results as it did at Munich. The view was that Asia was now in the same position Europe had been in, and the lessons we had supposedly learned from Hitler should have taught us how to face this situation because the circumstances were analogous. Widely heard was the expression that "if we don't stop the Reds in South Vietnam, tomorrow they will be in Hawaii, and next week in San Francisco." It was altogether fitting that our expanding military power be used to blunt supposedly national-liberation wars and stop subversive aggression tactics. Surely a sudden strike by our advanced techniques against a small and primitive nation would win quick results. Most agreed that we must stand and fight in Vietnam or lose all Southeast Asia and the faith of the world in our will and capacity to meet the Communist challenge anywhere.[33]

It was especially essential by air strikes against North Vietnam to avenge the cruelties of Hanoi upon South Vietnam and also to boost the morale of the nearly collapsed government at Saigon. However small South Vietnam might be, it was still a part of a larger world struggle which we could not abandon in whole or in part. Further, by fighting local wars and quelling local disturbances, we would avoid far costlier global catastrophies and hence would be working for the noble ideal of a universal peace. With this outlook, we did not understand that others might see our efforts differently, interpret our actions as those of a possibly imperial-minded policeman rather than those of a noble man seeking universal peace. Hoopes declared that Walt Rostow, a leading adviser and proponent of a broader war, saw Vietnam

as a centrally directed and coordinated Communist challenge, a deliberate testing of the national-liberation war theory with global implications. Success for Ho Chi Minh would set off a string of revolutionary explosions in vulnerable areas all across the world from which only Communism would benefit. But if the challenge in Vietnam were met and mastered by a determined Free World countereffort, similar Communist insurgencies in other miserable and restless areas—in Asia, Africa, and Latin America—would be deterred or discouraged.[34]

Judging from his experience in World War II he believed "tactical airpower could make the war unbearable for Hanoi." But, Hoopes observed, there were no industrial targets in that country whose destruction might cripple the economy of the nation and force its government to the conference table.

When the major decisions to enlarge the war were made in 1965, Hoopes continued, Rostow was the "channel through which President Johnson received almost all written communications on foreign affairs." Seeing the president several times each day and selecting the papers for executive study at night, he could influence the choice of options and revise the views expressed by responsible department heads and their staffs when passing them on to the president. Objective as he tried to be, it was easy for him to filter out evidence contrary to his fixed beliefs. He certainly used his position to argue his own case, "for a ground strategy of relentless pressure, for heavier bombing, even for invasion of North Vietnam," and he was not scrupulous, as had been McGeorge Bundy, about making certain that the president heard the full arguments on all sides of an issue:

The evidence is however that his ebullient interpretations consistently reassured President Johnson. They did so by reinforcing the President's own bellicose instincts about the Vietnam War, his patriotic pride in American power, his belief in the inherent righteousness of the United States and its capacity to apply limitless power for good, his sense of moral duty to meet commitments undertaken, and his conspiratorial view of life and politics.[35]

It appears that all the inner advisers, except George Ball and a few others, urged President Johnson to intervene directly with ground forces in the war in early 1965. Since this advice agreed with his own inclinations, the president began to inch us into the war—but in such a clever fashion that it appeared only an evolution of the policies and programs inherited from his predecessors. He declared that he did not get us into Vietnam, for we had already been there for ten years, ever since Eisenhower offered our assistance to Diem in 1954. However, he, not Eisenhower or Kennedy, sent in increasing numbers of ground combat forces beginning in 1965. Johnson did so, but at the deliberate request of the government of South Vietnam. He had not pressured Saigon to request the aid.[36] General Earle G. Wheeler declared that the summer of 1965 was the time of decision:

By the late spring of that year, due to a combination of causes, the Viet Cong/North Vietnamese Army was threatening to overwhelm the armed forces of South Viet Nam. That summer, at the request of the South Vietnamese, the United States made the decision to commit major forces to halt aggression.[37]

According to one able scholar, Theodore Draper, the major impulse to insert ground forces was therefore due to the "progressive deterioration . . . of General Nguyen Khanh's South Vietnamese regime and the subsequent near-breakdown of the South Vietnamese armed forces" toward the end of 1964. By this weakness, the United States was virtually "blackmailed" into this tragic step.[38] What few officials then realized was that it would be all too easy for the enemy to match our every escalation short of his total annihilation by nuclear warfare.

Steinberg wrote that at his first foreign policy meeting on November 24, 1963, Johnson expressed his opposition to the Diem coup. With little faith in other tactics, he declared the only way to win was to kill the Vietcong, "not bring the New Frontier to South Vietnam"; he appeared pleased when Rusk, long silent under Kennedy, now spoke strongly to the effect that the war "had nothing to do with nationalist aspirations or so-called yearnings for social justice," was not a civil war, but "was simply an aggression on South Vietnam by North Vietnam aided by Red China." All the trouble there would end if China and Ho would leave their neighbors alone, Rusk thought. Johnson believed Ho was another Hitler carrying on aggression and if not stopped would bring on a larger war or require cowardly appeasement. Johnson ended the meeting with the decision to "increase the pressure and press on."[39] He ignored the advice of de Gaulle to seek neutralization. Such an easy out would only open the way for a speedy Communist takeover, and he would not be a party to any solution that would let Ho take South Vietnam against the wishes of the South Vietnamese.

When U Thant told LBJ that Ho was willing to start peace negotiations in private unofficial talks, Johnson felt such gestures lacked substance and sincerity of purpose, were aimed at gaining a propaganda victory over Saigon and

Washington, and would merely deceive millions. In truth, Ho would really accept nothing short of victory and our withdrawal. The prolonged and stalled negotiations in Paris from 1968 to 1972 (in which the enemy, expecting our defeat and withdrawal, incessantly demanded terms that amounted to victory for them and total defeat for us and Saigon) would appear to support the claims of Rusk and Johnson that the enemy had nothing to offer and was not yet willing to engage in serious negotiations. Therefore, the many rumors of genuine peace offers from Hanoi and the charges that Johnson sabotaged, evaded, and ignored sincere efforts for peace were unfounded. They were a clever enemy design to deceive the world and discredit Johnson. Yet for many American critics it was easier to believe our enemy than our president and his advisers.

General Curtis LeMay, Chief of Staff of the Air Force, urged pulverizing North Vietnam from the air and told Johnson, "We are swatting flies . . . when we should be going after the manure pile." Such attacks, coupled with dire warnings of more to come, Strategic Air Commander General Power believed, would turn the tide and bring us satisfactory terms in the war. Walt Rostow had his scheme for a bigger war—intensified fighting in the South, bombing in the North, reconnaissance over Laos, and the bombing of the Pathet Lao bases. From Richard Nixon and Barry Goldwater came further suggestions to bomb North Vietnam and lure China into the war so we could destroy "her budding nuclear plants." The ancient advice of Eisenhower, Ridgway, and others to avoid a land war in Asia was thus readily ignored by powerful groups in the United States.[40]

Johnson rejected all proposed compromises as insincere, abandoned Kennedy's vision of troop withdrawals by the end of 1965, and told Saigon officials in his New Year's message of 1964 that neutralization would be merely another name for Communist seizure. We would continue furnishing Saigon with our full support in this bitter fight: "We shall maintain in Vietnam American personnel and material as needed to assist you in achieving victory."[41] This statement bolstered Saigon's program of stern repression and encouraged her generals to spread hopes of total military victory.

Under Kennedy and Johnson were official advisers who questioned the prevailing rationale for the war and sought to influence events in whatever way they could. George Ball, Townsend Hoopes, in time Robert McNamara, and finally Clark Clifford, McNamara's successor, sought to caution against rash actions, which unbalanced our global commitments, wasted our energies and resources, and caused us to neglect pressing domestic needs. No one stated more clearly and forcefully this critical view of events than Hoopes, who was among the first few insiders to lift, however slightly, the veil of secrecy and obscurity that clouded so many of the decisions and accounts of the war. To his superior, Assistant Secretary of Defense John T. McNaughton, Deputy Secretary Hoopes felt compelled to relay his views of the rising tragedy. He symbolized the dovish trend inside the official family and revealed the spirit and philosophy that would ultimately persuade the president to halt the bombing, begin the reduction of our military involvement, and work for peace through the futile negotiations that began at Paris in 1968.

Encouraged by Johnson's wide-range peace effort just announced in December 1965, Hoopes sent a memorandum to McNaughton declaring the nation was at a grave crossroads. The official peace gesture revealed that the president was wisely reluctant to plunge deeper into the morass of war if it could be avoided. The suspension of the bombing was wise and should continue, for it would help improve the "psychological climate in the neutral world" and among many of our allies; it might in time help Hanoi to resist Peking's hardnosed policy of no concession; and, in truth, it risked little real loss for the United States except a possible letdown in Saigon. The very poor transportation system of North Vietnam combined with abundant coolie labor, Oriental resignation, and the ingenious use of bicycles on numerous trails had managed to neutralize the effect of the bombing. The bombing also failed to stop the infiltration of the South; in fact, it stiffened Hanoi's resistance, strengthened the Chinese argument for the policy of no concessions, and made Russia's efforts at moderation more difficult.[42]

The Korean War, Hoopes continued, had revealed the ineffectiveness of rear-area bombing attacks on primitive countries. We could possibly annihilate the whole population of North Vietnam but we could not bomb Hanoi to the conference table. Further efforts to destroy Hanoi and North Vietnamese irrigation ditches would most likely bring Russia and China into the war, tend to unify, not to split, the Communist world, and "increase US diplomatic isolation." China was just across the border, able to provide sanctuary, manpower, and equipment. Also the country suffered both an unfortunate North-South regional split and the existence of two established governments. In South Vietnam, no matter how deeply the United States was involved, China and Russia could never permit an American victory. They could drag out the issue at great length.[43]

Beyond these arguments for less war and commitment were the dangers to our total global posture. We had no major or vital interests at stake in that distant theater. The war consumed too much of our time, energy, manpower, and resources, and caused us to neglect other areas and problems. Our desire to have "more flags," especially European, fighting alongside us was unwise and unattainable. Asians would not welcome such a quick return of their late imperial masters. The war strained our relations with European nations, whose wealth and support we needed for other purposes. Nor was there any real likelihood that Europe could afford or would even try to help us in a war many Europeans deemed both immoral and wasteful.[44]

During the Johnson years and at times thereafter, antiwar forces seemed to have, without any genuine basis for it, the faith that diplomacy at Paris or elsewhere, if Washington and Saigon would but try it, would surely end the war. They never ceased pressing for a return to Geneva and a resort to the United Nations, urging Washington to seek the assistance of Russia in launching direct talks between the belligerents. What they did not openly admit was that the enemy through war or negotiation sought but one objective—total victory. When they pressured us for cutbacks, opposed escalation, and advocated negotiation, they in substance were either ignorant of the true nature and purpose of the enemy or were actually aiding and abetting his objectives. From 1968 until 1972, we offered the enemy publicly and privately every possible chance to negotiate an honorable solution of the war, but all in vain. They wanted total victory—which meant our total humiliation. The antiwar forces were unable to show that the enemy wanted an honorable settlement, and they could never quite hide their own willingness to accept, if nothing else availed, our total humiliation. It was this dissension and disunity here and abroad among free men that sapped the will and the strength of the free world.

By 1964 all our aid—sharply increased—proved insufficient. Saigon's efforts were no match for the Vietcong, then heavily supported by Hanoi, Moscow, and Peking. Diem's removal did improve its situation, but it was painfully clear that his successors were unable to save the country. Some Saigon generals, including the daring, aggressive, and youthful General Cao Ky, favored bombing North Vietnam. Prime Minister General Khanh publicly urged extension of the war to the North. Saigon naval raiders constantly invaded the coastal waters of North Vietnam and attacked ships bringing supplies to the Vietcong. United States ships gave naval protection to such attacks and raids, sometimes possibly inside the territorial waters of Hanoi. Anxious to pry electronically into enemy radar installations, detection devices, and radio frequencies, our "spy ships" often came very close to North Vietnam.

These developments stirred global fears of a wider war. U Thant urged negotiation and was strongly supported by General de Gaulle, who feared a more "generalized conflict." In the midst of an election year, when such hawks as Nixon and Goldwater were breathing down his neck and no real peace offers came from Hanoi, Johnson brushed aside all advice to strive for peace by negotiation. He did not wish to be guilty of the charges already being made by Goldwater that he was soft on communism. He would engage in no "conferences to ratify terror" and betray no people to communism. He believed concession would further weaken the shaky Saigon government, sap the will of its people to fight, and most likely lead finally to a Communist takeover. He was not ready for such a surrender. However, he de-emphasized the militancy of his policies during the campaign and repeatedly told the American people he would never send American boys to fight the wars Asian boys should be fighting—this at the same time he was asserting that he would never permit Communist expansion in Vietnam.[45]

Steinberg wrote that as early as February 1964 Johnson opposed the restriction of the war to South Vietnam and suggested we needed to shut off the supply routes, the Ho Chi Minh trails, the naval supplies shipped down by sea, and the privileged sanctuary of North Vietnam and the Demilitarized Zone. Hanoi and Peking, he felt, were playing "a deeply dangerous game," which might have to be stopped. This trial balloon, if that was what it was, brought fears of a wider war, and Dean Rusk gave reassurances that the war would be confined to South Vietnam. Nevertheless, Johnson ordered "a step-up in the program to drop Saigon guerrillas in the North," and permitted the use of United States naval vessels to escort and protect Saigon boats raiding North Vietnam. Further, the president brought large numbers of South Vietnamese pilots to the United States for training to bomb North Vietnam. He also developed for possible future use plans to create "sonic booms" over Northern cities; to employ electronic ships in Northern waters "to snarl radio communication" between Hanoi and the Vietcong; and to bomb and blockade, if not invade, North Vietnam.[46]

Air Vice Marshall Cao Ky stated on July 23, 1964, that South Vietnamese commando teams were already executing sabotage missions in North Vietnam by "air, sea and land." Hanoi, complaining two days later that Saigon and Washington forces had fired on North Vietnamese fishing craft, lodged a formal protest with the International Control Commission. On July 30, 1964, Hanoi also charged Saigon with further raids against its fishing vessels in the Tonkin Gulf. Protected by a United States destroyer, Saigon naval vessels bombarded two North Vietnamese islands. This brought a second protest by Hanoi to the commission on July 31.

On August 2, three North Vietnamese motor patrol boats, a part of Ho's "mosquito fleet," attacked without damaging the United States destroyer *Maddox* about thirty miles off the North Vietnamese coast. Hanoi said our repeated violation of her territorial waters justified its action. Although Washington denied that our warships fired upon their islands or installations, motor patrol boats manned by United States-trained Vietnamese and other nationals fired upon two North Vietnamese islands harboring radar installations. The *Maddox* when first attacked, Rusk admitted, was "six to eleven miles" off the coast of North Vietnam, which claimed twelve miles as the legal limit. Its skipper fired a warning shot across the bow and then sank two of Hanoi's PT boats. The Defense Department admitted that our destroyers on patrol sometimes collaborated with the hit-and-run raids on North Vietnamese cities.[47]

Hanoi's admission of the first attacks upon our destroyer stirred little public reaction in the United States, Steinberg noted, but its second attack upon the *Maddox* and the *C. Turner Joy* within two days, Johnson felt, required a response. On television before a late night audience August 4 he declared our ships, sixty-five miles from the enemy coastline, had suffered a second unprovoked attack. With great patriotic resolution, although not quite equal to Roosevelt's "day of infamy" speech denouncing the Pearl Harbor attack of December 7, 1941, the president said:

These acts of violence against the armed forces of the United States must be met not only by alert defense, but with positive reply.... That reply is being given as I speak to you. Air action is now in execution against gunboats and certain supporting facilities of North Vietnam which have been used in these hostile operations.[48]

LBJ later wrote that his advisers unanimously agreed that the United States could not ignore the second attack. It required retaliation. The decision was for "air strikes against North Vietnamese PT boats and their bases plus a strike on one oil depot." Enemy messages intercepted by us revealed that the enemy knew he was attacking us, and one even boasted: "Enemy vessel perhaps wounded."[49] Although others then and later strongly protested their belief that no attacks were ever made upon our vessels, the president authorized a prompt investigation of the event; and Admiral Sharp, Commander in Chief in the Pacific, who checked "all the reports and evidence," reported that "he had no doubt whatsoever that an attack had taken place."[50] Later and more detailed examinations "confirmed this judgment."

The president immediately summoned his advisers, including the National Security Council, and told them he wanted "a congressional resolution of support for our entire position in Southeast Asia. . . ." It was necessary to strengthen his hand because he felt we might be forced into further action and he did not want "to go in unless Congress goes in with me." Also a strong congressional endorsement would help persuade Hanoi to refrain from accelerating aggression—so he hoped. He told his audience that he had given the same advice to Eisenhower, who "had followed it in the Middle East and Formosan crises." In both instances Congress had backed Ike, and Johnson now sought the same support. Both men had tried to avoid the trouble Truman had in 1950 when he intervened in Korea without congressional sanction. In fact, Johnson sought from the first moment he became president to enlist the fullest support of Congress for any action he took in foreign or domestic affairs. Concerning Vietnam, he told Rusk and McNamara repeatedly that he "never wanted to receive any recommendation for actions we might have to take unless it was accompanied by a proposal for assuring the backing of Congress." In fact, it became routine, he noted, "for all contingency plans to include suggestions for informing Congress and winning its support."[51]

He had not sought such congressional support earlier because he had "continued to hope that we could keep our role in Vietnam limited." However, the Tonkin Gulf attacks changed the picture, wrote the president:

We could not be sure how Hanoi would react to our reprisal strike. We thought it was possible they might overreact and launch an all-out invasion of South Vietnam. They might ask the Chinese Communists to join them in the battle. Any one of a dozen things could have happened, and I wanted us to be ready for the worst. Part of being ready, to me, was having the advance support of Congress for anything that might prove to be necessary. It was better to have a firm congressional resolution, and not need it, than some day to need it and not have it. This was the thinking behind my decision to ask Congress for its backing.

My first major decision on Vietnam had been to reaffirm President Kennedy's policies. This was my second major decision: to order retaliation against the Tonkin Gulf attacks and to seek a congressional resolution in support of our Southeast Asia policy.[52]

In his speech prepared for the public on the issue, Johnson used the word *limited* to describe our action against Hanoi. When one adviser suggested the use of "determined" and leaving the "limitation" to speak for itself, Johnson replied that he wished the enemy to know we would not take the attack "lying down," but added "we are not going to destroy their cities and we hope we can prepare them for the course we will follow." Rusk felt there was an advantage "in not leaving in doubt that we are *not* doing this as a pretext for a larger war." A long discussion of the advantages and disadvantages of a congressional resolution followed, and Rusk declared his belief that most desirable was a resolution that applied not just to Vietnam alone but to all Southeast Asia. LBJ agreed with Senator Bourke Hickenlooper of Iowa that the president clearly had the right to order the armed forces of the nation into action, but he had no doubt that Congress would take "concrete action" on the issue and would support the proposal. The assembled inner advisers agreed. While the president thus spoke to the nation, our "retaliatory air strikes damaged or destroyed twenty-five enemy boats and 90 per cent of the oil storage tanks at Vinh. We lost two planes."[53]

Immediately after the initial air strikes in response to the enemy attacks in the Tonkin Gulf, Johnson's advisers recommended further actions. They suggested we resume our naval patrols in the Tonkin Gulf and be prepared to retaliate against further possible attacks. Air force and marine corps leaders felt extensive air strikes against the North would be necessary. There were great fears of a strong enemy reaction, which Saigon might be unable to confront, to any drastic action on our part. In the midst of one gloomy discussion LBJ suddenly asked his advisers a fundamental question: Is Vietnam "worth all this effort?" The answers reassured him. They told him we could not afford to let Hanoi win because of "our overall position in Asia and the world." If we lost South Vietnam, we would lose Southeast Asia—not immediately but eventually. All agreed—Rusk with even greater emphasis. But they proposed only limited measures, not total war. The decision was for limited expansion of the war.[54] Finding no shortcuts to success through retaliatory strikes, we moved steadily toward a set policy of sustained reprisal.[55]

Thus began a policy of bombing the North, of limited selection of targets, and of gradual expansion of the air war. By such gradualism Johnson hoped to persuade Ho to give up his effort to conquer South Vietnam and reunite it with North Vietnam under Communist authority.[56] Had the United States then used its full air strength, not to mention its full naval and greatly expanded armed might, would the results ultimately have been better? Would victory have quickly come or a much larger and far more dangerous war, possibly with Russia and China? Neither the wider effort that would risk nearly total world war nor the inaction that would most likely bring Saigon defeat and a consequent loss of confidence by our friends and allies seemed attractive to the United States. There was no easy way out.

Between the advice of the extreme hawks and doves, the president decided upon a course of moderate increase of our war effort. Although he said Asian boys should do most of the fighting in this war for their freedom, he believed that without an increase in our aid, South Vietnam would quickly fall to communism. Since the challenge of revolutionary warfare must be met somewhere and here was the place of its application, here it must be faced and defeated. However, he would take no reckless action that would risk world war and nuclear destruction. Whatever the extreme hawks might wish, he would not loose upon the world nuclear warfare:

It has never been the policy of any American to sympathetically or systematically place in hazard the life of this nation by threatening nuclear war. No American President has ever pursued so irresponsible a course. Our firmness at moments of crisis has always been matched by restraint—our determination by care. It was so under President Truman at Berlin, under President Eisenhower in the Formosa Straits, under President Kennedy in the Cuban missile crisis—and I pledge you that it will be so so long as I am your President.[57]

Asked if he felt the United States had overestimated its power to influence events in Asia, Secretary of State Dean Rusk answered that in Asia there were a billion and a half people, half Communist and half free. We could not settle their problems for them, but:

We can help those Asians who are determined to be free to develop the strength and the structure of the organization and the economic base, develop their public services, so that they have the strength and the capacity to meet their problems themselves. And this is what we have been trying to do for the past 10 years in South Viet-Nam.
. . . . .
So these pressures from the outside have to be met, have to be resisted. But these are matters which Asians themselves must have a full part in as their own problem. We can help and assist. And we can also be sure that these do not become matters of all-out, wholesale invasions with organized armed forces and things of that sort, that these people have a chance to—these 14 million people in South Viet-Nam—have a chance to resolve their problems themselves.[58]

In the dilemma Johnson and his advisers tried the middle course between total victory by use of our full armed might and certain defeat by withdrawal. They sought to insert just enough strength to insure Saigon and its friends against defeat, but not enough to assure their ultimate victory. That success through such a gradual and limited effort might require decades, give the enemy time to prepare for wider warfare, exhaust the patience, resources, and manpower of even a nation rich and powerful as the United States, and eventually and unexpectedly develop into a war beyond our initial calculations, even get out of control—all this did not disturb Johnson's advisers. It told the enemy in advance what we would do, thus denying us the advantage of surprise. Limited warfare was a concept not easily swallowed by millions of Americans— who preferred victory, and whose ancestors had *won* their wars.

In his speech to the nation of August 4, 1964, Johnson said he was sending to Congress for its approval a resolution to inform the world "that our Government is united in its determination to take all necessary measures in support of freedom and in defense of peace in Southeast Asia."[59] With far too little thought and discussion, on August 7, the Senate endorsed the resolution by a vote of 88 to 2, Senators Morse and Gruening being the two negatives, and the House by 416 to 0. Hereby the Congress gave the Johnson administration much authority:

Southeast Asia Resolution

Whereas naval units of the Communist regime in Vietnam, in violation of the principles of the Charter of the United Nations and of international law, have deliberately and repeatedly attacked United States naval vessels lawfully present in international waters, and have thereby created a serious threat to international peace; and

Whereas these attacks are part of a deliberate and systematic campaign of aggression that the Communist regime in North Vietnam has been waging against its neighbors and the nations joined with them in the collective defense of their freedom; and

Whereas the United States is assisting the peoples of southeast Asia to protect their freedom and has no territorial, military or political ambitions in that area, but desires only that these peoples should be left in peace to work out their own destinies in their own way: Now, therefore, be it

Resolved by the Senate and House of Representatives of the United States of America in Congress assembled, That the Congress approves and supports the determination of the President, as Commander in Chief, to take all necessary measures to repel any armed attack against the forces of the United States and to prevent further aggression.

Sec. 2. The United States regards as vital to its national interest and to world peace the maintenance of international peace and security in southeast Asia. Consonant with the Constitution of the United States and the Charter of the United Nations and in accordance with its obligations under the Southeast Asia Collective Defense Treaty, the United States is, therefore, prepared, as the President determines, to take all necessary steps, including the use of armed force, to assist any member or protocol state of the Southeast Asia Collective Defense Treaty requesting assistance in defense of its freedom.

Sec. 3. This resolution shall expire when the President shall determine that the peace and security of the area is reasonably assured by international conditions created by action of the United Nations or otherwise, except that it may be terminated earlier by concurrent resolution of the Congress.[60]

In seeking the Gulf of Tonkin Resolution, Johnson noted that speed was essential because "we are entering on three months of political campaigning. Hostile nations must understand that in such a period the United States will continue to protect its national interests, and that in these matters there is no division among us."[61] In this almost thoughtless fashion Congress once again officially endorsed the doctrine of containment, of anticommunism, of support for peoples who wished to establish the strength and unity essential to the preservation of their national freedom. It was a considerable extension of the Greek-Turkish Program of 1947. Every later act in support of the rising involvement in Vietnam, every appropriation bill for the men and materiel sent there gave additional support to the Johnson program. Here we assumed the role of policeman over a vast area. This was clearly unilateral action by the United States, taken hastily and with little approval by allies in Europe or Asia.

Whatever blame may be attached to the decision to intervene belongs to both the Congress and the president—and ultimately to the American voter who supported them.

Our official version of the affair declared the two attacks were unprovoked by the United States because our destroyers were outside the territorial waters of North Vietnam. The resolution was necessary to express our national unity and reassure Saigon and its long-suffering people. It also reendorsed officially the SEATO Treaty of 1954 and gave wide emergency authority to the president, amounting to a virtual declaration of war or blank check to make war in Southeast Asia as he alone might deem necessary. In the early summer of 1964 Johnson's advisers drew up for congressional approval a draft resolution which would give the president a sort of vote of confidence such as Eisenhower sought and obtained in the Formosan crisis. The president carried this draft in his pocket for weeks waiting for the right moment to introduce it to Congress. McGeorge Bundy, who drafted the initial resolution, later explained: "We had always anticipated . . . the possibility that things might take a more drastic turn at any time."[62] Such a resolution would check divisive debates about executive policy in the many crises that might suddenly appear and prevent sharp criticism of Johnson for actions such as that of Truman in authorizing the defense of South Korea without formal congressional endorsement in June 1950.

This major commitment and its origins were widely and most bitterly debated. Congressmen and scholars had grave doubts about the accuracy of the official version of the Tonkin Gulf affair. Hindsight revealed we took a bigger step by this military reply and official resolution than many then realized, and we did it without enough time or information to afford an honest and full review of the risk and scope of the action taken. Certainly but a few people outside government circles really saw that the resolution was to become the equal of a congressional declaration of war.

President Johnson virtually admitted in 1969 that he considered the Tonkin Gulf Resolution was the equivalent of a declaration of war. He observed that Senator Morse, who at the time voted against the measure and termed it a predated declaration of war, had given it the correct label. He also observed further that the resolution might just as well have been called the Fulbright Resolution, because the chairman of the Senate Foreign Relations Committee had endorsed and pushed it through the Senate, and it was that example that won its support unanimously in the House of Representatives. The president noted that Fulbright, a Rhodes Scholar and a very bright man, knew precisely what he was doing in 1964, but that later, when the troubles, losses, costs, and the going got tough, he "chickened out" on his commitments. The president said he had not sought a simple declaration of war, fearing that secret treaties might have pledged Russia and China to aid North Vietnam. He wanted no war with those major powers.[63]

Critics of our response to the Tonkin Gulf attack raised serious questions. Did Johnson have conclusive proof that Hanoi's motor boats had attacked our destroyers? Were the attacks unprovoked, or had our destroyers repeatedly zigzagged in and out of the Hanoi twelve-mile limit, with a large "black box" of electronic equipment operated by a special crew with sophisticated equipment for monitoring Hanoi radio and radar signals? In early 1968 a congressional investigation of the affair raised questions still not answered.

The Defense Department unsuccessfully sought in December 1967 to persuade the Foreign Relations Committee not to reopen the Tonkin incident. Undersecretary of Defense Paul H. Nitze, Secretary of the Navy Paul R. Ignatius, and Senator Richard B. Russell, then Chairman of the Armed Services Committee, pleaded with Fulbright to abandon any thought of reopening the incident, because it would be a "bad show" for the United States. Nitze denied that the *Maddox* and *C. Turner Joy* were in any way implicated in the attacks by South Vietnamese boats on the North Vietnamese islands of Hon Me and Hon Ngu on July 31 and against the North Vietnamese radar security stations on August 3, 1964. Since our destroyers were not serving as a cover or decoy for the Saigon attacks, Nitze insisted that Hanoi had no provocation for the attacks upon our destroyers. Nitze did admit there had been some "initial doubts" about the details of the August 4 engagement because of "reporting and communications 'snafus' but that all questions had been resolved before [President] Johnson ordered the [retaliatory] air strikes [12 hours later on August 5]."

The main witness in the initial inquiry prior to the Tonkin Gulf Resolution was Secretary McNamara, whose testimony persuaded Congress quickly to endorse the resolution, which the president used to justify the bombing of North Vietnam and the commitment of our soldiers to combat.[64] The Defense Department privately told Senator Fulbright that it had conclusive proof that Hanoi had ordered a deliberate attack against our destroyers on August 4 and offered as proof its possession of "special intelligence" information consisting of North Vietnamese radio messages monitored by our electronic intelligence stations. Many doubted that Johnson had enough time to secure such proof before he decided to launch air strikes against the North. The administration claimed it had "verified evidence" before issuing the order, but as late as 1968 Congress felt it unwise to pursue too far an investigation that might impugn the integrity of an administration in the midst of a war.[65]

However, a staff study of the Senate Foreign Relations Committee revealed that the *Maddox* had technical difficulties with its sonar shortly before detecting a torpedo attack. This knowledge stirred further doubts as to the reliability of official assurances of verified evidence. Official conclusion rested upon reports from the *Maddox* that its sonar had detected numerous torpedoes fired by Hanoi's PT boats. The *C. Turner Joy* had detected no torpedoes, which the Defense Department explained on the ground that it had a more advanced, lower-frequency type of sonar not well adapted to picking up shallow-running torpedoes. The *Maddox* alone had been attacked on August 2, and some six hours before the August 4 attack began, it reported a "material deficiency"—meaning simply that its sonar equipment was not working properly. The Defense Department later explained the equipment was working well at the actual time of the attack, a fact higher officials making the decision to bomb the North did not know at the time. The Senate staff study found no subsequent message from the *Maddox* that the deficiency had been corrected, nor did the study show that any inquiries were sent the *Maddox* about its technical troubles. Doubts were raised by some that a second attack ever actually occurred, but more doubt sprang from the belief that official decision preceded accurate information and conclusive verification of any attacks. The eight hours between the attack and the order to bomb the North gave too little time to get the facts.

Initial explanations did not accord with later studies and reports. On August 6 Senator Morse asked if a few days before the attacks our destroyers had participated in or known of the South Vietnamese raids upon the two North Vietnamese islands in the Tonkin Gulf. Secretary of Defense McNamara had then answered, "No." Staff study had revealed the opposite was the truth. The presence of our destroyers in the neighborhood of those island attacks, thought the fiery senator from Oregon, could not help but persuade Hanoi that they were somehow related to the attacks themselves. Others questioned how destroyers engaged in high-speed maneuvers could detect torpedoes with their sonar in the August 4 engagement, when at speeds of about eighteen knots such turbulence builds up around the sonar dome beneath the hull of a destroyer that the sonar has only a limited capacity to detect such small objects as torpedoes. Possibly the sonar could have detected the torpedoes had it been operating in the passive mode, listening for the whine made by the torpedo screws rather than in the active mode, attempting to bounce sound signals off the torpedoes.

The Defense Department would not reveal the truth here. Defense changed its account several times on several points. Initially it contended that the destroyers came under automatic weapons fire, that many torpedoes were fired, and that Hanoi PT boats came at our destroyers with speeds of more than forty knots. Later evidence stirred doubts as to these points. The Pentagon admitted that perhaps one or two torpedoes were fired and conceded that enemy PT boats may have operated at a lower speed. These changes raised further doubts about the reliability of the first reports showing the boats to be first paralleling and then closing in on the destroyers. Defense would not clarify many questions. Information about radar performance was classified.[66]

Broader questions were raised. Did the two Hanoi PT boat attacks justify the response we made? We suffered no damage, but in retaliation we bombed their installations, ships, ports, and harbor facilities and rapidly expanded air warfare over North Vietnam. Were not Hanoi's attacks against our ships protecting Saigon's armed vessels really defensive, not offensive? Many asked why Hanoi had stirred up such a crisis. McNamara said he could not explain it. Speculation suggested it was to test our reaction to direct military attack, create a domestic controversy over the whole question of the war in Vietnam, and put us in a most unfavorable light before world opinion. Our vicious response to this painless attack would appear to support this expectation. Some believed it was to put Russia on the spot—to see what she would do when faced with a choice between supporting Communist causes everywhere and her commitment to "peaceful co-existence" with the West.[67] Some believed China called the play.

A question could be raised: Were the suicidal attacks upon our destroyers by Hanoi motor boats designed by Hanoi and Peking to lure us into a wider land war in Asia? A guerrilla-type war, unlike that of Korea, in which we could be drained of our resources and men? If so, in the larger sense the enemy won here. In a world of rumor and suspicion, others at the time expressed the fear that we had provoked an incident off North Vietnam to justify our attacking Hanoi, bringing on a wider war, uniting Saigon and South Vietnam, and achieving victory. And some believed our Defense Department, especially the air force, would welcome a war with China and a chance to destroy her nuclear program in a preventive war.

Although officials announced a plan to send an additional five thousand men—the United States at this time already had more than sixteen thousand "technical advisers" stationed in South Vietnam, widely engaged in direct military action alongside the Saigon forces and suffering casualties—we wanted no wider war then. Talk in the post Diem era of invading the North caused friction between the South Vietnamese government and our officials in Saigon. However, Washington grasped the fact that the war could not be won as long as the Vietcong had sanctuaries in the North and in nearby countries and access by sea by which they received men and materiel.

If China sought to prove us a paper tiger and split us in an election year, she miscalculated badly. Senator Goldwater and virtually everyone else endorsed the Gulf of Tonkin Resolution and approved of the immediate response we made to the attacks. Hanoi now knew that more attacks would invite a greater response. Our stern reply deeply worried many of our European and Asian friends, who feared it would bring on a larger war; but it reassured Saigon, brought increased Chinese aid to Hanoi, and increased the tempo, size, and cost of the war for the United States.

Johnson made a most carefully limited response: He did not attack Hanoi or Haiphong, nor did he leave it up to Saigon to counterattack, as he might well have done. His initial decision was to limit his reaction to an attack upon the naval installations of Hanoi; but, as was noted at the time, he made his own decision, acted first, and told Saigon and his SEATO allies about it later. Nor would he be pressured into an international conference, in which the Communists could practice their "talk and fight" tactics while consolidating and expanding Communist gains and weakening Saigon morale. Peace by negotiation was our hope then and later, but Johnson would not be forced to accept a Communist and French proposal for a fourteen-nation Geneva conference.

In defense of our response and the Gulf of Tonkin Resolution, the president told the American Bar Association that for the past ten years our government had but one clear aim—observance of the 1954 agreements which guaranteed the independence of South Vietnam, "the consistent target of aggression and terror." In execution of that purpose our response to such attacks had followed a consistent pattern: "First, that the South Vietnamese have the basic responsibility for the defense of their own freedom. Second, we would engage our strength and our resources to whatever extent needed to help others repel aggression."[68] In analyzing his options, the president rejected as "morally unthinkable" our retreat—which would allow the freedom of a brave people to be handed over to tyranny. To others who proposed a larger conflict, he replied that such a reckless action would "risk the lives of millions," "engulf much of Asia," "threaten the peace of the entire world," and still "offer no solution at all to the real problem of Vietnam." We could and would meet any wider challenges, but our aim here was to restore peace and order. We would not be provoked into rashness or worn down, but would meet with firmness and "measured reply" all unprovoked attacks. His hand would never trigger the release of nuclear weapons.[69]

Just a few days earlier, but after the Tonkin Gulf attack, the president had told a Syracuse University audience that Eisenhower and Kennedy had sought the same objectives as he then sought:

That the Governments of southeast Asia honor the international agreements which apply in the area.
That those governments leave each other alone.
That they resolve their differences peacefully.
That they devote their talents to bettering the lives of their peoples by working against poverty and disease and ignorance.

He then based our action in South Vietnam upon previous commitments—the Geneva Accords of 1954, the SEATO Treaty, and the 1962 Declaration of Neutrality of Laos. In violation of the Geneva and Loas agreements, Hanoi was engaged in aggression against Saigon, Laos, and now, contrary to all law, the United States sixty miles off shore in the Gulf of Tonkin. So to all, including our Western allies under NATO, he proclaimed:

The challenge that we face in southeast Asia today is the same challenge that we have faced with courage and that we have met with strength in Greece and Turkey, in Berlin and Korea, and in Lebanon and in Cuba. And to any who may be tempted to support or to widen the present aggression I say this: there is no threat to any peaceful power from the United States of America. But there can be no peace by aggression and no immunity from reply.[70]

That was the Johnson answer to Hanoi's challenge in Southeast Asia. In this broad perspective he sought and won adoption of his Tonkin Gulf Resolution authorizing his action against Hanoi in 1964.

Critics of the war, led by Senator Fulbright, contended after 1964 that the Johnson administration stretched the Gulf of Tonkin Resolution far beyond the Senate's intention. The resolution was not meant, they said, to give the executive a blank check, a predated declaration of war, or an endorsement of a wider war. However, Johnson repeatedly cited the resolution to justify whatever action he took in Vietnam toward a wider war. The Congress did not mean to support by its resolution an extension of the war anywhere. It did mean to endorse our right of self-defense. Senator Gaylord Nelson of Wisconsin noted that the resolution did not limit the president's power under the Constitution, "neither does it offer Congressional endorsement and support for an expanded new course of action." The Wisconsin senator discussed with Senator Fulbright a possible amendment to the resolution:

> The Congress also approves and supports the efforts of the President to bring the problem of peace in Southeast Asia to the Security Council of the United Nations, and the President's declaration that the United States, seeking no extension of the present military conflict, will respond to provocation in a manner that is "limited and fitting." Our continuing policy is to limit our role to the provision of aid, training assistance, and military advice, and it is the sense of Congress that, except when provoked to a greater response, we should continue to avoid a direct military involvement in the Southeast Asian conflict.

Nelson wished to make it clear that in his opinion most senators felt our basic mission in Vietnam was "one of providing material support and advice. It is not to substitute our armed forces for those of the South Vietnamese Government, nor to join with them in a land war, nor to fight the war for them."[71]

The president did not have to consult Congress at all. He already had all the power necessary to defend our forces against attack, but he sought to achieve a broad political base for whatever actions he might wish to take. The Nelson amendment debate revealed that some congressmen, aware of the broader possibilities of the resolution, would limit presidential discretion. They expressed their fears of unlimited executive power, of too many facts kept secret from the people, and of attacks we had possibly provoked. Some believed our ships were or had been inside North Vietnamese territorial waters; but, no matter: the administration was using the incident to stampede the Congress into granting unlimited power to the president to escalate the war. Many could not explain why Hanoi would attack two United States destroyers so far off shore and protected by two United States airplane carriers. Why such an attempt at suicide? Some charged we had deliberately sought to expand the war.

Whatever the ultimate truth, by the resolution the United States Congress authorized the president "to take all necessary steps, including the use of armed forces, to assist" the members of SEATO, Laos, Cambodia, or South Vietnam if any of them sought "assistance in defense of their freedom." The wording of the resolution further stated that the operation of the resolution would expire when the president determined that "the peace and security of the area is reasonably assured by International conditions created by action of the United Nations or otherwise." It could expire also by a concurrent resolution of Congress, which would not require executive approval. Later, when congressional criticism of the war mounted, the president and his supporters snapped: Let Congress refuse the funds necessary to execute the war; let them repeal the resolution if they wish.

A larger war resulted from the raids and our heavy if measured response. Since the late 1950s Hanoi, backed by Peking and Moscow, had supported the efforts of the Vietcong with money, material, advice, and propaganda. In early 1964 Russia gave her full support to wars of national liberation, such as then existed in South Vietnam. This was the Soviet reply to Johnson's hint a few days before that the war might be expanded into North Vietnam, the base of the Vietcong guerrilla forces operating inside South Vietnam. The weakness, disunity, and lack of popular support for the various governments of Saigon made it clear that without our expanded support Saigon would soon collapse, the Vietcong would win, and a reunited Communist Vietnam would soon appear. The system and the people we had supported for ten years would surely collapse.

Johnson had no easy options. Withdrawal was unacceptable, and continuation of the 1964 situation would not save Saigon, its militarist rulers, or those popular elements who wished to struggle on for a possibly richer freedom. Hence the United States felt forced to increase its efforts to frustrate Communist conquest, but without the risk of world or nuclear war. From France came repeated talk of possible neutralization; but by this solution she only wished to extricate us from the war and permit a peaceful Communist takeover of South Vietnam. This would duplicate and justify French abandonment of North Vietnam in 1954. Our conception of neutralism, should that be the solution, was that both sides, Hanoi and Saigon, Communists and non-Communists, would accept agencies and guarantees by all powers, possibly under the United Nations, to preserve the true neutrality of the peoples involved, with appropriate forces of neutral nations stationed in the regions where and when necessary to preserve and protect such neutrality. Both Hanoi and the Vietcong would accept neither true neutrality nor United Nations advice.

All these options were being urged upon the president inside and outside the United States. Hard-line Republicans urged full military victory and condemned all who would seek an easy or cowardly peace. Nixon urged that we stand firm everywhere—in Panama, in Cuba, and in Vietnam—unless we wished in a few years to be faced with "immense problems that could lead to war." Barry Goldwater stumped the nation from "sea to shining sea" accusing the administration of lacking firmness, saying he would send ships to stop trade with Cuba and do what had to be done to win the war in Southeast Asia.

In 1964 a *New York Times* editorial pointed up the sharp contrast between Johnson and Goldwater. It declared:

> The world has seen and admired the judgment President Johnson has exercised in three Tonkin Gulf incidents. A sensible balance has been struck between firmness and restraint. Whatever the contrary advice he has received from some around him, it has been clear to friend and foe alike that Lyndon Johnson seeks "no wider war."
>
> But with Barry Goldwater in the White House, a volatile nature, a penchant for military solutions and a philosophy of brinkmanship could combine to create a situation of great danger. . . .
>
> Mr. Goldwater has indeed called for "victory" and "a new winning strategy." He clearly favors more vigorous American military measures, including air attacks on Communist supply lines in North Vietnam, if not in South China. After the single retaliatory American air strike in Tonkin Gulf, he argued that "if

we had kept up our attacks," the Communists would have given up the war. He has raised the possibility of an ultimatum to the Communist Chinese. In San Diego May 26 Mr. Goldwater said he would not use nuclear arms in Vietnam if conventional weapons could do the job, but he nevertheless "would leave it up to the commanders."

The *New York Times* found it alarming that Goldwater would delegate to the military so much of the executive authority he then campaigned to secure and quoted Goldwater's observation to the German correspondent of June 30, "I would turn to my Joint Chiefs of Staff and say, 'Fellows, we made the decision to win, now its your problem.' "[72] It then accused Goldwater of seeking to convert an Asian into an American war, declared he and his vice-presidential candidate, William Miller, saw Vietnam only as part of a global Communist conspiracy that we must defeat. The candidates attached no significance at all to the Sino-Soviet split.

The hawks had never liked the concept of limited or measured response. Their advice was to win, win, win! To use the power fate gave us to prevail where our interests were deemed vital. The situation worsened in Southeast Asia during 1964, and all our past efforts to help Saigon seemed not enough to prevent total disaster. In this crisis, with repeated and ominous reports from Saigon, the Defense Department still carried the ball and exercised more influence than did the State Department. While one agency of the executive branch seemingly worked for peace, another worked for a larger war, and often neither one knew what the other was planning and doing. Carefully and secretly laid plans for negotiation with Hanoi, reporters lacking the full facts declared, vanished into total futility with an air raid or sudden attack—not exactly conducive to good faith in the conduct of peace efforts. The nation and the world split on the issue of the war.

Not the Vietcong and the Communists. They meant to win any way possible. In late 1964 and early 1965 reports came to Washington that Hanoi was now sending sizable numbers of her regular forces to help the Vietcong inside South Vietnam. When by the close of 1964 the intelligence from Saigon revealed "that at least three regular North Vietnamese regiments—the 95th, 32d, and 101st—had left their bases in North Vietnam and were moving south for possible commitment in South Vietnam," our worst fears proved well-founded.[73] South Vietnam had not invaded the North with ground forces, but our air attacks equalled such an invasion in their devastation and brought a wider involvement by Hanoi directly in the ground war. We estimated, wrote Robert Shaplen, that Ho in "1964 had infiltrated at least 10,000 hard-core" Communist troops into the South, and that by the end of the year such forces "totaled at least 30,000." South Vietnamese officials put the figure at 45,000. Political weakness and instability, especially in the rural areas, had encouraged the Communists. Floods in Central Vietnam killed thousands, made other thousands homeless, and added great burdens to an already overburdened Saigon government. The Vietcong quickly seized every advantage, moved into every possible nook and cranny, and boldly attacked our air base at Bien Hoa, killing four and wounding nineteen Americans, and destroying five B-57 bombers. These events raised anew the issue of more bombing attacks upon the North and of a wider American participation and a greater American effort.[74]

In February 1965, Shaplen continued, while Kosygin was on a visit to Hanoi, where he praised the inspiring example of the North Vietnamese and offered full Russian support for the war against "American interventionists and their puppets," came a vicious night attack by the Vietcong on the American barracks at Pleiku. The Vietcong left eight Americans dead and more than a hundred wounded. They attacked other installations simultaneously and with similar losses to us. Twelve hours later Johnson ordered air attacks on the barracks, installations, and "major staging areas at Donghoi, just beyond the Seventeenth Parallel in North Vietnam." Although he told Moscow the "attacks were retaliatory and were not meant to expand the war," thereafter the air war increased step by step until it included the fringes of Hanoi and vast areas and targets within a few miles of the Chinese border. While we soon demonstrated that we could prevent a Vietcong victory, we could never quite win the war ourselves without a nearly total destruction of the land and its people.[75]

Without our aid Saigon was doomed to defeat, so Senator Mansfield reported to Congress and the nation in January 1966:

The most important new factor in the war in Vietnam has been the introduction of large numbers of U.S. troops into South Vietnam and their direct entry into combat. This augmentation of the U.S. military role in Vietnam was a response to a near-desperate situation early in 1965. There is no question that the Government of Vietnam in Saigon was faced with a rapidly deteriorating position at that time.

After the assassination of Ngo Dinh Diem, repeated coups had weakened the cohesiveness of the central authority and acted to stimulate public disaffection and indifference to the war. At the same time, there was a greatly accelerated military drive by strengthened Vietcong forces. Their control expanded over large areas of the country, particularly in provinces adjacent to the western borders. Communications and transportation between population centers became increasingly hazardous, except by Vietcong sufferance. In short, a total collapse of the Saigon government's authority appeared imminent in the early months of 1965.[76]

Without our aid Saigon's defeat was sure, it was true, but escalation bred escalation. Problems beyond our capacity to solve plagued us. Two cultures found it difficult to understand one another. Language barriers existed; the coordination of plans and the execution of programs for peaceful or military purposes were difficult. Corruption at every level of government and society wasted vast resources. At no point were we able to establish a government in Saigon acceptable to the vast majority of the people, especially in the countryside. In spite of our vast efforts at pacification, land reform, education, health, and welfare, the Vietcong could readily destroy faster than we could build. We could clear vast regions, but could not hold them unless we could put millions more men into the effort. A limited war of limited resources and perhaps limited will was never able to overcome the diabolically clever maneuvers of the Vietcong. Without stability, pacification was impossible. Force would have to precede, certainly accompany, the stability, but force was never enough to achieve stability. The Vietcong would not stand idly by and permit us the time successful pacification required.

We expanded the war to compensate for the collapse of our protégé Diem and the weakness of the anti-Communist forces in South Vietnam, to boost the sagging morale of the South Vietnamese, to prevent the collapse of their government, and to silence the ever-pressing hawks in America. By October 1965 our troops exceeded those of the regular South Vietnamese army. As Saigon further collapsed and its will to fight weakened, we made up for the loss with more and more of our own forces. In such fashion their war became ever more our war. The broad anti-Communist base of all the South Vietnamese so essential to victory in our struggle with the Vietcong was never established. The anti-Communists never loved their country or freedom enough to unite to save either. We threw in enough force to save the cities for a while, but could never find enough to protect simultaneously all the countryside. Security had to come first, before the people could risk a full and honest anti-Communist effort. Our forces were too often here today but gone tomorrow, while the native Vietcong were everywhere and forever present, if not always identifiable. We tried the search-and-destroy method to clear the villages of the Communists; but, in clearing the villages and herding the people into centers for protection, our methods of destruction were often ruthless and our care for the people in the new centers was not adequate to win them over. Rather it often promoted resentment or sullen neutralism.

The gradual rise in our economic aid and military commitment proved ineffective. The Pentagon long favored a greater effort to extend the war to North Vietnam. This argument gained force when Goldwater, strongly advocating military victory, won the support of millions. Ambassador Lodge ended his term as ambassador in 1964 with a recommendation that the United States continue to expand its efforts to win a victory in Southeast Asia. The Saigon government took all this as a sign of American support and roared louder for a greater effort to march to the North.

Neither before nor after the sharp expansion of the war and the use of combat troops in South Vietnam was there a formal declaration of war by the United States government, but we had fought many undeclared wars. The latest and most prominent example was the Korean War. David Rees noted in *Korea: A Limited War* that in 1950 at the very moment when he was taking actions that involved widespread combat operations, President Truman told the world, "We are not at war." In his view, "the United States was supporting a United Nations police action in Korea," and the urgency for action did not permit the time essential for a possibly prolonged debate over a declaration of war. It was to our great advantage to stress the collective nature of the United Nations intervention. By the United Nations Charter, member nations were already automatically committed to actions deemed necessary to preserve the peace. Shrewd as that interpretation of the Charter seemed in 1950, it left the president exposed as the one solely responsible for the actions taken thereafter under the exercise of his war powers.[77] Senator Taft and others referred to the crisis as "Truman's War," and Congress, which never refused to vote the funds to support the war, could hide behind the president's initial decision and let him take the rap for any consequences.

After 1965, the State Department, in the publication *The Question of a Formal Declaration of War in Viet-Nam,* explained the omission of a formal declaration of war on the following grounds. First, from the international viewpoint it was undesirable to request a formal declaration of war, because our policy in Vietnam was to assist Saigon, at its own request, "in thwarting an armed aggression from North Viet-Nam and to achieve a workable settlement of the dispute among the principal parties involved." This policy had limited aims: it sought to end the aggression "without threatening the destruction of North Vietnam," widening the war, or giving any basis for enemy miscalculation of our intentions. The United States believed that "the struggle must be won primarily in South Viet-Nam" and hence was "a defensive military effort." Secondly, a declaration of war would add a new and possibly explosive element to the world situation, since twentieth-century wars had widely come to imply "the total destruction of an enemy." It would therefore greatly increase the danger of Communist "misunderstanding of our true objectives in the conflict" and "of their expanded involvement in it."[78] There was also the possibility that Russia and China had secret treaties with Hanoi that committed them to help defend North Vietnam in case of war.

In defense of his belief that unfortunate as was the war in Vietnam, it was far better that Congress made no formal declaration, Senator Jacob Javits of New York wrote in 1970:

The Viet Nam action issues from executive decision; it is not a commitment of the national honor.
If the Congress had declared war, a tremendous complex of international agreements, a whole area of international law would have been invoked in such fashion as to unloose unforeseeable consequences. Public opinion might very well have required the bombing of Haiphong harbor and probably a land invasion of North Viet Nam.[79]

He added that had the Congress formally declared war in 1965 it would not have been as easy for its members to dissent from the war later. He appeared to feel that an executive decision for war did not commit the national honor so deeply as a formal declaration by Congress would have and noted that "the power not to declare war is a legitimate check on foreign policy."[80]

Further, continued the State Department analysis, such a declaration would permit doubts as to "the continued validity of the President's statements concerning his desire for a peaceful settlement allowing the various nations of the area, including North Viet-Nam, to live together in economic cooperation and his reiteration that we do not threaten the existence of North Viet Nam" itself. A declaration of limited warfare did not seem possible, believable, or feasible.[81]

"On balance," a war declaration might "significantly reduce the flexibility" of our efforts and means of seeking a solution among so many complex factors and lessen the chances that our enemy would take a reasonable approach to a solution. From the very first, our policy aimed to avoid closing any possible road to peace; rather it hoped to make Hanoi more, not less, rational in its response to our desired peaceful solution of the conflict. The State Department contended further that modern international law did not require a state to declare war "before engaging in hostilities against another state, nor would a formal declaration of war impose any obligations on an enemy by which we would not otherwise be bound." Absence of a formal declaration was not a factor that made the "international use of force unlawful. The only relevant legal question is whether the use of force is justified." The State Department release then observed:

Examples of hostilities begun without prior declaration of war abound in recent history. The fighting in Korea from 1950 to 1953, that in Indochina from 1947 to 1954, that in and around the Suez Canal in 1956, and that in West New Guinea between the Dutch and Indonesians in the spring and summer of 1962 all took place without benefit of declarations of war. We are not aware that the absence of declarations of war in these cases has been alleged to constitute a violation of international law.[82]

The international law relating to armed conflicts applied to all such conflicts, declared or not. "All that is required is armed conflict between two or more international entities." The State Department brief cited the 1949 Geneva Conventions for the Protection of War Victims, which specifically were made to apply to any "armed conflict of an international character" between two or more parties. The rules of war formed early in the twentieth century in the Hague Convention and deemed "binding on all states" as a "part of customary international law" were applicable without relation to a formal declaration of war.[83]

The State Department argued that for several reasons domestic considerations made it undesirable for the president to seek a declaration of war. It was not necessary "to authorize the actions" taken or to express the intent of our action in Vietnam. "The President has the power under Article II, Section 2, of the Constitution as Commander-in-Chief to deploy United States military forces to Viet-Nam" to help South Vietnam defend itself against invasion from Hanoi. The State Department brief declared there had been one hundred and twenty-five instances since the Constitution was adopted of presidential prosecution of war without congressional authority or formal declaration of war. In the case of Vietnam, congressional intent was expressed by the Joint Resolution of Congress of August 7, 1964, adopted by a combined vote of 504 to 2, explicitly approving all necessary steps including the use of armed force to defend the freedom of Southeast Asia. A formal declaration was not necessary to provide emergency power for the president. Many laws become operative in wartime, and most of those in effect after 1964 were "operative . . . by virtue of the state of emergency proclaimed by President Truman in December 1950. . . . However, there are only a few laws which can become operative only in time of war, and they have not been found necessary for the conduct of hostilities in Viet-Nam."[84] It is needless to add that antiwar forces rejected all these arguments and termed the war illegal, obscene, and immoral. In their view, however, a formal declaration would not have lessened its obscenity. They sought to discredit the involvement in every possible way, used the lack of a formal declaration for the purpose, and ignored the repeated examples of struggles without formal declaration.

In September 1964 Ambassador Taylor flew to Washington for a quick and urgent review of the situation which posed the possibility of the immediate political collapse of the Saigon government. Taylor told Johnson that Saigon controlled only about 30 percent of the country's territory; approximately 20 percent of the land belonged to the Vietcong. The rest was a no-man's-land in dispute, and the Vietcong had expanded their hard core of twenty thousand men in 1961 to about fifty thousand in 1964.[85] Kahin and Lewis stated that Taylor thought victory was impossible unless the cost to Hanoi and the Vietcong became unbearable; hence all possible effort must be made to increase our commitment and share in the war. The basic question then before us was: How much longer would there be any government or organization for us to support in South Vietnam? While Johnson kept saying publicly that we did not want to get tied down in a land war in Asia, his advisers secretly were suggesting a different course. In late September in Tokyo, William P. Bundy, Assistant Secretary of State for Far Eastern Affairs, said that although we did not wish the war expanded outside South Vietnam, such a course could be forced upon us by an increase of Communist pressure, "including a rising scale of infiltration." Threats of air action against the North and the belief it could successfully counter any rising guerrilla action lay behind such statements. A division of opinion between the need for a wider war with American ground forces involved and the fear that such a course would risk total war split our government. Some wished to be reassured that our ships were in Tonkin Gulf to end the war and not to provoke incidents that could bring a larger war.[86]

With the election over, Kahin and Lewis wrote, powerful forces inside the Johnson administration pressed strongly for a wider war. All the members of the Joint Chiefs of Staff reportedly worked for a broader commitment of our forces. Ambassador Taylor, former Chief of Staff, openly urged us to bomb the North and the infiltration routes through Laos. Senator Richard Russell, Chairman of the Senate Armed Services Committee, after a conference with the president on November 25, 1964, stated:

We either have to get out or take some action to help the Vietnamese. They won't help themselves. We made a big mistake in going there, but I can't figure out any way to get out without scaring the rest of the world.[87]

How can we really ever help people who "won't help themselves"? This was surely the time for most sober reflection.

Rushed back to Washington, Ambassador Taylor painted such a gloomy picture of the situation in South Vietnam that McNamara was heard telling the president: "It would be impossible for Max to talk to these people without leaving the impression the situation is going to hell." A press conference scheduled to follow the talks was cancelled.[88]

Peace negotiations in such a situation, still urgently sought by United Nations Secretary General U Thant, were deemed an unacceptable embarrassment by the United States and Saigon. On January 31, 1965, Moscow announced that Premier Kosygin would lead a delegation to Hanoi. Washington considered this a gesture of Russian support for Hanoi and a warning to us against a wider war; but possibly it was the beginning of an effort by Moscow to mediate a settlement, which in that situation would have greatly favored Hanoi. While Kosygin was in Hanoi, Johnson reiterated our determination to help more effectively the people of South Vietnam resist aggression and preserve their freedom. The Vietcong raid of February 7 against the American barracks at Pleiku, Johnson felt, justified a further expansion of our military aid.

Alfred Steinberg, a biographer highly critical of Johnson's war record, declared that Sunday, February 7, 1965, was the day LBJ departed from previous administrations, widened the war, and called for air strikes against the North. At 3 P.M., the previous Saturday, in the cabinet room with Cyrus Vance, Bill Moyers, George Ball, and General Earle Wheeler, he received the news from General William Westmoreland of the Vietcong raid on Pleiku and two other installations. This was what the president had been "impatiently waiting for." That Saturday evening he told a meeting of the National Security Council: "I've had enough of this." For months he had studied the excellent pictures of the North Vietnamese terrain taken by our U2 spy planes, "and he was more familiar with the terrain, installations, farms, factories, villages, cities, roads, and rivers than most of the air reconnaissance experts at the Pentagon." He knew the targets he wished to hit. He sent word to our ambassador to the United Nations, Adlai Stevenson, to excuse our action to U Thant as "defense actions," as a reply to "intensified Communist aggression in South Vietnam." Then he ordered our planes "to flatten the targets." Jack Valenti, proud of his master, said, "There is something about an emergency that puts an extra hunk of steel in his spine." Once again the Vietcong raided another American station, and Johnson ordered another attack. And so it expanded into an ever-wider air war. The war was spreading like a prairie fire:

At the beginning of 1965, an estimated twenty thousand American "advisers" were stationed in South Vietnam to man bases and train South Vietnamese troops, of whom an estimated ninety thousand were deserting annually. When an additional 3,500 Marines landed in March, Johnson had McNamara tell reporters they were sent merely to relieve South Vietnamese soldiers who had been assigned to protect American bases and not to "tangle with the Viet Cong." At the end of March Viet Cong guerrillas bombed the American Embassy in Saigon, and Johnson in retaliation dispatched another forty thousand American soldiers to South Vietnam. Instead of being called advisers, these June arrivals were referred to as combat-support troops, and their stated function was to fight the

Viet Cong only in emergencies when South Vietnamese troops were busy elsewhere.

The emergencies started coming in increasing numbers, and American casualties began to grow. By the end of the year they totaled 1,350 Americans killed and 5,300 wounded. There were now 190,000 American troops in South Vietnam, and despite the assurances by Defense Secretary McNamara that all was going well, stories made the rounds in Washington that Johnson and the Joint Chiefs of Staff were discussing putting perhaps a half million or even a million soldiers into Vietnam before long. This was now the American War that Johnson had campaigned against in 1964.[89]

By 1968 the American forces in South Vietnam exceeded the half million mark, and victory was not in sight for either side when the Paris talks began between Hanoi and Washington.

After the Vietcong raid at Pleiku, our planes attacked North Vietnam in force. It was "a test of will," when inaction would have certainly indicated weakness and defeatism, and it would stiffen the resistance spirit of our ally in South Vietnam. Although Johnson again declared we sought no wider war, in the next few days came two further air raids against selected targets in North Vietnam. Washington insisted that there was a difference between retaliation and outright war. However, words could not conceal the truth that a major expansion of the war had occurred. Since we refused negotiation from weakness, we apparently had decided to make a greater military effort in order to achieve a position of greater strength for eventual negotiation.

Thus, the United States was getting ready for a peace-through-pressure plan. It was an effort to bomb Hanoi to the conference table. At least by bombing we would be doing something we could later stop doing in return for possible concessions. An expanded war might also spur South Vietnam to renewed efforts. Political shifts in Saigon brought power into the hands of those favoring a larger war and victory. Here began the rising role to be played by Thieu and Ky, who declared that the Armed Forces Council, under the chairmanship of Thieu, would replace any government that tried to betray the country. These men soon gained full control of the government and long opposed any negotiated settlement. In March Saigon publicly announced that the war was obviously a case of self-defense, that there could be no peace until Hanoi and the Vietcong ended the war they had provoked and ceased their infiltration. The day after this statement United States bombers attacked North Vietnam in the first of a long series of raids that were not described as retaliatory.

Governments before Johnson's administration sought to limit our role in the war, to prevent any locked-in collision course of action that might, with mutual increases, eventually bring total global war. Johnson followed a policy of gradual or limited expansion, but he set no upper limit to the amount of force we might use. Critics said he was more concerned with our global military posture than the immediate war needs of Vietnam. The most powerful nation on earth must demonstrate to the world its firm determination and reliability as an ally. We increased our power and role in Vietnam, therefore, because of transcending global considerations. Containment of global communism and the effective performance of the role of world policeman in Southeast Asia required an effective demonstration of power and a resolution to succeed at whatever we decided to do. In any case, Johnson, concerned with objectives in and beyond Vietnam, insisted he would not be the first president to lose a war, betray an ally, and appease Communist despotism. Weakness in Southeast Asia, he thought, would invite trouble elsewhere, create a bandwagon psychology in the direction of communism, and demonstrate the truth of the domino theory.

Some in his official family believed a military victory was the only way to obtain a favorable political solution. Critics saw a sharp distinction between the limited objective of a favorable negotiating position and the rising aim of total military victory. The latter would require a far greater military effort, mean far greater losses of men and materiel, and undoubtedly cause a prolonged and bitter war. Some called the expanded effort "strategic persuasion." The casualties, the taxes, the devastation, and the length of the war increased.

Chinese and Russian efforts to aid with technical assistance, labor battalions, and materiel enabled Hanoi and the Vietcong to expand their efforts. Bomb as we did, the Vietcong received ample supplies by seizure from Saigon and the United States depots, by bicycles and shanks' mare along the various roads and trails not totally cut off by our air power, and even by sea. The enemy lived off the land and brought down only the barest and most essential supplies.

The crucial decision to deny the enemy a safe sanctuary in North Vietnam, in the DMZ, and in nearby Laos was the initial departure from earlier administrations. Then came the fatal decision to commit our ground forces when marines were first introduced from March to July 1965.[90] The first air attacks in the Tonkin Gulf in August 1964 and the attacks upon North Vietnam in retaliation for Communist raids upon Pleiku and other installations in February 1965 were soon superseded by sustained raids. Claims of success against enemy supply lines were refuted by McNamara's statement and the president's speech of June 30, 1966, in which he noted that Chinese coolie labor had transformed "jungle trails into all weather roads" able to permit Russian trucks to carry supplies southward. Thus, by mid-1966 a further enlargement of the war was necessary to counter the North's response to our previous expansion.[91]

One of Johnson's closest advisers, Walt Rostow, gave his enumeration of the key dates leading directly to the initial involvement and commitment of our ground forces:

January 27: A McNamara-Bundy memorandum asserts "the time has come for harder choices" and leans toward the "use of our military power in the Far East . . . to force a change of Communist policy."

February 7: Bundy, back from a trip to Vietnam in wake of attack on U.S. barracks in Pleiku and the retaliatory air strike on North Vietnam, urges "graduated and continuing reprisal" through air and naval action.

February 13: Johnson decides in principle on "measured and limited air action jointly with GVN" against military targets below the 19th parallel, 120 miles deep into North Vietnam.

March 13: Regular bombing of North Vietnam begins.

March-May: Marine and Army airborne units are dispatched to protect key U.S. air bases.

May-June: ARVN suffers major military setbacks in battles against regular North Vietnamese units; Nguyen Van Thieu and Nguyen Cao Ky take over government and ask for additional U.S. forces.

July: McNamara goes to Vietnam and recommends on July 20 that Johnson "expand promptly and substantially the U.S. military pressure against the Viet Cong in the South," including increased U.S. ground forces: Johnson announces prompt dispatch of an additional 50,000 troops, July 28, 1965, with "additional forces" to follow.[92]

That was the day, July 28, 1965, that "the die was cast," so he thought. Three reasons justified the action. For at least a year Hanoi had decided to commit its regular units to the battle and to seek a direct military victory. Rostow believed this enemy action was inspired by one of our great failures—that of Kennedy to respond "decisively to Hanoi's systematic violation of the Laos Accords of 1962." The enemy had with impunity broken its pledges, and we had simply stood by and done nothing. Enemy trails through this supposedly neutralized state continued in full use by Hanoi moving its forces southward. Rostow noted that "as in 1917 and 1941, 1947 and 1950, the American weight was thrown into the scale late, long after the aggressors had committed themselves to the venture." Further, Johnson's decision came only after "the Vietnamese were almost beaten to their knees in mid-1965." The first task now was above all to avoid defeat, not just to cut off the trails by which enemy supplies filtered southward.[93]

Finally, Johnson pondered the options before him and decided our ground forces were necessary, but he would gradually introduce them to avoid "a sharp political and psychological change in course." Rostow explained the reason for caution:

His diplomatic advisers urged strongly that this was the route best calculated to minimize the likelihood of Soviet or Chinese Communist military intervention. Johnson's nuclear responsibility bore heavily upon him. . . . He was determined to defend American security interests and honor the nation's treaties in ways consistent with the survival of civilization. The memory of Chinese intervention in Korea also played a part. . . .

These considerations suggested a defensive pattern of military operations. The strategy for our "victory" over "time" was to break the enemy will by denying him victory. Westmoreland believed he had been told to defeat aggression so the South Vietnamese might "be free to shape their own destiny." Thus we committed our strength to the degree deemed essential to permit self-determination; but the critical, if not uncontrollable, variant in this plan was always the capacity and will of the South Vietnamese to "shape their own destiny."[94]

In early 1965, the crucial period, the situation looked ominous for Saigon.

Northern troops—fighting units, not just replacements for Vietcong losses—were entering the South. Hanoi obviously sought a quick military victory. Ho then saw only weakness and disunity in South Vietnam and judged that war, open and aggressive, plus intensified terror, assassination, and destruction would speed the final defeat of South Vietnam. Thus LBJ wrote: "In March I agreed to General Westmoreland's request that we land two Marine battalions to provide security for the Danang air base."[95] Then through February and March increasing numbers of North Vietnamese regulars moved southward. Johnson was urged to consider sending sizable increases in United States forces to South Vietnam. Enemy atrocities against our installations and near the American Embassy accented the danger. We escalated the war to prevent Communist takeover.

By June 9 our forces were told not only to protect our base areas, but to assist Vietnamese units when they were in serious trouble. In late June that was extended to permit our troops to take either independent or allied action when that was deemed necessary to strengthen South Vietnamese efforts. This expansion was strongly urged by the Saigon government. Thieu and Ky believed no fewer than two hundred thousand American soldiers were immediately necessary. The military and economic situations were sharply deteriorating. The only answer seemed to be for us to expand our involvement. McNamara recommended sharp expansion, possibly a hundred thousand men by early 1966. He wished it made clear that we meant no invasion of North Vietnam. The major dissident, George Ball, offered these opinions: "We could not win a protracted war against local guerrillas in Asian jungles"; there was great danger of Chinese intervention; we would "lose friends and influence in Europe and elsewhere"; it would be best "to cut our losses and pull away"; expansion invited risks, and retraction raised problems, but its advantages outweighed the dangers of a larger war.[96]

Dean Rusk, LBJ later wrote, expressed a major worry which the president also entertained: "If the Communist world finds out that we will not pursue our commitments to the end . . . I don't know where they will stay their hand."[97] LBJ felt sure they would not stay their hand, and he could see that if we abandoned Southeast Asia, there would be trouble everywhere. Retreat from the challenge here "would open the path to World War III." However, Clark Clifford, an "old friend" of LBJ (so wrote the president) bluntly warned: "I don't believe we can win in South Vietnam . . . . If we send in 100,000 more men, the North Vietnamese will meet us. If North Vietnam runs out of men, the Chinese will send in volunteers. Russia and China don't intend for us to win the war."[98] He urged that over the coming months we quietly probe the possibilities with other nations for an honorable escape from the involvement because "I can't see anything but catastrophe for my country. . . ."[99]

After days of serious reflection and discussion, his inner advisers in Congress and the administration favored giving Westmoreland the forces needed to save South Vietnam from defeat. The only person to express serious doubts and opposition to that decision was Mike Mansfield. Although he would support the president in whatever action he undertook, he spoke of the "deepening discontent in the country. He thought the best hope was 'a quick stalemate and negotiations.' "[100]

Then the president had to decide for himself what would happen to the nation and the world if we failed to act with courage and stamina, if we let South Vietnam fall to Hanoi. Historians may long argue, as did the generation that lived during the war, the causes of our military intervention; but, in truth, the man who made the decision, the president, could most surely best know why *he* acted. His opinion therefore becomes the paramount factor. Here was Johnson's justification:

This is what I could foresee: First, from all the evidence available to me it seemed likely that all of Southeast Asia would pass under Communist control, slowly or quickly, but inevitably, at least down to Singapore but almost certainly to Djakarta. I realize that some Americans believe they have, through talking with one another, repealed the domino theory. In 1965 there was no indication in Asia, or from Asians, that this was so. On both sides of the line between Communist and non-Communist Asia the struggle for Vietnam and Laos was regarded as a struggle for the fate of Southeast Asia. The evidence before me as President confirmed the previous assessments of President Eisenhower and of President Kennedy.

Second, I knew our people well enough to realize that if we walked away from Vietnam and let Southeast Asia fall, there would follow a divisive and destructive debate in our country. This had happened when the Communists took power in China. But that was very different from the Vietnam conflict. We had a solemn treaty commitment to Southeast Asia. We had an international agreement on Laos made as late as 1962 that was being violated flagrantly. We had the word of three Presidents that the United States would not permit this aggression to succeed. A divisive debate about "who lost Vietnam" would be, in my judgment, even more destructive to our national life than the argument over China had been. It would inevitably increase isolationist pressures from the right and the left and cause a pulling back from our commitments in Europe and the Middle East as well as in Asia.

Third, our allies not just in Asia but throughout the world would conclude that our word was worth little or nothing. Those who had counted so long for their security on American commitments would be deeply shaken and vulnerable.

Fourth, knowing what I did of the policies and actions of Moscow and Peking, I was as sure as a man could be that if we did not live up to our commitment in Southeast Asia and elsewhere, they would move to exploit the disarray in the United States and in the alliances of the Free World. They might move independently or they might move together. But move they would—whether through nuclear blackmail, through subversion, with regular armed forces, or in some other manner. As nearly as one can be certain of anything, I knew they could not resist the opportunity to expand their control into the vacuum of power we would leave behind us.

Finally, as we faced the implications of what we had done as a nation, I was sure the United States would not then passively submit to the consequences. With Moscow and Peking and perhaps others moving forward, we would return to a world role to prevent their full takeover of Europe, Asia, and the Middle East—*after* they had commited themselves.[101]

The implication of that last statement clearly anticipated that our retreat would surely invite World War III and nuclear devastation.

As it became our war, too many Saigon officials and South Vietnamese were ever more willing to let us fight it for them, while they sat back and reaped whatever rewards war profiteering offered. By mid-1966 our units suffered more casualties than did Saigon's. Our use of nonlethal gas warfare to uncover the enemy by defoliation of the dense jungles was originally presented as a humanitarian measure to save innocent lives. By May 1966 it was justified as an easier way than using men to drive the enemy out of his complex system of tunnels so that he could be easily killed by high explosive bursts above ground. Even our helicopters and low-flying air attacks, which initially so nonplussed the enemy, soon found him devising effective countertactics and bringing in Russian antiaircraft weapons, which soon made Hanoi and North Vietnam one of the most dangerous runs our air power ever faced.

Our efforts, critics contended, merely hardened the will of the enemy to endure. In raising the cost of the war for our enemy, we had raised it for ourselves. Oriental patience and suffering, it was soon demonstrated, could likely outlast ours and accept indefinitely the rate of sacrifice of the years 1965-1968. Yet, we expected our forbearance in the further use of our vast destructive powers to cause Hanoi and the Vietcong to yield in order to avoid worse destruction and death. Hanoi, knowing we had the power to wipe out the entire country, was seemingly willing to risk that in preference to surrender. Did Johnson, Congress, or the American people realize when they gave the president the power to protect our destroyers in Tonkin Gulf that they were giving him the power to throw the full and awesome might of the greatest power on earth against a small, backward, primitive people of Southeast Asia, scarcely yet in the nineteenth, not to mention the twentieth, century?

Senator Fulbright, who led the debate in the fight for the Tonkin Gulf Resolution, later stated in defense of his support:

I did so because I was confident that President Johnson would use our endorsement with wisdom and restraint. I was also influenced by partisanship: an election campaign was in progress and I had no wish to make any difficulties for the President in his race against a Republican candidate whose election I thought would be a disaster for the country.

Although in sympathy with its purpose, he also helped to persuade the Senate to defeat the Nelson Amendment to the resolution, which sought to limit our commitment to aid, training, and advice, and to avoid a direct military involvement.[102]

Fulbright admitted in 1964 that our bargaining position was weak: "Until the equation of advantage between the two sides has been substantially altered in our favor, there can be little prospect of a negotiated settlement." At that point it seemed clear to Fulbright that we had but two realistic choices: "the expansion of the conflict in one way or another, or a renewed effort to bolster the capacity of the South Vietnamese to prosecute the war successfully on its present scale."[103]

Only after continued bombings and our introduction of ground forces did Fulbright begin to object—first through private memos to Johnson and then in public debate. The long-time friendship between Fulbright and Johnson suffered increasing strain in the years after 1964. The Senator from Arkansas, Chairman of the sometimes powerful Senate Committee on Foreign Relations, became the leader of a rising opposition to the wider war brought on by the president. A large part of the intelligentsia of the United States followed Fulbright in denouncing administration policies. He refused in 1964 to manage the foreign aid bill because it combined in a single package military and economic aid. The senator also sharply attacked Johnson's roughshod tactics against the Dominican Republic, his lack of generosity toward Panama, his rigid insistence upon fulfilling all commitments, his defense of the domino theory, and his stern adherence to the monolithic theory of global communism, when polycentrism had been rising since Tito's deviation of 1948.[104]

Further criticisms from inside the Democratic family came from Senators Mike Mansfield, Wayne Morse, Ernest Gruening, George McGovern, Eugene McCarthy, Robert Kennedy, and others. Fulbright was soon saying loud and clear that neither he nor the Congress meant the Gulf of Tonkin Resolution to become a blank check for all-out war. Mansfield, present at Manila in September 1954, strongly objected to the presidential citation of the SEATO Treaty as full endorsement of everything he was doing in Indochina:

I was a member of the three-man American delegation to Manila, along with Secretary of State Dulles and Senator Alexander Smith of New Jersey, in the writing of the SEATO agreement....We agreed on an alliance of anti-Communist countries there, but the American-type action in Vietnam was not included in that pact.

Nor did Mansfield agree with LBJ that current actions toward Vietnam had been forced on him by Eisenhower's letter to Diem in 1954.[105]

In June 1964 Johnson told a news conference that four basic themes governed our policy in Southeast Asia:

First, America keeps her word.
Second, the issue is the future of Southeast Asia as a whole.
Third, our purpose is peace.
Fourth, this is not just a jungle war, but a struggle for freedom on every front of human activity.
On the point that America keeps her word, we are steadfast in a policy which has been followed for 10 years in three administrations. That was begun by General Eisenhower, in a letter of October 25, 1954....

He read the letter Eisenhower had written ten years earlier offering our help to President Diem, declared "that it was a good letter then and it is a good letter now," and implied that Eisenhower had made a commitment which he must keep:

We will keep this commitment. In the case of Viet-Nam, our commitment today is just the same as the commitment made by President Eisenhower to President Diem in 1954—a commitment to help these people help themselves.

We are concerned for a whole great geographic area, not simply for specific complex problems in specific countries.[106]

Even Eisenhower objected to this interpretation and declared in 1965 Johnson's military action had no basis in his offer of economic aid in 1954. Mansfield, George McGovern, and others raised sharp doubts about the domino theory, which Secretary Rusk and McNamara also never accepted, except as a handy tool to win popular support. Steinberg noted that Mansfield scoffed at Johnson's hand-wringing claim that "if we quit in Vietnam, tomorrow we'll be fighting in Hawaii and next week we'll have to fight in San Francisco." McGovern wondered how "a flotilla of Chinese junks is going to get by the Seventh Fleet en route to San Francisco."[107]

Mansfield felt his role as majority floor leader in the Senate precluded an open conflict with the administration, but behind the scenes he repeatedly objected to wider war policies, especially to the commitment of ground troops and all the emphasis upon military victory. He rejected Johnson's contention that our retaliatory attacks did not expand the war, that he was just doing what had been done before because the troops there had already served as more than "advisers." Mansfield denounced such deception, noting that the very presence of combat troops and Johnson's announced plans of sending forty thousand more men introduced a new and dangerous dimension to the war. His first shock had come when LBJ, after the Pleiku attack of February 1965, sent thirty-five hundred marines, the first ground combat soldiers. To Mansfield that was the beginning of a big war for the United States, and the later expansions of troops, air strikes, and American efforts to win a military victory merely confirmed his initial fears. A long-time student of Southeast Asia, he had been convinced that a military victory was impossible. Only a political solution, accompanied by rural pacification and negotiation with the Vietcong and other dissident groups, could eventually bring an end to the crisis.[108]

Needled by Mansfield, Fulbright, and others, LBJ found it necessary to make some conciliatory gesture toward a peaceful solution. On April 7, 1965, at Johns Hopkins University, he pledged a billion-dollar investment to aid the economic development of Southeast Asia when the war ended and declared his readiness to engage in "unconditional discussions" to reach a peaceful solution. However, he defended his enlarged war program as necessary to honor national pledges to help preserve South Vietnam's independence and to prevent the total defeat of South Vietnam by a world communism bent on ultimate global conquest. To appease the doves, he declared he would never be second in the search for peace and would generously give full aid to develop all Southeast Asia, including the Mekong River Valley "on a scale to dwarf even our own TVA." This speech had been read and approved by war critics, among them Walter Lippmann, whose former enthusiastic support of the president had vanished in disillusionment over the tragic and deepening war in Vietnam. The president was so carried away by his own roseate scheme that he even persuaded Eugene R. Black, the esteemed wizard of finance, urbane banker, and ex-president of the World Bank to agree to manage this grandiose aid program for Southeast Asia. The gesture was soon lost along with the other hopefully announced possibilities of peaceful solutions that marked this tragic war.[109] Deepening war efforts, interspersed by brief moments of insincere enemy gestures toward peace, Saigon's slowness at pacification and land reform and our brief bombing pauses, marked the years after 1964.

Why did Johnson feel compelled to enlarge the war after 1964? Certainly because he wished to prevent the fall of South Vietnam to Ho and to check any further aggression against the rest of Southeast Asia. He accepted the domino theory. Communist wars of "national liberation," guerrilla or any other style, must be defeated and the whole threat of guerrilla subversion frustrated. Mao Tse-tung's classic three-step formula for subversion must be proved faulty:

Step One (Creation of Bases)

Secretly establish control of the rural people by the use of selective terrorism (murder) and propaganda.

Gradually eliminate government influence by the assassination of village chiefs and other notables.

Establish a political and military base among the people through force and persuasion.

Conduct guerrilla operations against the forces of law and order.

Step Two (Equilibrium)

Form squads, platoons, companies, and battalions from among the controlled population.

Increase guerrilla operations against remaining forces of law and order.

Expand the military and political base in order to build forces as strong as the government forces and in order to:

Destroy isolated government forces;

Extend political control of the people.

Step Three (Counteroffensive)

Create large military formations capable of attacking and destroying the government forces.

Extend political control over the entire population, eliminating by execution those who resist.

Attack and destroy the remaining forces of law and order.[110]

If communism could win here by the method of secrecy, terror, and subversion, no areas would be safe. Hanoi must be taught that aggression did not pay. In principle, Johnson believed we would either meet the Communist challenge here or later have to face it on our own shores.

Honestly, he believed that our treaty commitments under SEATO and earlier pledges of aid had committed us to give whatever assistance was essential to stop global communism. There should be no more Munichs. Once Rusk was heard to justify the war as necessary ultimately to stop the Yellow Peril—"a billion Chinese armed with nuclear weapons." If the United States failed to honor its commitments to defend nations seeking our aid in Southeast Asia, people elsewhere would not trust an American pledge, would seek peace with communism, and the world would sink into anarchy if not despotism and suffer greater future wars. If Kennedy increased our advisers to save Diem from defeat, Johnson did the same later in the belief that defeat was sure if we refused to put in ground combat forces in 1965. We fought, Johnson believed, to preserve the independence of South Vietnam and to give the South Vietnamese a chance to avoid the harsh fate that befell the North Vietnamese in 1954. By our involvement, we hoped to advance freedom in South Vietnam. Urgent as reform, pacification, and peasant support were, the administration believed that physical security was essential before those objectives could be won.

As problems arose and Hanoi expanded its efforts, it was easier to increase our commitment of men and materiel than to do anything else. And, as we expanded our military efforts, so did the enemy expand theirs. Escalation seemed always easier than negotiation. Certainly it was deemed preferable to appeasement and cowardice. When our every effort to negotiate a reasonable end to the war was rebuffed by Hanoi and the Vietcong, and the eternal demand that we withdraw and abandon South Vietnam to communism was the only option left us, it seemed ever easier to seek the defeat of the Vietcong than to persuade Ho to abandon his efforts to conquer the South. We expanded the war to persuade Ho to negotiate.

Not to be ignored was the immense pressure of the hawks inside and outside the Johnson administration. They insisted persuasively upon victory, upon humiliation of the enemy, and denounced any concept of even limited warfare. As our involvement deepened and casualties increased, the case for withdrawal, moderation, and compromise with communism weakened and the demand for victory grew. Sneak attacks in the Tonkin Gulf, upon Pleiku and Saigon—against civilians and soldiers alike—inspired little trust in Communist reason and peaceful intent. The picture of communism on the march ever since 1939 permitted little faith in rational solutions of problems in conflict between us. Rising support of the Vietcong by Hanoi, Moscow, Peking, and all world communism persuaded Washington that the Communists planned our ultimate humiliation, defeat, and conquest.

Be it partial or total war, one small slice or big slice at a time, the danger was rising, and the enemy plan seemed clear: spread communism over the globe. Just as in December 1941, when Japan chose to attack Pearl Harbor, leaving us no choice but to fight, so now it appeared that Communist attack, invasion, and aggression in Southeast Asia and elsewhere left no other honorable choice to us in 1965. The Johnson administration could never forget that a large, if indefinite, number of South Vietnamese had courageously undertaken to defend themselves and their country against

Communist attack and subversion and had asked us for help, which the SEATO Treaty and other pledges of assistance justified. The president truly believed he had no choice left him but to intervene to prevent a Communist seizure of South Vietnam. The betrayal of North Vietnam by the Western nations at Geneva in 1954 would not be repeated by his administration for the rest of that tragic nation and its people.

Later, doubts were repeatedly raised in public discussion and journalistic reports that South Vietnam ever officially requested our ground forces be introduced into the war. In their official report on the war in Vietnam the two ranking American commanders in charge of the naval and military operations declared in 1969 that it appeared that the Communists would succeed—

perhaps in a matter of months, as things were developing. Acting on the request of the South Vietnamese government, the decision was made to commit as soon as possible 125,000 United States troops to prevent the Communist takeover. At the same time President Johnson indicated that additional forces would be sent as requested by the Republic of Vietnam and the Commander of the United States Military Assistance Command, Vietnam.[111]

War critics had long been unconvinced that we had ever officially been requested to send such aid, and some accused Johnson of forcing our assistance upon Saigon for our own and broader objectives.

Thus a great nation, unaware of the enormous costs compared to the minor gains that could possibly be won in Vietnam, plunged tragically into a war in the expectation and hope of a clear-cut, if limited, victory over a concealed enemy backed by combined populations in excess of one billion people. In truth, nothing inherited from past regimes locked the president into such a collision course. His great election victory in 1964 freed him to make his own decisions, and his campaign rhetoric certainly pointed in the direction of peace, not war. Beyond that, the wisdom of hindsight should have suggested a reconsideration of whatever commitment we had in Vietnam. Certainly, if with all our aid over the last ten years Saigon's forces could not defeat or contain the Vietcong forces it outnumbered six to one, escalation was not the answer we should have found.

Critics felt the president and his advisers had lost all sense of proportion. Although he said repeatedly that all he wished was to permit South Vietnam's people a free choice, his terms left no room for compromise with the Vietcong and Hanoi. They should simply stop trying to conquer South Vietnam. The Johnson administration went into the war without ever developing a cost estimate of the effort and with no limit upon the commitment. Some felt the president regarded virtually every commitment as a blank check to cover the costs of the effort whatever they might be. No one calculated what such an effort might ultimately cost. The nation took a big leap into the dark, but Johnson did not and could not hide the action. Both the people and their government were well-informed and knew precisely what was done. Although many ultimately rejected the grounds on which we fought, no one could truthfully deny that Johnson repeatedly told the world why he decided to intervene. Furthermore, Congress voted the funds to foot the bill. Had the enemy quickly faded away, as innocents hoped and initially expected, the bitter dissension that followed would have been aborted and Johnson would have become a national hero.

CHAPTER TWO

LIMITED WAR

For Johnson, the American people, and many others Vietnam was a major tragedy. It split his party, betrayed the promise, and frustrated the fulfillment of his great electoral victory of 1964; checked the full development of his once-golden concept of a "Great Society"; stirred deep fears and wide denunciation in Western Europe; served to justify in undiscriminating minds Communist aggression around the globe; and weakened the strength, will, and unity of the whole free world. This seemingly endless war spent funds desperately needed to solve the housing, educational, crime, ecological, ghetto, and urban problems of a rising national population. However, with limited power and limited resources, simultaneous progress on both the peace and war fronts was impossible. For Johnson the problem to be solved was how to respond to the demands of the hawks for victory and the doves for domestic progress. Unfortunately he tried both. Peace gestures, bombing pauses, promises to go anywhere and confer at any time with anyone about a reasonable settlement were accompanied by an expanding military commitment of more men, materiel, air strikes, and broad ground sweeps to "search and destroy" or "clear and hold" to increase the pressure upon an enemy who would never quit or admit defeat. While Fulbright argued that Ho would no more likely surrender under such air raids than the British did in World War II, Dean Rusk contended that the raids would weaken popular support of Ho and bring him to the bargaining table.

In February 1965, Rusk declared Southeast Asia had "a right to live in peace," to be "free from aggression," which threatened its existence in freedom. In violation of the Geneva Agreement of 1954, the Declaration on the Neutrality of Laos, the Protocol of Geneva of 1962, and international law, North Vietnam had "directed and supplied the essential military personnel and arms for a systematic campaign of terror and guerrilla action aimed at the overthrow of the Government of South Viet-Nam and the imposition by force of a Communist regime." In citing our past efforts to reassure the people of South Vietnam of our friendliness and support, he included Eisenhower's offer of aid to Diem in

1954, the Manila Pact ratified in February 1955 by a vote of 82 to 1, and the Tonkin Gulf Resolution approved in 1964 by a congressional vote of 502 to 2. Worth a reminder, he felt, was President Johnson's statement upon signing the Tonkin Gulf Resolution:

> To any armed attack upon our forces, we shall reply.
> To any in Southeast Asia who ask our help in defending their freedom, we shall give it.
> In that region, there is nothing we covet, nothing we seek—no territory, no military position, no political ambition. Our one desire—our one determination—is that the people of Southeast Asia be left in peace to work out their own destinies in their own way.[1]

Repeatedly our officials had stated that the key to peace there and elsewhere was the readiness of all "to live at peace and leave their neighbors alone." There was no mystery about this, and there should be no mystery about the turbulence there. Those who refused to leave their neighbors alone knew what that meant. The Geneva pledge of 1954, the Laos agreement of 1962, and international law forbade "the illegal infiltration of military personnel and arms. . . ." Such acts could never "be described as 'leaving your neighbors alone.' " In repeated consultations the statesmen of Southeast Asia had sought ways to achieve freedom from aggression and subversion, but without any indication from Hanoi of the slightest willingness to cease its aggressive acts. On February 17, 1965, the president had firmly declared that our objective in South Vietnam was to defend and protect the freedom of South Vietnam from all aggression. Our actions would be only those held necessary to stop the assault. In this speech Johnson again stated:

We have no ambition there for ourselves. We seek no dominion. We seek no conquest. We seek no wider war. But we must all understand that we will persist in the defense of freedom and our continuing actions will be those which are justified and those that are made necessary by the continuing aggression of others.[2]

One month later on March 25, 1965, the president also advised the nation to keep a "cool and clear view of the situation in Viet-Nam." In a review of the war, then beginning its rapid expansion, he said the "central cause of the danger there is aggression by Communists against a brave and independent people." Although the Vietnamese people faced other dangers, he believed, if the aggression were stopped, "the people and Government of South Viet-Nam will be free to settle their own future, and the need for supporting American military action there will end." He noted that the people suffering from this Communist assault were Vietnamese; it was "no struggle of white men against Asians"; it was "aggression by Communist totalitarians against their independent neighbors." The chief burden of resistance had fallen upon "the people and soldiers of South Viet Nam," and we had lost only a few hundred of our men while they had "lost tens of thousands." However, he reaffirmed here and hereafter:

The United States still seeks no wider war. We threaten no regime and covet no territory. We have worked and will continue to work for a reduction of tensions on the great stage of the world. But the aggression from the North must be stopped. That is the road to peace in Southeast Asia.[3]

We anticipated a day, the president continued, when Southeast Asia could be "free from terror, subversion, and assassination," when it would no longer need "military support and assistance against aggression but only economic and social cooperation for progress in peace." Even then in Vietnam we supported major programs for pacification and economic expansion, and in the future we could expect "bolder programs." Furthermore, we would never be second in seeking solutions to end Communist aggression; instead, we would always be ready "to go anywhere at any time and meet with anyone whenever there is promise of progress toward an honorable peace." To all who might be interested in our desire for honorable negotiations, he said we sought only a return to the essentials of the agreements of 1954—"a reliable arrangement to guarantee the independence and security of all in Southeast Asia." At the moment he saw no sign of Hanoi's willingness to accept such a solution, but he felt a change might occur in their outlook as they recognized the cost of their current course—"if we all remain united." Meanwhile we would continue to aid South Vietnam "for as long as is required to bring Communist aggression and terrorism under control."[4]

On April 1, 1965, seventeen nonaligned countries meeting in Belgrade petitioned the United States to begin negotiations with Hanoi to end the war as soon as possible,

without posing any preconditions, so that a political solution to the problem of Vietnam may be found in accordance with the legitimate aspirations of the Vietnamese people and in the spirit of the Geneva Agreement on Vietnam and of the Declaration of the Conference of Non-aligned Countries held in Cairo.[5]

These nonaligned nations expressed their concern at "the aggravation of existing tensions and conflicts in Southeast Asia," Africa, the Middle East, and Latin America springing from "oppression and foreign intervention"; they expressed their regrets at the inability of a deadlocked United Nations to solve the problems of these areas and safeguard the peace. They reaffirmed: "the right of peoples to self-determination and the principle that all states shall refrain in their international relations from the threat or use of force"; their dedication to the principle of "the sovereignty and territorial integrity of states"; their conviction that the use of force and pressure was against "the rights of the people of Vietnam to peace, freedom, and independence" and could only worsen the situation and likely bring on a larger war with "catastrophic results." The aggravation of the situation in Vietnam, they believed, was "the consequence of foreign intervention in various forms, including military intervention, which impedes the implementation of the Geneva Agreement on Vietnam."[6]

Our reply to the seventeen nonaligned countries of April 8, 1965, welcomed their concern and interest, as we did the initiative of any people for peace in the world. It was "a constructive contribution," whose principles we accepted and whose fulfillment was "the purpose of our presence in Vietnam." If the nonaligned nations sought self-determination, so did we; when they condemned the resort to force against Vietnam, we did so, too. We were "deeply concerned" by the worsening situation and would end the war "by ensuring the independence of South Vietnam." However, we declared:

The basic cause of the conflict in Vietnam is the attack by North Vietnam on the independent nation of South Vietnam. The object of that attack is total conquest.
The regime in North Vietnam has sent trained military personnel and weapons of war on an increasing scale into South Vietnam. It has directed and supported a mounting campaign of terror, assassination, and military action against the Government and people of the Republic of South Vietnam.
The Government of South Vietnam has requested the help of the United States in its defense against attack. In fulfillment of our long-standing commitments we have given such help. We will continue as long as we are needed, and until the aggression is halted. In these actions we seek only the security and peace of South Vietnam, and we threaten no regime.
The war against South Vietnam is a war of great brutality. Simple farmers are the target of assassination and kidnapping. Women and children are strangled in the night because their men are loyal to the government. Small and helpless villages are ravaged by sneak attacks. Large scale raids are conducted on towns; and terror strikes in the heart of cities.
We hope that the anger of people in every country will extend to those who commit these daily acts of violence in the South. We hope that the sympathy and compassion of every land will be held out to these victims of unprovoked attack. These are men and women, and even children, who die because they are attacked—not because they are attackers.[7]

Our reply further stated that the way to peace in Southeast Asia demanded an independent South Vietnam securely guaranteed and able to fix its own relations with other nations, "free from outside interference—tied to no alliance—a military base for no other country." Go to Hanoi, we virtually said to the seventeen countries; don't come to us. We will accept your program today. Only Hanoi stands in the way. We were ready now for "unconditional discussions." In our view peace could be achieved the moment aggression from Hanoi ceased:

That aggression has many elements. It has meant the training and infiltration of agents and armed forces—the procurement and supply of munitions—the bombing of compounds by night and Embassies by day—murdering secretaries and soldiers alike—in short, a whole campaign of terror and military action that is externally supported and directed. When these things stop and the obstacles to security and stability are removed, the need for American supporting military action will also come to an end.[8]

We would eagerly withdraw our forces when South Vietnam was left alone to determine its own future, and we would gladly cooperate in any way possible to develop better relations between North and South Vietnam. But, we stated finally, "Because the aggressor has made great efforts to hide his actions, it will also be important to have new ways and means of assurance that aggression has in fact been stopped." Our hope was that other nations would participate in helping Southeast Asia improve the life of its own people, and we recalled our suggestion of a large-scale program for the economic development of the region and expressed the hope that other industrialized nations would join.[9]

Stephan Pan and Daniel Lyons noted that in a radio broadcast, April 19, 1965, Hanoi bluntly rejected the appeal of the seventeen countries. The reason was that any United Nations intervention in Vietnam was inappropriate because it would be an undesirable variation from the 1954 Geneva Agreement on Vietnam. Two days later the *Peking People's Daily* called Johnson a "hangman" and a hypocrite because while he announced his willingness to enter unconditional discussions, he was actually expanding the war. The British, Canadian, and French governments earnestly sought the support of Russia in persuading Hanoi to negotiate, but to no avail. In Vienna, April 1965, Rusk asked Gromyko about a possible cease-fire in Vietnam, but the reply was curt and negative.[10]

Although he had long and ably demonstrated as a majority leader of the Senate and in his first White House years his wondrous powers of persuasion, Johnson found it impossible to pressure or persuade Hanoi, Peking, and Moscow.[11] His political techniques of cronyism, consensus, patronage, and policy were inadequate for the world arena he entered in 1963. "Let us reason together" was possible amid reasonably like-minded people, but as Dean Acheson was often quoted as saying: It is extremely difficult either to reason or negotiate with one whose aim is to annihilate you. James Reston of the *New York Times* observed that President Nixon in 1969 also faced the evident objective of Hanoi to humiliate both him and the United States into total surrender.[12] Johnson often tried peace gestures to allay the doves and expansion of the war to appease the hawks. Just before he made his Johns Hopkins speech, which pledged our efforts to extend the Great Society to Southeast Asia, he declared that if he had not retaliated against Ho for the sneak attack upon Pleiku, he would have been impeached. The peace bloc puzzled Johnson by its ability to ignore the many willful and planned Communist outrages against our secretaries, billets, Saigon and village leaders, cities, and innocent civilians while incessantly condemning our air attacks, relocation efforts, and accidental acts of tragedy that accompany all wars. The doves condemned only the tragedies caused by Saigon and Washington and ignored or excused the deliberately willful murder of helpless civilians by the Vietcong, while the hawks found excuses for our accidents, apologized, and would make what amends we could to those who suffered from our actions. The need to relocate entire populations from insecure areas to safer places of refuge caused much physical and emotional strain for our allies, but it was essential.

The defoliation of the jungle trails, the use of napalm and fire bombs to smoke the Vietcong out of their complex of tunnels and underground installations, the wide and necessary shoot first "at anything that moves" practices of guerrilla warfare, and the secret ambush from field, forest, and city street required a prompt response which sadly often brought death and pain to friend and foe alike. But the enemy alone chose this method of warfare. he could not be allowed to violate long and painfully won rules of "civilized" warfare, while we absorbed thereby repeated losses. Only after many attacks and much loss did we strike back with whatever means we found effective. Certainly our manpower was too limited to permit a man-for-man combat. Our advanced technology—short of nuclear obliteration—whatever edge it gave us, we had to use or quit the effort. Furthermore, it was standard Communist practice to enlist the support of every person in the villages they controlled. The enemy was everyone—old, young, men, and women. Without uniform or identification, they had all too frequently made war against us. The guerrillas in the villages and rural areas, wherever chance offered, made total war against the forces and people of South Vietnam and the United States. This total effort required the response we made, if defeat was to be avoided and this type of protracted warfare successfully frustrated.

To pleas for bombing pauses, military cutbacks, renewed diplomacy for peace, resort to the United Nations, or return to Geneva, the president replied repeatedly he was ready to try virtually anything whenever the enemy was willing to reciprocate in some reasonable fashion, but he would not unilaterally withdraw, reduce our effort, or accept any alternative without enemy concession. Under him there would be neither appeasement nor betrayal.

The Vietcong on March 22, 1965, drew up a statement denouncing the United States imperialist aggression against the people of Vietnam, declaring Americans "the most brazen warmongers and aggressors and the sworn enemy of the Vietnamese people." They noted the vast assistance the United States gave to French colonialists, charged that we violated the Geneva Accords, and denounced SEATO as a military bloc to "protect" Indochina and turn it into a United States colony. They pledged an heroic effort to liberate the people of Vietnam, establish their independence, democracy, and neutrality, and promote their reunification with North Vietnam. They warned Johnson: "Pull out of South Vietnam. If you stubbornly continue plunging headlong into the war you will sustain the biggest and most shameful failures." South Vietnam would never cease fighting until its goals had been won:

All negotiations with the U.S. imperialists at this moment are entirely useless if they still refuse to withdraw from South Vietnam all their troops and all kinds of war materials and means and those of their satellites, if they still do not dismantle all their military bases in South Vietnam, if the traitors still surrender the South Vietnamese people's sacred rights to independence and democracy to the U.S. imperialists, and if the South Vietnam National Front for Liberation—the only genuine representative of the fourteen million South Vietnamese people—does not have its decisive say.

They expressed their full determination to expel the foreign invader and liberate South Vietnam and thanked the "peace- and justice-loving people all over the world" for their aid.[13]

This and similar enemy statements constituted the background for Johnson's famous Johns Hopkins speech of April 7, 1965. In this, possibly his ablest statement on the war, he announced: "We are joining those 17 countries" who last week sent their views to some two dozen countries having an interest in Southeast Asia. This full statement of our policy, he believed, would contribute to peace in Asia. Solemnly he observed that both "Americans and Asians are dying for a world where each people may choose its own path to change." This was the same principle for which our ancestors fought at Valley Forge. In Vietnam, a very long way from the quiet Johns Hopkins campus, Johnson declared: "We have no territory . . . , nor do we seek any. The war is dirty and brutal and difficult." It had already cost us the lives of four hundred young men. Why did we take this painful road? "We fight because we must fight if we are to live in a world where every country can shape its own destiny, and only in such a world will our own freedom be finally secure." Such a world could "never be built by bombs or bullets," yet human weaknesses were "such that force must often precede reason," war must come before peace. The true world of Asia was not "serene or peaceful." Ugly reality prevailed there. North Vietnam had attacked an independent nation, South Vietnam, and "its object was total conquest." Although some South Vietnamese participated in the attack on their own government, trained men, supplies, orders, and arms came from North to South.[14]

Why were we there? Because we had "a promise to keep." Since 1954 every president had supported South Vietnam. This aid, by example and expansion, constituted in itself our "national pledge"—certainly a trust in its continuance—to help save the independence of South Vietnam, and he added: "I intend to keep that promise." To dishonor that pledge would expose the people of South Vietnam to unspeakable terror. We were there also to "strengthen world order." From Berlin to Thailand were people whose well-being depended upon their ability to count on us if attacked. To sacrifice Vietnam to its sure fate would shake the confidence of all those people in our sacred word. The result would be unrest, instability, and wider war.

We were there further because great stakes were involved. To those who later favored pulling out, "bugging out," or reliance upon "Vietnamization"—that is turning the war over to Saigon—he might thus be heard saying directly:

Let no one think for a moment that retreat from Viet-Nam would bring an end to conflict. The battle would be renewed in one country and then another. The central lesson of our time is that the appetite of aggression is never satisfied. To withdraw from one battlefield means only to prepare for the next. We must say in Southeast Asia—as we did in Europe—in the words of the Bible: "Hitherto shalt thou come, but no further."[15]

To those who said all our efforts there were futile, that China's power was so great it was "bound to dominate all Southeast Asia," he said there was "no end to that argument until all of the Nations of Asia are swallowed up." To anyone who asked why we had any responsibility there, he said it was the same reason we had for defending Europe in World War II. That war was fought in Europe and Asia, and its end left us "with continued responsibility for the defense of freedom." We wanted "nothing for ourselves"—only that South Vietnam be left to shape its own destiny. We would do everything necessary to attain this and we would do "only what is absolutely necessary." If there had been a recent step-up in the scale of the war, such was "not a change of purpose," but rather it was a "change in what we believe that purpose requires." It was "to increase the confidence of the brave people of South Viet-Nam" and to convince Hanoi's leaders and all its allies that we would "not be defeated," we would "not grow tired," and we would "not withdraw," openly or "under the cloak of a meaningless agreement." He wished he could persuade Hanoi with words rather than guns and planes "because we fight for values and we fight for principle, rather than territory or colonies." The essentials of any final peace settlement and the only path for reasonable men to follow toward peace demanded an independent South Vietnam, "securely guaranteed and able to shape its own relationships to all others," freed from outside interference, tied to no alliance, and assured of being a "military base for no other country."[16]

The president observed that to such a peace there might be many ways, "in discussion or negotiation with the governments concerned; in large groups or in small ones; in the reaffirmation of old agreements or their strengthening with new ones." Such proposals we had stated fifty times over to friend and foe alike, "And we remain ready with this purpose for unconditional discussions." Until that bright day came, we would try to keep the war from spreading, for we had no desire to see additional thousands—Asians or Americans—die in battle. We had "no desire to devastate" what North Vietnamese at such pain and sacrifice had built. Rather, we would use our power with restraint, "with all the wisdom we can command," but we would use it. And he held out the high hope of a billion-dollar United States investment to rebuild both sections of that divided and tragic country. Meanwhile we must try to prevent one nation from imposing its will upon another: "We will do this because our own security is at stake." We would do this to help make the centuries-old dream of peaceful and orderly solution of disputes among people come true.[17]

Kahin and Lewis observed that while Johnson declared, in this and other speeches, his readiness for unconditional discussions, his speech contradicted that statement. The words, "in discussion or negotiation with the governments concerned" would seem to omit the National Liberation Front from the talks. The declaration that a peaceful settlement "demands an independent South Viet-Nam—securely guaranteed and able to shape its own relationships to all others—free from outside interference" squarely countered the wishes of Hanoi and the Vietcong for reunification under communism and with no outside guarantees, supervision, or protection. And the ringing words "We will not be defeated. We will not grow tired. We will not withdraw, either openly or under the cloak of a meaningless agreement" in the situation of Hanoi's relation with the NLF and the South Vietnamese of the past decade made a positive response by Hanoi out of the question.[18]

If there were doubts about our pledge to engage in absolutely unconditional discussions, Saigon quickly let it be known it had conditions to impose and found Johnson's speech at Johns Hopkins could be variously interpreted. Saigon stated its own preconditions for peace talks: previous withdrawal of the Vietcong armed units and political cadres and negotiation only with recognized representatives of the opponent, which did not include the South Vietnamese National Liberation Front. Saigon further declared that its conditions must also be met before peace negotiations could begin. A split between Saigon and Washington arose over the preconditions to peace talks. Negotiation with the Vietcong was one of the bitterest snags in the peace efforts. Saigon opposed any recognition of the Vietcong, and official Washington was reluctant to resort to pressure. However, others believed no peace was attainable without direct talks between all the parties engaged in the struggle. Obviously the Vietcong, who had fought longer, harder, and more successfully, would have to be included in any talks. Without their approval nothing could be finally settled.

Senator Joseph Clark of Pennsylvania admitted that we would never get a peace in South Vietnam without direct negotiations with the Vietcong. Asked about this, President Johnson declared the idea of including the Vietcong in negotiations had been carefully considered by Secretary Rusk, George Ball, the Undersecretary of State, and the National Security Council. He felt the Vietcong "would have no difficulty finding the government to negotiate," but he added, "I don't believe we'd ever agree to someone negotiating that is not a government." He added also that a territorial district, like Mississippi, could exist, but was not a sovereign government that could negotiate with foreign states.[19]

Rusk declared there was "a certain artificiality about this issue" of talking with the Vietcong. Who are the Vietcong? he asked, and then observed that they were mainly infiltrators from Hanoi who were "responsible for the presence of American forces today in South Viet-Nam." The Vietcong elements indigenous to South Vietnam were a relatively small number compared to the rest of South Vietnam. If South Vietnam could return to peace and normal political practices, the people who termed themselves the National Liberation Front could then join other elements in the country in a search for solutions of its problems:

But the mere fact that there are tens of thousands of military personnel sent in there from Hanoi does not seem to us to give the Viet Cong any special status to be treated as a government or to be taken into account by special negotiation on the question of how you deal with the future of South Viet-Nam. I don't know of any other government in the world that would permit negotiations with a group of that sort under these circumstances.[20]

Asked if the United States would permit Hanoi to have Vietcong agents represented on their team, Rusk replied that the question of credentials at a conference was an issue usually handled by the governments actually represented. The governments participating could name their delegations; it was not normal for a conference to check on who sat behind the leading delegate at the peace table; therefore "if Hanoi wants any of these people there in their delegation, that is up to them."[21] At a news conference of July 28, 1965, the president reiterated his pledge to negotiate with any government any time and place and noted that the Vietcong would have no difficulty in being represented and having their views presented "if Hanoi for a moment decides that she wants to cease aggression, and I would not think that would be an insurmountable problem at all. I think that could be worked out."[22]

In a lengthy review of the war, June 23, 1965, Rusk noted that the Communists refused all discussion or negotiations and still sought the total conquest of the South Vietnamese people. The attacks upon women and children in the night continued. South Vietnam had suffered since 1961 some twenty-five thousand dead and fifty-one thousand wounded, figures greater by ten times than our losses in the Korean War and in proportion to population even larger than our losses in the Second World War. Even more terrible were the civilian losses from murder, kidnapping, and terror. Intelligence estimated that by the end of 1964 some forty-thousand men from North Vietnam had infiltrated the South. This was Hanoi's long-matured decision to raise the stakes of the war and its answer to our repeated affirmation that we did not wish a wider war. Rusk declared Hanoi wrong in thinking "*they* can have a larger war without risks to themselves. And hence the airstrikes against military targets in North Viet-Nam." Our attacks made the infiltration more difficult, "increased the cost of aggression," and took some of the pressure off South Vietnam. Air attack alone could not bring peace, but he defended it as necessary to hit the logistics of aggression because: "It is the aggression itself that is the wrong. Those who worry about bridges and barracks and ammunition dumps would do well to give their sympathy instead to the daily victims of terror in South Viet-Nam."[23]

On April 8, 1965, in answer to President Johnson's Johns Hopkins speech, Hanoi announced its famous four-point program, so hard-lined and tough that few Americans could support any negotiation on those terms. The four points which became the repeated answer of Hanoi and the Vietcong to all peace efforts in summary called for our virtual surrender. They demanded first that we recognize the basic national rights of the Vietnamese, withdraw all our troops and weapons, dismantle all our military bases, end our military alliance with Saigon, cease our intervention and aggression against the country, and stop all acts of war against North Vietnam. Next, pending the peaceful reunification of Vietnam, the two zones must refrain from joining any military alliance and allow no foreign military bases, troops, and military personnel in their respective territories. The third demand was that the "internal affairs of South Vietnam must be settled by the South Vietnamese people themselves, in accordance with the programme of the South Vietnam National Front for Liberation, without any foreign interference." Finally, the peaceful reunification of Vietnam must be settled by the Vietnamese people in both zones themselves, without any foreign interference.[24]

Only Communists and appeasers could accept such harsh terms as Ho here proposed in his formal answer to Johnson's Johns Hopkins speech. The official American view was that the administration had to accept the four points as conditions before negotiations could begin at all. The third point was the most unacceptable to Washington and was the subject of considerable debate. War critics noted that Washington took its copy of the four points directly from a radio broadcast from Hanoi which, of course, contained no punctuation. It read: "The internal affairs of South Vietnam must be settled by the South Vietnamese people themselves in accordance with the program of the NFLSV (the National Front for the Liberation of South Vietnam) without any foreign interference." Scholars claimed that as originally published in Hanoi, the third point separated with commas the vital phrase, "in accordance with the program of the National Liberation Front." Although this left the meaning a little ambiguous, the punctuation was believed to make the condition possibly acceptable to the United States.

The Chinese *People's Daily* published the third point in a manner that was translated to read: "According to the program of the Southern National Liberation Front, the affairs of the South must be settled by the southern people themselves without foreign interference." This wording would make the point seem even more innocuous.[25] Washington rejected the Chinese reading and accepted the broadcast version, which attributed the dominant role in settling the peace to the Vietcong and its National Liberation Front. The Communists contended that the four points constituted a return to the Geneva Accords formula and were in harmony with the desires of the people of South Vietnam. Washington officially rejected both these contentions. Repeatedly, before and after the initial publication of these four points, the Vietcong and Hanoi had made the same demands in language as strong as they had here.

This fact the war critics ignored in their accusations of insincerity against the Johnson administration. Pan and Lyons observed that Radio Hanoi and Radio Peking repeated the harsh demands of total surrender on many occasions. Communist China said unofficially as late as February 1966, "the United States was willing to allow National Liberation Front participation in any future South Vietnamese Government," but then added, "the Communists would accept only complete control." Hanoi also turned down repeated offers and peace overtures from all sources and insisted that its own harsh terms be accepted before it would even come to a peace conference. An indirect but official reply to such overtures, including one from Pope Paul, broadcast from Hanoi January 4, 1966, reaffirmed in greater detail the four demands, and the Vietcong's National Liberation Front reiterated the same terms then and thereafter.[26]

U Thant, Secretary General of the United Nations, tried to get negotiations started and secretly engaged in repeated efforts to that end. He even went so far once as to say that much as he respected the "wisdom, moderation, and sensitivity to world public opinion" of President Johnson, he was sure the great *American people, if only they know the true facts and the background to the developments in South Viet Nam, will agree with me that further bloodshed is unnecessary.* And also that the political and diplomatic method of discussions and negotiations alone can create the conditions which will enable the *United States to withdraw gracefully from that part of the world.* ... [27]

The Johnson administration found these hints that it was not being honest with the American public most unwelcome and unfair. Neither Johnson nor Rusk appreciated these remarks, and they expressed their feeling "to U Thant through the American Mission at the United Nations." Also the American press reaction to U Thant's speech was cool. Both Hanoi and Peking rejected U Thant's peace efforts and suggested bluntly that he had "knocked at the wrong door" and insisted that "Viet-Nam had nothing to do with the United Nations." Neither China nor North Vietnam was a member of the world organization. Also some Americans believed U Thant had overstepped the boundaries of his authority.[28]

Had we accepted Communist terms we would have surrendered the whole cause to communism. Acceptance would have meant our total withdrawal from the war, the end of all bombing, the dismantling of all bases. The Communist interpretation of no "foreign interference" did not include Hanoi or North Vietnam—only non-Vietnamese elements present in the South. That would have yielded to Hanoi and the Vietcong a free hand in the reunification of the country under Ho. Ho never would have accepted genuinely free elections in the North, and the Vietcong already in control of many areas of South Vietnam would have refused such freedom there also.

Such a farce of rigged elections neither Washington nor Saigon would accept. Hanoi then and thereafter rejected every reasonable peace offer made to it, but critics of the war managed to persuade a good many people that Washington and Saigon were the culprits responsible for the failure of the peace efforts. They believed that while Washington held out high hopes of peace, it actually sabotaged repeated and genuine offers from the Vietcong and Hanoi. No genuine or reasonable offers came from Hanoi or the Vietcong. They were willing only to talk about our surrender and their total takeover. Also charges of insincerity were made against President Johnson, who was accused of talking peace while expanding the war, of answering every peace feeler and crushing every peace hope with outrageous deeds of violence and surprise attacks. Heard often was the charge that his State Department did not know what his Defense Department either planned or did, until the bloody deeds were done. However, those who distrusted Washington, while seeming to trust the enemy, found it easy to ignore and condone the standard Communist practice of surprise attacks, violation of every truce, and talking while fighting. The enemy refused officially to admit that North Vietnam actually engaged its troops in South Vietnam. The war critics also "knocked on the wrong door." They should have sent their objections to Hanoi and the Vietcong.

Ho's stern and humiliating demands constituted a propaganda victory for

Johnson, who sought to use such tough terms to enlist European support and to confuse the academic community inside the United States. Steinberg observed that it took some of "the starch out of the teach-ins," in which many teachers and students throughout the nation engaged in daylong and nightlong denunciations of our involvement in the war.[29]

In behalf of his objectives and to the great disgust of the war critics, when he sought from Congress an additional $700 million to meet the mounting cost of the war in Vietnam, Johnson repeated strongly his whole thesis of the war:

> This is not a routine appropriation. For each Member of Congress who supports this request is also voting to persist in our effort to halt Communist aggression in South Vietnam. Each is saying that the Congress and the President stand united before the world in joint determination that the independence of South Vietnam shall be preserved and Communist attack will not succeed.

It was a war of aggression, but not the same type man had long known:

> Instead of the sweep of invading armies, there is the steady, deadly stream of men and supplies. Instead of open battle between major opposing forces, there is murder in the night, assassination, and terror. Instead of dramatic confrontation and sharp division between nationals of different lands, some citizens of South Vietnam have been recruited in the effort to conquer their own country.
>
> All of this shrouds battle in confusion. But this is the face of war in the 1960's. This is the "war of liberation." Kept from direct attack by American power, unable to win a free election in any country, those who seek to expand communism by force now use subversion and terror. In this effort they often enlist nationals of the countries they wish to conquer. But it is not civil war. It is sustained by power and resources from without. The very object of this tactic is to create the appearance of an internal revolt and to mask aggression. In this way, they hope to avoid confrontation with American resolution.
>
> But we will not be fooled or deceived, in Vietnam or any place in the world where we have a commitment. This kind of war is war against the independence of nations. And we will meet it, as we have met other shifting dangers for more than a generation.[30]

After this reiteration of his general thesis of past pledges and a half century of experience with aggression, he declared we should make no mistake about this war and Communist purpose:

The aim in Vietnam is not simply the conquest of the South, tragic as that would be. It is to show that American commitment is worthless. Once that is done, the gates are down and the road is open to expansion and endless conquest. That is why Communist China opposes discussions, even though such discussions are clearly in the interest of North Vietnam.

Then citing the overwhelming votes to support the formation of SEATO and the approval of the Gulf of Tonkin Resolution, he declared:

Thus we cannot, and will not, withdraw or be defeated. The stakes are too high, the commitment too deep, the lessons of history too plain.

At every turning point in the last 30 years, there have been those who opposed a firm stand against aggression. They have always been wrong. And when we heeded their cries, when we gave in, the consequence has been more bloodshed and wider war.[31]

We would not repeat that mistake, he added, nor would we heed those who urged a reckless use of our power. We did not wish to expand the war; we would do what we must do, and only that:

For, in the long run, there can be no military solution to the problems of Vietnam. We must find the path to peaceful settlement. Time and time again we have worked to open that path. We are still ready to talk, without conditions, to any government. We will go anywhere, discuss any subject, listen to any point of view in the interests of a peaceful solution.[32]

He regarded congressional approval of his request as approval of his Vietnam war policy.[33]

To aid his peace efforts, wrote Steinberg, Johnson suddenly announced a bombing pause over North Vietnam to start May 12, 1965, and, urged by McNamara, secretly sent a message through Russia to Hanoi, telling Ho that he would be "watchful" for any indications from him of a serious desire to negotiate for peace. If no serious sign came, we "would end the bombing pause." A quick reply came from Paris that "Hanoi would negotiate on condition that Johnson recognize in principle the four-point program." This supposedly meant that once we recognized the principle of the four points as a basis for negotiation Ho would not press for its practical application.[34] How does one "accept" a principle which he does not intend to practice?

Gruening and Beaser wrote that Rusk replied that the four points did not agree with the Geneva Accords because reunification elections under the Geneva settlement "were to be supervised by the International Control Commission." We would talk about the four points or other proposals any party to the dispute might wish to make, but we would not accept prior to any talks the surrender of our position that South Vietnam must be recognized as a separate and independent nation. Rather, North Vietnam must withdraw its troops and cease its aggression against South Vietnam. Also any reduction of military activities by us would require "an equivalent cessation" by Hanoi and the Vietcong.[35] Since Hanoi refused to admit any direct participation in the war by its regular forces or to concede in any way the sovereignty of South Vietnam and denounced our presence itself as the only aggression being committed in all Vietnam, constructive negotiations were not likely to succeed.

The secretary of state felt that such violent rejections of our peace efforts clearly proved that Hanoi wanted a military victory, not peace. To domestic critics who charged that our bombing pause was not long enough, Rusk noted: "the harsh reaction of the other side was fully known before the attacks were resumed. And I would also recall that we held our hand for more than 4 years while tens of thousands of armed men invaded the South and every attempt at peaceful settlement failed." He added: "Hanoi is not even prepared for discussions unless it is accepted in advance that there will be a Communist-dominated government in Saigon, and unless too—so far as we can determine—American forces are withdrawn in advance." In support of his statement, he observed that Senator Fulbright also had concluded: "It seems clear that the Communist powers still hope to achieve a complete victory in South Viet-Nam and for this reason are at present uninterested in negotiations for a peaceful settlement." As long as one side was bent on victory, there was no magic formula, no procedural miracle through which peace could be obtained.[36]

After a review of the progress of the war, Rusk set forth his own peace formula, his "four steps for peace" program, which he took from Tran Van Do, the foreign minister of South Vietnam:

An end to aggression and subversion.
Freedom for South Viet-Nam to choose and shape for itself its own destiny "in conformity with democratic principles and without any foreign interference from whatever sources."
As soon as aggression has ceased, the ending of the military measures now necessary by the Government of South Viet-Nam and the nations that have come to its aid to defend South Viet-Nam; and the removal of foreign military forces from South Viet-Nam.
And effective guarantees for the independence and freedom of the people of South Viet-Nam.[37]

For these objectives the president in late July stated: "We will stand in Vietnam." Hanoi's repeated rejection of these fundamental steps and objectives, Rusk believed it now should be clear for all to see, showed that the enemy sought conquest rather than reasonable peace and freedom in South Vietnam.

In a July 1965 news conference Johnson declared fifteen efforts had been made to launch peace discussions with the help of forty nations over the world, but without answer or reciprocity from the enemy. Our objectives in Vietnam had been widely stated and debated, but he reiterated that he was ready to discuss any and all proposals, "for we fear the meeting room no more than we fear the battlefield."[38] Reflecting on our mistakes of half a century and his desire to avoid their repetition, the president declared that three times in his own lifetime, in two world wars and Korea, we had supposedly learned that "retreat does not bring safety and weakness does not bring peace." Here we fought "a different kind of war," of "no marching armies or solemn declarations," a war in which some citizens of South Vietnam, with understandable grievances, joined in attacks upon their own government.

But we must not let this mask the central fact that this is really war. It is guided by North Viet-Nam and it is spurred by Communist China. Its goal is to conquer the South, to defeat American power, and to extend the Asiatic dominion of communism.

Again he said there were "great stakes in the balance." Most non-Communist nations of Asia could not alone resist the expanding might of Asian communism.

Our power was their "vital shield." If it vanished, the rest of the world was lost. If an American promise was worthless, in every nation the forces of independence would weaken,

and an Asia so threatened by Communist domination would certainly imperil the security of the United States itself.

We did not choose to be the guardians at the gate, but there is no one else.

. . . We learned from Hitler at Munich that success only feeds the appetite of aggression. The battle would be renewed in one country and then another country, bringing with it perhaps even larger and crueler conflict, as we have learned from the lessons of history.

Thus again he said we could not betray the word and honor of three presidents who promised to help this small and valiant nation. He emphasized: "We just cannot now dishonor our word, or abandon our commitment, or leave those who believed us and who trusted us to the terror and repression and murder that would follow."[39]

Other members of the Johnson circle loved to rattle off the numerous occasions on which we had sought to achieve a negotiated settlement instead of a military victory only to meet total rebuff from the enemy. In a letter to the president of the security council of the United Nations of July 30, 1965, Ambassador Goldberg began with our acceptance of the Geneva Accords of 1954 and listed:

Various approaches to Hanoi, Peking and Moscow.

Support of peaceful overtures by the United Kingdom, Canada, and the British Commonwealth of Nations.

Favorable reactions to proposals made by the seventeen non-aligned nations, and later by the Government of India.

Approval of efforts by the Secretary-General of the United Nations to initiate peace talks.

Endorsement of a larger role for the United Nations in Southeast Asia, including a U.N. mission of observers along the frontier between Viet-Nam and Cambodia, a U.N. mission to investigate alleged suppression of minority rights in Viet-Nam, and a U.N. invitation to Hanoi to participate in Security Council discussions of the incident in the Gulf of Tonkin.

Major participation, directly and through the United Nations, in economic and social development projects in Southeast Asia.

A direct appeal by the President of the United States to the members of the United Nations to use their influence in bringing all parties to the peace table.

Repeated assertions on the highest authority that the United States is prepared to engage in negotiations or discussions of any character with no prior conditions whatever.

On at least fifteen occasions in the past four-and-a-half years, the United States has initiated or supported efforts to resolve the issues in Southeast Asia by peaceful negotiations.[40]

The State Department released to the press in late December 1965 a statement of our official position on Vietnam. It included fourteen points which constituted our recommendations for peace:

1. The Geneva Agreements of 1954 and 1962 are an adequate basis for peace in Southeast Asia;
2. We would welcome a conference on Southeast Asia or on any part thereof;
3. We would welcome "negotiations without preconditions" as the 17 nations put it;
4. We would welcome unconditional discussions as President Johnson put it;
5. A cessation of hostilities could be the first order of business at a conference or could be the subject of preliminary discussions;
6. Hanoi's four points could be discussed along with other points which others might wish to propose;
7. We want no U.S. bases in Southeast Asia;
8. We do not desire to retain U.S. troops in South Viet-Nam after peace is assured;
9. We support free elections in South Viet-Nam to give the South Vietnamese a government of their own choice;
10. The question of reunification of Viet-Nam should be determined by the Vietnamese through their own free decision;
11. The countries of Southeast Asia can be non-aligned or neutral if that be their option;
12. We would much prefer to use our resources for the economic reconstruction of Southeast Asia than in War. If there is peace, North Viet-Nam could participate in a regional effort to which we would be prepared to contribute at least one billion dollars;
13. The President has said "The Viet Cong would not have difficulty being represented and having their views represented if for a moment Hanoi decided she wanted to cease aggression. I don't think that would be an insurmountable problem."
14. We have said publicly and privately that we could stop the bombing of North Viet-Nam as a step toward peace although there has not been the slightest hint or suggestion from the other side as to what they would do if the bombing stopped.[41]

In a statement on January 3, 1966, entitled "The Heart of the Matter in Vietnam," Vice-President Humphrey gave his version of both the origins of the war and the initiatives for peace in Vietnam. To him the simple fact was that Hanoi had trained and armed tens of thousands of men, including units of Hanoi's regulars, and sent them into South Vietnam for the purpose of conquest. This external aggression alone was responsible for the presence of U.S. combat forces. Not until the summer of 1965 did our forces there reach the number of those infiltrated from Hanoi. Our commitment to secure South Vietnam from external aggression sprang from bilateral agreements between Washington and Saigon, the SEATO treaty, the annual actions by Congress in financing aid to South Vietnam, the Tonkin Gulf Resolution, and the solemn declarations of three presidents of the United States: "At stake is not just South Viet Nam, nor even Southeast Asia: there is also at stake the integrity of a U.S. commitment and the importance of that commitment to the peace right around the globe."[42]

Further, Humphrey reminded the many critics of the war who kept charging Johnson with fostering a "credibility gap" and hiding honest peace moves from Hanoi and elsewhere, that:

A. We are not aware of any initiative which has been taken by Hanoi during the past five years to seek peace in Southeast Asia. Reports of "peace feelers" have to do with initiatives by third parties. Hanoi has denied that it has ever made any "peace feelers." We ourselves know of none. During 1965 Hanoi has consistently insisted that its four points must be accepted as the sole basis for peace in Viet Nam. The third of these four points would require the imposition of the program of the liberation front upon South Viet Nam, whether the South Vietnamese wanted it or not.

B. The initiatives for peace undertaken by our side, and by many other governments, would be hard to count. They began with President Kennedy's talk with Premier Khrushchev in Vienna in June 1961 and have not ceased. The publicly known initiatives have been multiplied many times by private initiatives not yet disclosed. . . .

On the public record, Humphrey noted the following instances of peace gestures:

1. The Kennedy-Khrushchev talks in June 1961;
2. Geneva Conference on Laos;
3. U.S. reference of Gulf of Tonkin matter to the U.N. Security Council in August 1964;
4. The Polish proposal to convene the two Co-Chairmen and the three members of the ICC (India, Canada and Poland) to take up the question of Laos;
5. The call of the 17 non-aligned nations for negotiations without preconditions;
6. Attempts by U Thant to visit Hanoi and Peiping;
7. President Johnson's call for unconditional discussions;
8. The British Commonwealth Committee on Viet Nam;
9. Attempted or actual visits by Patrick Gordon Walker, Mr. [Harold] Davies (MP), and Ghanaian Delegation.[43]

Rumors of offers to negotiate filled the air in late 1965 and thereafter, but further inquiries usually revealed that the Vietcong, resting on the four points, merely expected our acceptance of their program, and spread rumors—too readily termed credible by Johnson's critics—to discredit our sincerity and make us appear unreasonably bent on military victory alone. Critics charged that too often Washington committed some dramatic act of war at almost the precise moment it announced its peace efforts and asserted that such steps to expand the war obviously destroyed all hopes of a peaceful solution. From Italy came a warning that Ho would not start peace talks if we bombed the Hanoi-Haiphong area, and yet the very day Rusk replied to Hanoi, our planes bombed the Hanoi-Haiphong area for the first time. Shortly thereafter reports out of Hanoi called the stories of Hanoi's peace feelers groundless lies. Acts expanding the war in hopes of a military victory were never conducive to persuading the enemy of the sincerity of peace gestures on a basis of mutual compromise. Nor was the enemy practice of talking while fighting and insisting upon our total withdrawal without reciprocity any more helpful.

On July 27, 1965, when Johnson gave a preview of his plan to increase our force gradually until Ho cried enough and to avoid the extremes of all-out war or pullout, Mansfield bluntly told the president before his cabinet and many leaders of Congress that he was turning the crisis into an American war. The senator added, wrote Steinberg, that there had been no truly legal government in Saigon since Diem's murder, and that we could not bomb North Vietnam to the conference table or surrender; in conclusion he stated strongly that this was not "an American war, . . . and the United States must not make it one." When Johnson asked Mansfield what he would do, the senator made no reply but stared straight into his face.[44] The next day before a television audience Johnson said Hanoi left him no choice because the loss of South Vietnam would endanger our national security and he must honor the commitments of Eisenhower, Kennedy, and his own administration, which Congress and the people had accepted and supported.[45]

All during the year 1965, the year of the crucial decision to turn the crisis in Southeast Asia into an American war of global significance, our role expanded momentously, the air raids over the North increased, and in vain hopes of a quick victory our ground forces entered the war. Although Johnson invested heavily in men, materiel, and the creation of a giant infrastructure as a base for effective military action, enemy strength also increased alarmingly in 1965 over 1964: from 32,000 Vietcong regulars in 1964 to 75,000 in 1965; from 60,000 Vietcong irregulars in 1964 to 100,000 in 1965; and from 7,400 Vietcong infiltrators from the North in 1964 to 19,000 in 1965. The Vietcong and its political arm, the National Liberation Front, retained effective control of the rich and vital Mekong Delta, where 60 percent of the South Vietnamese people lived and owned 60 percent of the country's wealth. Our expansion of the war caused "a stalemate in the South and prevented a Viet Cong victory," which had seemed possible at the beginning of 1965. Neither side could now claim a military victory.[46]

It was victory enough to assure that Johnson's peace efforts were not the result of defeat, weakness, or irresolution. As 1965 passed, the feeling grew that we could afford to be magnanimous, reasonable, and possibly generous—enough for Johnson to permit congressional critics of the war to use the presidential plane on a global tour for talks with the heads of sixteen governments on how to end the war. Anxious to avoid trouble with Mansfield and his friends, whose help he needed in so many ways, he told the senator to tell everyone that he only wanted to find a way to peace. Mansfield asked: "Did you mean what you said about not remaining in Vietnam and acquiring special privileges after the war?" The president answered, "All I want is to negotiate an honorable settlement that will allow the people of Indochina to choose their own government."[47]

Mansfield and his colleagues received a friendly reception wherever they went. They also obtained an earful of advice because the various officials knew it would quickly reach the president. Mansfield's thirty-page report evidenced a most independent view. It informed the president that he could not conquer Hanoi and impose puppet regimes upon South Vietnam, no matter how much he expanded the war. It recommended that he reduce our military objectives, establish a holding operation, and seek political and land reforms to wean the peasants and dissidents away from the Vietcong and help the people establish a broad-based anti-Communist government, which all could wholeheartedly support. To induce the enemy to negotiate, it also urged the president to halt all bombing immediately.[48]

The doves urged bombing halts more frequently than the hawks suggested escalation of the air attacks and the war generally. There had been one brief bombing pause earlier. The original suggestion for the second pause came from McNamara, who seemed to be changing his mind about the war, the effectiveness of the bombing, and the possibility of any strictly military solution at all.[49] Among those inside the Johnson administration he was almost alone in his support of an air pause to speed peace negotiations and counter world disapproval of the bombing. Strong opposition to the pause came from such outside advisers as Clark Clifford and Abe Fortas, who believed it would only give the enemy time to prepare for greater future offenses. Dean Acheson had little faith in peace negotiations and urged more earnest efforts for military victory.[50]

Inside the administration Rusk and Bundy initially strongly favored continuation of the bombing without any pause. The president once noted that Rusk and Bundy "are always a little bit readier to hit than McNamara."[51] The thirty-seven day bombing pause began December 24, 1965. With great fanfare and expectations the president launched it by sending key administration leaders around the world to enlist the support of various nations and explain our actions to many governments. Our ambassadors could have conveyed presidential concepts and policies just as well and much cheaper, but the president wished to dramatize, "Texas style," his peaceful intentions. His critics considered his efforts doomed because he would negotiate only with North Vietnam, not the Vietcong or the National Liberation Front. In vain, he sought to make Ho admit he was the aggressor and agree to withdraw his aid and troops from South Vietnam. One inside dove, Townsend Hoopes, declared of Johnson's peace gesture: "As a public relations effort it had dramatic scale and spontaneity; as a serious diplomatic effort it was a nullity."[52]

While Johnson's agents were hopping around the world on their dramatic and widely publicized jet flights in a fruitless search for peace, our State Department, January 7, 1966, published its fourteen-point peace program, which was to become the basis for much future discussion of the war and its possible settlement. Later in the same year, September 22, 1966, our objectives in Vietnam were again summarily stated by Ambassador Goldberg at the United Nations. Our aims were strictly limited. We fought no "holy war" against communism; in Asia we sought "no empire or sphere of influence," no permanent military bases, no permanent alliances or American presence of any kind; nor did we desire to impose any alliance policy on Saigon or in any way threaten China's "legitimate interests." We did not ask Hanoi to surrender unconditionally or yield "anything that belongs to it." Nor did we seek to exclude any segment of the people of South Vietnam from any "peaceful participation in their country's future." We preferred a political solution of the war and rejected Hanoi's "right to impose a military solution." For the South Vietnamese people, we sought the same right of self-determination that the United Nations Charter affirmed for all nations. The reunification of Vietnam should be decided by the free choice of all Vietnamese peoples north and south, without any "outside interference." Hence in any peace talks we would discuss Hanoi's four points along with those that any others might wish to raise.[53]

In defense of the American record and in answer to those who declared the basic obstacle to peace was the bombing of North Vietnam, the able ambassador noted that while there was no bombing of North Vietnam at all for five years and while there were no United States combat forces at all in Vietnam, Ho steadily increased his infiltration of South Vietnam in violation of the Geneva Agreement. Yet during all that long period we made strenuous efforts to reach a peaceful settlement. Johnson's two bombing halts, Goldberg declared, had failed to produce any concession, military letup, or sign of willingness to negotiate from Hanoi. He added: "We are prepared to order a cessation of all bombing of North Viet-Nam the moment we are assured . . . that this step will be answered promptly by a corresponding and appropriate deescalation on the other side."[54] At any time, we would withdraw our forces, and we urged Hanoi to accept a time schedule for a supervised and phased withdrawal of all outside forces from South Vietnam. Once again, our United Nations ambassador declared that participation by the Vietcong elements in the negotiations was not "an insurmountable problem." That obstacle to negotiation, he said, was more imaginary than real. Perhaps to Goldberg and the United States, but certainly not to anti-Communist South Vietnamese.

Repeated demands that the United States ask the United Nations to help in the search for a peace settlement were answered by the many efforts of Goldberg and others to work with that body. Serious chances of success were marred by the fact that North Vietnam and China, whose agreement was vital to any solution, were not members of the United Nations, and any proposal injurious to Communist hopes faced the certainty of a Russian veto in the Security Council and considerable obstructionism in the Assembly. Our every effort to enlist UN support also faced blatant Communist propaganda, which accepted no solution except our total abandonment of South Vietnam to communism. No effective action to end the war rationally could be taken by the United Nations, since the Communists would accept nothing but total victory and eternally countered all our efforts with the NLF's four points. Our acceptance of those terms would have condemned South Vietnam to the same fate Ho had meted out to the North Vietnamese dissidents from 1953 to 1956. Furthermore, Hanoi and the Vietcong, supported by Peking and Moscow, seemed determined to prove to the world that wars of national liberation could succeed against even the most powerful nation on earth.

CHAPTER THREE

NO VICTORY—NO PEACE, 1965-1968

After 1966, most Americans believed that any peaceful settlement of the war would eventually have to include full participation of the National Liberation Front of South Vietnam, but they rejected its precondition that we negotiate only with the NLF as the legitimate government of South Vietnam and abandon completely our Saigon allies. Neither the Vietcong nor Hanoi would pledge to match our steps toward reducing the war. They demanded we cease bombing the North, but without any reciprocity on their part at all. That we would not accept. We offered to reduce our forces if Hanoi would evacuate its troops from South Vietnam, but Hanoi refused to admit it invaded the South, regarded the two sections always as one country, and repeated endlessly that the only aggressor against South Vietnam was the United States.

The United Nations, many Americans believed, should lead in all peace efforts. Doves everywhere urged a return to Geneva and the terms of 1954. This the Russians could support without risking the charge of abandoning Hanoi or turning soft about orthodox Communist objectives. The Geneva Accords had been a victory for communism, a major defeat for freedom. However, Moscow refused to do anything that might advance Chinese influence.[1] Hanoi meant to have a peace that would leave the Communists in sole command of South Vietnam, and Washington would never agree to any solution that would betray its Saigon allies to be liquidated by the Communists. Although there seemed no middle ground that anyone could trust, total military victory increasingly appeared impossible. The price of absolute victory was too high. It would demand a near-total obliteration of all Vietnam, an enlarged effort that would risk world war, and the nuclear destruction of a vast portion of mankind. How far could we go toward military victory before we brought Russia, China, and the whole Communist world into war against us? That was ever a main question after 1966.

Critics of the war attributed the failure of many reported peace efforts more to the president's stubborness than the enemy's refusal to accept anything less than total surrender. Rumors kept spreading after 1965 of peace offers, secret missions, and near successes. Steinberg noted that some Johnson associates believed the president halted the bombing in December 1965 and sent his agents around the globe on their highly publicized peace mission to offset the very bad publicity he received from a *Look Magazine* article on our ambassador to the United Nations, Adlai Stevenson, who had been quoted as sharply critical of the president for not aiding U Thant's peace efforts. The president was vexed because U Thant would not agree that the war was an invasion of South Vietnam and part of an international Communist plot, not simply a civil war. Although many scholars and Asian statesmen did not agree, U Thant declared it was nationalism, not communism, that motivated the resistance movement in Vietnam against all foreigners, and especially against Americans, who were meddling most in local affairs. He bluntly stated that Vietnam was not even vital to Western interests. Because he sternly held and publicly proclaimed such views, Washington officials began a campaign of slurs against him.[2]

Johnson's dislike of the secretary general had developed as early as August 1964. After a visit to Johnson in Washington, U Thant returned to New York believing he had presidential approval of his suggestion for secret and unofficial talks with Hanoi. He then sent word to Stevenson, who in turn excitedly passed the word on to Rusk that Ho was willing to confer privately with us on preliminary peace talks. No response then or later appeared. A possible explanation of the Washington blackout, wrote Steinberg, was that the war was going very badly and Johnson did not wish to embarrass the unstable Saigon government.[3] Furthermore, the president and the secretary of state had ample ways of learning from other contacts that no serious or sincere offers of reasonable settlement were forthcoming from Hanoi.

Johnson felt compelled, however, to make repeated efforts to satisfy both the hawks and the doves in his administration. Fighting and negotiating, making war and peace simultaneously, posed a dilemma. In early 1965 while Johnson studied the possible expansion of the war, U Thant asked Stevenson if the United States was still interested in peace negotiations. Rusk told Stevenson that secret evaluation of the situation revealed that from Hanoi would come only a negative response. Rusk's information came from a middle-level North Vietnamese government official, not Ho Chi Minh or any high-ranking Hanoi official. The reaction from this minion was totally negative. Hanoi was not ready for any serious peace efforts. Johnson's critics deemed this a most slipshod way to check such a serious matter. Stevenson believed a stronger effort should be made and asked U Thant to try again. On January 18, 1965, U Thant suggested that a secret meeting of American and North Vietnamese envoys be held on January 18, 1965, in Burma. The government of Burma agreed to meetings at Rangoon. Again the news was passed on to Washington, and ten days of silence followed:

Then came a strong *No*, with the explanation that "any rumors of such a meeting might topple the Saigon Government." This was ridiculous, Thant told a dispirited Stevenson, for Saigon Governments were toppling with regularity.

"What Saigon Government are they talking about?" . . . "Minh, Khanh, Suu, Tri—or what?"[4]

Aware that he would look like a warmonger after the full knowledge of U Thant's peace efforts was known and angered at this slur upon his integrity, Johnson permitted his press secretary to report that the United States had received no proposal from U Thant. Rusk later said he did not tell Stevenson to reject the Rangoon meeting, but merely expressed grave doubts of any positive results from it. Steinberg wrote that Johnson flatly stated in a press conference: "Candor compels me to tell you that there has not been the slightest indication that the other side is interested in negotiation." He probably meant "serious" negotiation.[5]

Until the full story can be told any evaluation of these most critical events is incomplete, but enough uncertainty and conflict appeared here to advance the rising fear, so adverse to the Johnson administration, of a "credibility gap." U Thant's comment that in wartime "the first casualty is truth" also did not help restore popular faith in Johnson's strict adherence to nothing but the whole truth.[6]

In this most unusual war, in which seizure of territory was not the major objective, but the winning of conflicting political aspirations was, Johnson was hard pressed by both hawks and doves to pursue sharply conflicting objectives. In this war the peace we sought could be won only by a greater military investment than popular approval would permit. From 1965 until the end of his presidency, Johnson kept searching for a diplomatic solution:

Few Americans realize how intensive—and extensive—that effort was over the years. Only a handful of my closest advisers knew of all the many attempts we made to get into a dialogue with Hanoi. The fact is that from 1965 until January 1969 we were in virtually continuous contact, either directly or through intermediaries, with leaders in Hanoi or their representatives. Hardly a month passed throughout that period in which we did not make some effort to open the gateway to peace. Until March 31, 1968, every attempt we made was ignored or rejected by the North Vietnamese.[7]

We told the enemy repeatedly:

We are ready to talk in private or in public; we will meet quietly in any capital; we will stop the bombing if you will do something on your part to lower the level of fighting. These numerous appeals through so many channels may well have convinced the North Vietnamese that we wanted peace at any price.

Never once was there a clear sign that Ho Chi Minh had a genuine interest in bargaining for peace. Never, through any channel or from any serious contact, did we receive any message that differed significantly from the tough line that Hanoi repeated over and over again: Stop all the bombing, get out of Vietnam, and accept our terms for peace. The North Vietnamese never gave the slightest sign that they were ready to consider reducing the Communists' half of the war or to negotiate seriously the terms of a fair peace settlement.[8]

"Free-lance" peacemakers, rumors of sincere peace efforts, hints of Johnson's sabotage of honest approaches, and spreading disbelief in the sincerity of his desire for any settlement short of total military victory caused bitter dissension at home and reinforced enemy efforts to fight on. Again and again we offered to talk, cease the bombing, draft lines to limit the area of the bombing or do other things essential to peace, when and if the enemy assured us such actions would lead "promptly" to "productive discussions" rather than the usual barrage of propaganda against us before the whole world. It was a diplomacy of total frustration; even after the Paris talks began and during the Nixon years until October 1972, the diplomatic deadlock held tight.

The bombing pause in May 1965 affords a good illustration. It was, judged the president, a "total failure"; it produced nothing, as usual, but permitted the critics to shift grounds and insist that it was too short.[9] A review of the secret history of the diplomacy of these years shows how stubborn both sides could be.[10] They could not reach a settlement because they could not agree on the question of who should hold power in South Vietnam. In spite of ever greater punishment, Hanoi meant to unite all Vietnam, if not all Indochina, under communism, and Washington and Saigon meant to preserve a non-Communist South Vietnam. Hanoi would never really negotiate on any proposal other than total victory or its ultimate possibility under Ho Chi Minh's four-point total surrender program. The no-longer-secret history clearly showed no lack of contact or shortage of intermediaries between the opposing sides. The opportunity for peace was missed for reasons of substance, not want of diplomatic contact. Neither side would yield, because from its own perspective nothing could be conceded. The ultimate question was: Who was to govern South Vietnam? The problem could not be accommodated. Washington believed the enemy would not accept the increasing punishment we imposed, but he did. Hanoi would compromise only to "the extent of giving Washington a face-saving method of withdrawal from the South and of postponing the achievement of its long-term objective for a few years by the formation of a supposedly neutralist regime in the South."[11]

When Washington talked of negotiations, it meant we sought a similar face-saving means for Hanoi to halt the war in exchange for a cessation of our bombing and the withdrawal of our ground forces. Hanoi did not try to use the peace movement in America as a means of spurring negotiations, but rather deemed that movement to be a sign of weakness and disunity of will that would eventually bring our defeat and withdrawal.

One reason for the short bombing halt was Johnson's concern over Russia. On April 5, 1965, our intelligence spotted the first Soviet antiaircraft site under construction fifteen miles southeast of Hanoi, and this activity raised the risk of a more direct Russian confrontation. The week-long bombing halt began May 12, and in a top-priority message, May 10, 1965, to Maxwell Taylor, the United States ambassador to South Vietnam, the president said he would not announce the pause but would simply privately call it to the attention of Moscow and Hanoi and seek some reciprocity. The United States intelligence community informed the president of the situation broadly. The current program would likely bring little change in the war; the enemy would continue and intensify his efforts to win a victory with more men and equipment and with air defenses strengthened by Soviet and possibly Chinese aid. If the United States expanded its efforts, the enemy would:

likely count on time being on their side and try to force the piecemeal engagement of U.S. troops under conditions which might bog them down in jungle warfare, hoping to present the U.S. with a de facto partition of the country. The Soviet Union . . . would almost certainly acquiesce in a decision by Hanoi to intensify the struggle.[12]

The report noted there was no real prospect of any "give" on Hanoi's part. Our limited bombing and ground forces would not likely change that mood. Nor would the enemy be apt to negotiate seriously unless our air attacks brought severe damage and destruction to Hanoi's major economic and military targets. The advice to the president was that any increased bombing should leave the enemy an opportunity to explore negotiations without complete loss of face, would not preclude Russian pressures on Hanoi to avoid expanding the war, and would not stir sudden world animosities against us.[13]

In his message to Ambassador Taylor, May 10, 1965, Johnson expressed the hope that the bombing pause, especially planned to coincide with Buddha's birthday, could be used "to good effect with world opinion." Although he would tell Moscow and Hanoi privately, he would watch closely to see whether they might respond in any way. Their reaction would guide his future decisions. He said his purpose in this plan was

to begin to clear a path either toward restoration of peace or toward increased military action, depending upon the reaction of the Communists. We have amply demonstrated our determination and our commitment in the last two months, and I now wish to gain some flexibility.[14]

Meanwhile, Rusk sent a message to Foy D. Kohler, our ambassador to Moscow, May 11, 1965, to be delivered to Hanoi's ambassador to Russia; but Ho's embassy in Moscow refused to receive Kohler or the message because of the lack of diplomatic relations. Kohler then sought to deliver the message to the Soviet Union since it was a Co-Chairman of the Geneva Conference on Indochina. In his brief but sharp encounter with a Soviet deputy foreign minister, Nikolai P. Firyubin, he asked:

Does the Soviet Government agree to transmit the oral communication to the D.R.V.? I said this was the whole purpose of my visit.

Firyubin said the D.R.V. embassy had not put such a request to the Soviet Government. I must agree that for Soviets to act as intermediary between us and D.R.V. is very unusual. Naturally he would report my request to his Government and if the D.R.V. should request this service he would not exclude the possibility of transmitting the communication to the D.R.V. Government.[15]

While they talked briefly about Hanoi's official reaction to our offer, Firyubin passed a note to another Russian official, who left the room and after some time returned with a note to Firyubin, who read it and—probably upon an order from his superiors—told Kohler his government would not transmit the message to Hanoi, since that government had not requested this service. The Russian added that it was our responsibility to get the message delivered. When Kohler pressed the Russian to be sure he had correctly understood his refusal to cooperate with us in our search for peace and a reduced level of warfare, Firyubin bluntly stated, "I am not a postman," and said, "we could find our own ways of transmitting messages." They argued further about the niceties of diplomacy, but without success. However, Kohler had handed the Russian a note which contained the text of the oral communication just delivered. Firyubin did not return it.[16]

The note Firyubin had refused to send on to Hanoi had informed the enemy of the bombing halt to begin May 12. Why this action? We declared it took into account repeated suggestions from various quarters, including public statements from Hanoi's representatives, that there could be no progress toward peace while the air attacks continued against North Vietnam. It stated our conviction that the cause of the war was armed action against the people and government of South Vietnam by forces decisively affected from North Vietnam and said we would carefully watch to see during this pause if there were any significant reductions in these aggressive actions. It stressed that the road toward the end of such armed attacks was the only route that could end our air attacks against North Vietnam. It noted that the pause risked being misunderstood and being characterized as weak, adding that if such were the outcome,

it would be necessary to demonstrate more clearly than ever, after the pause ended, that the United States is determined not to accept aggression without reply in Vietnam. Moreover, the United States must point out that the decision to end air attacks for this limited trial period is one which it must be free to reverse if at any time in the coming days there should be actions by the other side in Vietnam which required immediate reply.[17]

The effort was in vain, and the bombing resumed within a week. Both Moscow and Hanoi had been almost insulting and hostile. Russia probably wished to avoid charges, almost certainly to be made if she cooperated with us, of collusion between the Soviet Union and the United States. Kohler suggested that Russian action not be deemed a final or hard-line rejection, but possibly a reflection of the bind she found herself in at that moment. The Rusk message to Hanoi was not an ultimatum.[18] It was no final condition, no threat of total annihilation; it contained no final proposition which if declined meant the use ultimately of all our power to destroy. There was no fixed or immediate time limit. The use of such a word to describe a will merely to take further steps to prevent the Communist conquest of South Vietnam was just one of many examples of how war critics stretched words beyond their truth and, as the word then went, "badmouthed" our effort to establish freedom in Indochina.

The end result of our renewed bombing was to stiffen enemy determination to fight on; it did not force him to compromise. In a further discussion with
Hanoi about a bombing halt and negotiations, Premier Pham Van Dong of North
Vietnam spelled out the price of peace to two French friends of Henry Kissinger,
then a Harvard professor, who arranged and supervised a mission to Hanoi. The
two French friends, Raymond Aubrac and Herbert Marcovich, outlined as a
private idea a two-part proposal: an end to the bombing coupled with an
assurance that Hanoi would not increase its terms of war efforts after we
stopped the bombing. The problem of controlling any possible Communist
efforts to spread the war while we halted the bombing was discussed. Marcovich
said part of the control might be through overflights for reconnaissance
purposes. The premier stated that the country under discussion was "our
country," and it could not be thus discussed, adding: "We want an
unconditional end of bombing and if that happens, there will be no further
obstacle to negotiations." Asked what he meant by unconditional, the premier
answered that he could not negotiate while being bombed, but then went on to
say that he would be satisfied with a de facto end of the bombing, rather than an
official declaration that it had stopped. Would there be a delay between the end
of the bombing and the beginning of negotiations? He answered: "This is not a
problem."[19]

Then at some length the premier observed that the problem ahead was
very simple, yet very complex, and of great importance for the world. Simple,
because it concerned the freedom of a people; complex, because many
considerations were involved in any solution; and important, because it
concerned so many people. He felt that the United States government was trying
to solve the problem within its present limits, which the Frenchmen took to
mean that he did not believe we were then in Vietnam as a prelude to an attack
upon China. And then the premier expressed his belief that America sought to
get a clear picture of the present position. This was as of July 1967.

Our view is this: U.S. power is enormous and the U.S. government wants to win
the war. President Johnson is suffering from a pain and this pain is called South
Vietnam. We agree that the situation on the battlefield is decisive; the game is
being played in South Vietnam. From the newspapers we see that some people
want to confine the war to the South. However, the White House and Pentagon
seemed determined to continue the war against the North. Therefore we think
that attacks on the North are likely to increase. We have made provisions for
attacks on our dikes; we are ready to accept the war on our soil. Our military
potential is growing because of aid from the U.S.S.R. and other Socialist
countries.

Now I shall talk to you about negotiations and solutions. We have been
fighting for our independence for 4,000 years. We have defeated the Mongols
three times. The United States Army, strong as it is, is not as terrifying as
Genghis Khan. We fight to have peace at home; we have no wider aims. . . . We
are ready to talk at any time provided that actions against the North are
unconditionally ended.[20]

Pham Van Dong said ending the war required two conditions: a permanent and unconditional end to the bombing and a withdrawal of United States forces. He denied that Hanoi meant to impose socialism upon the South; nor did he think the NLF wished such a result. It rather anticipated a broad coalition government, a political settlement in the South, and after that might come gradual efforts toward unification.[21] Obviously that was a near-total misreading of both truth and fact. The United States never sought to conquer Vietnam as did the forces of Genghis Khan; it never sought to destroy Hanoi's Communist society; and Hanoi obviously meant through NLF coalition in the South to unite all Vietnam and Indochina under Ho Chi Minh. The people of South Vietnam had nothing to fear from us, but everything to fear from their northern neighbors and their own local traitors and saboteurs. The Pentagon historians concluded that the two sides clearly understood each other as the war began rapidly to expand. They knew a painful contest lay ahead, but were not inclined to find a peaceful way out. Neil Sheehan of the *New York Times* reported: "They held very different estimates of the efficacy of U.S. military might. We thought its pressures could accomplish our goals. The Communists did not."[22]

After 1965 the rising debate about our involvement in the war vitally affected the course of the war itself. Opposition to the war broadened, and demands for peace efforts grew. In and out of Congress bitterness arose over the tragedy, the losses, the cost and the consequences of the war. In developing their indictment of the war and their program to end it, the critics declared we must recognize and negotiate with the Vietcong rebels, who controlled large areas and sizable numbers of the people of South Vietnam. Although they received aid from outside sources, the Vietcong were not mere puppets of Hanoi or anyone. We should concede that it was a civil war, in which we should not meddle at all. Our involvement was a mistake; all Vietnam should be free to determine its own fate. Indochina for centuries had not wished to live under Chinese or any other foreign hegemony. The bombing should stop; it was not effectively impairing Hanoi's ability to aid the Vietcong. This was admitted by both McNamara and Clifford, secretaries of defense between 1963 and 1969. Our demand, when neither we nor Saigon had won the war, that Hanoi stop its aid to the Vietcong was merely a vain call for surrender and acceptance of defeat by Hanoi and the Vietcong. Every appropriation for the war should be denied, since it supported an evil, immoral, and unnecessary war.

Critics noted that every appropriation perpetuated the deception of the Gulf of Tonkin Resolution and was a further endorsement of this tragic war. Rubber-stamp approval of requests for money, which implied continued endorsement of the war, the president could use before the world to justify his Vietnam policy. Congressmen long ago abdicated to the president the major responsibility for the determination of most foreign policies. Senator Russell of Georgia and others deplored the slow erosion of congressional power, regretted the inaction of Congress before the escalation of the war, and declared it had followed like sheep behind the executive's war policy.

Congress, while told by high administration officials that victory was just around the corner, troop cutbacks were coming soon, Saigon was nearly ready to assume a major role in the war, and rural pacification was proceeding successfully, continually but reluctantly approved rising appropriations for the war after 1964. As late as June 1969, Saigon officials told Washington they would not be ready for our troop reduction until late 1970, if that soon, and our estimate also was that the ARVN (Army of the Republic of Vietnam) was still no match for the Vietcong. When Johnson requested an appropriation in 1965, he said it was more for the approval of Congress of his war effort than for the money itself. This brought from young Representative John Lindsay of New York, in explanation of his vote for the measure, that he did so only because "the President has requested us to present a united front to the world on our involvement in Vietnam."[23] He warned that his vote was not to be interpreted as an approval of the administration's whole policy in Vietnam. Nor did it imply a blank check endorsement of unexamined billions more for the war, or for the further expansion of our armed forces in Vietnam without allies or resort to diplomacy to end the tragedy. Others had similar misgivings and reservations.[24]

Gruening and Beaser noted that the expansion of our anti-Communist efforts in Vietnam, the Dominican Republic, and elsewhere raised grave doubts about our intentions and their possible consequences. Senator Fulbright published his *Arrogance of Power;* editorials on "The Illusion of Omnipotence" appeared in the *New York Times;* and perhaps millions questioned the wisdom of our assumption of the role of global policeman. Senator Gaylord Nelson of Wisconsin denounced the presidential practice of citing every military appropriation for the war as proof of congressional endorsement of both the war and the Gulf of Tonkin Resolution. That resolution did not give eternal approval of war anywhere the president wished. It conferred power to protect our forces in Southeast Asia; it did not sanction the containment of communism. He predicted that Congress and the public would live to regret their hasty and thoughtless action, and, when voting against the resolution that would authorize funds admittedly not then needed, said to the administration: "obviously you need my vote less than I need my conscience."[25]

Senator Joseph Clark of Pennsylvania declared we had no "mission to conduct a holy war against godless Communism"; holy wars "never succeeded in the past" and were not apt to in the future. Emphatically he asserted that Vietnam was not "essential to our national security"; we had "no business getting sucked into a ground war on the land mass of Asia"; military solutions to political problems were not "likely to succeed in the world today"; rather the only true approach to peace was through "an earnest effort, painstakingly pursued by the diplomats of all countries, to settle the differences between the nation-states . . . without recourse to war." The bitterest critic of the war, Senator Wayne Morse of Oregon, reminded his Senate colleagues in 1965 that in the previous summer they had widely proclaimed that their vote for the Tonkin Gulf Resolution did not mean their approval of a wider war, the bombing of North Vietnam or the use of ground troops, yet within the past eight months "all those things had come to pass." In the final vote on the appropriation bill of May 1965 only three Senators—Morse, Nelson, and Gruening—opposed the measure. In a July press conference the president announced both sharp increases in our fighting forces and additional efforts to achieve peace in Vietnam.[26]

Appeasing both doves and hawks continued to be a major problem for the Johnson administration. The night before the press conference, Mansfield secretly promised to support the president publicly, but declared his opposition to any further expansion of the war and "just about everything else the United States had done in Vietnam since Diem's murder, particularly the bombing in the North."[27] Nevertheless, LBJ had his congressional appropriation and, by implication, a resolution approving his policies and supporting once again the Tonkin Gulf Resolution. Now he could move ahead to the wider war he had pledged to avoid the previous year. Morse reminded the Senate that the Pentagon and the White House recognized votes, not words. Gruening and Beaser concluded: "Thus the Congress had abdicated its power to de-escalate the war in Vietnam for the second time,"[28] when the Senate approved, May 8, 1965, an additional $700 million for prosecuting the war.

When Congress met in January 1966 the bombing pause, launched December 24, 1965, still prevailed, and a major peace offensive was proceeding. Over the Christmas holiday congressmen faced constituents full of questions and doubts about the war; now back in Washington they were in a more critical mood than when they left the previous October. In a very much troubled election year, Pentagon predictions of a long war and requests for troop increases to possibly four hundred thousand men greatly disturbed the Congress. In the months ahead, dissent increased in volume and extent. By the time Johnson ended the bombing pause January 31, 1966, he had acquired some new and powerful opponents in Congress. In his report on Vietnam, filed January 8, 1966, Mansfield concluded glumly that our expansion of effort had "blunted but not turned back" the Vietcong.[29] Instead the enemy merely matched our expansion by local recruitment in the South and reinforcements from the North. Most likely it would be necessary for us greatly to magnify our strength and involvement before the conflict could end; there was no information to permit a precise judgment of the forces necessary to prevent the defeat of South Vietnam. If the American commitment were "open-ended"—a term the critics so widely used thereafter—so seemed the Vietcong's determination and commitment to win. There was no fixed or stable number of Vietcong, no known maximum strength available to the enemy.[30] Would China, Russia, and other Communist nations stand by while we overwhelmed North Vietnam?

Mansfield's study concluded that as we expanded so also would the Vietcong. Thus we were caught on a "rising escalator" without any forseeable limits to future needs. The report accurately noted that in spite of our increased bombing of the North, the Vietcong could commit at will terrorist attacks on Saigon and other South Vietnamese cities.[31] If Hanoi, Haiphong Harbor, and the Red River dikes were open to our bombing at will, so were South Vietnamese cities and our vast installations to Vietcong terror attacks at almost any time, as the increasing attacks in the South, most notably the surprise Tet offensive of 1968, alarmingly confirmed. Even the best efforts of General Abrams, who replaced Westmoreland, could not prevent such raids and attacks upon Saigon and other sections.

No area escaped the war. Our bombs hit widely in North and South Vietnam. Their range and effectiveness were awesome, but the Vietcong also destroyed and ravaged as they wished. There was no front, no recognizable enemy; the war was everywhere. Daily infiltration into any city was possible; the potential for sabotage, murder, and terrorism was always present, ready to erupt when required. One soldier, noting how the war in Vietnam differed from the one in Korea, commented: "This is the first war I know of where a ground soldier can be in the middle of the blood, stink, and death one minute and be in a cool bar drinking a gin and tonic twenty minutes later."[32]

In his Annual Message to the Congress on the State of the Union, on January 12, 1966, the president told the nation the war had no foreseeable end: "We may have to face long, hard combat or a long, hard conference, or even both at once." However, he added, "we will stay as long as aggression commands us to battle."[33] Events appeared to prove him correct on both scores. War critics sharpened their attacks thereafter. Senator Young of Ohio, just back from Saigon, said the conflict was a civil war, revealed that Westmoreland had admitted that the bulk of the Vietcong were native South Vietnamese, and urged the president to resist the advice of some hawks to bomb North Vietnam "back into the stone age."[34] All over the Western world ever louder voices urged the president to stop the bombing, a request which soon became a chant of increasing numbers of demonstrators, antiwar protesters, pacifists, war critics, and Communists. Nowhere in the Communist world did people march or protest to Hanoi, Peking, and Moscow to stop their war, to end their aggression against South Vietnam. The crusade for peace was entirely one-sided.

The administration sought ever larger appropriations for the war and added its usual reminder that each grant was in accord with previous commitments to defend Southeast Asia, including the Gulf of Tonkin Resolution of August 1964: "While that resolution remains in force, and until its obligations are discharged, we must persevere."[35] This official request of January 19, 1966,[36] for funds to carry on the war did not win the "instant" and overwhelming approval of Congress that the Gulf of Tonkin Resolution in 1964 and the $700 million appropriation resolution in 1965 had received. The new request "triggered a bitter debate," stirred widespread opposition to the war, and evoked urgent demands for a full peace effort. On January 21, 1966, seventy-seven Democratic members of Congress urged the president by letter to support all possible peace efforts, applauded the bombing halt, and advised him to seek the full support of the United Nations for a cease-fire.[37]

Johnson replied on January 22, 1966, that he and Ambassador Goldberg determined to make every effort to obtain United Nations support and achieve a cease-fire, but he noted that the continuation of Hanoi's infiltration of the South and the Vietcong attacks all during the bombing pause were causing unacceptable hardships upon our men and our allies.[38] On January 26, 1966, the president received a letter from fifteen senators, led by Senator Vance Hartke of Indiana. It proclaimed their agreement with the Mansfield report and other late critics of an ever expanding war, especially Senator Fulbright. Fulbright stated openly his opposition to any resumption of the bombing; Mansfield said the suspension should be "indefinite"; and Senator George Aiken of Vermont believed the bombing "should be suspended until it becomes perfectly clear that the Communist nations intend to fight the war to the finish." The fifteen senators felt the president should have their collective judgment in front of him before he made a decision.[39]

In a short reply, January 28, 1966, to the senators, the president declared:

I continue to be guided in these matters by the resolution of the Congress approved on August 10, 1964 . . . by a vote of 504 to 2. My views of the present situation remain as stated in my recent reply to a group of members of the House, of which I enclose a copy.[40]

This bitter exchange between Johnson and his critics set the Washington cloakrooms humming with complaints about Johnson's war policy. Two biographers of the president, Rowland Evans and Robert Novak, observed that the open denunciation of the official war policy by Senators Hartke and McCarthy "dramatized the harsh political fact that Johnson's problems had assumed a new and far more ominous dimension."[41] A more positive reply of the administration to its congressional critics was the order to resume the bombing of North Vietnam on January 31, 1966. However, on the same day, Goldberg was instructed to seek the aid of the Security Council of the United Nations in search of a solution to the war. The council met the next day, and on February 2, 1966, voted to consider the Vietnam War. "The vote was 9 in favor, two opposed"; but since it was a procedural question, the Russian and Bulgarian vetoes did not check the procedure. At the request of Prime Minister Harold Wilson of Great Britain the United States did not press for further United Nations action. We had refused Wilson's request to continue the bombing halt and felt we could facilitate his personal efforts in his forthcoming visit to Moscow to achieve something without the expected "forensic slugging match in the Security Council."[42]

The war critics, lead by Morse and Fulbright, were not silenced by the two-pronged effort of talking and fighting. Morse declared that we approached the United Nations "with an olive branch in one hand and bombs in the other. Members of the United Nations are still talking about the bombs."[43] In February 1966 LBJ's troubles with Fulbright mounted: the senator, concerned about the course of the war, the perversion of the Gulf of Tonkin Resolution, and the nearly total abdication of responsibility by Congress for policies and decisions affecting the war, was anxious to inform the public of the diverse views on our war and held lengthy televised hearings on the issue. The critics had a field day. General James Gavin, once army research chief who resigned in protest against Eisenhower's inadequate response to the Sputnik challenge, urged the reduction of our role in Vietnam. He proposed our withdrawal into strong regions or enclaves, urban areas, and port sites, and there, with our sea and air power, through attrition, defense, and endurance, stay on the course until the Vietcong decided to negotiate.[44]

His suggestions received but a limited hearing and understanding by the people. He told the Fulbright Committee that we had enough forces there to hold the coastal areas, where sea and air power could be most fully effective. We should do our best with the forces already there and remember our responsibilities elsewhere around the globe. He noted that "tactical mistakes that are allowed to escalate at the initiative of an enemy could be disastrously costly. . . . We should maintain enclaves on the coast, desist in our bombing attacks on North Vietnam and seek to find a solution through the United Nations." The $10.5 billion budgeted for the fiscal year 1967, together with "all the other commitments we have world wide," were excessive.[45]

In support of Gavin, General Ridgway continued his more than a decade of opposition to our involvement in any massive ground war in Asia.[46] George Kennan, once called the father of Truman's containment policy, now regretted the use of that word *containment*. He felt the situation had changed, because the danger of a monolithic Communist global conspiracy had passed; he declared that a polycentered, national deviationist Communist world had developed. Ancient fears of Communist imperialism were no longer justified. With others he rejected the domino theory and the Munich analogy, so often made by anti-Communist defenders of the war. Although he supported the Gavin enclave approach, he and the other critics did not favor an outright abandonment or betrayal of our Saigon allies. All opposed resumption of the bombing, favored stronger efforts to negotiate a political solution, believed military victory in any meaningful sense was impossible, and sought to extricate us from the war in the most honorable way possible.

Evans and Novak believed Johnson flew to Honolulu in February 1966 primarily to upstage the Fulbright hearings.[47] The two-day meeting between the president and the Saigon leaders, Ky and Thieu, seemed a repetition of earlier journeys. Once again all vowed their friendship, in war and peace, and proclaimed that broad reforms, including the establishment of a democratic political system for South Vietnam, were of vital importance in winning the war. Saigon's leaders pledged their best efforts to defeat the Vietcong and those "illegally fighting with them on our soil"; their dedication to the eradication of social injustice; the establishment and maintenance of a stable, viable economy and a better material life for the people; and the construction of "true democracy for our land and for our people." They also invited the Vietcong to abandon the war and join Saigon through the Open Arms Program: "Stop killing your brothers, sisters, their elders and their children—come and work through constitutional democracy to build together that life of dignity, freedom, and peace those in the North would deny the people of Vietnam." For the United States, the president pledged to aid in every possible way the achievement of these goals, to help them build while they fought, to stabilize their economy, to increase their food production, to spread the light of education, and to erase disease.[48] The Honolulu conference was followed by highly dramatized visits to Saigon by Secretary Freeman and Vice-President Humphrey, who sought to reassure the South Vietnamese of our deep concern for their welfare and our sincere belief in ultimate victory.

However, official efforts neither erased the impact of the Fulbright hearings nor stopped the rising criticism of the war. While Thieu and Ky faced troubles with the Buddhists and the ever powerful Vietcong, Johnson suffered antiwar demonstrations, academic denunciation of the war, de Gaulle's ouster of NATO headquarters from France, and hard-line hawkish demands for military victory. In the belief we could win, Richard Nixon favored a massive expansion of the military effort, even at the risk of war with China. The evangelist Billy Graham even found "higher" endorsement of the war when he declared:

There are those who have tried to reduce Christ to the level of a genial and innocuous appeaser! . . . But Jesus said, "You are wrong—I have come as a fire-setter and a sword-wielder. . . . I am come to send fire on the earth. . . . Think not that I am come to send peace on earth: I came not to send peace, but a sword."[49]

Nothing could hide the ugly nature of the war or quell disturbing doubts about its wisdom. The meeting in Honolulu neither silenced public debate nor reduced the rising dislike of our backing military cliques which did not really represent the people they claimed to govern. Our support of Ky and Thieu made them less, not more, willing to execute the reforms necessary to ultimate victory and peace. The 1966 critics did not endorse the abandonment of South Vietnam to such torture as Ho imposed upon North Vietnam from 1953 to 1956; but they did favor cutbacks, and they opposed the whole concept of military victory at all costs.

On February 17, 1966, General Maxwell Taylor rejected the Gavin policy. He declared it would sacrifice both our unique ability to move speedily and our great firepower; assign a humiliating role to our forces; have a disastrous effect upon our allies, who would be made more defenceless than ever; and destroy the confidence of all Vietnamese in their ultimate success. It would be tantamount to an abandonment and betrayal. The Tet holiday offensive of 1968 and other Vietcong attacks thereafter demonstrated too well that any fixed areas of defense were targets of effective attacks and gave the enemy the too easy option of time and place, without fear of full retaliation or surprise attack. Enclaves were unacceptable. Kennan also urged that we limit our aims and military commitments in Vietnam and, believing we could safely hold there, suggested we dig in, hold, and see if any possibilities for a solution might develop. This widespread dissent over the war and domestic policy brought a sharp loss of Democratic strength in the mid-term election of 1966.[50]

By mid-February 1966 the half dozen or more opponents of the official war policy, wrote Steinberg, had grown to some thirty of the sixty-seven Democratic senators. Among the many critics of the war, Robert Kennedy was by far the most powerful. By nature he was not a dissenter, one who mingled closely with the other war critics and doves to discuss the means of influencing an administration deaf to their proposals. At such a meeting, Senator Eugene McCarthy reportedly observed, "We've got a wild man in the White House, and we are going to have to treat him as such," and Senator Gore called him a very desperate man apt to get us into a war with China, "and we have got to prevent it." Such statements from the regular doves and critics disturbed Johnson much less than criticism coming from Kennedy, who inherited the mantle, ideology, philosophy, imagery, and charisma of John Kennedy. On February 19, 1966, Kennedy admitted that our withdrawal was impossible, but he offered a solution that would tell Hanoi we sought not surrender, but rather peaceful negotiation to end the war through the establishment of a coalition government that included the National Liberation Front. Shocked by such a suggestion from so powerful a source, high-ranking officials of the Johnson administration attacked Kennedy as both naive and unpatriotic. Humphrey compared coalition to "putting a fox in the chicken coop or an arsonist in a fire department."[51]

Satisfied with thus discrediting Kennedy, Johnson then faced Fulbright. On March 2, 1966, a resolution by Senator Morse to repeal the Tonkin Gulf Resolution came to a vote on the Senate floor. Fulbright opposed this maneuver because it would give the White House a chance to tell the people that repeal would betray our fighting forces in Vietnam. The doves did not wish to risk popular repudiation, but Morse would not abandon his effort, and it failed by a vote of 92 to 5, with Fulbright on the losing side. The next day Johnson further expanded the war by ordering another thirty thousand soldiers to Vietnam. With Fulbright in the audience he told a Democratic dinner, "You can say one thing about those Foreign Relations Committee hearings, although I don't think this is the place to say it."[52]

Steinberg observed that Fulbright's standing with the intellectuals vexed Johnson. The former Rhodes scholar, university president, and sponsor of the world-renowned Fulbright scholarship program certainly helped to turn much of the academic world—long supporters of Wilson, Franklin D. Roosevelt, and Kennedy—into opponents of Johnson. With Truman, Eisenhower, and many others, Johnson believed that the ultimate dangers of Munich and Vietnam were identical and the domino theory was legitimate; but many professors and authors praised Fulbright's rejection of such oversimplifications of history. The sophisticated scholar from Arkansas declared: "The treatment of slight and superficial resemblances as if they were full-blooded analogies—as instances of history 'repeating itself'—is a substitute for thinking and a misuse of history." He told the president, in Churchill's words: "Appeasement from strength is magnanimous and noble and might be the surest and perhaps the only path to world peace." Then he added that the president, once the father of the Great Society, had now become its pallbearer because war had sapped the "inspiration and commitment" behind it:

In concrete terms, the President simply cannot think about implementing the Great Society at home while he is supervising bombing missions over North

Vietnam. There is a kind of madness in the facile assumption that we can raise the many billions of dollars necessary to rebuild our schools and cities and public transport and eliminate the pollution of air and water while also spending tens of billions to finance an "open-ended" war in Asia.

Slightly later at Johns Hopkins University he delivered the famous Christian A. Herter lectures—later part of his book *The Arrogance of Power*—in which he denounced the president and his advisers for seeking unlimited power and empire, for their "self-appointed mission to police the world, to defeat all tyrannies, to make their fellow men rich and happy and free."[53]

Congressional consent, however reluctant, to appropriations for a war, which ever larger numbers of people opposed, continued, and every appropriation for its support afforded a chance to debate and denounce the war. A supplemental appropriations bill reached the Senate February 16, 1966, and for the next few weeks once again the whole war policy was debated, mainly in the relatively quiet chambers of Congress, away from the television cameras. Both Republicans and Democrats expressed their dissent from the war policy. Critics said Johnson sought to limit further television hearings and reserve such nation-wide audiences for presidential and official statements by the executive branch of the government.[54]

Congressional defenders of the administration pleaded their case. Senator Russell Long of Louisiana denounced the dissenters as "advocates of retreat, defeat, surrender and national dishonor" who harmed the nation by saying that we had no commitment to fight aggression in South Vietnam. He reminded his senatorial colleagues of our commitments from Eisenhower to Johnson, of the Gulf of Tonkin Resolution, and of our many appropriations for the war. The repeated expression of fears of Chinese entrance and our eternal carping about the loss of American boys did not advance our national defense of freedom and the defeat of Communist despotism. Nor was it helpful to suggest that we were the international criminals when in truth we were the good guys of the world: "Our children will call us blessed and courageous if we stand fast and defeat Communist aggression."[55]

The critics charged that a careful review of recent history would reveal we had no commitment to use ground forces in Asia. McGovern noted it was easy to talk about our children calling us blessed if we got into a war with China, but asked what if, in that event, no children were left to call us anything. Although Lincoln once opposed our intervention in a war with Mexico, he managed to survive with some glory. Other critics noted that General MacArthur once said that anyone who committed us to a major war in Asia should have his head examined, and General Ridgway once opposed the use of ground forces in Asia as "a harebrained idea." Surely no one would suggest that Generals MacArthur, Gavin, and Ridgway lacked patriotism, intelligence, or knowledge of the problems of war in Asia. Senator Gore of Tennessee said the issue was not "defeat, retreat, surrender," but was rather the problem of limiting the war to manageable proportions.[56] Was it an open-ended war for total military victory against whatever forces might enter? Was it a global war? Whether it aided the enemy or not, it was necessary to debate the vital question of the means and ends of this war, especially if democratic processes were to be respected at all.

Critics declared the requested defense appropriations were already provided in other measures and opposed the effort now made to obtain funds in the belief, born of previous experience, that it was another attempt, a deceptive ruse, by the administration to secure a further endorsement of a wider war policy. As evidence to support their suspicion, they cited the president's statement, requesting the money, that it was "in the letter and the spirit of the [Tonkin Gulf] resolution." Hence congressional support of the measure, the critics contended, would again be used to claim congressional support for the war policy. Senator Richard Russell of Georgia sought to persuade everyone that the bill was merely an authorization for defense: "It could not properly be considered as determining foreign policy, as ratifying decisions made in the past, or as endorsing new commitments."[57] Senator John Stennis of Mississippi agreed and added that sanction of the request for supplemental appropriations meant neither approval nor disapproval of our Vietnam policy. Aiken of Vermont wished no such future misinterpretation or stretching of the measure as marked that of the Tonkin Gulf Resolution of 1964. Gore approved the appropriation, but wanted it clearly understood that his vote for the measure did not mean he backed any measure we had taken to get involved in the war, which he deemed a great historical mistake and, he feared, greatly increased the danger of a world war. He recalled his opposition to Eisenhower's initial pledge of aid and his advice to Kennedy and Johnson against widening our commitment; apologized for his mistake in not speaking out sooner; and noted how we had inched into this bog through three administrations, how three presidents had assured us that combat forces would not be sent to Vietnam.[58]

Fulbright agreed with Gore that Vietnam was vital neither to our security nor to a balance of power between the major powers, expressed regrets for his delay in initiating his televised hearings, and admitted he had not realized earlier how serious was our commitment in Southeast Asia:

At the time of the 1964 resolution I really had no realization of what we were about to get into, or how it was about to escalate, or certainly I would have held hearings then. I regret that we did not do this earlier. However, it is better to have the hearings now than not at all.[59]

When Russell sought to cut off the debate after but twelve hours of discussion in the Senate and warned that we might lose the war "by a process of attrition and a lack of ammunition," McGovern snapped back: "a few days of discussion of an authorization of nearly $5 billion should not quite so quickly be labeled a 'filibuster.' " Anxious to reflect the wish of many to avoid any wider war, he was willing to support an amendment to limit our troops to the present level. Little wonder the administration feared the critics of the war received too much publicity by the debate and the televised hearings. It also feared the possible adoption of an amendment, being widely discussed, to prohibit any further expansion of the war in Vietnam.

One of the bitterest critics of the war, Senator Ernest Gruening of Alaska, on February 24, 1966, told of a White House conference of August 1965. "Mr. Alaska," an honorary title given to Senator Gruening, long an opponent of the war, was called to the White House for a discussion. In detail he told the president why he opposed our military involvement in Vietnam, disagreed completely with the oft-repeated statement that three presidents had pledged support for such a policy, and bluntly declared Johnson had no commitment at all. Rather, the senator said, we had invited ourselves into Vietnam; it was a war we could not win; and its continuation would only bring ever greater disaster.[60]

The president persuaded him not to present his amendment, which would prohibit draftees from being sent to Vietnam without their consent unless Congress, by law, thereafter permitted them to be sent involuntarily. He declared that "no draftees would be sent to Vietnam before January," and, after repeating his request, assured him that "if we were not out of Vietnam by January, I would be free to do anything I pleased." Gruening had refrained thus from introducing his amendment, but now on March 1, 1966, he called it up and saw it voted down after "the briefest of debates" by a "sudden death" motion—a motion to table it, which is not debatable—by a count of 93 to 2 (only Morse and Gruening opposed). Another motion by Morse to rescind the Gulf of Tonkin Resolution was similarly tabled by a vote of 92 to 5. Senators Fulbright, Gruening, McCarthy, Morse, and Young opposed. However, many people supported the appropriation out of loyalty to the troops in the field, but without endorsement of the war itself.[61] So Congress continued to consent to measures in support of the war while many of its members dissented from the whole war policy.

In explanation of their votes for the measure many congressmen sought to justify their action by such words as: my vote does not constitute a blanket endorsement of the war; with reluctance and apprehension; my vote does not mean that I am wholly satisfied with the administration's policies with respect to Vietnam; and my vote should not be construed as an unqualified endorsement of all aspects of our policy in Vietnam and does not constitute a mandate for unlimited expansion of the war. To the general public the vote for the supplemental appropriation in the House of 392 to 4 appeared an overwhelming approval, but the numerous doubts expressed by so many congressmen might have raised questions in many quarters. Congress failed to apply any brakes to the escalation of the war.

Why such a failure? Especially when such widespread fears, doubts, opposition, and turbulence existed virtually everywhere—openly in Congress, at the numerous and lengthy sit-ins over the country, in academic halls, in teach-ins, and in the nearly endless open letters in newspapers by many of the most highly esteemed persons of the land. Senator Russell felt the failure to stop the escalation of the war was due to the erosion of congressional power. Gruening and others believed it sprang rather from a refusal or reluctance to use the power Congress had under the Constitution. Congress had the power of the purse and could cut off the funds any time it wished. Many noted the inexcusable haste that accompanied the Tonkin Gulf Resolution, the popular emotionalism, spurred on by executive persuasion, that caused many men to vote not their honest convictions, but what they feared the people back home would more likely approve. Any actions that might be interpreted as a failure to support our fighting men abroad would most surely be misunderstood by the people and most surely reflected in the next election. Thus quiet decisions made and actions taken by Eisenhower, Kennedy, and Johnson—on a rising scale—slipped us into war. Congress felt compelled to finance this war, for many of its members, although they honestly opposed it, sacrificed their convictions in favor of their political careers. Conscience lost, opportunism and expediency won. Seldom in history have representatives in any legislative body so consistently voted one way while speaking the other.

Others thought differently. Right or wrong, unnumbered millions believed communism was a genuine danger; the global conspiracy was not ended; the domino theory was right; the SEATO commitment and the numerous programs of aid for nations seeking the strength to establish and preserve their freedom since the days of Pearl Harbor, the Marshall Plan, technical assistance and foreign aid had not been mistakes at all. They did not accept the scholarly refinements of Fulbright, Kennan, and others; the doubts and unproved accusations of Morse and Gruening; the suggested reductions, cutbacks, and retreats proposed by Gavin and Ridgway; and the subversive efforts of appeasers, cowards, Communists, and fellow travelers among students, teachers, and authors who condoned every crime of our enemy and blandly ignored the millions of South Vietnamese who wished to avoid the great tragedy that befell North Vietnam in 1954.

Millions of Americans believed it was our war, the war of freedom versus slavery, in which all men who sought or cherished freedom should participate. Possibly Congress and the people failed to put brakes on the war policy because they were not sure in their hearts that the policy was wrong. The refusal of Ho to accept all reasonable peace offers; the Russian crush of Czechoslovakian moves toward liberalism in August 1968; Russia's entrance into North Africa and the eastern Mediterranean in support of the Arabs; her continued supply of Hanoi; and the return of the hard line in Soviet policy and the Soviets' continued firm determination to expand Communist imperialism at every opportunity—all these revealed that the war critics of the Johnson years may not have had the full and final truth on their side. One fact emerged from the debate: the rising denunciation of the war encouraged Ho and the Communists to fight on in the plausible belief that they could wear out the will of Americans impatient for victory. Seldom in history did internal dissension so erode the unity and strength essential to victory.

While the debate continued, so did the war. Increases in ground-troop strength, napalm and explosive bombing, and air strikes all failed to bring the expected and oft-predicted victory. Both sides increased their efforts and suffered greater losses of men and materiel, but no one could predict when victory would come. It was not only a civil war in process but a civil war within a civil war. When Buddhists refused to cooperate with the Ky government, Ky, with our backing, crushed the Buddhist threat. Because of our support of this Buddhist defeat, slogans of "Yankee Go Home" and "End the War" appeared in a Saigon parade of thousands, and ARVN troops clubbed the marchers into flight. Meanwhile air strikes hit near Hanoi and Haiphong on April 17, 1966, and giant B-52 bombers from Guam began daily flights over Vietnam. Rumors spread around Washington of an Inchon-type landing in North Vietnam, with its attendant egging of China into a showdown (which some feared the hawks desired to justify attacks upon Chinese nuclear installations).

One irrepressible critic of the war was Senator Stephen Young of Ohio, veteran of two world wars, friend of President Truman, and victor over the oft-denounced John Bricker. At Truman's request, Johnson, then majority floor leader in the Senate, assigned Young to top committees, and in return for such past favors, Young long delayed joining in open opposition to Johnson's war policy. However, within a year after Johnson became president and the course of his war expansion program was clear, Young began to speak out forcefully. A trip to South Vietnam, a tour of our bases, and talks with many officials, especially with General Westmoreland (who told him: "The bulk of the VC's fighting us in South Vietnam were born and raised in South Vietnam") convinced him that a giant miscalculation had been made. Back home, Young publicly declared the president had "made the most serious mistake that any President of the United States has ever made by involving our armed might in a civil war more than eight thousand miles from Washington."[62]

Nor would Young accept the official assertion that the Korean and Vietnam wars were equally justified. In the Korean War few South Koreans, if any, supported the North Korean invasion of the South. That was a real invasion by part of a once-united nation of another section of the same country. There was no indigenous South Korean organization in opposition to the government of Syngman Rhee, nothing equal to that of the Vietcong, with its roots in South Vietnam. Also Young claimed that while we had a definite commitment to South Korea, derived from the diplomacy of World War II, we had no such positive or binding obligation to Saigon. Truman had turned the Korean War into a "United Nations effort," but Johnson had been unable to do this in South Vietnam. Finally, the Western world more widely approved the Korean War than the Vietnam War under Johnson. When Dean Rusk condemned the Vietcong for their sneak attack upon Pleiku in February 1965, Young asked the secretary of state: "Would you call George Washington's crossing the Delaware on Christmas Eve in 1776 to capture the Hessians at Trenton a 'sneak attack?' "[63] When Young admitted publicly that he would sleep better if Rusk were no longer secretary of state, the president told a conference of congressmen: "I'm sorry I'm a little late, but I stopped at the drugstore and bought some sleeping tablets for Senator Steve Young because Steve ought to get his sleep, because Dean Rusk is going to be Secretary of State a long, long time."[64]

At a presidential briefing of June 22, 1966, attended by twenty-eight congressmen who had just visited Vietnam and ranking officials of the government and the armed forces, most of whom were hawks calling for victory at almost any cost, Mansfield, Aiken, and Young opposed expansion. Young cited one Ohioan in the House who sought to please the president by attacking congressmen identified in *Pravda* as opposed to the war, and who then added, "I don't exclude some U.S. Senators from my remarks, because they are giving aid and comfort to the enemy." In support of Mansfield and Aiken in opposition, Young declared:

It's a miserable civil war. And it does not involve in any strategic importance the defense of the United States or any real commitment. We don't have a mandate from Almighty God to police the entire world. This talk about there being an international Communist conspiracy that we must repel wherever it rears its ugly head is a myth. Southeast Asia, Mr. President, very definitely is not within our sphere of influence. South America? Yes.[65]

Nevertheless, Johnson meant to "raise the price of aggression" Ho must pay and made his opening move with the bombing attacks on the oil installations near Haiphong and Hanoi June 29, 1966. The president felt he must do something to boost the morale of the Joint Chiefs, who were frustrated because we were not winning. This was also his answer to Ho, who expressed his willingness to fight a long war against the United States and then admitted he did not think it would be necessary because in the coming November American election the hawks would lose.[66]

Johnson's popularity surged ahead ten points as a result of the bombing escalation, and official optimism spread over the nation at the possible end of the war with victory. As he toured the country in the summer of 1966, crowds cheered him loudly when he attacked his critics as un-American and noted how they seldom denounced the North Vietnamese for bombing hospitals for American servicemen or the atrocities of the Vietcong and the Communists. However, when the hoped-for victory did not come, presidential popularity waned, and the people wanted to hear Bobby Kennedy, not LBJ. Instead of surrender, reports came of greater expansion by Ho of his war effort. He told his people: "Hanoi, Haiphong, and other cities and enterprises may be destroyed . . . but the Vietnamese people will not be intimidated." He sent more than six hundred thousand people out of Hanoi, called up his trained reserves, accepted the help of fifty thousand Chinese road and railroad laborers to help repair the bomb damage, and welcomed the vast Russian military aid plus some missile crews into North Vietnam.[67] The trap grew tighter and the bog deeper.

As Johnson's popularity declined, the president changed once again from the man who favored raising the price of aggression to Ho through expanded war to the statesman of peace and reason, of magnanimity and compromise. Such shifts in the pendulum from war to peace and the reverse puzzled many who believed the president was genuinely sincere in his actions. Others doubted every presidential action and referred to the man as above all "a wheeler-dealer," a political opportunist whose every thought was motivated only by its possible political effect. For the much-belabored president, it should be said that steering any course satisfactory to everyone was most difficult, but trying to satisfy both hawks and doves proved impossible. He was well aware of the possible consequences of his choices.[68] If he pressed hard for total victory, most likely Chinese and Russian intervention would bring on global warfare and possible nuclear disaster. If he abandoned Saigon to its fate, faith in an American promise, power, and will would vanish around the globe. Truly the most reasonable approach to the future was to continue the past policy of limited warfare, seek to persuade Ho that aggression did not pay, and simultaneously urge every reasonable effort for a peaceful solution.

In the fall of 1966 the pendulum swung once again toward peace. Ambassador Goldberg told the United Nations we wanted peace in Vietnam and would halt the bombing of North Vietnam when Hanoi made an appropriate gesture toward reduction of the war. Repeatedly after this our policy was to suggest negotiations and pledge bombing halts and other efforts for peace—but only when Hanoi indicated to us a willingness to reciprocate. Goldberg added now a promise that the presence of the Vietcong at the peace conference would not be "an insurmountable obstacle." (Rusk, however, believed that Ho was quite capable of representing the Vietcong.) The president also asked U Thant to use his influence with Ho to obtain an agreement to negotiate. His visit with U Thant on October 7, 1966, at the United Nations was marred by hecklers outside the building, who yelled: "Hey, hey LBJ! How many kids did you kill today?" The same day the president made a speech to a Newark audience, attacking Richard Nixon. The loudest cheering during his speech came when he mentioned the name of John Kennedy.[69]

On October 10, Johnson in a conference with Andrei Gromyko, the Soviet foreign minister, defended our policy in Vietnam on grounds of humanity, but the Russian told him no settlement was possible "as long as American planes are bombing North Vietnam." Johnson then told Gromyko he halted the bombing for thirty-seven days less than a year before in response to a private plea from Soviet Ambassador Dobrynin, but "you kicked me in the . . . by sending in large amounts of Soviet weapons." Russia could easily and quickly end the crisis by stopping its flow of supplies to Hanoi.[70]

On October 17, 1966, the president began a seventeen-day, thirty-one-thousand-mile trip to Southeast Asia. Some antiwar demonstrations accompanied his visits to New Zealand and Australia along the way. A two-day conference with his Southeast Asian allies was held at Manila, October 24 and 25. The host, President Marcos of the Philippines, favored a halt in the bombing, but still signed the hard-line communiqué which Johnson's staff had prepared. It pledged that all the seven powers present, allies of South Vietnam, would remove their forces from South Vietnam six months after Hanoi withdrew its "military and subversive forces." Johnson's close advisers, Rusk and Clark Clifford, argued in vain against such a pledge. The Manila pledge actually hardened our terms for negotiations because it ignored a promise to stop the bombing. Also Premier Ky there defined "subversive forces" to be sent to the North to include "the Viet Cong guerrillas, who were native to the South." At

Manila Johnson declared the United States would enforce peace in Southeast Asia, a pledge Walter Lippmann termed this "messianic megalomania which is the Manila madness." Humphrey defended the Manila pledge as a great addition to the earlier "Spirit of Honolulu," as significant for Asia as had been the Atlantic Charter for Europe.[71]

After Manila, the president went to Thailand, governed by a dictatorship but a base for some fifty thousand American forces and for daily air strikes over Laos and North Vietnam. His visit was jolted a bit by the announcement that China had just exploded a missile with a nuclear warhead, but he told a formal state dinner audience that the war in Vietnam was about ended, in spite of the fact that there were "rivers still to cross and mountains to climb." His adviser and speech writer, Walt Rostow, inserted in the presidential language frequent mention of "Munich," "appeasement," and broad anti-Communist slogans. Johnson said his objective in South Vietnam was to establish "the principle of self-determination," of "one-man, one-vote" by secret ballot.[72] Thus the principle enunciated by the Supreme Court in the case of Baker versus Carr would be extended to Southeast Asia.

At Dulles Airport upon his return to Washington November 2, 1966, he told the American people the war effort would be increased beyond the 326,000 men already there. "We shall never let them down." To the large crowd come to welcome his return, including Senator Fulbright, he said criticism of his war policy must end: "When there is deep division in a land, there is danger."[73]

Division there was, and it was to grow in the coming months. The war so absorbed the executive energies and attention that the president had or took little time to keep his political fences repaired. Even his closest friends needing his help in their efforts at reelection had cause to complain. The Ninetieth Congress, elected in November 1966, showed an increase of forty-seven Republicans in the House and three in the Senate.[74] Many of those defeated had been staunch supporters of the president and his war policy.

The election results warned of troubles ahead for the president. Johnson's double policy of talking peace while increasing the fighting confused his critics and puzzled his friends. When he asked the enemy to make the smallest gesture for peace, to indicate in even the slightest way that he would join him in talks and said he would go anywhere, any time, he certainly gave every impression of deep sincerity of purpose. Both Hanoi and his war critics everywhere noted, however, that when the test came he always flatly rejected the two basic requirements experts deemed most necessary to win Communist acceptance: an immediate end to the bombing of North Vietnam without any pledges or concessions in return from Hanoi and the recognition of the National Liberation Front as an independent political body in the South. One biographer, Alfred Steinberg, sharply critical of Johnson, noted: "Because of his adamant stand on these two issues, Johnson knew he could prevent negotiations from taking place while, at the same time, gaining great political mileage as a man who wanted peace."[75] To this anti-Johnson and bitter antiwar critic, it seemed the president was thus insincere and deceptive. In truth, the president knew those terms meant total defeat for freedom. Peace on those terms could have easily been obtained, but peace with justice, no. Somehow Steinberg seemed to think our defeat was the honorable way to peace, that Johnson, not Ho, was the obstacle to peace. He turned reason and truth upside down.

Pressure for a bombing halt was a constant during the war, yet it rested upon a misunderstanding of both Johnson and the nature of this war. We could not match the Asian masses man for man. Our technical superiority had to be used. We feared a land invasion of the North out of concern for China and Russia, but air strikes offset Hanoi's land invasion of the South and boosted the morale of South Vietnam, which had to suffer so much devastation and terror. LBJ declared that in spite of various reports to the contrary, the vast majority of our airmen strenuously sought to avoid civilian casualties and had clear orders to attack carefully selected military and industrial targets. LBJ agreed with McGeorge Bundy that bombing was less important to a successful outcome of the war than ground operations in the South. His advisers never believed, as did some military men, that the bombing campaign could be decisive.[76]

Of that we will never know for sure, but Albert Speer's inside observation of Hitler's defeat expressed the belief that allied air attacks could have brought German defeat without a land invasion. Also Nixon's awesome air attacks of 1972 appeared to have influenced serious peace talks later in the year and in 1973. Many military men in the United States believed the full use of our air power from the beginning could have changed the course of events. The "steady barrage" of enemy demands for an entire cessation somewhat reinforced the belief that bombing was hurting the enemy more than he cared to admit. In any case, it was for him a good issue to use in his incessant propaganda attack upon Johnson's hawks and his appeals to the sentiments of the doves, appeasers, and antiwar forces. LBJ strongly noted:

The cry was picked up by some of our friends abroad and, with increasing intensity, by a few of our own citizens. These demands were generally accompanied by the warning that only a total and permanent bombing halt offered any chance for starting serious talks. Most people forgot, or ignored, this central fact: We had stopped the bombing, not once or twice, but eight different times from 1965 to the beginning of 1968. Five other times we had ruled out attacks on military targets in or around Hanoi and Haiphong for extended periods. The net result of all these bombing pauses was zero. Indeed, it was less than zero for us, because the enemy used every pause to strengthen its position, hastily pushing men and supplies and equipment down the roads of North Vietnam for massive infiltration into the South.[77]

After the thirty-seven-day bombing pause, which ended January 31, 1966, Johnson's advisers unanimously agreed that only one development would end the war—"Hanoi's conviction that North Vietnam could not win militarily." Clearly Ho and his advisers had not reached that conclusion. Their forces had suffered heavy losses in 1965, but their total strength had increased through infiltration and intensive recruitment and in 1966 was rising to a high level.

Johnson later wrote:

> Under the military rule of thumb—that in a guerrilla war the defending forces need ten men for every guerrilla—more than 2 million men would be needed to cope with the Viet Cong-North Vietnamese forces then in the South. My military advisers and I were certain that we had lowered that commonly accepted ratio—through heavier firepower, increased mobility, the use of airpower both as a weapon and for transport, and other factors. But we knew that the defense still needed considerably more manpower than the offense in this kind of fighting.[78]

When he totaled his allied force he revealed that it numbered a little more than eight hundred thousand—a ratio of less than 4 to 1. Allied forces never reached the 10 to 1 ratio.

Almost everyone had his peace plan, and never before in our history had any government seemed so anxious for negotiations to end a war. In fact, some criticized the administration for seeming to beg the enemy to negotiate. The suggestion was heard—from Eisenhower and General Omar Bradley, among others—that we should once and finally state our peace terms and fight on until the enemy accepted them without further humiliation before the world. De Gaulle reiterated in late 1966 his belief we should withdraw and let Vietnam settle its own affairs in its own way. Many critics long termed the whole war Asia's affair, a family squabble, not related at all to global communism, and of no business to the Western world. U Thant kept urging us to halt the bombing as proof of our sincere desire for peace, and Hanoi never stopped demanding a cessation of the bombing and all other acts of war without indicating any willingness to initiate genuine peace negotiations.

The British foreign secretary, George Brown, visited Moscow November 23, 1966, to win approval of a plan under which the United States would stop bombing the North while a conference negotiated a cease-fire and settlement. Kosygin passed back Hanoi's reply that first the bombing must stop without any preconditions or reciprocity. Johnson deemed this proof of Communist insincerity and immediately expanded the war by ordering heavy air strikes over Hanoi in early December 1966. At the same time a Polish offer to promote peace talks between Washington and Hanoi at Warsaw without prior end of the bombing, private reports declared, had been accepted by Hanoi only to be suddenly withdrawn when Hanoi was bombed once again December 13 and 14. When U Thant strongly criticized Washington for bombing Hanoi during these delicate negotiations, Johnson through Goldberg asked U Thant to take whatever steps he felt necessary to launch any discussions that might bring a cease-fire.[79]

Hanoi's demands obviously doomed to failure any efforts U Thant might make. Goldberg communicated to U Thant our established fourteen-point peace program, but the three points which U Thant believed essential to peace were not included: an unconditional end to the bombing; a mutual scaling down of the fighting; and the inclusion of the Vietcong in all negotiations.[80] Johnson said we were willing to make every concession except unconditional surrender to the enemy, but Hanoi wanted nothing less than that, then and long thereafter.

In negotiations to conclude a war which we had not won and they had not lost, it was difficult for either side to yield. War critics felt the United States, as the greater power, could afford to be magnanimous and make the first concessions to get off a collision course that might destroy a major portion of mankind and civilization. Senator Mansfield urged the president to extend the three-day Christmas truce until February 12 and suggest to Hanoi that both sides freeze their military strength to facilitate a cease-fire, but the president ordered the resumption of the air attacks and declared: "You just can't have a one-sided peace conference or a one-sided cessation of hostilities." We could not "cease" while they "fired." At the same time Ambassador Lodge added that peace negotiations would most likely be unnecessary because the enemy would probably just "fade away"; if not, the Vietcong could earn a cease-fire only by ending their military activities. Hanoi rejected an international peace conference proposed by Mansfield and George Brown because Brown was unwilling to invite the NLF.[81]

U Thant then lectured Washington on the nature and price of peace in Southeast Asia. If we wished peace there, he said, we must accept certain propositions. One was that the Vietcong forces and the NLF were not puppets of Hanoi, no matter how much help they received from the North. The war was a civil war now in the South, as it was in all Vietnam prior to 1954. Before you could have peace, you would have to negotiate with your real enemy, the major force you were actually fighting, the Vietcong. Hanoi could not dictate to the Vietcong, who might continue to fight a more limited but costly guerrilla war even without Hanoi. The Saigon military clique, French oriented and mandarin educated, and the great landlords supported by us did not represent the masses of South Vietnam—rural, urban, Buddhist. The domino theory was not valid. Neither Ho nor the Vietcong had any interest in or intention to invade other adjacent lands or become the puppets of Peking or Moscow. No vital Western interests were involved in South Vietnam. These realities, U Thant declared, we would have to grasp and accept if we sincerely sought peace in Vietnam.[82] This, when Communists were already moving into Laos and Cambodia and using vast parts of these areas to aid their war effort.

Naturally, Rusk pounced on all these concepts, which diametrically opposed our interpretations of the situtation. From our truce efforts and periods of pause had been expected "some abatement of hostilities and . . . moves toward peace"; but, said the president, "unfortunately the only response we had from the Hanoi government was to use the periods for major resupply efforts of their troops in South Vietnam."[83] Johnson ordered new air attacks on Hanoi January 15 and 16, 1967, and assured us that the civilian population suffered no bombing, except possibly by accident. Critics long noted the rising number of such accidental deaths. Enemy peace terms continued to follow the hard-line four-point program of April 1965, but Ho's agent in Paris softened the statement in January 1967, stating that if we would halt the bombing unconditionally,

Hanoi would examine and study the situation. A few days later the foreign minister of North Vietnam added that when the bombings and other acts of war had ended, "there could be talks between the two countries." Johnson replied, February 2, 1967, that the bombing would continue until Hanoi matched us with some reciprocal concession or reduction of the war. He publicly admitted that he saw no serious signs of a desire or willingness to end the war on any just basis.

In all the rumors and peace negotiations there was more propaganda than truth. We would not accept the two basic conditions that we halt the bombing and recognize officially the NLF as an independent force in South Vietnam. For Hanoi that would offer an open-ended reinforcement of its troops in South Vietnam and for us mean the abandonment of our Saigon allies, the destruction of their morale, and the exposure of our own forces to unnecessary risks and dangers. Hanoi still refused officially to admit her direct military involvement in South Vietnam and universally proclaimed that Washington, not Hanoi, was the only genuine aggressor against South Vietnam. The war critics declared that Hanoi could not negotiate with us on our terms without giving up its whole rationale of the war. Hanoi refused to accept as legal or permanent the division of the two sections of the country by the 17th parallel. The conflict was a civil war involving all Vietnam. Had the Geneva Accords been honestly executed and the elections allowed in 1956, the Communists, north and south, would have won and would have long since governed the country. Since 1954 Saigon governments were only puppets of the United States, not entitled to recognition by anyone. In their definition of the war, Hanoi was not an aggressor; rather it was defending the homeland from a foreign invader, and all native Vietnamese enlisted with us were traitors to Vietnam. Hence pledges to reduce the war, to accept conditions for a cease-fire, to stop reinforcing the Vietcong and Hanoi's regular forces would be a pledge to betray the cause, the country, and the Communist troops in the field. How could one be an aggressor against oneself? In Hanoi's view the interests of Ho and the Vietcong were in major part the same. No matter that many non-Communists had supported Ho prior to 1954 against France and now against the United States; the dominant leaders of both movements were Communists, and their interests were largely identical. If Vietnam were to be one country, they meant it should be Communist ruled; if it were to be, for whatever time, two countries, then both Ho and the Vietcong meant that both should be under Communist governments. In any case, Ho could not for a moment abandon his former friends and supporters in the South any more than in the North. Separately or together, it was still the same fight, the same war, the same cause—oust the foreigner and establish Communist regimes everywhere in Vietnam. Nowhere in Communist doctrine or practice was there any provision for official admission of defeat or the surrender of the ultimate objectives of power.

Neither side could negotiate its annihilation, but talk of peace had to go on. Possibly patched-up deals to paper over differences or other means might be found, but the conflict between the two systems would endure. Out of Paris in early 1967 came a story of a possible peace solution arranged by Senator Robert Kennedy. Johnson had enough trouble with the brilliant and dedicated young senator without having him seize any credit for ending our most unpopular war. Headlines hit the world with the hope that Kennedy could arrange a peace Johnson failed to win. The martyred president's brother toured many parts of the world and enjoyed virtually everywhere a most wondrous reception. There seemed no place he had not visited, no problem he had not studied, and no end to his energies and commitments. In Paris he talked about the war with the director of the Far Eastern Section of the French government, Etienne Manac'h, who told him of a peace proposal by Mai Van Bo, head of the Hanoi diplomatic office in Paris. It was a three-stage proposal for ending the war, but only after we had stopped the bombing. In truth, it was but another statement of the by now well-established Hanoi formula. Kennedy recognized it offered nothing essentially new or hopeful, but an employee of the United States embassy in Paris felt it was important enough to cable a full report to the State Department, and from there the news leaked to the public. Headlines blared: Kennedy bringing home peace proposal from Paris!

Then followed a series of bitter and ugly events between Kennedy and the Johnson administration. The two men never managed to achieve any harmonious relation, and at times the bitter recriminations marred even the most formal intercourse between the two possibly most powerful men in the United States. Humphrey once declared that when the two got together often "all sense flies out the window, and they become two animals tearing at each other's throats." Kennedy told the Senate March 2, 1967, that the president did not want a peace in Vietnam because he asked the enemy to surrender unconditionally as a precondition. He offered his own peace program: suspend the bombing unilaterally and be ready to negotiate immediately; neither side should build up its forces during the negotiations; and Hanoi and Washington should both gradually withdraw their troops from South Vietnam.

In answer to Kennedy, Rusk said all our bombing pauses had in response met only hostile action. Later, November 14, 1967, Rusk told the Foreign Policy Association that we should search soberly for the essence of the Vietnamese problem and declared that it did "not clarify the issue to call Viet-Nam 'just a civil war,' " when over twenty Hanoi regiments then sought "to impose their will upon the South." He added:

Of course both sides are Vietnamese, but it should be clear that the problems, the special problems of the divided states—Germany, Korea, and Viet-Nam—are to be solved not by force but by peaceful means.
    It does not clarify the issue to speak of "unconditional surrender," when all that is being asked of North Viet-Nam is that they get their troops out of South Viet-Nam and Laos and stop training guerrillas for Thailand.

Those who would "negotiate now" should know that if an enemy representative should present himself anywhere to discuss peace, Rusk "would be there." To those carrying banners calling for peace in Vietnam, he hoped that "through some reciprocal extension of the presumption of good faith" they would realize that the president had asked him and others to carry that banner of peace to "every capital of the world over and over again." He challenged the demonstrators outside the building in which he then spoke "to produce a representative" from Hanoi "willing to discuss the problems of peace" with or without conditions. That would be more helpful than what they were then doing.[84]

Those who deplored violence, as he did, Rusk declared, should know "that all the violence could end within hours if we could get some minimum cooperation from the authorities in Hanoi." Those for de-escalation should know that he had tried repeatedly to reduce the level of fighting "only to face a categorical rejection from the other side. Those who would brush aside a security treaty as a scrap of paper should reflect soberly on the dangers which would arise if it should be discovered that our security treaties do not mean what they say." Although he had never claimed God was on his side, he had done his best along the way. He would leave the final judgment to the Almighty, but to those who were so certain of their righteousness in denouncing the war, who wanted to speak in moral terms, he suggested that they should look at the total moral context and consider

whether it is moral to send men and arms to impose a political system upon a neighbor or to sign the 1962 agreement on Laos and treat all of its provisions with contempt; whether it is moral to try to destroy the elections in South Viet-Nam by murder and assassination during the election campaign; whether it is moral to refuse any forum, public or private, bilateral or in conference . . . to engage responsibly with the issues of bringing the situation to a peace. Is it not also moral to know what the effect is upon the capacity of the nations of Asia to have some aspiration toward freedom, to enjoy that freedom?

He asked that we "try to embrace the total moral problem."[85]

He noted that in recent decades it had made a great difference to world history "that we and others were concerned about what happened in Iran and Greece and Turkey and Berlin and Korea and the Philippines and Malaysia and the Congo and in Southeast Asia." People should

bear in mind that we have undertaken a most difficult task since 1945. We have had to place ourselves across the path of aggression with firmness and have been branded as the aggressor by those in whose path we stood. In doing so we have had to act with a restraint which has taxed our patience to the utmost, because we could not turn the human race on to the slippery slope of general war. This combination of firmness and restraint requires the utmost of understanding and nerve from a people who are as impatient as are we here in this country. Indeed, our impatience has made us a great nation.

But impatience is pretty dangerous in this modern world.[86]

To hawks who urged us on to victory, he suggested that they seriously ponder the possible consequences of our using fully our awesome power to get anything done quickly. Finally, he noted that he was "rather afraid of people who are so absolutely right." To negotiate with such a people and to reason with them at all was a "strenuous exercise." In any case man must find the answer to the question of peace or else he would not need to "worry about the future, because there wouldn't be any."[87]

In Saigon, where General Westmoreland asked to increase his strength to four hundred thousand American troops, Goldberg defended the administration, declared our pledge to the Vietnamese stood strong and firm, and demanded that they be allowed to determine their own lives free from outside interference. At home, Johnson told state governors he had made thirty-three offers to Hanoi in four months. More likely he had made approximately the same offer thirty-three times in the same period. At least, the example the president used in refuting Kennedy's accusation that he was a war lover suggested it. Johnson told the governors: "If I propositioned a gal thirty-three times . . . and I didn't get one proposition in return, I just wouldn't have anything more to do with her."[88]

Of peace efforts there seemed no end in 1967. The president sent five letters to Ho Chi Minh in the backstage maneuvering that marked this period. The fifth letter (February 2, 1967) expressed the wish for a quick end of the war, noted the heavy toll caused by it and predicted history's harsh judgment upon their failure to find a just solution. It recalled the several vain efforts of past years and recent public statements from Hanoi of a willingness to begin bilateral talks with the spokesmen from Washington, "provided that we cease 'unconditionally' and permanently our bombing operations against your country and all military actions against it." The president saw two great difficulties with those conditions:

In view of your public position, such action on our part would inevitably produce worldwide speculation that discussions were under way and would impair the privacy and secrecy of these discussions. Secondly, there would inevitably be grave concern on our part whether your Government would make use of such action by us to improve its military position.

However, he was prepared to move even further than Hanoi had yet proposed publicly or privately; in brief, he would halt the bombing and any further increase of our forces in South Vietnam, "as soon as I am assured that infiltration into South Vietnam by land and by sea has been stopped."[89]

Meanwhile, in London, February 6-13, 1967, Kosygin expressed the belief that Hanoi's statement that "there could be talks" with Washington after an unconditional halt in the bombing might serve as the basis for a compromise. He told Wilson he "had some influence with Ho Chi Minh" and could virtually "guarantee negotiations in three or four weeks if a fair compromise were found" between the positions of Hanoi and Washington. In lengthy communications between them, Johnson told Wilson that besides ending the bombing he would delay the arrival of an additional seventy-five thousand new troops to South Vietnam, but would expect Hanoi, in return, to withdraw its troops from South Vietnam and cease any further infiltration of weapons, ammunition, and troops.

While these communications proceeded, Pope Paul VI urged continuation of the Tet truce until the peace negotiations could be arranged. Kosygin returned to Moscow before any reply came from Ho, and Johnson resumed the bombing February 14, 1967. Wilson defended Johnson, blamed Hanoi, and stated his belief that peace was almost within our grasp: "One single act of trust could have achieved it . . . one gesture by North Vietnam–which would have cost them nothing in terms of security or even face."[90]

Johnson received an answer from Ho February 15. Ho would not accept the status of an aggressor; rather, he proclaimed, that was the guilt of the United States; Vietnam had never harmed the American people; it was a little country thousands of miles from our shores. Ho's reply continued at length, and it was a most persuasive piece of deceptive propaganda for his cause. The United States for over two years with its air and naval forces attacked North Vietnam; it had meddled in Vietnam, launched an aggressive war in South Vietnam, sought to perpetuate the partition of the country, and committed various crimes against peace and mankind. It had used most inhumane weapons and methods of warfare, "such as napalm, toxic chemicals and gases," to raze villages, destroy crops, and murder innocent people. Its planes had dropped tons of bombs on "towns, villages, factories, roads, bridges, dikes, dams and even churches, pagodas, hospitals, schools," and helpless people. United States acts of terror and aggression must cease. The people of Vietnam must be left free to settle their own affairs. If Washington wanted peace, it should stop immediately and unconditionally its bombing raids "and all other acts of war against the D.R.V."[91] Vietnam would never submit to force or talk under the threat of bombs.

Johnson's reply was to expand the war. By air, mines were dropped into North Vietnam's rivers. The Seventh Fleet moved up the Tonkin Gulf near the North Vietnamese coastline to shell the area, and American troops just below the DMZ began to lob shells over the zone into North Vietnam. The president saw no alternative. Apparently Hanoi saw no alternative to escalation either, because the enemy increased his terror by killing and seizing thousands of civilians, attacking cities and air bases on a larger scale, and using Russian rockets for the first time. Innocent South Vietnamese civilians were caught in the squeeze between the two enemies and forced to endure the napalm, bombs, and strafing mistakes of American planes and simultaneously the taxes, forced drafts, and ceaseless atrocities of the ever present, if unidentified, Vietcong.[92]

LBJ believed the conflict in Vietnam was different from any other war. He noted that it included elements of the Korean War, the Huk rebellion in the Philippines, and the Greek civil war, but was unlike any of them:

Our goal was not to destroy the enemy's army on its home ground, nor did we try to eliminate the enemy's dictatorial regime. This was a war of no fixed front. The "enemy" might be two or three divisions at one time, as at Khe Sanh, or two or three armed men sneaking into a village at night to murder the village chief. It was a war of subversion, terror, and assassination, of propaganda, economic disruption, and sabotage. It was a political war, an economic war, and a fighting war—all at the same time.

In spite of the fact that television screens, for the first time in history, brought all the horrors of war into the living rooms of America, I think that the American people never had a real chance to understand the Vietnam conflict in all its dimensions. There were many reasons for this failure in communications. Complex problems always have trouble competing with oversimplifications. Economic development and the building of political institutions rarely get the same attention in the press or on television as the violence of war. Nor is the average American reporter or reader nearly as interested in what the Vietnamese are doing as in what Americans are doing.

But the Vietnamese themselves, in Saigon and in Hanoi, knew very well the kind of war it was. The Communists recognized that cutting off the rice supply to a district town could be as disruptive as an attack by three battalions. They knew that killing one able village chief could do as much damage as wiping out a squad of soldiers. They were aware that effective propaganda could have more impact than a division of troops. Throughout the war, and especially after the fall of the Diem government, the Viet Cong and North Vietnamese were not satisfied with trying to destroy the military forces that opposed them in the South. They attempted in every way possible to disrupt the economic life of the country. Through propaganda and terror, they worked daily at keeping the political life of the South in turmoil. Until the introduction of American combat forces into Vietnam in the summer of 1965, the downward slide was not restricted to the military arena. The South Vietnamese economy was increasingly disrupted, and the political front came close to chaos.[93]

Our intervention changed this condition and gave South Vietnam another chance to save itself.

In late March 1967 Johnson flew to Guam for a war conference. Stopping on the way at Nashville, Tennessee, he said he would persevere to the end because his course was just, and noted that two years earlier he was "forced to choose, forced to make a decision between major commitments in defense of South Vietnam or retreat . . . in the face of subversion and external assault."[94] The elaborate retinue of aides and reporters with the president, who termed the coming conference merely "a routine review of the war," stirred serious misgivings in the minds of Mansfield and Fulbright, who observed that in the past an extension of the war generally followed such gestures.[95]

Perhaps the president hoped to avoid the necessity of inviting General Ky to attend the conference at Guam. However, the dapper little air force general, more aristocrat and autocrat than democrat, who, when asked who his heroes were, once answered that he had only one—Hitler—turned out to be the center of attention at the conference. For the occasion, he wore plain civilian clothes and left at home his usual gaudy uniform, oversize glasses and pistol. Now, in the guise of a civilian, he gave the president a copy of the constitution for South Vietnam just completed.[96] The president appeared most happy over the document, as though it were his own child, and looked forward to the elections planned under its authority for the coming September. Ignoring its flaws, its rigged provisions, he felt it offered great hopes for future success and noted that it took the American people thirteen years between 1776 and 1789 to draft and launch a successful and durable form of government. Under the severe conditions of a bitter war it seemed to him that the little Republic of South Vietnam was making remarkable progress.[97]

The Guam conference broadly discussed General Westmoreland's estimated need for increasing our troops to above 475,000 men by the end of the year. The "search and destroy" tactics might require an additional 200,000 men. When our battle deaths averaged 750 a month at the time, it was hardly reassuring to the president to be told that enemy losses were considerably higher than ours—an enemy who was reduced to using thirteen-year-old boys. McNamara observed that air raids over the infiltration routes and base areas already reached about 13,000 a month. By 1966 he had begun to have doubts about our war policy. Now he would limit the bombing to military targets below the 20th parallel, the Hanoi-Haiphong line, and take other steps to reduce the war.[98] This put the brilliant defense secretary on a course in conflict with administration policy, which tended to favor escalation, and finally brought his peaceful departure from the cabinet in early 1968. For years, McNamara had declared that destructive and effective as it was in devastating the North and complicating Hanoi's supply lines, air power could not bomb the enemy to the conference table. The nature of guerrilla warfare enabled the enemy to carry on the war, even expand it, with a very limited amount of supplies, which he could move by foot, bicycles, small trucks, and coastwise boats. The enemy could not win that way, but, on the other hand, he could not be easily or soon defeated.

The Guam conference also concerned itself with the long discussed rural pacification program. Efforts to build a successful economy and stable social system based upon it had been underway since the first grants by Truman in 1950. All succeeding administrations sought to advance the concept of economic growth through improvement in land use and land diffusion among the people who worked the land. Perhaps free men have falsely believed that the main answer to communism is economic progress. Kennedy put considerable thought and energy into his strategic hamlets and aid program; Johnson, in his famous Johns Hopkins speech of April 7, 1965, promised to invest a billion dollars to advance the economic development of Southeast Asia "after the fighting ended." He had gone so far as to persuade the able Eugene R. Black, former head of the World Bank, to head a proposed team of experts to initiate plans for a TVA-type scheme to rehabilitate the entire Southeast Asian area. Little was heard of it thereafter. At Guam the "other war," meaning the war against poverty, in Vietnam was again discussed. Robert Komer, ex-CIA agent and Johnson aide, was in charge of this program. The president and the American public now wished to know how the pacification program was proceeding. Just five months earlier Johnson blandly promised to lead much of Asia out of disease, hunger, ignorance, and its fear of aggression.[99]

The Revolutionary Development (R.D.) program had begun in 1966 to carry on more successfully the old Kennedy scheme of strategic hamlets. Steinberg ably briefed the plan:

The R.D. team for each hamlet consisted of fifty-nine persons trained in specialties such as police work, farming, and military techniques. The function of each native team was to move into a hamlet to manage its affairs and develop it into a support area for the Saigon Government. However, with the war rapidly moving to an *hourly* cost of four million dollars for the American Government, an *annual* expenditure of forty million dollars on pacification could not provide for many fifty-nine-man teams. And even if more money were available, the emphasis of R.D. on police vigilance, with each hamlet resident privately interrogated on the political opinions of his neighbors, was hardly conducive to a growing love for the Saigon Government.[100]

Overoptimistic reports had too long been made of the pacification program. The credibility gap between the reality and the reports was about as great as the real progress of the military phase and official reports of the war. Komer was accused of telling the president and the American people what he thought they wished to hear. Even advisers to Ky called the Komer report on pacification of 1966 too optimistic. However, the United States embassy officials in Saigon called the program a glowing success and based their optimism on the fact that the Vietcong, grown desperate, had lately increased their attacks on the pacification teams to halt the program that would nullify the Vietcong program.

Senator Edward Kennedy adopted the South Vietnamese refugee problem as his own "special project." His travels to South Vietnam and his extensive studies there convinced him that the situation of over a million refugees had been somewhat ignored and minimized. In the spring of 1967 these million people lived crowded in temporary quarters, "coastal-area camps and towns," with little provision for health, food, education, job training, and general care. Even the Vietcong often fled to our side to avoid our air raids and artillery attacks.[101]

Nor did the reports at Guam and later adequately stress the "gross corruption" that infested Saigon and thousands of provincial governments. Enormous "waste and extravagance" marked the AID and United States military construction programs. In May 1967 one large construction combine was officially charged with running a billion dollar contract without normal management controls:

Among a host of detailed findings, the GAO found the combine guilty of losing accounting control of 120 million dollars; of "goldplating," or needless buying of super-quality supplies; shipping items such as business envelopes by airfreight from the United States; and failing to build warehouses or fence off the mile-long Cam Ranh Bay Depot, so that local sampans beached nightly and stole millions of dollars worth of diesel engines, electric cable, roofing etc.[102]

Spasmodically Saigon would undertake efforts to erase the corruption among its officials and subordinates. In 1968 Premier Tran Van Huong reported that 21 of his nation's 44 province chiefs and about one-fifth of its 250 district chiefs had been dismissed for corruption or inefficiency. The number dismissed would have been higher if adequate replacements had been available. He noted that people paid large sums of money to secure political appointments "because they knew they could get it back many times over." Although the Thieu-Ky regime promised reforms, the regime jailed no province chief or high-ranking official.[103] Corruption, nepotism, favoritism, black marketeering, open theft and profiteering had long been a way of life in Vietnam. Any reports that anticorruption drives were a glowing success should have misled no one.

Nevertheless, Johnson came home from Guam full of optimism about future victories, about our now being "at a favorable turning point." Premier Ky assured our newsmen that the enemy was "on the run," his transportation and supply system "in near paralysis." The Guam answer was that ceaseless warfare would soon break the Communist will to fight. If so, critics felt, it would have to be done by United States soldiers alone, for with but few exceptions, ARVN units were still fleeing from battle and were deserting at an annual rate of nearly one hundred thousand. They also harshly mistreated their own civilian population, "stealing, raping, burning down villages, generally kicking people around."[104]

After numerous peace proposals and the Guam conference, the president felt he had but one option—to expand the war. So out went new orders to pound North Vietnam harder, send more shells across the DMZ, increase the search-and-destroy missions, and widen the air warfare. Furthermore, spy plane flights over China should be stepped up and hot pursuit of the enemy into Cambodia and Laos permitted. Military victory seemed to be the answer. The failure of the peace efforts and such a stiffening of attitude and determination to frustrate aggression stirred wide doubts and misgivings everywhere. The president appeared to feel he had tried in vain every reasonable approach to peace. All his efforts brought from the enemy was an incessant demand for the four-point NLF program, which meant our surrender. Gestures toward peace, a prolonged truce, possible halt to the bombing he might accept, but he would take no unilateral steps to peace. Hanoi would have to make some reciprocal offer, some gesture, some effort to reduce the war.[105]

By July 1967 McNamara and Westmoreland had come to a sharp disagreement over our war policy. The general wanted more men immediately, and Premier Ky urged Johnson to supply a total of 600,000 soldiers, "or 137,000 more than the number there at that time." For a closer look, McNamara made his ninth trip to Southeast Asia and found the general's "insatiable appetite" most unwelcome; he could see little improvement in our situation since 1965 when Westmoreland first demanded a major increase. Although rosy predictions of ultimate victory, the ARVN's greater assumption of the military burdens, and the withdrawal of our forces sought to silence public criticism of the conduct of the war, currently vast increases of men and materiel were deemed essential. To McNamara it seemed strange that just two years earlier,

before the bombing of North Vietnam, no regular North Vietnamese troops were in the South; now ten regiments had crossed the Seventeenth Parallel. Two hundred thousand Viet Cong were said to have been slain, but great doubts existed in the Pentagon regarding the credibility of Westmoreland's "body count" of the enemy, for the same number of VC troops and guerrillas were in the field as had been present in 1965. In addition, McNamara's statisticians had figures to show that "Westy" was not making efficient use of the men he had. Only 37 per cent of his American troops were assigned to combat duty. And what about his own afternoon tennis games? Furthermore, in his April 28 speech before Congress, Westmoreland had incorrectly given the impression that South Vietnam's ARVN forces were carrying a large share of the fighting burden when he told the legislators, "Vietnamese troops have scored repeated successes against some of the best Viet Cong and North Vietnamese army units." Nor was there as much success in the pacification program as had been anticipated when Johnson transferred that function from the civilian hands of Ambassador Bunker to General Westmoreland. It was progressing "very slowly," McNamara complained.

McNamara also had strong doubts about the declared value of bombing the North. The number of American plane losses was approaching the one thousand mark, yet the expected breaking of the will in the North was not occurring even though the tonnage dropped on the Communists exceeded that dumped on Germany during the whole of World War II. As for the effectiveness of bombing the supply routes to the South, the amount of matériel customarily shipped was so small (one hundred tons) that no significant decrease had taken place. As for the persistent military demand to bomb and mine the harbor at Haiphong and take the risk of having Red China and the Soviet Union join the conflict directly, McNamara pointed out again that though 4,700 tons of North Vietnam's daily supply imports of 5,800 tons came through Haiphong, North Vietnam's seacoast ran four hundred miles and contained many locations suitable for "over-the-beach" nighttime unloading operations.[106]

When rumors of conflict between McNamara and Westmoreland spread, Johnson sought to squelch both the rumors and the dispute by ordering McNamara to tell reporters that political progress in South Vietnam over the past year had been "noteworthy," economic change "remarkable," and the Vietcong offensive "blunted."[107]

A war neither won nor lost, a bitterly divided inner council, the absence of reliable information to guide policy, the spreading distrust in the credibility of the Johnson administration stirred an ever rising criticism of the war and brought the president and his war program to a new low in popularity. Steinberg observed that by August 1967 the polls revealed that over 50 percent of the people disapproved of his handling the war, 41 percent felt the troops should never have been sent to Vietnam, and 56 percent believed the war was either lost or stalemated. Still the president refused to believe he was wrong or the war was lost. However, those losing faith in him and his policy increased in number, and amid this distrust and uncertainty the president began to lose control over the Congress, the budget, and his own executive bureaucracy. Riots and violence were so widespread in 1967 that the president and his cabinet suffered abuse, heckling, and often found it necessary to avoid contact with the public at all. Antiwar demonstrators met them wherever they appeared. It seemed to many that the big man in the large oval room of the White House was himself losing touch with reality. Somehow, some day, peace would come, but until that day, the president believed, we should persevere along current lines with gradual enlargement of the war. Eventually Ho would surely be willing to talk, to offer some reciprocity for actions we had often indicated a willingness to take.[108]

His critics and others believed that if he would unconditionally stop the bombing of North Vietnam, peace talks could and would begin. Secretly he told Ho he would halt the bombing of Hanoi to permit him in safety to ponder our conditions for negotiations, but when Ho would not accept reasonable terms, he ordered Hanoi bombed repeatedly. Hanoi told us, also repeatedly, there would be no negotiations until the bombing and all other acts of war against North Vietnam were stopped unconditionally: "There will be no reciprocity ... no bargaining ... no blackmail."[109] Hanoi refused even to speculate about what it might do if we stopped the bombing of the North, and Washington always qualified its offers to cease the bombing with some sort of demand for reciprocity—for "mutual military restraint" or scaling "down of the conflict."

Opposition to our peace efforts came not only from Hanoi but also from the National Liberation Front of South Vietnam. Any final solution of the war would obviously require the approval of the Vietcong, the primary enemy indigenous to South Vietnam. An NLF official told us in September 1967:

If America stops bombing the North, Washington will be able to talk to Hanoi, but that will have no effect on the war in the South. If you want peace in the South, then you must talk with the Front there, for it is the Front that is fighting in the South, and you can't end a war except by dealing with the men fighting it.[110]

This basic fact took a long time to win acceptance inside the Johnson administration, and even longer in Saigon. Thieu and Ky filled South Vietnam's jails with tens of thousands of political prisoners, whose only crime was to favor coalition and talks with the Vietcong.[111] In the absence of a total military victory over the Vietcong, obviously any negotiated solution would require direct contact and compromises with the Vietcong. For Saigon this was one of the very hard facts of life.

Republicans often appeared more hawkish than Johnson and the Democrats, but notable exceptions occurred. Especially significant was Senator Thruston Morton's blunt declaration that the Johnson war policy was "bankrupt" because it was committed to a military solution. He called for an immediate end to the bombing of North Vietnam and to all search-and-destroy missions in the South. Possibly in answer to this and other attacks, the president made his San Antonio Declaration of September 29, 1967. By its formula we would "stop all aerial and naval bombardment of North Vietnam when this will lead promptly to productive discussions. We, of course, assume that while discussions proceed, North Vietnam would not take advantage of the bombing cessation or limitation."[112] Hereafter Johnson stressed the need for Hanoi to show some sign of restraint, reciprocity, and concession before he would agree finally or unconditionally to stop the bombing. This San Antonio formula caused disagreement within the administration and raised serious doubts about Hanoi's possible compliance with it. The enemy denounced it.[113]

In both early summer and October of 1968 came lulls with a sharp decline in casualties on both sides. Key administration officials, including Harriman, who later said we missed the chance here offered to speed peace negotiations, urged the president to accept these actions as signs of the necessary restraint we had sought,[114] but he was slow to accept the evidence as sufficient to justify a cessation. He feared for the security of our troops below the DMZ and elsewhere, noted the speedup of Hanoi's efforts to supply the Vietcong and its own armed forces in the South, and bluntly observed that he certainly was not going to accept Hanoi's one-sided view of de-escalation: "that the United States lower its level of military operations while the enemy is free to increase its operations." By taking such a reasonable position, our government hoped to persuade Moscow to win Hanoi's acceptance and end the deadlocks in the peace efforts, but Hanoi stubbornly held out for a total cessation of the bombing and all other acts of war before agreeing to talk about anything with the United States.

During the war there were nearly endless reports of genuine peace efforts, which upon later and fuller study turned out to have been largely false. Heard were calls for a return to Geneva, which had been a betrayal of North Vietnam to communism. The efforts of our British friends to effect a return to Geneva were rebuffed. There was a call for a Soviet-American conference, which obviously could not succeed unless approved by the other parties. To Johnson's every approach to Russia came the incessant reiteration of the Hanoi and National Liberation Front four-point program. Further, there came demands to turn to the United Nations. Twice we had sought discussions with Hanoi and Peking through the United Nations, first in the Security Council after the Tonkin Gulf attacks of 1964 and again in April 1965, when U Thant considered visits to Hanoi and Peking to explore the possibilities of peace (but they had refused to participate). Both deemed the United Nations incompetent to deal with the matter. We had tried to clear the way for a conference on Laos and Cambodia, in the hope that progress toward peace there might be reflected in Vietnam also, but our efforts had been blocked by Hanoi and Peking.

Of private and semi-official efforts, secret and open, there was nearly no end. In the spring of 1964, for example, a private line to Hanoi through a Canadian diplomat tried to test the mood in Hanoi only to meet its stern demand: withdraw your forces, abandon your Saigon puppet, and let the NLF take over power in South Vietnam. Out came reports in the summer of 1964 of Rangoon talks between Hanoi and Washington, arranged by U Thant, but which somehow became entangled, confused, and lost in the Washington bureaucracy. U Thant received no reply to his offer. Johnson never even heard of the proposal until much later, and U Thant found no real solution prospects from Hanoi, just a hazy offer to talk. We have long since learned the sharp distinction between talk and serious negotiations with Communists. When the seventeen nonaligned nations called for unconditional discussions, we agreed. The enemy labeled the authors of the suggestion "monsters and freaks" and refused to talk at all. In April 1965, when the distinguished Englishman, Sir Patrick Gordon-Walker, sought to explore Hanoi-Peking views on ways to end the war, he was refused permission even to enter North Vietnam or China. The enemy termed the president's offer in his Johns Hopkins speech of unconditional discussions a hoax. The president of India also made constructive proposals to end hostilities and establish an Afro-Asian patrol force, but these interesting and hopeful suggestions Hanoi and Peking rejected as a betrayal. Third-hand assurances filtered into Washington throughout 1965 of enemy readiness to negotiate, but always on the basis of the tough proposition: stop the bombing permanently without conditions; then Hanoi might "do something." It would not commit itself in advance—beyond the four points.

Chester L. Cooper, the Assistant for Asian Affairs on the White House staff, wrote that in late October 1965, Rusk discussed with him a proposal supposedly relayed to him by Janos Peter, Hungary's foreign minister, "on authority from Hanoi" of the enemy's willingness to negotiate if the bombing stopped. Upon inquiry, this, too, turned out to be entirely false. The Hungarian initiative was a hoax. Peter had not been to Hanoi, had no authority to speak for North Vietnam, and had no reason to believe Hanoi was ready to reduce its demands. Cooper observed:

If the North Vietnamese were, in fact, receptive to negotiations on any terms but their own and to a political settlement on any terms other than the surrender of the United States, it was not evident from their public statements during 1965 and 1966. Every American offer of negotiations, no matter how forthcoming or unconditional, was called a "swindle," "deceitful," or a "trick." Every reported North Vietnamese "peace feeler" was vigorously denied by Hanoi—a tactic that frequently pulled the rug out from under those who claimed that the United States was ignoring or rejecting Communist overtures. The plain fact of the matter was that by the summer of 1966 the positions of both Washington and Hanoi were non-negotiable.[115]

Yet the rumors went on spreading and antiwar critics repeatedly accused the administration of sabotaging these "sincere" efforts in its stubborn determination to seek victory in a "winless" war. The Paris talks, deadlocked for years, should have dispelled these false accusations because we knew all the enemy was ever willing to negotiate was our unconditional surrender.

While the defenders of the administration war policy applauded Johnson's San Antonio formula as a sincere peace gesture, the critics ever more bitterly denounced the war and our peace overtures as inadequate and insincere. They never seemed to think the enemy was insincere. Nor could they show he had anything to offer but our humiliation. They ridiculed Johnson's contention that he only sought to protect our security. General David Shoup, ex-marine corps commandant and winner of the Congressional Medal of Honor, bluntly declared: "They just keep trying to keep people worried about the Communists crawling up the banks of Pearl Harbor, or crawling up the Palisades, or crawling up the beaches of Los Angeles, which is of course a bunch of pure unadulterated poppycock."[116] In a famous column Walter Lippmann, bitter critic of the Johnson war policy, reminded all Americans that although Mao's troops could march, they could not swim, and suggested our withdrawal seaward out of the quicksand of Asian land warfare. Senator John Sherman Cooper of Kentucky blamed Johnson for the failure of negotiations to end the war. Charles Percy, able young senator from Illinois, noted that our every step expanding the war was easily matched by the enemy and added that administration policies, not its critics, as the president liked to assert, must surely be wrong.

Criticism of the war grew to full fury in late 1967. The president denounced his critics as "Nervous Nellies," "cussers and doubters," nonpatriots, "lefties," and cowards, whose only policy was to cut and run, whose words and deeds endangered the lives of our forces in Vietnam, gave the enemy false hopes, and came near to open treason against the nation. Dissension at home prolonged the war by holding out for Ho the hope of eventual American withdrawal. As the antiwar protest mounted in fever and fervor, official denunciations of the critics also increased in intensity. Some accused Walter Lippmann, Martin Luther King, Jr., and others of nearly treasonous actions and moral turpitude. In April 1967 General Westmoreland came home from Vietnam to help defend the war against its home front critics. Fulbright feared that such criticism of dissent would lead to charges of disloyalty, then "treason," and ultimately to censorship of all dissent. He declared that Westmoreland had "neither the competence nor the right to discuss U.S. foreign policy on Southeast Asia." The historic ideal of civilian supremacy suffered in these years.

The war critics believed the war in Vietnam checked our efforts to reach any understanding with Russia or reduce the tensions of the cold war. They thought Russia was anxious to end the war in Indochina. The truth was difficult to discover. Russia may have had reasons for wishing the war to continue. Johnson's defenders, who believed in the global Communist conspiracy thesis, noted that we suffered far more from the war than Russia did and asked why Russia should wish to end a war that cost us so much and her so little. She was investing only a very small fraction of the nearly $30 billion a year we were spending by 1968. Nor could Russia risk further criticism inside the Communist area by posing as the champion of peace or any settlement short of victory for communism in Indochina. For years China had accused Russia of betraying Lenin and the world proletarian revolution and of collaboration with capitalism. Dissension within the Communist world had brought on a sharp Chinese-Russian split. Obviously Ho would follow the nation that helped him most. Further the war had stirred animosities against the United States around the world and at times offset the very bad image created by Russian actions toward satellite nations—for example, the brutal repression of Czechoslovakian liberal tendencies in 1968. Neutral nations and fellow travelers everywhere ignored the vital differences in the conduct of the two great powers.

The United States intervened only at the official request of South Vietnam, whose government sought our aid in its fight for a richer freedom, while Russia crushed the slightest tendency toward freedom in Czechoslovakia against the obvious will of the people and their government. While the United States would withdraw from South Vietnam if an official request to do so were made, Russia was asked to leave Czechoslovakia and stubbornly refused. One was an effort at national and individual freedom from oppression, the other was the exact opposite—it was the conquest and subjugation of an entire nation and its people. However, the war in Vietnam complicated in many ways our relations with Russia and made very difficult the efforts of both sides to reach agreements. It lessened the possibility of success of any pressure upon Russia in Europe and left us little will or strength to frustrate Russian ambitions in other areas. By fighting in faraway Southeast Asia we were engaged in a sideshow, not the main tent, where lay our greatest potential and actual enemy. Why should Russia wish to end a war that so successfully bled us, stirred internal attacks upon the establishment, and gave little promise of any quick solution?

Negroes grew bitter at the inequities of the draft, which found so many of them fighting a war which whites and educated people somehow managed to evade. Young people, who had to do the fighting in an increasingly unpopular, possibly "winless" war, marched in giant demonstrations against the Pentagon to protest against the president and his official family, who felt it essential to move around the nation under strict armed guard and arrange secret routes and rear door entrances and exits. Johnson spoke more and more to the armed forces under the protection of a mighty retinue of secret service men. Young men burned their draft cards, evaded the draft, and deserted from the armed forces and fled to Canada, Sweden, and elsewhere. Intellectuals and others led antiwar protests and demonstrations. Students took charge of university campuses, interrupted classes, seized administration buildings, and demanded control of university education. From nearly everywhere came the cry: Stop the war, halt the bombing, talk with the NLF and the Vietcong, bring the boys home, and use the money for rebuilding the ghettoes, for education, for reconstruction, and for construction here at home.

All the bickering, dissension, and bitterness between the hawks and the doves erupted in a giant and tragic confrontation at the Democratic party convention in Chicago in 1968. It brought catastrophic retaliation against the demonstrators and protesters by the police of that city. It may have encouraged Russia and Ho to believe that victory might be dumped in their lap by the self-destruction of American society and the subversion of its established institutions. A new word slipped into the terminology of United States politics—the politics of confrontation or the "new politics" of the extremists—radical left and the radical right, and both against the moderate center. As the extremism of both sides grew in noise, if not in numbers, the young radicals, black panthers, students, hard-line Communists, fellow travelers, extreme right wingers, John Birchers, Dixiecrats, many followers and supporters of George Wallace, men of great wealth and power under cover of antiwar, anti-Johnson, antiliberalism, and anti-intellectualism—sought ominously to grab power, betray the entire democratic spirit and procedure, and force traditional leadership and system everywhere to yield to extremist minority programs. Many lost all patience with the slow processes of representative government. They wanted instant reform, instant progress, and instant change. Whatever it was, they lacked the patience to work for it in the democratic tradition of reason, persuasion, and evolution and too readily turned to the tactics of revolution and violence.

The dominant trend of the administration policy, at least until March 1968, was hawkish in nature. It had thought in terms of winning the war and invested more efforts in that hope than in pacification and reform. All our peace efforts seemed in vain; every attempt met the Vietcong four-point program that demanded our dishonorable surrender and total withdrawal. The only other option, which long seemed the easiest of all to pursue, was to try for military victory. The official policy was to talk peace, profess a desire for peace, and offer to negotiate on any reasonable terms; but when Hanoi responded with silence or blunt rejection, the administration generally proceeded with an expansion of the war. Powerful hawks had little faith in pacification or any negotiations short of victory and pressed incessantly for military victory. A tragedy for all mankind in the 1960s sprang from the fact that a military response and repression so often seemed the easier way to solve so many problems. Hugh Sidey observed that the president found the central theme of these years was that "when the United States weakened its defense structure or ignored its world responsibilities or when its leaders hesitated or vacillated, rarely did we escape trouble and when it came the trouble was usually worse than it would have been earlier." Johnson once declared: "We're not going to have any men with any umbrellas." He could not forget the image of Neville Chamberlain, who went to see Hitler three times seeking "peace in our time" at the sacrifice of free and innocent people.[117] The sad and lonely president observed, "You pay more dearly later on if you appease."[118] The weakness, disunity, lack of will, and military unpreparedness of the nations in the 1930s, Johnson felt, as Truman, Eisenhower, and Kennedy before him, had permitted the rise of Hitler, Mussolini, and Tojo and the spread of aggression and conquest, which by unity and strength might have been stopped before it became so nearly fatal.

CHAPTER FOUR

ABOUT FACE

Behind Johnson's historic decision to reverse direction lay many factors, and doubtlessly many will claim credit for the change. Hindsight judgments have already posted priorities. Dean Rusk, the one man other than the president best able to tell the story, has remained silent and has even indicated no intent to crowd the field with memoirs. Only the president could really know why he acted as he did, and his explanation was supplied by the publication in 1971 of the history of his White House years, in *Vantage Point*. His critics fault the study as something less than the whole story, as not quite what he once termed history with the bark on it. However, he was in a far better situation to judge his actions than his staff members and inner circle of advisers, than Clifford, McNamara, Rusk, Bundy, Walt Rostow, and all the rest. His explanation deserves more emphasis than theirs.[1]

His four major decisions, the presidential package of March 31, 1968, included: his retirement from politics; a halt in the bombing of North Vietnam, as a step toward eventual withdrawal and peace; the expansion and modernization of the South Vietnamese Army, as an effort to Vietnamize the war; and only a small increase in our own military forces—far short of the approximately 206,000 additional men requested by his field commanders after the Tet offensive. Why these steps, this de-escalation of our involvement? To 1968, efforts had failed to persuade Hanoi to cease its attempts to conquer South Vietnam. The enemy had matched our every step in expansion of the war, and the future seemed to invite only more of the same with ever greater risks, higher casualties, and the likelihood of Chinese and Russian intervention. We had been unable to bomb the enemy to the conference table; rather our expansion of the war with all its attendant tragedies had brought on a chorus of despair inside the United States and the Western world, a cry for cessation of the bloodshed and destruction. Although he believed his course had been right, the president feared we had lost the will to continue the struggle to halt totalitarian aggression. The antiwar argument had undercut the resolve of the nation. No one understood any better than the president the need for domestic progress, with the nation unhampered by endless war, toward better homes, schools, health, and employment opportunities. He felt he could not take the risks of a deeper involvement and a wider war which the hawks urged after the Tet offensive, yet he was aware that continuation of the limited war held little promise of victory at any future date. He wrote:

However, I rejected the suggestion that we use air power to close the port of Haiphong and knock out part of the dike system in the Red River delta. I felt that there was too grave a risk of Communist Chinese or even Soviet involvement if those measures were carried out, and I wished to avoid the heavy civilian casualties that would accompany destruction of the dikes. I emphasized again to my military advisers that we were going to avoid actions, in the air or on the ground, that might trigger a wider and more destructive war.[2]

Requests for military increases were being considered along with the issue of bombing during the last two years of Johnson's administration. Options including a maximum force, minimum essential force, increased air strikes over broader areas and at more targets, and possible ground actions against at least the southern part of North Vietnam were all studied on a contingency basis. Johnson must have been influenced by a detailed memorandum given him by McNamara May 19, 1967. It revealed the defense secretary's serious doubts about the wisdom of the war and his opposition to its further expansion. He told the president that probably Hanoi would not negotiate seriously, if at all, until after the 1968 election. Continuation of the war at the current rate—or with modest increases in our force levels—would neither change Hanoi's mind nor satisfy the American people. It would most likely get us in deeper and risk a confrontation, possibly war, with China and Russia. All options were imperfect; there were no easy ones. He advised retreat from further involvement and avoidance of greater risks.[3]

McNamara's disenchantment really began in July 1966. By then he had reached the conclusion that we could not win the war. Air power had failed to decrease the rate of infiltration or cripple Hanoi's logistical support of the war, and these cumulative failures "tipped the balance in his mind against any further escalation of the air attacks." The growing antagonism, domestic and foreign, to the bombing, which was the major impediment to negotiations reinforced his change of direction. Also he then believed that his proposal to establish a multisystem anti-infiltration barrier across the DMZ and the Laos panhandle would effect the stabilization of air warfare at current levels.[4]

The Jason Summer Study Reports on our air campaign concluded that our bombing to July 1966 had no measurable direct effect on Hanoi's ability to carry on the war; air damage to Hanoi's facilities and equipment had been more than offset by increased aid from Russia and China. Although our bombing cost Hanoi approximately $86 million in losses by July 1966, in 1965 alone Hanoi received military and economic aid from her friends estimated at somewhere between $250 and $400 million, and they had shown an ability to increase the amount:

The low volume of supplies required, the demonstrated effectiveness of the counter-measures already undertaken by Hanoi, the alternative options that the NVN transportation network provides and the level of aid the USSR and China seem prepared to provide, however, make it quite unlikely that Hanoi's capability to function as a logistic funnel would be seriously impaired. Our past experience also indicates that an intensified air campaign in NVN probably would not prevent Hanoi from infiltrating men into the South at the present or a higher rate, if it chooses.[5]

No basis existed for us to assume Hanoi could not expand its war efforts to match any escalation we would feel we could afford. What Hanoi's limits might be ultimately, we had no way of knowing, but they certainly had not been reached in 1966. Nor was there any evidence that our bombing had reduced enemy morale:

It would appear to be equally logical to assume that the major influences on Hanoi's will to continue are most likely to be the course of the war in the South and the degree to which the USSR and China support the policy of continuing the war and that the punitive impact of U.S. bombing may have but a marginal effect in this broader context.[6]

The more significant observation was that the bombing had clearly reinforced the popular support of the enemy regime by engendering patriotic and nationalistic enthusiasm to resist and endure. The attacks also improved Hanoi's political relations with its allies. Our experience to date disappointed our hopes, showed we had overestimated the disruptive effects of our air strikes, underestimated enemy recuperative capacities, and had forgotten how peoples generally unite in hours of great common danger. Only the most extensive expansion of the war could conceivably change the situation. These reflections lay back of McNamara's gloomy assessment of our prospects, which he reported to the president. The president could not possibly have ignored the thoughts of one of his closest and most respected advisers.

To halt the bombing, to reduce its level, and confine the areas subject to attack became a major debate within the administration from 1966 to 1968. To McNamara and others such a reduction of the level of the war seemed the only "out" from a stalemated war—at whatever level we might choose to conduct it. He suggested we simply reduce the air war, "without fanfare, conditions, or avowal, whether the stand-down was permanent or temporary,..." Just stop the bombing of North Vietnam and see what might follow. Virtually all reports from Hanoi strongly urged that peace negotiations could not even begin without a total end to bombing attacks upon North Vietnam. This option would provide a face-saver for Hanoi, if that were the obstacle to negotiations; it would permit a reduction of the bombing to the DMZ and Ho Chi Minh trails; and it would lower the "international heat" on the United States. It could be resumed at any time, with spot attacks to keep Hanoi off balance—if that proved necessary.[7]

The Joint Chiefs of Staff strongly objected to McNamara's program for a bombing halt. They said a reduced air attack would be a serious blow to airmen and others, who risked their lives to advance our political objectives, and would sharply weaken the morale of all air force personnel. There was little evidence to justify any belief that the war was likely to be settled by negotiations. The enemy would most certainly view any pause or halt as a sign of our weakness and lack of determination to win. It was justifiable to state very clearly our war aims and peace policies once, but to reiterate them incessantly, almost to beg the enemy to negotiate, was a sign of weakness and certainly apt to be counterproductive. It also could only confuse our allies as well as the general public. Better it would be to give the enemy a "sharp knock" against his military assets and war-supporting facilities than the past and current campaign of slowly increasing pressure, which only deprived us of "the military effects of early weight of effort and shock, and gave to the enemy time to adjust to our slow quantitative and qualitative increase of pressure."[8] Others argued that we could not simultaneously pursue negotiations and build up the ARVN, and stated their preference for a buildup of South Vietnam.

Westmoreland sharply opposed any curtailment of the air war in the North. He declared it was "one of two trump cards" (the other was American troops in South Vietnam); it had definite military value in slowing the southward movement of supplies, diverted manpower, and created great costs for Hanoi. Rather than stabilize or de-escalate, he advocated lifting the restrictions, cited the high level of aircraft attrition on low priority targets, and advised expanding the bombing to include "MIG airfields, the missile assembly areas, the truck maintenance facility, the Haiphong port facilities, the twelve thermal power plants, and the steel plant." In any case, Hanoi, he felt, would use any pause in the bombing to strengthen its air defenses and repair its airfields. It would do little to advance negotiations for any rational solution. If bombing had failed to achieve its purpose, it was rather because too many restrictions had been imposed upon its use.[9] How much influence this running debate from 1965 to 1968 exercised upon the president no one knew. He was undoubtedly aware of the dialogue.

Meanwhile, from Communist capitals and perhaps well-intentioned Americans came a steady propaganda barrage against our "aggressions" in Vietnam, along with demands for a bombing halt. McNamara again urged Johnson on October 31, 1967, to change course. The present trend could only be "dangerous, costly, and unsatisfactory" to the American public. The defense secretary foresaw rising demands from the generals for more ground forces and more air attacks on Hanoi, Haiphong, and additional targets. "He described ways to increase our military actions, but opposed these on the grounds that they involved 'major risks of widening the war.' " Rather, he advocated other choices that might stabilize our operations, risk fewer casualties, lower the level of the fighting, and avoid anything that might deter peace negotiations. Especially, he sought the creation of the conditions under which the South Vietnamese could assume "greater responsibility for their own security." He wished no intensification of the bombing. McGeorge Bundy, frequent adviser to Johnson, also opposed an expansion of the bombing and believed there should be no large-scale expansion of existing forces.[10] Virtually all his inner advisers favored a larger role for South Vietnam in the fighting. Vietnamization of the war was a policy which all presidents from Truman through Nixon sought, largely in vain.

Hawkish advisers, including Walt Rostow, Maxwell Taylor, and others, opposed the bombing halt and military cutbacks on the ground they would signify our weakness to Hanoi and our own people, ease Hanoi's burdens, delay peace talks, or bring endless negotiations. They felt such a retreat would degenerate into a pullout, discourage South Vietnam and even our own troops, and would finally convince Hanoi they could win, not on the battlefield but through weakened public support inside the United States. To cut back the war without concessions from the enemy would be the height of folly. Even stabilization of the war would tell the enemy that we lacked the zeal to stay on course, had lost our will and dedication. "Win or get out!" the hawks shouted.[11]

Ambassador Ellsworth Bunker took a similar line: a bombing pause would not bring serious negotiations. Limits on further troop levels should depend only upon "Hanoi's willingness not to expand its side of the war." Bunker "favored shifting increased responsibility for combat operations to the South Vietnamese," but said we should help them achieve the capacity to do so Westmoreland strongly opposed a bombing halt and argued that an effective air program against Hanoi's logistical system was "absolutely essential" up to the 20th parallel. He thought it would be foolish to place any absolute limits especially to announce them, on troop levels. He said his major purpose also was to shift the fighting to the natives and begin our withdrawal, which he anticipated might take two years.[12]

At the president's request Rusk offered his suggestions on November 20 1967. The secretary of state thought the stabilization of force levels was desirable, but declared a public announcement would be entirely unwise because it would help the enemy by giving him a firm base of knowledge for his future plans. He favored the Vietnamization of the war as quickly as possible, but declared:

> I am skeptical of an extended pause in the bombing because I don't know who would be persuaded. Hanoi would call any pause (i.e., not permanent) an ultimatum. We know of their "fight and negotiate" strategy discussions. For those in the outside world pressing for a halt in the bombing, no pause would be long enough. No one has said to me that his view would be changed if we had a prolonged pause in the bombing and there were no response from Hanoi.[13]

He was for reducing our bombing operations in the Hanoi-Haiphong area, but not for permitting it to become a complete sanctuary and thereby eliminate Hanoi's incentive for peace.

On December 18, 1967, Johnson, in one of his rare exceptions, wrote a memorandum for his permanent files stating his own view of the McNamara proposals:

I had decided that a one-sided and total bombing halt would be a mistake at that time, that it would be interpreted in Hanoi and at home as a sign of weakening will. I thought we should continue to hit significant military targets but I insisted we weigh heavily in each case whether U.S. losses might be excessive and whether any strike might increase the risk of Peking or Moscow becoming more involved. . . .

I also expressed my opposition to announcing a policy of stabilization. I felt that such an announcement would only make things easier for military planners in Hanoi. On the other hand, I saw no basis for increasing the already approved level of U.S. forces. Finally, I accepted McNamara's suggestion that we review our military operations with a view to cutting our casualties and speeding the turnover of responsibility to the South Vietnamese.[14]

Johnson admitted, in retrospect, he had erred in not accenting strongly enough in his State of the Union report of January 17, 1968, the likelihood of a coming test of our strength and will in Vietnam. Although he would have preferred to, he had not warned of the enemy buildup and the likelihood of major combat near at hand because he did not wish to alert the enemy to our knowledge of his plans. He admitted he had been "too cautious."[15] However, it is very doubtful that he or others inside his official family expected the intensity, nature, and size of the coming attack, for surely if they had, it would have been neither such a surprise nor disaster.

Clifford's summation of the events in early 1968 was fairly accurate.[16] The conditions of 1964-1965 had changed. The Korean situation had suddenly become explosive, due to the *Pueblo* affair. When that electronic spy ship and its crew were seized by North Korea, and we felt unable to respond effectively, that revealed our weakness of will and strength. While this disturbed us, there was also the warning of a possible Berlin crisis, and other disturbances loomed over the horizon, so much so that some hawks proposed calling up the reserves, expanding draft calls, and preparing for larger dangers ahead. On February 1, 1968, Johnson consulted General Matthew B. Ridgway, former Army Chief of Staff, and heard of his deep concern over the problem of our strategic reserve. It was so weak, he feared, "we were in no condition to react to any new crisis" anywhere, and he urged the president "to take steps to remedy the situation."[17]

In late February, just a few days before Clifford took office officially on March 1, 1968, events occurred in South Vietnam and Washington that brought major problems for the new secretary of defense and his president: the Tet offensive of January and February 1968 and General Westmoreland's request for 206,000 more men. Added to the more than 500,000 already there, this would have made an unexpected demand upon our resources. Its presentation raised most serious doubts in official Washington about the whole war policy followed since 1964.

On February 28, 1968, just back from his hurried trip to Saigon, where he received the request for more troops, General Earle G. Wheeler, Chairman of the Joint Chiefs of Staff, rushed from Andrews Air Force Base, paused just long enough to change his clothes, and drove through the rain to the White House. His report, designed to encourage the president and his advisers, had the opposite effect: "It served only to shock them into extended debate." After eight years of effort, the generals had thought and hoped the recommendations at long last would bring military victory. Such expressions of victory, through the use of more troops, had supported too many previous requests only to be followed by failure. This time the answer would be no.[18]

General Wheeler tried vainly to reassure everyone at the White House breakfast that morning. He declared the Tet attacks had not caused a military defeat—which was genuinely true. The people had not risen against Saigon as the Communists had hoped, nor had they panicked. In fact, the offensive alarmed the non-Communists, who now began to cooperate. Enlistments in Saigon increased, and in their hour of great danger the people rallied behind Saigon instead of Hanoi and the Vietcong.[19] Wheeler declared that many more troops would be immediately needed because our forces had been caught off balance and were vulnerable to another such attack. Massive reinforcements would guard against a quick repetition of the Tet offensive, allow us to regain the initiative, exploit enemy losses, and speed the day of victory. Then he told the men around the breakfast table that he personally endorsed the request, which added up to approximately 206,000 more men.[20]

Although General Westmoreland did not actually use the above figure—he regarded the proposal as "a planning paper"—the president and others treated it as a request. Without a precise total they "sensed" how much was being sought. Wheeler's "shopping list" called for three more combat divisions along with sizable air, naval, and land support. This plan was then fed through the Pentagon's computers, which gave the precise number, which became "so secret that to this day some officials will not utter it—a reminder of the President's wrath when it did leak to the press during the March debate."[21]

The sheer size of this request, a 40-percent increase in the 535,000-man force already committed to Vietnam, shocked the civilians present, including the president. Their initial thought was to ascertain how Westmoreland's needs might be met. One participant commented that "It was a hell of a serious breakfast. . . . It was rough as a cob." Some inside the official circle believed sizable increases might revive the argument for a wider war to permit our forces to pursue and destroy enemy sanctuaries in Cambodia, Laos, and possibly North Vietnam, but Johnson was most wary about any massive new commitment. He had for years tried hard to avoid too wide a popular disturbance over the war and had managed to send half a million men to Southeast Asia without calling up the reserves, imposing economic controls, or seeking a formal declaration of war.[22] Repeatedly generals had asked for "a little bit more to get the job done," but now with a nation badly divided over the war "they were asking for mobilization." The Wheeler-Westmoreland report confronted Johnson with a major dilemma: give us a big increase in strength or accept failure. That morning no one advocated lowering our objectives, but it was a time when many pressures for a change of direction were crowding in on the White House. The sober thoughts came too late. Such an analysis should have been undertaken before a single combat soldier was sent there.[23]

Now began a debate that took a strange twist: "One dramatic record of its progress appeared in the twelve versions of a presidential speech that evolved during the month of March 1968—the last draft pointing in the opposite direction from the first."[24] A group of *New York Times* writers declared in March 1969:

The catalytic event in the policy reappraisal—and the centerpiece of General Wheeler's vivid report—was the enemy's Lunar New Year offensive, which began Jan. 30, 1968, and swelled into coordinated assaults on 36 South Vietnamese cities and included, in Saigon, a bold penetration of the United States Embassy compound.

Confident and secure one day, Gen. William C. Westmoreland, then the American commander in Saigon, found himself on the next dealing with a vast battle the length of South Vietnam.

The psychological impact on Washington had outrun the event: The capital was stunned.[25]

Even the president himself apparently had no expectation of the tension within his immediate circle over coming events. Clifford played a major role in this shift of policy, but it "was not a one-man show."[26] Fresh from civilian life without fixed convictions about the war, he was open to diverse views and able to ask the hard questions. To persuade him was not easy. Civilian dissenters from the hard-line war policy at the Pentagon, given a more sympathetic ear, now pressed strongly their views. They believed the war was deadlocked, questioned our objectives in the war, and believed the time to restore balance and sanity to our policy was fast running out.

Thus began the final round of debate over the expansion of the war and over the coming speech of the president. Again all the possible options were reviewed, but the debate centered chiefly upon the suggestion to reduce the level of forces and seek peace through negotiation and a bombing halt. Advocates of reduction contended: further expansion might persuade the South Vietnamese to do less for themselves; Vietnamization could never work while it was our war; self-reliance could come to South Vietnam only when it again became their war. No one could tell the president when victory might come, what precise number of men would be required to win, or hold out any hope of honorably ending the war. It was more of the same old approach—just give us more men and then hope they will suffice to persuade the enemy to abandon his dreams of conquest. Such an open-ended war policy no longer seemed justifiable. And the world financial situation, the crisis of the dollar, was noted: how could sharply increased military expenditures, required by expansion of the war, possibly relieve the imbalance of payments and curb the rising inflation inside the United States? Although there were questions to be asked, no one had the answers. Among others, Johnson asked Clifford's board of review to explore these:

What objectives would additional forces achieve?
What dangers would additional forces, if recommended, aim to avoid?
What would our budget problems be and could we meet them?

What problems would be created in our balance of payments, and could they be met?

If we increased forces, what negotiation posture should we take?[27]

These and several other similar problems required full analysis before final decision could be made.

The Tet offensive punctured "the heady optimism" over our military progress which had accompanied previous reports out of Saigon from Westmoreland and Ambassador Ellsworth Bunker as late as November 1967. By late February 1968 "the pool of disenchantment" had spread to the

fence-sitters in Congress, to newspaper offices and to business organizations. It had also reached the upper echelons of Government.

If tolerance of the war had worn thin, so had the nation's military resources—so thin, indeed, that there was almost nothing more to send to Vietnam without either mobilizing, enlarging draft calls, lengthening the 12-month combat tour or sending Vietnam veterans back for second tours of duty—all extremely unappealing.[28]

Other problems, Clifford noted, pressed Congress for solution. Our dollar was then battered by the gold crisis in Europe and inflation at home, but most ominous, the nation was badly divided and an ugly polarization of views had formed. Leading congressmen and others refused to accept the Tet offensive and its defeat as a victory for us, as the administration initially sought to proclaim. If it was a victory, why the call for a 40 percent increase in troops?

Clifford, as head of a special task force, had to prepare an answer to the request for more troops. As Clifford later explained, "We were not instructed to assess the need for substantial increases in men and matériel; we were to devise the means by which they could be provided."[29] He took the oath of office as secretary of defense at 10:30 A.M. March 1, 1968, and three hours later gathered his task force around the oval oak table in the private Pentagon dining room of the secretary of defense. Of considerable significance, for the first time in seven years, Secretary of State Dean Rusk went to the Defense Department for a formal meeting.[30] Too often during this war Defense and State had failed to cooperate. Other veterans of the long war and of many bitter debates over it attended this meeting. In their hands rested considerable responsibility for the dramatic reversal of the war policy.

Clifford noted that in heading this special task force, "My work was cut out." He lacked the long experience of the others with the war and its direction:

I had attended various meetings in the past several years and I had been to Viet Nam three times, but it was quickly apparent to me how little one knows if he has been on the periphery of a problem and not truly in it. Until the day-long sessions of early March, I had never had the opportunity of intensive analysis and fact-finding. Now I was thrust into a vigorous, ruthlessly frank assessment of our situation by the men who knew the most about it. Try though we would to stay with the assignment of devising means to meet the military's requests, fundamental questions began to recur over and over.[31]

No transcript or full record of the discussions was made. Had one been kept, Clifford said, "it would run to hundreds of closely printed pages," and the documents brought in for study would have reached many hundreds more.

Clifford later said that no civilian present advocated compliance with the request for so many men, nor did anyone wish flatly to reject it. However, in his review of the event, Walter Rostow subsequently wrote that his initial reaction was to support Westmoreland's request. He stated that the heart of his argument was:

The outcome (say) two months from now of the whole battle since Tet depends on what happens between now and then. If we send some forces now—and Westy knows others are on their way—he will be able to do much more than if he has to work off thin margins.[32]

Some later suggested that a smaller request for possibly thirty to fifty thousand men would likely have been granted and the crisis facing Johnson would have been avoided or at least delayed. Instead, the task force soon collided over the war strategy and the possibilities of victory. In spite of variations, two broad views arose. One took the Westmoreland view that the strategy of attrition by intense pounding of the enemy was the proper approach, and the Tet offensive offered more of an opportunity than a setback. It would justify our seizure of the initiative, demoralize the enemy by greatly enlarged attacks, and pave the way for a favorable settlement. Hard-liners still thought in terms of military victory. Those who favored continuing the old program aiming for victory included Rusk, Rostow, and the two generals—Wheeler and Taylor. Rusk, the staunchest defender of the war, patiently bore the burden of the ciriticism, but Rostow and Taylor, once envoys to Saigon for Kennedy, even more strongly opposed any relaxation of the pressure upon the enemy.

The hard-liners, observed Hoopes, declared that the Tet offensive offered a new opportunity because now the guerrillas had come out of their hiding and openly faced our superior firepower in battle. This revealed, they believed, that the Vietcong could no longer withstand "the relentless pressure of U.S. military power" through a long drawn-out war. If Washington would but promptly comply with the request for more troops, we could much more quickly bring the enemy to the conference table. In any case, Wheeler warned that Westmoreland would deem a failure to grant the additional forces an indication of no confidence in his leadership.[33]

The second group opposed these views, continued Hoopes, urged a less aggressive ground war, asked for renewed efforts to negotiate, and prepared for political compromise to speed the end of the war. Nitze, Warnke, Katzenbach, and later Clifford most forcefully favored the road to peace. They did not see Tet as a military victory of any sort for the United States, found no "convincing evidence that the enemy's attack was motivated by desperation" or the desire to spur a popular uprising against Saigon. Rather, they believed, the enemy had more limited objectives: "to capture one or more major cities," cause widespread panic in the ARVN, retake the countryside in order "to destroy the pacification program," and gain again access to recruits for the Vietcong in the rural areas. Above all, however, these men sought "to show public opinion in America that, contrary to the optimistic projections of November, the U.S. was not winning the war and in fact could not seriously attempt to win it without undermining its domestic and global interests."[34]

Paul C. Warnke, Assistant Secretary of Defense for International Security Affairs, admitted that both sides were disappointed with the results. The Communists captured no major cities and suffered terrible losses, possibly thirty thousand, and the ARVN fought better than expected, with few desertions and no popular uprisings against Saigon; but the attacks devastated both cities and countryside with heavy loss of life, civilian and military. The fact that the enemy could still wreak such havoc over the countryside showed the futility of the pacification program, and tied down large and powerful United States forces in remote places like Khesanh and Con Thien, where enemy artillery pounded them mercilessly. In truth, public opinion in the United States had been stunned, and the view became almost unanimous that the United States could not win the war in any meaningful sense.[35]

Clifford's role was the most remarkable because it was the most unexpected. McNamara left the government, so it was widely believed, because he had increasing doubts about official policy. Hence it was commonly assumed that Johnson chose Clifford as his successor in the belief that he supported the course of the war to date without doubts or reservations. When he entered the government, Clifford, a backroom counselor to the president, had the reputation of being a hawk, one who had faithfully supported official policy, opposed the bombing halt of December 1965, and would continue such support. However, his trip to Asia in 1967 had revealed that our allies in the war did not share our view of the danger in Southeast Asia. Although he continued to support Johnson's policy, he was more encouraged by the president's peace than his war efforts. Possibly his thoughts on the war were not fully known to the president. On the other hand, perhaps at the assumption of direct responsibility, he took a fresher and closer look at the question. He tried to reassure the leaders of North Vietnam, who had sharp reservations about the San Antonio peace offer.[36]

At his Senate confirmation hearings of January 25, 1968, he stated it was his understanding that the president's formula would tolerate "normal" levels of infiltration Southward by Hanoi. Johnson had not approved this statement in advance, and one source declared that "all hell broke loose at the White House and the State Department."[37] Even though Rusk for two days urged the president to reject Clifford's interpretation, on January 29 the State Department confirmed that Clifford's remarks represented our official policy.

On becoming defense secretary and chairman of the task force, Clifford worked long and energetically to understand the situation, prodigiously researched the Vietnam issue, and pumped everyone available for first-hand knowledge and advice, especially McNamara, whose own misgivings influenced his departure from the cabinet post. Clifford initially had to rely upon many of his civilian subordinates for information and advice, and many of these young men, hitherto silent before the most brilliant management of McNamara, quickly seized this great chance to be heard. One of them said that the Tet offensive gave them an answer to the seductive charts of the hard-liners who never tired of promises of victory while repeatedly seeking a few more men.[38]

Although the Clifford task force and others initially took the request for additional troops as a sign of panic by Westmoreland, ranking officers in Saigon headquarters during and after the Tet attacks asserted that "there was no thought of asking for many more troops until shortly before General Wheeler's visit in late February." A Pentagon official declared that Johnson had asked Wheeler to go out there to find out what "Westmoreland thought he could use." This approach vexed one civilian official in the State Department, who said, "It was a mistake to ask a damned-fool question like that."[39] The Joint Chiefs of Staff for months had feared their strategic reserve was inadequate and sought a chance to rebuild it by persuading the president to mobilize the national guard. Bunker had suggested we give priority to the reequipment and expansion of the South Vietnamese army. This was approved by the Pentagon civilians, but the Wheeler-Westmoreland plan "called for 206,000 men by June 30, 1969—roughly 100,000 within a few months and two later additions of about 50,000 men each." Such an increase, the Pentagon believed, would assure victory.[40]

Mr. Warnke, among other soft-liners, challenged this military thesis head-on: Hanoi would match our reinforcements as it had in the past: "the result would simply be escalation and 'a lot more killing' on both sides"; and "the financial costs would be immense," possibly an additional "$10-billion to a war already costing $30-billion a year." He urged de-escalation, a pullback from Westmoreland's "aggressive search-and-destroy tactics and the abandonment of isolated outposts like the besieged Marine garrison at Khesanh." Rather our forces should be used as "a mobile shield" for the population centers, while the ARVN should bear a greater share of the fighting. Now we should make a full effort toward a peaceful and diplomatic solution.[41]

The complexity of the troop issue stirred doubts in Clifford's mind, and he began asking questions the others, more familiar with the details, would never have asked. Perhaps he feigned ignorance and stupidity, for he could never get the exact figures on troops straight. A colleague recalled, "He drove Bus Wheeler mad. He would say, 'Now I understand you wanted 22,000 men for such and such,' and Wheeler would point out this didn't include the support elements, and if you added them, it would be 35,000 in all."

"This happened again and again every time Clifford wanted to get the numbers down as low as possible, and it had a psychological impact on him," the source added. Thus was spent the first weekend in March. Johnson heard that the study was not going well and had hit a "discordant note," but "Clifford's doubts had not hardened into convictions" when he made his first report to the president on March 5. It was a short memorandum which recommended giving Westmoreland 50,000 men in the next three months and set a schedule for getting the rest of the number sought ready over the next fifteen months. Two differing interpretations of even this small beginning arose: the Pentagon saw it as the beginning of the process to comply with the hard-line program, "to get the pipeline going," while State Department officials saw it as part of a process of whittling down the 206,000 figure. Even Clifford was uneasy about his own report because he feared the president's approval of the first batch would commit him irrevocably to finish the whole program. "But the Secretary did not challenge the report directly; he tried to stall," suggesting that the task force "check General Westmoreland's reaction to be sure the 'mix' of forces was right." Wheeler wished to move speedily ahead, but Rusk, Rostow, and others were willing to ponder the issue longer. The task force carried on.[42]

The postponement appeared to suit the presidential mood. An aide said Johnson's instinct was to delay the execution of the plan, and, "He kept putting off making an initial decision. . . ." He, too, had most obviously become conscious of the complaints rising throughout the nation and the grumbling in Congress over the gold drain, the rising costs of the war, and the alarming size of the troop request. Even ancient friends like Senator Richard B. Russell of Georgia, who was chairman of the Senate Armed Services Committee, found Westmoreland's request most unwelcome. "Influential men like Senator John Stennis, the Mississippi Democrat, were privately warning the President to go slow on mobilizing reserves."[43]

As the task force persisted in its studies, Clifford, beginning to grasp some of the issues, further questioned the generals ever more deeply and insistently. What was our military plan for victory? How would we end the war? Would two hundred thousand more men do the job? If not, how many more might be needed? And when? What would the call-up of such numbers involve? Increased draft calls? Extension of duty for those in service and bringing in the reserves? To these and many other questions he could get no precise answers. Could not the enemy match us with his own buildups? What would our increases really cost? What would be their effect upon our total economy? Would they require credit restrictions, tax increases, possibly wage and price controls? Would not our balance of payments be further weakened by possibly another half billion dollars a year? Could bombing ever stop the war? The answer was: Never by itself. It could inflict severe damage of life and materiel, but it would not stop the war. Would a bombing increase lessen our casualties? Very little, if at all, because they were due to the ground fighting in South Vietnam. Clifford learned:

We had already dropped a heavier tonnage of bombs than in all the theaters of World War II. During 1967, an estimated 90,000 North Vietnamese had infiltrated into South Viet Nam. In the opening weeks of 1968, infiltrators were coming in at three to four times the rate of a year earlier, despite the ferocity and intensity of our campaign of aerial interdiction.[44]

How long must we keep sending men and doing most of the fighting? When would South Vietnamese troops be able to replace us? He was told the ARVN forces were improving, but were not yet ready to assume the major burden of the war, and "we did not know when they would be." When he asked for a presentation of plans for ultimate victory, he found there was "no plan for victory in the historic American sense." Why not?

Because our forces were operating under three major political restrictions: The President had forbidden the invasion of North Viet Nam because this could trigger the mutual assistance pact between North Viet Nam and China; the President had forbidden the mining of the harbor at Haiphong, the principal port through which the North received military supplies, because a Soviet vessel might be sunk; the President had forbidden our forces to pursue the enemy into Laos and Cambodia, for to do so would spread the war, politically and geographically, with no discernible advantage. These and other restrictions which precluded an all-out, no-holds-barred military effort were wisely designed to prevent our being drawn into a larger war. We had no inclination to recommend to the President their cancellation.[45]

Under these conditions, then, how could we ever expect to win? The hope was that if we continued our superiority over the enemy, pressed our attacks, hurt him through search-and-destroy tactics, some time, preferably soon, he would decide he could not win and would cease his aggression. The generals believed he could not absorb the punishment we inflicted upon him forever, and our strength was increasing all the time. Well, asked Clifford, how long would it then take? Six months? One year? Two years? There was no agreement or exact answer. Nor did anyone have any confidence in his own guesses. No one in the task force could see any "light at the end of the tunnel" or foresee when our troops could come home, even after seven years of active warfare. Such intensive analysis went on for days and greatly deepened the concern of Clifford and others. It was most difficult to reach any firm conclusion, to make any positive recommendations to the president in such uncertainty of judgment. Clifford wrote:

I could not find out when the war was going to end; I could not find out the manner in which it was going to end; I could not find out whether the new requests for men and equipment were going to be enough, or whether it would take more and, if more, when and how much; I could not find out how soon the South Vietnamese forces would be ready to take over. All I had was the statement, given with too little self-assurance to be comforting, that if we persisted for an indeterminate length of time, the enemy would choose not to go on.[46]

Then he asked if anyone saw any decline in the enemy's will after four years of our active warfare, after the great destruction and vast casualties, and the answer was negative. This reply was most impressive to Clifford, who daily became more conscious of the domestic unrest, draft card burnings, street marches, and problems on school campuses that dramatized the great bitterness and divisions in the nation. Equally disturbing were the costs of continuing to expand the war. He was also aware of our obligations and involvements elsewhere in the world. The possibility of improving relations with Russia was hampered by the war. Our interests in the Middle East, Africa, Western Europe, and elsewhere had been neglected. In many ways, we were paying too high a price for the war. The nagging doubts from his previous August-September trip to Asia kept disturbing his thoughts. If nations living in the shadow of Vietnam did not believe the domino theory, felt they were in no danger from Communist expansion, "perhaps it was time for us to take another look." Since 1954, if not earlier, we had invested huge amounts of money, materiel, and men trying to build independence and security in South Vietnam. In 1968, Clifford saw no reason for us to increase further such a commitment, especially when there was no assurance that even a 40-percent increase of our troops would appreciably improve our situation. All that we could certainly predict was that if we raised our strength they would, too.[47] An early end to the war could come "only if the GVN [government of Vietnam] took the steps necessary to provide effective military and political leadership to its population."[48]

Clifford's recommendation was a rejection of the requested increase of forces. It called for sending 22,000 additional personnel and deploying three tactical fighter squadrons, which with additions would bring us slightly above the 525,000 authorized level. It urged "a highly forceful approach" to Saigon "to get certain key commitments for improvement, tied to our own increased effort and to increased US support for the ARVN." Most urgent was the modernization of the equipment of the South Vietnamese armed forces. The task force especially urged the president to impress upon Thieu and Ky the need for their maximum effort to save the nation. Government reform and the end of corruption were imperative, and a united front was essential. At the least, the Tet offensive should have taught this lesson. Meanwhile, events could decide which way we should go—escalation, as requested by Westmoreland, or de-escalation, which McNamara and now Clifford seemed to approve. The editors of the *Pentagon Papers* concluded:

> Thus, faced with a fork in the road of our Vietnam policy, the Working Group failed to seize the opportunity to change directions. Indeed, they seemed to recommend that we continue rather haltingly down the same road, meanwhile consulting the map more frequently and in greater detail to insure that we were still on the right road.[49]

This report of March 4, 1968, left Johnson to face alone a profound political-military dilemma. Should he meet the request for troops—to stabilize the military situation—and risk the political turbulence that decision would almost surely inspire? Or should he totally reject it and accept the likely fall-out around the world of our allies and the certain denunciation of domestic hawks? Against Westmoreland's request, senior civilian officials in the Defense Department concluded their case:

> Since the United States military build-up began in 1965, Hanoi has gradually increased its forces in South Vietnam and maintained a reasonable ratio to the fighting strength of the American Forces. There is every reason to believe, these officials contend, that Hanoi is able and willing to continue to do so if more American troops are sent to Vietnam within the next year.
> The reinforcements that General Westmoreland wants would thus not restore the initiative. They would simply raise the level of violence. The United

States would spend billions more on the war effort and would suffer appreciably higher casualties.

North Vietnam would likewise endure substantially greater losses. But the experience of the Tet offensive shows, according to this line of reasoning, that American Military commanders have gravely underestimated the capacity of the enemy to absorb such punishment and to be still able to launch bold offensive operations.

"So there would just be a lot more killing," one analyst said.

The White House is also reported to have received an analysis from the Central Intelligence Agency that supports this view of North Vietnam's manpower resources and its will to resist.

"Essentially," said one official, "we are fighting Vietnam's birth rate."[50]

Clifford concluded, therefore, the policy we were then pursuing was both endless and hopeless:

A further substantial increase in American forces could only increase the devastation and the Americanization of the war, and thus leave us even further from our goal of a peace that would permit the people of South Viet Nam to fashion their own political and economic institutions. Henceforth, I was also convinced, our primary goal should be to level off our involvement, and to work toward a gradual disengagement.[51]

Thus Clifford's earlier doubts now became convictions. The restrictions upon the war laid down by the president and accepted by the task force permitted no military answer. Therefore by mid-March 1968 Clifford and many of his committee felt it was time to state the case for a fundamental change in our policy, to emphasize peace, not a larger war. He then began the search for a path to disengagement. He now challenged the initial recommendation of his own task force for more troops and told the president, "This isn't the way to go at all. . . . This is all wrong."[52]

Clifford's words carried weight, if not exactly greater affection for him personally, at the White House. He told the president that with our situation of bitter internal division and desperate domestic needs it would be immoral to consider investing greater efforts in Vietnam—a "military sinkhole." This division of sentiment at the heart of Johnson's official family deeply disturbed the president, who always preferred "a consensus among his close advisers." He never turned his famous temper on Clifford, but the latter's arguments chilled their personal relations "and left the Defense Secretary, a friend for 30 years, feeling oddly frozen out of the White House at times."[53] Rusk did not differ with Clifford's suggestions on troop numbers as much as with the long-range implications of his argument that we would have to accept something much less than we initially had sought. Rostow said the defense secretary had come under the influence of "professional pessimists" inside his own department. The morale of the civilians in the Pentagon rose sharply when they discovered a new ally in Secretary Clifford.[54]

Also unknown to the soft-liners in the Defense and the State departments was a new ally inside the White House staff, Harry McPherson, a presidential speech writer, who was then at work on a major speech on Vietnam, which in final version became the famous renunciation speech of March 31, 1968. This speech was initially conceived in late February from Rostow's thesis that since the Tet offensive had not been a setback, we should hang on until the enemy sensibly realized he could never win. While Clifford's task force continued its famous debate, McPherson developed his first draft, which included "an open-ended commitment to the war—a willingness to carry on at whatever the cost." However, as the debate in the task force continued and the numbers considered for reinforcement sank to fifty thousand, the tone of his speech softened. Johnson would not initially commit himself to any speech then drafted or to any specific figure.[55]

Further events influenced the president's decision: Senator Eugene McCarthy's stunning upset in the New Hampshire Democratic primary on March 1; the report that our dead and wounded in Vietnam had reached 139,801, higher than our overall Korean War losses; the emergency meeting of American and West European bankers to find a way to stop the gold drain; and Senator Robert F. Kennedy's March 16 announcement of his candidacy for the Democratic nomination for president.[56] Kennedy suggested to the president through Clifford that if the president would change his Vietnam policy, he would not feel obliged to seek the presidency himself. Sorensen, former special counsel to President Kennedy, who was present at an interview between Kennedy and Clifford, laid out the plan. Johnson should announce that because of the current uneasiness, he had found it necessary to conduct a full and complete review of the Vietnam policy and had decided to choose a commission to investigate and report its findings to the president and the people. When Clifford observed that this action would be a presidential confession of error, Kennedy answered that no one expected the president to use such words, but the words would have to be strong enough to indicate he now doubted the wisdom of the present course of escalation. The senator also suggested a list of distinguished Americans including himself to man the commission, but declared unnecessary Sorensen's suggestion that Kennedy be its chairman. To Clifford's comment that a Kennedy candidacy faced the great difficulty of displacing an incumbent president seeking reelection, Sorensen bluntly said 1968 presented "an entirely different situation."[57]

Later that day (March 14), Clifford presented Kennedy's plan to Johnson and received the "immediate and positive" reply that the offer was not acceptable because it would be deemed a political deal that would tie his Vietnam policy to the presidential race. Such a statement as Kennedy sought would cast grave doubts on the wisdom of his present policy; the choice of an outside group would usurp the functions and powers of the presidency; and such an effort would be a great boost to Hanoi's morale. There was no need for the people suggested for the commission to meet in any case because the president already knew their thoughts. He also knew they could hold no objective inquiries because they had already made up their minds. He agreed to talk to any individuals or groups, but not such a group and in the manner—accompanied by a public statement—Kennedy proposed. For this reason Kennedy announced March 16 his intention to seek the presidency. Clifford felt Johnson's reasons for refusing the Kennedy proposal were fully justified.[58]

Arthur J. Goldberg, our ambassador to the United Nations, on March 15 sent a long memorandum to the president urging him to halt the bombing of North Vietnam in order to get negotiations started. This step was favored by Katzenbach and Ambassador-at-Large W. Averell Harriman; but Goldberg, long frustrated by his inability at the United Nations or elsewhere to move on the Vietnam issue, was the one who dared risk Johnson's anger by raising and pressing the issue directly. Few knew of his efforts, which he had made quite secretly. His note had been sent labeled "For the President's Eyes Only." Rusk, Clifford, and Rostow saw it, but "Goldberg discussed it with none of them." Others opposed the halt, and, among them, Bundy favored a delay of several weeks in the fear that another offensive might be near. A day after Goldberg's letter had been received, the subject of the bombing halt arose in Johnson's inner circle. Johnson exploded. His patience "sorely tested," he sat up in his chair and said:

Let's get one thing clear! I'm telling you now I am not going to stop the bombing. Now I don't want to hear any more about it. Goldberg has written me about the whole thing, and I've heard every argument. I'm not going to stop it. Now is there anybody here who doesn't understand that?[59]

Dead silence followed this outburst, but the issue was not dead. Clifford believed Goldberg's courage had opened the way for further effort.

Johnson did not say anything about massive troop reinforcements in that outburst. The dissenters from the war policy, now led by Clifford, shifted their tactics, took the initiative, and proposed that the bombing be halted "to the Panhandle region of North Vietnam south of the 20th Parallel." This was an issue on which no one knew the president's opinion, but it afforded a chance to reopen the bombing halt effort, break out of the long deadlock, and set in motion further efforts to disengage. It might also help win popular support for the war awhile longer and focus attention "on what we could do without significant military drawbacks to make clear to people we were serious about peace."[60]

Clifford cleverly pleaded for the restriction of the bombing; it would not violate the president's insistence that there be no halt without matching restraint from Hanoi; it would not endanger, as the military feared, our troops in outposts just south of the demilitarized zone; the region south of the 20th parallel offered some of the best targets because most of the supplies and North Vietnamese troops had to pass through this region; and it might offer a diplomatic opening; "If Hanoi and Washington were not able to walk directly to the negotiating table . . . perhaps they could begin to 'crawl.' " Such a cutback had been suggested before by McNamara and Rusk. The theory was that if we made the first move, Hanoi would match it, and thus we just might begin to scale down the war and extricate ourselves without negotiations.[61] It would be an easy way to save face all around, especially for Communists, who never liked any formal treaties or written pledges that implied anything less than total victory.

Initially the president followed the Joint Chiefs of Staff, who strongly objected to the plan. There were reports that some senior generals threatened resignation if it were accepted. However, the very delicate and indirect soundings through "quasi-disavowable" channels made in Hanoi found the reaction negative. They passed the word that "only a halt could produce talks." In fact, the talks actually began in May 1968, while the bombing did not come to a full halt until November 1. Privately the president had made no decision on the halt in March 1968, but publicly he was just as insistent as ever that there would be no halt. With Robert Kennedy now in the presidential race and attacking him viciously for his war policy and with the opposition mounting from diverse sources inside his own party, he struck back, attacked his critics, recalled the Munich betrayal, and derided all those who would "tuck our tails and violate our commitments" in Vietnam.[62]

The Clifford dissenting faction took this as a counterattack aimed at them by the hawkish faction inside the administration led by Rostow. Johnson ridiculed dovish proposals for shifting the ground strategy from the mountains to the cities in order to save lives. Clifford, then exhausted by his tough first weeks in office and ill from a renewed bout with hepatitis, felt he had lost the argument. The bombing halt had been set aside. The only hopeful sign left was the president's continuing delay in approving the troop requests.[63]

In spite of the president's public outbursts and apparent hard-line attitudes, he was in mid-March 1968 uneasy and undecided. On March 20, Goldberg met with Johnson at the White House, in his first meeting since he had sent the memorandum of March 15. He was unaware of the angry outburst that first greeted his proposal. The president asked him to go through his arguments once more, listened carefully, asked additional questions, and in a friendly manner asked him to meet with a secret council of "wise men" to be held in Washington March 25, when he would be asked to present once again the views he had just offered. There were no angry words. The next hint, quite indirect and not widely understood then, came March 22, when the president announced he was making General Westmoreland Army Chief of Staff, effective in July 1968. He insisted, however, that the appointment meant no change of strategy. He was considerably upset over the general speculation that he was "sacking Westy because of Tet." Johnson observers believed, nevertheless, that the appointment signalled "a gradual transition to a new policy."[64]

Hoopes wrote that signs of rising trouble pressed hard upon the president in mid-March 1968. Even the public began to get a glimpse of events. Somebody leaked to the press the alarming size of the request for more troops for Vietnam. This aggravated the chronic balance-of-payments problem and seriously strained the international monetary system. The criticism of Westmoreland, the threat to the dollar, the wide opposition to any major call-up of the reserves, and the disturbing drift and indecision inside the administration alarmed Congress. Now 49 percent of the American people in a Gallup poll expressed the belief that our involvement in Vietnam with ground forces was wrong from the beginning. Intellectuals intensified their objections to the war and the request for more troops. Max Lerner said that the Washington response to the Tet attack was the same old mix that had been wrong so many times before: reappraisal, a visit by a high official to Vietnam, "the decision to hold tight," claim that whatever happened there was a basic gain, followed by another call for more soldiers in the hope that victory could soon be assured. He observed that repetition of this process, followed again by failure and disappointment, now produced only frustration and anger on all sides. It was obviously wrong, he continued, to fight a war of "corpse statistics on Asian terrain, with China's endless millions in the background. . . ." This would be "to move ever farther away from the world of reality."[65]

One of the world's ablest students of international relations, George Kennan, said the war was a great miscalculation and policy error almost unequalled in our history. The official policy lacked a plausible or realistic objective. The mouthpiece of a great number of American intellectuals, the *New York Times,* called the situation simply a "man-made disaster," while *Time* magazine noted that the debate in Washington proceeded in a vacuum, in which Johnson and his small clique of advisers had kept their views hidden from the outside. The prospects looked bleak and dark to most Americans. The Senate, led by Fulbright, was especially in deep gloom because the president made virtually all decisions without consulting Congress. In fact, Fulbright seemed to think the major issue was Johnson's effort "to expand the war without the consent of Congress." Robert Kennedy said he knew that what we had been doing was not the answer and that to continue it was immoral and intolerable. With all the pressure outside and inside the government crowding in on him, Clifford reached the firm conclusion that the war was not winnable in any military terms. He began stating firmly and strongly his case for change of direction—which aimed squarely at withdrawal. Although he had not yet found the exact formula, the basic ingredients were already penetrating the task force. In the summary by Hoopes, it contained these elements:

a bombing halt to get talks started, a shift to a less costly ground strategy, measures to strengthen ARVN, a clear warning to the GVN [Government of Vietnam] that U.S. military power would not remain indefinitely in Vietnam, and that therefore the GVN must posture itself for a serious political settlement involving compromise with the NLF.[66]

Although he continued publicly in a series of speeches around the nation to defend the war, the president was deeply disturbed at the events of early 1968. Being a sensitive soul whose skin was not as thick as it may have appeared, he could not ignore the cry against the war, its cost, its lack of popular support, and the sudden reversal of opinion and advice of so many close friends and advisers who had supported him faithfully for years. Among the many elder statesmen whom he consulted and whose advice, if unwelcome, was most highly respected was Dean Acheson, former secretary of state. Asked his opinion of the

Vietnam situation, Acheson told the president that on the basis of occasional official briefings given to him it was impossible to know what was really happening. He noted that he had "lost faith in the objectivity of the briefers," and then he told the president bluntly: "With all due respect, Mr. President, the Joint Chiefs of Staff don't know what they're talking about." When Johnson declared that was a shocking statement, Acheson told him that if it was perhaps the president ought to be shocked. Told that the president wanted Acheson's considered judgment, Acheson answered he could give this only if he could freely and fully make his own inquiry into the facts, so that he could be independent of the "canned briefings" from the Joint Chiefs, Rostow, and the CIA. Johnson gave him full support and the resources for a free evaluation.[57]

Then Acheson assembled an expert group of advisers and assistants, and over two weeks they talked and studied at length and in depth the problems and solutions. On March 15 at a luncheon alone with the president, he spelled out the hard, cold, and ugly facts for the president. Hoopes, who gave us the best inside account of these events leading to the historic reversal of 1968, summed up Acheson's conclusions:

Acheson told the President he was being led down a garden path by the JCS, that what Westmoreland was attempting in Vietnam was simply not possible— without the application of totally unlimited resources "and maybe five years." He told the President that his recent speeches were quite unrealistic and believed by no one, either at home or abroad. He added the judgment that the country was no longer supporting the war. This was tough, unvarnished advice in the Acheson manner, though served with the customary polish and elegance. The President obviously did not like it, but he greatly respected the purveyor.[68]

Unknown to his political advisers, Johnson was moving to settle the troop issue. He secretly sent Wheeler to meet Westmoreland in the Pacific to learn if he still needed massive reinforcements. In a ninety-minute interview at Clark Air Force Base in the Philippines, Westmoreland reported that our battlefield situation had improved, the crisis at Khesanh had eased, the enemy seemed to have lost steam, and the ARVN was rebuilding and moving back into the countryside. He told Wheeler that he would be satisfied to keep the two 5,000-man brigades rushed to him in February, if given about 13,500 support troops for them. With this information secretly gathered, the president assembled his inner advisers on March 22 to discuss the speech being prepared on the Vietnam question. Its still hawkish tone disturbed Clifford and others, who wished it to include some gesture for peace along with the scheduled reinforcements.[69]

Once again Clifford urged the president to accept a bombing halt or reduction in the belief it would improve the administration's image here and abroad. It might also help the president in the coming Wisconsin primary of April 2. Humphrey agreed that if there were to be any change, the bombing should be stopped, not just curtailed. A long discussion began, and again many questions arose. After seven hours of debate, Rusk, who had brought up the possibility of a bombing halt as early as March 3, summed up the discussion. He declared that there appeared a consensus favoring some step toward negotiation, but expressed doubt that Hanoi would be satisfied with a curtailment. Nice if it would work, said many—but few believed it had a chance. The doves felt they had lost another round to the hawks. The next morning McPherson sent the president a memo that "sought to strike a compromise between the general desire to make a peace gesture and the fear of rejection by Hanoi." It urged Johnson "to stop the bombing north of the 20th Parallel and, simultaneously, to offer to stop" it in the rest of the territory of North Vietnam if Hanoi agreed to show restraint at the DMZ and "left Saigon and other cities free from major attacks." Johnson passed the memo to Rusk, who returned it later with the comment that he had been entertaining similar ideas and they should be further developed. However, he made no specific recommendations.[70]

The president asked McPherson for another copy, which he sent to Bunker in Saigon—who offered no opposition. Still the president hestitated. His advisers thought he had about made up his mind, but he had not. One White House official commented that "He could keep everybody else lathered up the whole time. He just kept slipping back the deadlines for decision."[71] He kept sounding out diverse sources, outside Washington and outside the administration. To Washington he called the secret council of most highly trusted advisers, already mentioned to Goldberg. These elder statesmen had a special impact upon the president. In the previous fall they had unanimously backed the president, but, stunned by the Tet offensive, several of them had changed their minds. Most shocking to Johnson was the reversal of Clifford, who had been a member of that early group, but now had most dramatically changed. He encouraged Johnson to call these same men back to Washington, "in the hope that it would strengthen his argument." The men who gathered at the State Department on March 25 constituted a "Who's Who" of our foreign policy establishment:

> Dean Acheson, Secretary of State under President Truman; George W. Ball, Under Secretary of State in the Kennedy and Johnson Administrations; Gen. Omar N. Bradley, retired World War II commander; McGeorge Bundy, special assistant for national security affairs to Presidents Kennedy and Johnson; Arthur H. Dean, President Eisenhower's Korean war negotiator; Douglas Dillon, Secretary of the Treasury under President Kennedy.
>
> Also Associate Justice Abe Fortas of the Supreme Court; Mr. Goldberg; Henry Cabot Lodge, twice Ambassador to Saigon; John J. McCloy, United States High Commissioner in West Germany under President Truman; Robert D. Murphy, ranking diplomat in the Truman-Eisenhower era; Gen. Matthew B. Ridgway, retired Korean war commander; Gen. Maxwell D. Taylor, former chairman of the joint chiefs of staff and a constant Presidential adviser on Vietnam, and Cyrus R. Vance, former Deputy Defense Secretary and President Johnson's trouble-shooter.[72]

These well-informed men heard and questioned the special task force. In a two-day debate, the sharp exchange and change of views staggered the president. The high hopes of the past fall had now yielded to deep discontentment over the war. Johnson seemed especially impressed when Acheson, Bundy, "and to a lesser degree Vance" now joined Goldberg in opposition to any further military

commitments and in support of a peaceful solution. Especially unsettling was
the reversal of Bundy, who had been one of the "architects of intervention in
the early sixties and of the bombing of North Vietnam in 1965." A hard-line
faction was still present and forceful: Fortas, Taylor, and Murphy. "Mr. Murphy
wanted more bombing, not less." Lodge seemed to be on all sides of the issue,
while McCloy leaned toward the hawks. Dillon, Bradley, and Ridgway "were
now doubters," who were "war-weary if not yet ready to shift course." All were
deeply concerned at the waning popular support of the war.[73]

    "There was no consensus on the bombing issue." Goldberg and Ball
wanted a halt to open the way for negotiations; others were uncertain, but the
whole group left the impression that said: "We had better start looking for
another way to get this war settled."[74] Such shifts of opinion among these key
statesmen of several years carried more weight with Johnson than the New
Hampshire and other primaries. When advised to consider the impact of the war
upon the coming election, he "replied testily that the campaign was the least of
his concerns." Two days later on March 28, Rusk, Clifford, Rostow, McPherson,
and William Bundy met in Rusk's office to polish the president's speech. It was
still, said one of the participants, a "teeth-clenched, see-it-through" speech,
which announced that about fifteen thousand more troops would be sent, made
a formal plea for peace by negotiation, and said nothing about a bombing halt.
To this Clifford could not remain silent. He launched

an impassioned plea against taking this approach.
    "I can't do it—I can't go along with it. . . . I can't be in the position of
trying to polish a speech of this kind. This speech can't be polished. What's
needed is a new speech. This one is irrevocably setting the President down the
wrong road."[75]

    Then he went into a monologue that lasted nearly an hour, and, to his
surprise, not even Rusk cut him short. Further expansion of the war "would tear
the country apart"; the country needed a peace speech, not a louder war cry. He
appealed for compromise at which the group resumed the debate on the 20th
parallel suggestion. On this point the generals and commanders ceased raising
strong objections, although Admiral U. S. Grant Sharp, Commander of the
Pacific Fleet, "thought the cutback would fail" and fully expected the failure to
be followed within short order by a resumption, if not expansion, of the
bombing. Nor did Rusk, although anxious to find some way to negotiation,
think the cutback would satisfy Hanoi. However, at the end of this day, March
28, Rusk and Clifford agreed that McPherson should prepare a substitute draft.
So that night while the president was showing Senator Mansfield the hawkish
speech, his aide was writing another, quite different speech. By working through
the night he had it ready in the morning. With the draft to the president
proposing the bombing cutback to the 20th parallel, McPherson included a note
saying that "it seemed to reflect the sentiments of some of the President's
leading advisers." He offered to resume work on the original draft if the
president wished, but by the end of the day the president was conferring with

him about the draft of the new speech. This signified a major break in the debate.[76]

Undoubtedly, the president had been sorely troubled by the rising antiwar sentiment throughout the nation, the reflection of this in the counsel the "wise men" just offered, the great turmoil over the country, the European opposition to the involvement, the relative lack of concern of many Asian governments, the drain on our financial resources, and the failure of the escalation of the last three years to bring or promise victory although it had saved South Vietnam from defeat. These factors and Clifford's change of attitude finally persuaded the president to try a new tack. With this new approach in mind the presidential speech was rewritten five more times. No major dispute arose except over the 20th parallel as the cutoff point for the bombing. Katzenbach favored the 19th parallel instead of the one finally chosen. Clifford wanted to push the line as far south as possible. When the debate between the hard-liners and the soft-liners ended, Johnson had reversed himself, started us on the road to peace and disengagement, limited our military commitment to Saigon, ordered the reduction of the bombing of North Vietnam, and offered to negotiate with Hanoi, as well as to withdraw from politics. He abandoned the drive for victory in favor of the search for peace with compromise. However, the hawks in the White House inner circle fought the trend toward peace by withdrawal until Johnson left the White House in January 1969.

According to the *New York Times,* Johnson initially hesitated to announce his political retirement in the same speech with his policy reversal, but as he became convinced of the necessity for the bombing cutback he decided "it would be more effective if he made it clear that he was not just appealing for votes or pacifying domestic critics or serving some other personal interest." It would help restore public faith in the word and sincerity of the president. He also felt it would be more effective and dignified if he made both announcements before the Wisconsin primary.[77]

The speech brought a great sense of relief to Washington, the nation, and perhaps the president and his family.[78] However, as the world waited for Hanoi's response, our navy jets struck Thanh Hoa, 210 miles north of the DMZ, and people felt that once again perhaps a double-cross had destroyed all hopes for peace. The State Department accused the generals of sabotaging the president's peace effort.[79] Fears, doubts, and distrust plagued the efforts while Hanoi and Washington began sparring in Paris. They haggled over the size of the peace table. They contended over the presence of the Vietcong and the Saigon government. They argued over the seating arrangements. They disputed over who was to initiate troop withdrawals.

While all this quibbling and stalling was going on, Clifford could not ignore our many pressing domestic problems or the popular cry for peace rather than larger war. The enormous increase in troop strength the army initially sought after the Tet offensive would have meant that our forces would have been double the size of the regular South Vietnamese army. Clifford reminded the president that we had entered the war to prevent the subjugation of South

Vietnam and enable the people to determine their own future. These objectives had been largely assured by 1968. We had no commitment that required us to remain in the South until the North had been thrown out entirely or the Saigon government, whatever its nature, had won complete military control of the whole country. "The more we continued to do in South Viet Nam, the less likely the South Vietnamese were to shoulder their own burden."[80]

In reflecting upon the reversal from war to peace that began with Johnson and continued under Nixon, Clifford thought the world situation in 1969 had sharply changed from that of 1965, certainly enough to justify the new direction. Harriman and Vance, chosen by Johnson to represent our government at the Paris peace talks, agreed. Clifford's summation threw some light on the earlier decision to escalate the war: he declared that in 1965 North Vietnam's forces came close to a military takeover of South Vietnam. Saigon was then so militarily weak and politically demoralized, its situation had become hopeless. China and Russia had then announced their intention to support "wars of national liberation." Khrushchev's ouster from power in October 1964 and Chou En-lai's visit to Moscow in November 1964 stirred our fear of a Sino-Soviet effort to penetrate the underdeveloped nations. Acceptance by Sukarno of Indonesia of widespread Chinese Communist infiltration into his nation, the rising Chinese influence over all Southeast Asia, and its special hostility toward Malaysia raised ominous threats. Virtually all nations in this area needed time to consolidate their national freedom. Our indifference to their fate then could have had a most tragic effect.[81]

By 1968, Clifford continued, the above situation no longer existed. In fact, Clifford contended, there had been some dramatic changes. The ARVN had grown in size, proficiency, and morale. The South Vietnamese political system had become more stable and more representative, although political repression still prevailed. In the rest of Asia greater security existed. Sukarno was out of power, and the Communist challenge had been mercilessly crushed in Indonesia. The governments of Thailand and Singapore had used the last four years to win greater popular support. Australia and New Zealand had tightened their mutual defense arrangements. Also the remarkable growth and progress of Japan, South Korea, and Taiwan belied the predictions of Chairman Mao. Perhaps of just as much significance was the fact that since 1965, Sino-Soviet relations had steadily worsened. Numerous direct military clashes occurred along the Chinese-Russian land frontier, and in fact, "The schism between these two powers is one of the watershed events of our time." Russia's support for Hanoi greatly exacerbated the conflict with China and brought into clear focus their struggle for leadership in the Communist world. Furthermore, they sharply differed over the desirability of peace talks in Paris. Aware of the danger of wider war, Russia favored negotiations. China, anxious to speed the world revolution by any means, opposed all compromise. Russia's increased aid to North Korea lessened its dependence upon China, while Mao's cultural revolution and the destructive effects of the Red Guards stirred rebellious unrest throughout China and probably retarded the consolidation of any faction or ideology for some time in that impoverished country.[82]

A good many Americans agreed with Clifford that by 1968 the solution of critically urgent domestic problems, not so fully recognized in 1965, required more of our energy and resources and "set a chronological limit on our Vietnamese involvement."[83] Once we had started toward a de-escalation and de-Americanization of the war, both logic and events seemed to justify a continuation of the trend. Our bombing pauses before and after March 1968 had shown no dramatic change in the course of the war. The bombing halt and the acceptance of the 20th parallel as a line above which no further air attacks would be allowed, followed by Johnson's suspension of the bombing of all North Vietnam, October 31, 1968, did not noticeably increase enemy attacks or the likelihood of Saigon's defeat.

Some further elemental wisdom dawned upon some of the presidential advisers, especially Clifford, who recorded that whatever the problems to follow our gradual disengagement, these must be faced:

There is no way to achieve our goal of creating the conditions that will allow the South Vietnamese to determine their own future unless we begin, and begin promptly, to turn over to them the major responsibility for their own defense. This ability to defend themselves can never be developed so long as we continue to bear the brunt of the battle. Sooner or later, the test must be whether the South Vietnamese will serve their own country sufficiently well to guarantee its national survival.[84]

His own searching questions, which puzzled and disturbed the generals, revealed to him that within the presidential ground rules of limited warfare there was no precise number of soldiers that could guarantee victory. By 1969 he was convinced that the million ARVN forces, backed possibly by our air support and logistics, should be able, if they had the determination, to prevent a Hanoi-controlled regime's being foisted on them. Then he added: "If they lack a sense or a sufficiency of national purpose, we can never force it on them." In the long run Southeast Asia and other regions of the world must develop the ability, the courage, and the will to meet the needs of their own people, including their own defense. We could not forever, if at all, give them the stability, popular acceptance, and military strength required to save their freedom or nationalism. We could advise, urge, aid, but our power could no more build a nation in Southeast Asia than it could solve many of our domestic problems. To increase our forces would but destroy more of the country, advance the "Americanization" of the war, and further postpone for the South Vietnamese a chance to shape their own lives. Such advice coming from Clifford and others had a decisive impact upon the president.[85]

The president and his secretary of state played the most vital role in the dramatic reversal. In early March 1968, Rusk told the president that substantial additions to our forces might make the South Vietnamese too dependent and recommended that we should try to increase their ability to fight their own war. Why not just stop most of the bombing of the North during the coming rainy season? Then without any great military risk or prior announcement, just wait out the reaction of Hanoi? That way we could test the Communist tactic of "fighting and negotiating." Johnson accepted with full approval Rusk's recommendation:

At some convenient point this spring, America should do two things simultaneously, stop the bombing of the North and mobilize more men for Vietnam. It should announce that it will talk at any time, appoint negotiators, appeal to world opinion, remind Hanoi of its offers to talk and conduct a major peace offensive. At the same time, it would reinforce its armies in the South and continue the talk of pacification.[86]

Rusk declared that if Hanoi failed to react, we could simply resume the bombing. Meanwhile, we could give South Vietnam the best equipment possible. When he told Johnson about his proposed quiet bombing halt, the president urged: "Really get on your horses on that."

When the *New York Times* carried the story on March 10, 1968, about the debate inside the administration concerning the request for vast increases in our forces in the war, Johnson grew very indignant and expressed his belief that it came from lower-level "Pentagon civilians," whose attitude of pessimism and pacifism was already known to him. Although he did not know the exact source of the story, he later wrote angrily:

It was obvious that the sources for the story did not know or understand what was going on in my mind, and they were not party to my dealings with my senior advisers; nor did they understand the decision-making process. A few people with strongly held opinions were trying to put pressure on me through the press to see things their way. I also felt that there was more than a little political motivation behind their action, since the article appeared two days before the New Hampshire primary. I was convinced that this story, and others like it that would inevitably follow, would create controversy and solve nothing. Such reports would further arouse congressional critics and give Hanoi an impression of increased divisiveness in our country. It might help prolong the war. The fact was that I had firmly decided against sending anything approaching 206,000 additional men to Vietnam and already had so informed my senior advisers.

I have always believed that any public official has not only the right but the obligation to support his judgment inside government just as strongly, as eloquently, and as frequently as he can. But once a decision has been made, he has an equal obligation to carry it out with all his energy and wisdom. If he cannot do so in good conscience, he should resign. He has no right to sabotage his President and his own government from within. He has no basis for assuming that he has all, or even most, of the facts. He has no license to make official secrets available to unauthorized persons. Above all, he has no right to leak half-truths or lies or distortions to win backing for his position. This incident raised serious doubts in my mind about the integrity, judgment, and reliability of some lower-level officials in my administration. If I had known who was responsible, I would have fired him, or them, immediately.[87]

The president declared that during the fall of 1967 and the spring of 1968 his administration struggled with one of the most "serious financial crises" of his era. As he pondered the problem of greater aid to South Vietnam he discovered that he could not ignore the monetary difficulties at home. Obviously, calling up more troops and increasing our military expenditures would complicate these already grave problems. Rusk advised the president that his greatest concern about possible new military measures was over their effect on our financial situation. Should we adopt some of the programs then under study without passing a tax bill, there would likely be "new panic in Europe, heavy inflation at home, and possibly the collapse of the monetary system. 'If we do this without a tax bill,' he said, 'we are dead.' "[88]

Then, as the Tet offensive collapsed and Westmoreland was able to launch an offensive with the forces he already had, Johnson felt no great urgency to rush any further reinforcements beyond the limited additional commitments already decided upon. The president concluded:

By March 22 we had further refined our estimates of the additional troops needed for Vietnam and to build up our strategic reserve at home. We planned a call-up of about 62,000 reserves and proposed only 13,500 additional troops for Vietnam. These would be mainly support forces to back up the 10,500 combat troops we had sent in the days immediately following Tet.[89]

The Johnson administration in this way decided against any further expansion of the war and truly began a gradual withdrawal from involvement. The president said:

Four factors led to this further scaling down of our plans. First, and most important, it was our collective judgment that another massive Communist attack was increasingly unlikely. Second, the South Vietnamese were clearly improving militarily and getting in shape to carry a heavier combat load. Third, our financial problems remained serious, despite the solution we had found for the gold crisis. The Congress still had not passed a tax bill and we faced a large budgetary deficit. Finally, domestic public opinion continued to be discouraged as a result of the Tet offensive and the way events in Vietnam had been presented to the American people in newspapers and on television. Critics of our policy became more and more vocal as contention for the Presidential nomination heated up.

Had Westmoreland insisted that he needed more reinforcements to avoid disaster for his troops, Johnson said he would have found them, but "Westy" assured him he did not need them.[90]

After the famous meeting of the "wise men"—a large group of the most famous younger and elder American statesmen of the age—and a special study made for the president by the former secretary of state, Dean Acheson, Johnson noted: "At the end of our discussion ... six advisers favored some form of disengagement, one was in between, and four were opposed."[91] Johnson told Humphrey that because of our own pessimism, our doom and gloom fears, "We were defeating ourselves." He felt that even his inner advisers had also been unduly depressed, and observed:

I knew this group had not been reading the detailed reports on Vietnam each day, as I and my principal advisers had, but they were intelligent, experienced men. I had always regarded the majority of them as very steady and balanced. If they had been so deeply influenced by the reports of the Tet offensive, what must the average citizen in the country be thinking?

To this observation, Humphrey replied: "Tet really set us back."[92]

The conflicting advice offered the president reflected considerable pessimism and doubt about the course of the war. Men on the outside of the government who came to counsel the president lacked the tension and the detailed and accurate knowledge of events essential to decision. Rostow noted that such distinguished men who came at Johnson's call on March 25 and 26

with certain exceptions . . . came with their minds hardened in pessimism not only about the situation in South Vietnam but, I would guess, even more by their assessment of the impact of Tet on the mood of the country. As I heard their comments around the table in the State Department on the night of March 25, I wrote a note to Dick Helms sitting next to me: "Only the men in the field can save us." And they pretty well did, as the course of the war and pacification in the following ten months demonstrated . . . .[93]

A memorandum by Daniel Ellsberg, then an insider, believed Tet had ended the whole possibility of success in the war:

In terms of our earliest, most ambitious objectives . . . or even, most of our less ambitious goals—I think that the war is over; those aims are lost. I expect the Tet offensive—and those events I am quite sure will follow in the next two months—to have decisive impact on the course of the war, decisively foreclosing most evolutions favorable to us. . . . By that time things are going to get much worse; and then, they will not get better . . . . The TET offensive and what is shortly to come do not mark a "setback" to pacification; it is the death of pacification, as it has been conceived.[94]

However, the evidence began to pile up that South Vietnam was not collapsing; the South Vietnamese did not flock to the side of the Communists; and enemy troops that initially occupied South Vietnamese cities were soon forced out by stubborn fighting, much of it by South Vietnamese soldiers. By mid-February 1968 it was clear to Johnson and those who were most responsible for government policy that the Tet offensive had essentially failed. The key question then, thought Rostow, was what could be done "to exploit that failure, to convert a successful but somewhat disheveled defensive position into forward momentum?" At that point Westmoreland requested more troops: ". . . not because I fear defeat if I am not reinforced, but because I do not feel I can fully grasp the initiative from the recently reinforced enemy without them."[95] By that time South Vietnam, supported by a rising swell of popular approval, was moving to mobilize an additional 65,000 men, soon to be expanded to 135,000. However, in spite of these hopeful signs, a broader "gap opened up between the assessment of the situation" by insiders such as Bunker, Westmoreland, and

Johnson and that made by others outside and inside the government. The *Washington Post,* the *Wall Street Journal,* the *New York Times,* other media, and numerous persons of various ranks in the government deemed Tet a total disaster and pacification ruined, a setback that years could scarcely recover.[96]

On March 19, 1968, the "wise men" delivered their verdict to the president:

Continued escalation of the war—intensified bombing of North Vietnam and increased American troop strength in the South—would do no good. Forget about seeking a battlefield solution to the problem and instead intensify efforts to seek a political solution at the negotiating table.[97]

These recommendations, concluded the authors of the *Pentagon Papers,* backed by further consultations and confirmations, surprised the president. He now had to face the hard decisions:

In March of 1968, the President and his principal advisers were again confronted with a dilemma which they had faced before, but which they had postponed resolving. Although seldom specifically stated, the choice had always been either to increase U.S. forces in South Vietnam as necessary to achieve military victory or to limit the U.S. commitment in order to prevent the defeat of our South Vietnamese allies while they put their political-military house in order. In the past, the choice had not been so clear-cut. Progress toward military victory had been promised with small increases in force levels which did not require large reserve call-ups or economic dislocations. Military victory would then assure a viable South Vietnamese political body capable of protecting and gaining the support of the people.

In March of 1968, the choice had become clear-cut. The price for military victory had increased vastly, and there was no assurance that it would not grow again in the future. There were also strong indications that large and growing elements of the American public had begun to believe the cost had already reached unacceptable levels and would strongly protest a large increase in that cost.

The political reality which faced President Johnson was that "more of the same" in South Vietnam, with an increased commitment of American lives and money and its consequent impact on the country, accompanied by no guarantee of military victory in the near future, had become unacceptable to these elements of the American public. The optimistic military reports of progress in the war no longer rang true after the shock of the TET offensive.

Thus, the President's decision to seek a new strategy and a new road to peace was based upon two major considerations:

(1) The convictions of his principal civilian advisers, particularly Secretary of Defense Clifford, that the troops requested by General Westmoreland would not make a military victory any more likely; and

(2) A deeply-felt conviction of the need to restore unity to the American nation.[98]

After all the advice had been given, all the reviews and studies had been pondered, and the final decision made, Johnson, out of office with time to reflect and write his conclusions, had additional observations worth the reflections of posterity. He concluded:

My biggest worry was not Vietnam itself; it was the divisiveness and pessimism at home. I knew the American people were deeply worried. I had seen the effects of Tet on some of the Wise Men. I looked on my approaching speech as an opportunity to help right the balance and provide better perspective. For the collapse of the home front, I knew well, was just what Hanoi was counting on. The enemy had failed in Vietnam; would Hanoi succeed in the United States? I did not think so, but I was deeply concerned.[99]

He noted that every president in this century had faced opposition to the wars we had fought. It was never easy to accept war, its horrors and pains. Many Americans, even the men who had served him and the nation long and well and played a major role in past decisions, had grave doubts:

They seemed to feel that the bitter debate and noisy dissension at home about Vietnam were too high a price to pay for honoring our commitment in Southeast Asia. They deplored the demonstrations and turbulent arguments about Vietnam. So did I. They wanted money poured into the deteriorating cities and into other public programs that would improve the life of our disadvantaged citizens. So did I, though I knew there was no guarantee Congress would vote these additional funds even if the war ended. They seemed to be saying that anything that happened in Asia or the rest of the world was less important than the strains we were suffering at home.

I could never agree with this argument. My own assessment in 1965 and in 1968 (and today) was that abandoning our pledges and our commitment in Vietnam would generate more and worse controversy at home, not less. Such abandonment would bring vastly greater dangers—in Laos, Cambodia, Thailand, and elsewhere, including India and Pakistan—than would a policy of seeing our commitment through in Southeast Asia. In 1947 the British were able to pass on to us their responsibilities in Greece and Turkey. In 1954 the French knew they could transfer the problem of Southeast Asia's security to our shoulders. But if the United States abandoned its responsibilities, who would pick them up? The answer, in the short run, was: No one. As I had said in 1965, we did not ask to be the guardians at the gate, but there was no one else. There was no question in my mind that the vacuum created by our abdication would be filled inevitably by the Communist powers.[100]

As he reflected upon the problems and the options before him, he came to believe an acceptable answer—if we had the patience to stick with it—was that "we could shift an increasing share of responsibility to the Vietnamese and the other peoples of Asia." The increasing capacity of South Vietnam, demonstrated by its ability to withstand and then hurl back the Tet offensive, inspired his faith that we would not need to continue bearing indefinitely such a heavy share of the burden. He also believed other Asian nations had begun to demonstrate a growing will and capacity to take on more of the responsibility for their own defense. Thus he saw ahead the possibility that we might reduce our role and limit our commitments. We had not lost the war, and we had helped the South Vietnamese reach the stage where, we hoped, they could with our material and financial aid save themselves. In this belief he wrote:

At the beginning of March 1968 I was concerned that we might have to contribute considerably more to Vietnam—more men, more equipment, more money. I have described the various influences that eased my concern and shaped my final decision. For me, the key influence was the change in the situation in Vietnam. But other matters, especially our financial problems, played an important part in that final decision.[101]

Others may question this interpretation, may seek additional answers—perhaps in the rising disunity marked by violence, demonstrations, and dissent, in widespread global opposition to the war, in the belief we could not win in any rational sense.

Interminable debate, mountains of advice, and critical events at length persuaded President Johnson to announce on March 31, 1968, his retirement from politics, his desire to end the war as quickly as possible, a halt in the bombing over most of North Vietnam, and the establishment of a ceiling of 549,500 men for Vietnam. The "only new troops going out would be support troops previously promised." We would equip and train South Vietnamese forces to assume the major responsibilities at a sharply accelerated scale. He told Hanoi he was halting the bombing of North Vietnam north of the 20th parallel as an incentive to begin peace talks. By our unilateral restraint, nearly 80 percent of Ho's territory would no longer suffer aerial destruction.[102] This was an historic reversal of our seven-year-old policy of escalation. It was a welcome surprise to the doves and a severe shock to the hawks.

In his noble effort to restore credibility in his administration and in himself, he withdrew from politics. This would, he hoped, persuade Ho that he was sincere and the Congress that he had put aside all political considerations, wishing in the last months of his administration to be free to seek peace in Asia and harmony at home. No one had felt more keenly than he the deep divisions and hostilities current in the land. His renunciation of further ambitions might help heal some of the wounds and restore unity to the nation.[103]

His retirement from politics may have been an even greater surprise to most Americans than his reversal of his war plans. It was certainly related to the Vietnam question. The tragedy of Vietnam more than anything else brought on his reversal of policy and abandonment of leadership. However, the decisions to quit politics and downgrade the war were not sudden or impulsive; they had been long in evolution. His friends and careful observers offered the following explanation. There were reasons of health and personal desire.[104] He was not a good loser. The polls, and Senator Eugene McCarthy's victory in the New Hampshire Democratic primary, showed that a surprisingly large number of Americans did not like his Vietnam policy. The president might even have won the nomination and the election, some said, but the past few months had shown that it would be extremely difficult for him to govern the nation. The abuse and denunciation by members of his own party—Robert Kennedy, James Fulbright, George McGovern, Eugene McCarthy, and millions more—wore him down.

He told some friends: "A man gets tired of being hit over the head." No longer could he control or persuade even a Democratic Congress to cooperate in support of his war or domestic policy. His many detractors never let up. They questioned his every motive and even called him a murderer. Mobs formed to harass him wherever he went. His continuation in power would divide the country in the midst of a national crisis, whereas his departure might convince the American people, Hanoi, and the rest of the world that he sincerely sought peace and could put his country above all else. As he once said truly, he had tried hard, some thirty times, to secure an honorable peace; but Hanoi rejected his efforts, and many of his countrymen—clergymen, scholars, ranking congressmen, powerful politicians, and such Negro leaders as Dr. Martin Luther King, Jr.—doubted his sincerity, his intelligence, and his loyalty to their causes. Everyone had a cause which somehow the war obstructed. But for the war, ghettoes could be erased, domestic strife would be reduced to manageable proportions, Europe would be made safer from Russian infiltration, the problems of the Middle East, Africa, Arabia, Israel, and Latin America could be eased. Peace, whenever it might come in Vietnam, would most probably reveal how illusory such beliefs really were.

In spite of his outwardly abrasive manner, Johnson was a most sensitive spirit, who resented the refusal of Kennedy's supporters ever really to accept him. Since 1963 they had shown a remarkable inability to distinguish between style and performance. Admirable as style may be, posterity may have a greater respect for Johnson's performance than Kennedy's style. As time passed this was of reduced importance to Johnson, who in 1968 suffered for policies and actions for which he was not always responsible. Certainly his renunciation of March 1968 did much to restore his credibility. Few ever again called him a wheeler-dealer. The president wished to use the time left to him in office to be a statesman, above and beyond partisanship, and to work unceasingly to bring the war to an honorable conclusion. Both friend and critic admitted that he never looked nobler or stood taller than when he assumed the presidency and when he retired from it.

He surely would have agreed with the statement his much maligned and ever loyal secretary of state made later in answer to the question, What went wrong in Vietnam?

What went wrong in Vietnam was a persistent and determined attempt by the authorities in Hanoi to take over South Vietnam by force.

The thing which is wrong from the very beginning about the situation in Southeast Asia is that these authorities in Hanoi have employed their military forces in Laos, in South Vietnam, and with trained guerrillas and other activity in Thailand, to do things to their neighbors that they are not permitted to do under general standards of international conduct. That has been our problem.[105]

Only time will finally tell who was right: the president, or his detractors, who helped to bring the reversal in his policy to save Southeast Asia from communism and his retirement from the presidency.

After the historic speech of March 31, 1968, the defense secretary discovered he had gone almost full circle within one month. He began his duties with one immediate assignment: to devise the means by which to strengthen our forces in Vietnam and speed the war to a victorious end. Now, after the famous reversal, he was given two quite different and long-range tasks, "developing a plan for shifting the burden to the South Vietnamese as rapidly as they could be made ready, and supporting our government's diplomatic efforts to engage in peace talks."[106] The task was immense, and he never had the time to complete it. No one proposed to cut and run. The ARVN had to be prepared, supplied, and aided to assume an ever greater share of the fighting. First Johnson and then his successor, President Nixon, determined to de-Americanize the war, but not to abandon South Vietnam to communism.

On a visit to Saigon in the summer of 1968, Clifford discovered a shocking situation. Key officials of the South Vietnamese government seemed unaware of serious defects in their war effort in such matters as "troop training, junior officer strength and rate of desertions. They were, I felt, too complacent when facts were laid before them."[107] Asked about the gross desertion rate of ARVN personnel—then running at 30 percent yearly—Ky told Clifford it was because the men were so poorly paid. Asked what his government intended to do about the problem, Ky suggested we reduce our bombing and give the money thus saved to Saigon to be used for paying the troops. He was not jesting. The defense secretary came home

oppressed by the pervasive Americanization of the war: we were still giving the military instructions, still doing most of the fighting, still providing all the matériel, still paying most of the bills. Worst of all, I concluded that the South Vietnamese leaders seemed content to have it that way.[108]

To change this most unhappy situation would require years and billions more—if we were to save anything from our vast investment in that country. We could not stay there forever. Nor should we longer support a regime that delayed and obstructed reform. But for our presence, Thieu and Ky would have to broaden the base of their support or accept defeat.

Meanwhile, after weeks of silence and delay, Hanoi finally agreed to meet with us in May in Paris to initiate what some called peace talks. On April 3, 1968, the White House released the news that Hanoi had accepted our offer of negotiation and had declared

its readiness to appoint its representatives to contact the United States representative with a view to determining with the American side the unconditional cessation of the United States bombing raids and all other acts of war against the Democratic Republic of Vietnam so that talks may start.[109]

Here began another round of talking and fighting—long a Communist strategy—most recently illustrated in the negotiations to end the war in Korea. The fighting went on, but at each sign of a lull or of reduced casualties the doves hopefully noted signs of progress, while others saw virtually no gains in Paris and said that Johnson gave far more than he received. The world looked on with disgust as Hanoi stalled for seventy-seven days before it would agree on the size and seating of the table. By January 1969, it finally agreed upon a round table that equally balanced the United States and Saigon on one side and North Vietnam and the Vietcong on the other side; but Hanoi totally rejected any serious discussion of substantive problems.

Our chief negotiators in Paris, W. Averell Harriman and Cyrus R. Vance, for months sought some measure or gesture of restraint or reciprocity that would justify our total suspension of the bombing of North Vietnam with hopes for a cease-fire soon thereafter. All candidates in the 1968 election campaign openly supported the administration's peace effort and reiterated their common hopes for an honorable peace ending the tragic war. Initially Hanoi objected to having the Saigon government present, but Harriman and Vance were insistent. The president refused to order a bombing halt of all North Vietnam until Hanoi agreed to accept reciprocal restraints, and Hanoi refused to accept Saigon's presence and rejected our demands for reciprocal restraints. Hence began the long deadlock. The fighting went on.

In return for a total bombing halt of North Vietnam, Rostow declared:

Explicitly, the terms included the acceptance by Hanoi of the GVN as a negotiating partner—a valuable legitimizing of the South Vietnamese political process of 1965-1967. They also included the understanding that bombing could be resumed if there was infiltration across the DMZ or major attacks on cities in the South. In addition, it was understood that aerial reconnaissance of the North would continue.[110]

Implied clearly was that this halt would promptly lead to serious negotiations. This the October decision failed to bring. In Rostow's words:

And this violated the most fundamental understanding behind the bombing cessation: namely, that serious talks would begin when the bombing had ceased. By no stretch of the imagination did Hanoi engage in "serious talks" in the three and a half years following the bombing halt. On this ground it is my view that Richard Nixon was free at any time he thought necessary to resume the bombing of North Vietnam, quite aside from the gross violations of the DMZ and major attacks on the cities of South Vietnam that led to the resumption of the bombing in April 1972.

In the short run, he concluded that perhaps the bombing halt was a necessary test of enemy willingness to negotiate an end to the war. It may have reduced the level of warfare for a while, giving Hanoi a chance to recuperate and repeat the effort later.[111]

Bernard Gwertzman of the *New York Times* reported on October 17, 1968, that the Johnson administration dropped its use of the word "reciprocity" and declared it would stop all bombing of North Vietnam for "solid assurances" from Hanoi that this would improve the chances for peace. The slight change in the wording of our demands for some kind of restraint or concession offered a formula more acceptable to Ho, who had positively and long asserted his rejection of any reciprocity for a bombing halt. Washington still insisted upon "an element of fairness" by North Vietnam, some indication that enemy forces would not take advantage of a halt or stall endlessly the negotiations. We reportedly offered Hanoi several alternative ways to assure us that a halt would advance the cause of peace: "These include a pledge to restore the demilitarized zone to true neutrality; a pledge not to use a bombing cessation to step up infiltration of men and supplies into South Vietnam, and a pledge to decrease the number of attacks against cities and other populated areas." Beyond this hoped-for result lay the implication that Hanoi could bring representatives of the Vietcong or National Liberation Front into the more substantive talks, and Washington could bring in representatives from the government at Saigon. Certainly any final settlement would have to include the participation and support of the two opposing factions of South Vietnam.[112]

The diplomacy of the bombing halt—the decision of October 31, 1968—led to an enduring misunderstanding between the belligerents. Washington officials repeatedly cited the "understandings" that brought the halt, but Hanoi did not accept our interpretation of what was understood. By that decision, tacit or otherwise, we agreed to stop the bombing of North Vietnam, and the enemy agreed to negotiate at Paris with representatives of the South Vietnamese government. Participants in these negotiations have not clarified the precise details of the story, but a capable journalist, Max Frankel of the *New York Times,* tried to set the record straight. By his account, the enemy refused officially or otherwise to enter into any formal "understanding," to make any written or pledged agreement as to what it would do after the halt. Hanoi's view was that our bombing of North Vietnam was a violation of international law and our effort to impose "conditions" for such an illegal act was unacceptable blackmail. To escape the dilemma caused by this view, the diplomats used another method—the diplomatic device of "understandings."[113]

"Understandings" have marvelous flexibility in that they can be easily stretched by either side to mean so many various, even conflicting, things. Max Frankel wrote:

Understandings are to diplomacy what pantyhose are to underwear—they fit snugly when first tried but can be stretched out of shape at almost any time. . . .
Nonetheless, there is nothing very novel or sinister and no longer anything very mysterious about the understandings currently in vogue. Understandings in diplomacy develop when there is need for a horsetrade while it remains either inconvenient or impossible to reach a formal accord, contract or treaty. They can be dismembered, disowned or even denied from the start, as the North Vietnamese have denied any understanding whatsoever about the terms under which the United States stopped the regular bombing of Hanoi's territory two years ago.[114]

George Christian, Johnson's press secretary, revealed that part of the bombing halt understanding had been that each side could tell the story as it wished and, as Walt Rostow observed, preserve "its own mythology." This seemed necessary to save face for each side, especially since in the long negotiations leading to the bombing halt "Hanoi had vowed that there could be no negotiations on the war until the bombing had been stopped 'unconditionally.' Washington had vowed that it would not stop the bombing unless it obtained a degree of reciprocal military restraint."[115]

Washington declared it would cease the bombing unilaterally, and then stated its conditions for continuing the policy. If the enemy violated the DMZ or renewed its attacks on the cities of South Vietnam, we would resume the bombing. Then the Communist agents in Paris were asked if they "heard" these two points. They said they did. Asked if they "understood" what we said, they again replied that they did. This seems about all they "agreed" to by implication. Then we informed them that we intended to fly unarmed planes over North Vietnam, which we repeatedly thereafter did to protect our withdrawal from enemy attacks that might build up along many trails and areas. We said they were unarmed, but persistent reports said our reconnaissance planes were accompanied by armed escorts. The enemy always refused to recognize our right to violate his air space, on the ground that North Vietnam was a sovereign state and its government could not yield such a right. This was the extent of the October 1968 understandings. Each side took its own view of the arrangement. There was no formal statement of the terms, the promises, or the understandings. However, Washington at a subsequent time interpreted that arrangement to suit its own needs.[116]

Our later amendments stirred considerable protest from the antiwar forces, who feared they meant a return to a wider war rather than a continuation of our planned withdrawal. James Reston of the *New York Times* stated that in his news conference of December 10, 1970, and again later in speaking to television commentators, Nixon insisted that there was an understanding after the bombing halt that unarmed reconnaissance planes could fly over North Vietnam with impunity. Then he added another "understanding," which he laid down. No matter that the enemy did not agree; he used this means of telling him what we meant to do and unilaterally declared:

> Now the other understanding . . . is one that I have laid down. It is a new one. . . . If the enemy at a time we are trying to de-escalate, at a time we are withdrawing, starts to build up its infiltration, starts moving troops and supplies through Mugia Pass and the other passes, then I as Commander in Chief will have to order bombing strikes on those key areas. . . .

In his December 10 press conference, he was more specific. He told the world that if he concluded that enemy actions menaced our remaining forces by his continued infiltration, he would order "the bombing of military sites in North Vietnam, . . . the military complexes, the military supply lines. That will be the reaction I will take."[117]

This was a clear warning and a clear policy statement, justified as necessary—"protective reaction"—to secure our retreating forces; but obviously it was not part of any understanding or agreement with Hanoi or the Vietcong.

We might lay down many conditions and tell the enemy their nature and let him run whatever risks he wished, but the enemy did not agree to these new conditions. They were not part of any understandings. The enemy had never ceased his violations of these "understandings." Serious peace talks had not yet begun. Nixon's one-sided announcement of our policy was a long way from the enemy's acceptance of an arrangement by which he would not infiltrate the DMZ and bomb South Vietnamese cities. As James Reston wrote:

He is not waiting for that now. His policy is to bomb before they get to the DMZ or move into place to shell the cities. The military logic of this is obvious, but it is not a part of Hanoi's "understanding" or even of Washington's "understanding" of October 1968.[118]

In mid-October signs of movement in Paris appeared; agents of Hanoi and Washington reached understandings soon to become evident. Clifford wrote:

At last the North had accepted the participation of the South in peace talks. We would stop all bombing of North Viet Nam. Substantive talks were to start promptly. We had made it clear to Hanoi that we could not continue such talks if there were indiscriminate shelling of major cities in the South, or if the demilitarized zone were violated so as to place our troops in jeopardy.[119]

These events gave hope of faster progress toward a total cease-fire and a possible final solution of the tragedy.[120]

The president and his advisers, Clifford wrote, devoted a full day to a study and review of the situation, and the Joint Chiefs of Staff unanimously agreed that "the bombing halt under these circumstances was acceptable." The State Department told Saigon a seat for them had been won at the Paris conference table and urgently requested their "earliest possible presence." Washington was much relieved at this much progress, but then the relief turned to deep anxiety. Clifford described the cause:

These feelings were short-lived. The next three weeks were almost as agonizing to me as March had been. The cables from Saigon were stunning. The South Vietnamese Government, suddenly and unexpectedly, was not willing to go to Paris. First one reason, then another, then still another were cabled to Washington. As fast as one Saigon obstacle was overcome, another took its place. Incredulity turned to dismay. I felt that the President and the United States were being badly used. Even worse, I felt that Saigon was attempting to exert a veto power over our agreement to engage in peace negotiations. I admired greatly the President's ability to be patient under the most exasperating circumstances. Each day ran the risk that the North might change its mind, and that months of diligent effort at Paris would be in vain; each day saw a new effort on his part to meet the latest Saigon objection.[121]

While this haggling continued General Creighton W. Abrams was ordered home for a personal report. The president was assured that a bombing halt would not endanger our own forces or those of our allies. On October 31, therefore, he announced that the bombing of North Vietnam would cease, peace talks would begin promptly, and Saigon would have a seat at the conference table.[122]

By the time all the difficulties had been settled, Washington officials had formed a clear opinion about the Saigon government. The United States and South Vietnam neither shared the same views nor sought the same objectives, and doubts existed that they ever had. The conflict between our war aims was not total, but there were significant and disturbing differences. The United States entered the war to prevent the defeat of South Vietnam, to give Saigon the time, assistance, money, and material aid to avoid disaster. Beyond any reasonable doubt the American people wanted to end the war as quickly as possible. Clifford noted that Harriman had once said that it was "dangerous to let your aims be escalated in the middle of a war. Keep your objectives in mind, he advised, and as soon as they are attained, call a halt."[123]

Saigon's objectives, Clifford wrote, went beyond ours: it sought to win "the loyalty of villagers to the central government in Saigon," to fix the form of the postwar government to suit the Saigon ruling clique, to predetermine its leaders and their means of selection. Important as such objectives might be for Thieu and Ky, for the Saigon government, "these were clearly not among our original war objectives. But these were the precise areas of our differences with the Saigon government."[124] In the view of the ruling clique at Saigon, the longer the war—backed by our vast contribution—lasted, the more secure would be their power. They would have to make fewer concessions to other factions inside the country—and it could perhaps remain less democratic and less representative of the people. In fact, a few more years of war might so decimate Hanoi and the Vietcong that no concessions would have to be made to any group. Saigon apparently was not anxious to reach an early settlement of the war. A vast program of social reform and the restructuring of an entire society had little attraction to men who might suffer most by it. As long as we propped up this ruling elite they would not have to make any concessions. Clifford's conclusion, which most likely had been reached simultaneously by others— including probably the president—was:

The fact is that the creation of strong political, social and economic institutions is a job that the Vietnamese must do for themselves. We cannot do it for them, nor can they do it while our presence hangs over them so massively. President Thieu, Vice President Ky, Prime Minister Huong and those who may follow them have the task of welding viable political institutions from the 100 or more splinter groups that call themselves political parties. It is up to us to let them get on with the job. Nothing we might do could be so beneficial or could so add to the political maturity of South Viet Nam as to begin to withdraw our combat troops. Moreover, . . . we cannot realistically expect to achieve anything more through our military force, and the time has come to begin to disengage. That was my final conclusion as I left the Pentagon on January 20, 1969.[125]

The president had sacrificed his career and dedicated almost a year of his presidency to get this far.

When Johnson left office in January 1969, some progress had been made toward peace, but not much. The talks had begun; perhaps some infiltration through the DMZ had halted; and attacks upon the major cities had lessened, due more to General Abrams's brilliant defensive maneuvers or Hanoi's planned de-escalation—no one knew. Hanoi's officials had reluctantly agreed to talk with us before our troop withdrawal, which they had once declared prerequisite to any talk. Ho no longer claimed that the Vietcong was the only representative of South Vietnam. Saigon, too, made concessions. After vowing never to talk with the NLF, it began conversations with its agents in Paris and possibly elsewhere. However, while these negotiations went on, the fighting continued, with the loss of thousands of American lives. The military correctly claimed that Hanoi and the Vietcong were using the bombing halt and the lull to move massive amounts of supplies southward and rebuild their roads, bridges, and armies in preparation for greater drives later. Washington did the same. Although cutbacks were programmed for the future, contingent upon certain developments, they had not yet begun. Almost 550,000 troops were now in South Vietnam, and the war was costing us annually a little under $29 billion.

Johnson left office under a cloud of failure, almost humiliation, and his peace effort showed few signs of real promise. Under his direction the war had cost us more in both lives and money than anyone expected in 1964 or early 1965. The administration had never persuaded the American people or the Western world that our involvement was essential to our vital national interest. Beyond doubt, it seriously weakened the Great Society program, produced a serious gold drain and dollar crisis that threatened the world monetary system, and brought a nearly ruinous inflation that reached 4.7 percent in 1968. This in spite of a 10 percent tax increase adopted to prevent a huge budget deficit that, some predicted, might reach as high as $25 billion. The war had also chilled our relations with Russia and Western European countries.

Richard B. Morris and William Greenleaf, in a careful survey of the consequences of the war under Johnson, summarized:

The war had a profound effect on national politics and morale. It fractured the Johnson consensus and crystallized in the Democratic party a highly vocal opposition that included a disenchanted Senator J. William Fulbright, who became one of the most persistent critics of the Vietnam policy. The war energized an amorphous peace movement, lost Johnson the confidence of a vast part of the intellectual and academic community, sparked resistance to the draft, embittered Negro leaders who regarded Vietnam as a drain on America's obligation to help the poor, intensified the alienation of youth and the generation gap, and channeled the forces of student insurgency on the college campuses. By 1968 Vietnam was generally recognized as the single issue that compressed with explosive intensity most of the frustrations that beset Americans of every political persuasion. And for those who believed that the first need of the country was to lay out a set of social priorities, Vietnam was a forbidding roadblock in the path of progress.[126]

CHAPTER FIVE

NIXON'S SEARCH FOR PEACE, 1969-1970

In the summer of 1969 President Nixon went to Asia to reassure our friends. To demonstrate the durability and strength of our commitment to their security simultaneously with our retreat from direct involvement was no easy task. The president had to find both an honorable and fairly speedy way to get our troops out of Indochina. Yet the election mandate of 1968 was for honorable withdrawal. There would be no total abandonment, no precipitous or irresponsible retreat, he told them, but he would let ally and enemy know we wanted peace and would seek a solution through diplomacy. At Guam, Manila, Bangkok, Saigon, and other places—by speech and printed word—over the next four years he made significant statements, which collectively constituted a major shift in the direction of United States foreign policy. Observers carefully sorted out its elements and soon called it the Nixon Doctrine. Some called it a deceptive maneuver for a betrayal. For nearly thirty years we had followed a fairly straight line from "no more Munichs" into the bog of Vietnam, and in one week Nixon sought to chart a route to a new era of "no more Vietnams " For years this effort had been approved by Hubert Humphrey, Edmund Muskie, George McGovern and others of both parties. Had they known the ultimate course of the war and understood fully American impatience, Lyndon Johnson and Dean Rusk might have decided differently in 1965. Nixon sought security for Asia and for our interest there without our direct military involvement. He wanted no more of those creeping involvements. The United States was and would remain a "Pacific power" and had vital and durable interests in the region, but total commitment and military participation were not essential. A more limited and selective role would be required.[1]

Like it or not, the president said, geography made the United States a Pacific power. Indonesia was only fourteen miles from the Philippines at its closest point. For the United States World War II began in the Pacific; the Korean War came from Asia, as did the Vietnam war. Our involvement in the Pacific area was unavoidable; our destiny was tied to that vast region. From Communist China, North Korea, and North Vietnam came great dangers of aggression, such a menace to world peace that we must continue to play a significant role.[2]

At every stop he recognized the cry of Asia for the Asians and said: "That is what we want and that is the role we should play. We should assist it, but we should not dictate." What would be our policy in the future if any ally in Vietnam or under SEATO should ask: "Well, you are pulling out of Vietnam with your troops. We can read the newspapers. How can we know you will remain to play a significant role as you say you wish to do in the security arrangements in Europe?" The president replied that the question was not easy to answer, but when asked we would be greatly tempted to provide the military assistance to meet an internal or external threat. He wished to assure our Asian friends emphatically "that we would keep our treaty commitments, for example, with Thailand under SEATO," and he added most significantly:

As far as the problems of international security are concerned, as far as the problems of military defense, except for the threat of a major power involving nuclear weapons, that the United States was going to encourage and had a right to expect that this problem would be increasingly handled by, and the responsibility for it taken by, the Asian nations themselves.

Preliminary conversations with Asian leaders over the recent months had led him to believe that they were willing to undertake this obligation. However, he then observed: "But if the United States just continued down the road of responding to requests for assistance, of assuming the primary responsibility for defending these countries when they have international problems or external problems, they were never going to take care of themselves."[3]

Although currently collective security for Asia looked like a weak reed, within five to ten years he thought united action to meet internal threats other than that posed by a nuclear power, "was an objective that free Asian nations could see and which the United States should support." He did not regard internal threats unassisted from the outside as too serious; citing Thailand as an example, he said the danger there would not be too great "if it were not getting the assistance that it was from the outside." Generally, our policy would be to help them fight the war but not to fight the war for them. However, he added, one of the reasons for his trip was

to leave no doubt in the minds of the leaders of non-Communist Asia that the United States is committed to a policy in the Pacific—a policy not of intervention but one that certainly rules out withdrawal, and regardless of what happens in Vietnam that we intend to continue to play a role in Asia to the extent that Asian nations, bilaterally and collectively, desire us to play a role.[4]

Protecting our interests across the Pacific would require our involvement where a major threat arose from a nuclear power. We would keep our commitments to nations we deemed important, like India, whether they were formal allies or not. A brilliant journalist, Max Frankel of the *New York Times,* summed it up:

In other words, the United States will help defend countries, such as South Korea, that are clearly attacked across national boundaries or lines of demarcation by a Communist nation. It will also take a serious view and perhaps play a role in defending non-aligned nations against invasion and particularly if those countries should be threatened with nuclear weapons.

But these commitments will not be augmented by new treaties or attempts to resuscitate old treaties, such as SEATO and CENTO. And no general commitment, explicit or implicit, will be stretched to justify the use of American troops to put down domestic insurgents or rebels. The best defense against insurrection—so holds the doctrine—is preventive political and economic action, including social reform, land reform, civil liberty and the like. If all should fail and a government that Washington respects and deems deserving of survival is threatened from within it will help it against insurgency by providing material and technical assistance, training and perhaps even some advisory, but no ground forces as in South Vietnam in 1965.[5]

These principles should aid Asian schemes of self-help and collective security, which we would support but not dictate. It was not our role to prescribe

defense positions for countries that fail to design their own or to feel a greater concern for their safety than they themselves evince. Above all, not every military action will necessarily be seen as part of a grand Communist design of aggression and not every insurgency will necessarily be deemed part of a great conspiracy.[6]

We were a Pacific power, but our interests on the Asian mainland were "peripheral."

As late as his second inaugural address (January 20, 1973) Nixon strongly affirmed his faith in the principles of self-reliance domestically and internationally. Again he stated the basic principles of his Guam Doctrine, declaring that we would expect others to do their share:

The time has passed when America will make every other nation's conflict our own, or make every other nation's future our responsibility, or presume to tell the people of other nations how to manage their own affairs.

Just as we respect the right of each nation to determine its own future, we also recognize the responsibility of each nation to secure its own future. Just as America's role is indispensable in preserving the world's peace, so is each nation's role indispensable in preserving its own peace.

This was not, he said, a retreat from our responsibilities, but it was a better way to peace and progress. Abroad and at home, he favored a division of duties. Perhaps both Americans and others had too long looked to Washington and to government for the solution of problems they might better have solved themselves. From here on, he favored less paternalism and more self-reliance.

Essential elements of the Nixon Doctrine, as summarized by Frank N. Trager, included: letting other nations do their own fighting—Vietnamization, for example; "assisting allied states against nonnuclear aggression," provided they were willing to assume the "primary responsibility for their own defense";

offering a nuclear shield if our friends were threatened by a nuclear power; "maintaining our treaty commitments"—with a harder look at all future pledges; and a phased withdrawal of our military forces wherever feasible. Where this policy might ultimately lead no one could then know, but it stirred grave doubts among our friends in Europe and Asia. It signaled a new direction of policy that especially alarmed Japan and Taiwan when it was extended in 1972 to include a new approach to China. It became a means of escape for the United States from its overcommitments. It broke new trails when by our support it led to the admission of Communist China to the United Nations, our acknowledgment that Formosa's future was an internal question which China alone should ultimately settle. It motivated other nations to initiate new directions and new policies of peace with China and Russia. It broke many long-standing policies and assumptions associated with the cold war. Its unproved implication that the Communist conspiracy had ended, or in any case that peace through containment was not our responsibility alone, greatly endangered our friends and allies who were not yet strong enough to be equal partners or to defend themselves.[7]

In Bangkok, on July 28, three days after his announcement at Guam, Nixon puzzled many observers when he stated:

We will honor our obligations under that treaty (SEATO). We will honor them not simply because we have to, because of paper, but because we believe in those words, and particularly believe in them in the association that we have with a proud and a strong people—the people of Thailand.

We have been together in the past, we are together at the present and the United States will stand proudly with Thailand against those who might threaten it from abroad or from within.[8]

To many observers this statement seemed in conflict with the Guam Doctrine of no direct military intervention except where a nation might be threatened by a nuclear power; it was an "invitation to entanglement," which aroused considerable fear in the hearts of many doves, who had referred to Nixon as a statesman after his Guam policy, but after the Bangkok pronouncement labeled him a politician. His inner advisers denied there was any contradiction. They said the Thailand statement did not change the policy because all the president meant to say was that Thailand had the primary responsibility for its defense against internal subversion. Although they might count on our advice, training, technical aid and equipment, they could expect no combat forces. The emphasis upon military assistance and the ambiguity concerning direct combat assistance disturbed many observers and war critics, who felt that in a moment of enthusiasm the president tossed off remarks much too close to the old and discredited policies of the recent past. It sounded like more Vietnams were yet to come.[9]

In historical perspective, Max Frankel of the *New York Times* observed:

But real change depends not on how Asians react to their fears but how the United States deals with its own. From Munich to Vietnam, the great fear was of "appeasement" of any would-be aggressor. Will the great new fear now be of "involvement" and will it cause more or less trouble?

Mr. Nixon seems unsure and he is unlikely to answer the question until one day he must make a quick and far-reaching decision on some Vietnam or Cuba or missile crisis.[10]

Equally repulsive to antiwar critics was the president's similar declaration to American troops in a surprise trip to Saigon that the war effort in South Vietnam might go down in history as "one of America's finest hours." Such critics could not grasp that in a true sense the vast effort, sacrifice, and courage required of us to help save a small and defenseless nation from Communist despotism, without immediate benefit to the United States, was truly such a shining act as the president portrayed it. They had forgotten how welcome in the Korean War were the words of Nehru of India who reminded his fellow Asians in that tragic hour that this was the first time in history that the Western white man had ever sent his sons to die in a fight for Asians. In South Vietnam it was for the same cause—the freedom of Asians.

The full implications of this Guam or Nixon Doctrine will undoubtedly be long debated and thoroughly analyzed by historians and statesmen. John W. Finney of the *New York Times* wondered whether it meant, as Nixon described it, a "major shift in U.S. foreign policy"? Would it really change our involvement in Asia and elsewhere? At Nixon's request, Senator Mansfield toured Asia in August 1969 and upon his return issued a report giving his opinion, which led some to suggest the label should be the "Nixon-Mansfield Doctrine." Mansfield declared it meant that while we would maintain our treaty commitments, we expected Asia to be able to handle its own defense problems, with assistance from others but without outside manpower. He later went beyond what many conceived to be Nixon's Doctrine when he said that it meant:

That we did not intend to become involved there on a combat basis anymore, and that to our friends we would give logistical and economic support; the only way in which we would ever become involved again would be when our security was at stake and a nuclear showdown appeared to be in the offing—in other words when there was no possible choice.[11]

Some asked when our security would be at stake in the event of an insurgency or invasion in Asia if our interests there were only peripheral. Further confusion arose when other senators, after a meeting with the president in November 1969, declared the doctrine applied not just to Asia but to the whole world. Whatever he originally meant at Guam, the doctrine grew in meaning and scope. In his famous speech of November 3, 1969, Nixon said his Guam Doctrine set forth three principles as guidelines for our future foreign policy toward Asia:

First, the United States will keep all of its treaty commitments.

Second, we shall provide a shield if a nuclear power threatens the freedom of a nation allied with us or of a nation whose survival we consider vital to our security.

Third, in cases involving other types of aggression, we shall furnish military and economic assistance when requested in accordance with our treaty commitments. But we shall look to the nation directly threatened to assume the primary responsibility of providing the manpower for its defense.[12]

When these broad principles were given practical application confusion arose. In general, supporters of the doctrine assumed that no more Vietnamlike aggressions would occur in Southeast Asia, but the United States would stand by its commitments to protect South Korea, Taiwan, the Philippines, and Thailand, to whom, it was revealed, pledges had been made. Mansfield thought the doctrine implied a reduction in our military presence in Asia. On his own lengthy tour of Asia, Vice-President Agnew raised disturbing doubts about the "no more Vietnams" principle when he declared that the United States stood ready if requested by the Malaysian Commonwealth to assist its effort to maintain the Singapore Naval Base after Great Britain withdrew in 1970. Although he denied that this meant we would send combat troops, the tenor of the speech had implications not easily reconciled with the Guam formula for reducing our participation on mainland Asia. Agnew's aides explained that he meant we would aid Singapore with a commercial arrangement, but would not guarantee its defense.[13]

James W. Naughton of the *New York Times* reported that the reactions of the various countries the vice-president visited revealed that his tour left a wake of contradictions. After Agnew's departure, the Malaysian prime minister said the vice-president had convinced him the United States would not leave "us in the lurch. It is prepared to spread its umbrella for the security of the region." That same day, however, he dropped from his speech a line that said Malaysia "can expect help in the event of unprovoked aggression by enemies from without who have sinister designs against us." This switch may have come because he realized he had no written guarantee or treaty to assure this. Taiwan believed we were firmly committed to help them in case of attack from Mao, but its newspapers expressed sharp doubts, and one called Agnew's assurances "empty and perfunctory." In Thailand great fears sprang from the possible American retreat from Asia, and in Laos and Thailand officials remained jittery after Agnew's visit. In fact, Agnew and others did not dispel the serious doubts Asians now entertained about their future under our protection.[14]

Nor did Nixon's expression that he feared our continuing to give vast supplies to Asian nations might sap their fighting spirit and make them too reliant upon modern methods reassure many Asians. To peoples living next to Communist countries, such talk meant ominously: "The era of an unlimited American military commitment to Asia is over." They could well ask:

But if Communist goals, notably of capitals like Peking or Pyongyang, remain unlimited, what is to take the place of the American commitment? Will the kind of regional alliances that President Nixon seems to envisage prove sufficient to prevent a repetition of the Vietnam tragedy?[15]

Countries not so conscious of a direct Communist threat, including Japan, opposed regional military alliances. Japan was a member of the Asian and Pacific Council (ASPAC) founded in 1966 "largely on South Korea's initiative," but Japanese officials stated repeatedly "that ASPAC should have only economic and cultural functions, not military."[16] Taiwan and other free Asian countries wished to know what our intentions were and what role we expected to play. Unless we were specific about our obligations, the implication was clear that they would make other arrangements. Our retreat from an involvement, whatever assurances it gave the American people, gave little or none to Asians.

Reports from South Korea and from most of Southeast Asia, wrote Philip Shabecoff of the *New York Times,* outwardly appeared to approve the new policy of Asians for Asians. Pleasing to those in a mood of swelling national pride over the region was the exhortation to be more self-reliant in "shouldering the burden of defense and in guiding their own destiny." Nothing could be more delightful to people with memories of repressive colonialism than to be free of alien regimes "telling them what to do." However, observers quickly detected nagging fears of any sudden or total efforts by us to execute the doctrine. From South Korea came one of the strongest protests against the Nixon Doctrine. Although South Korea, one of the toughest and most self-reliant Asian countries, had been primed by twenty years of United States aid "to take care of itself," the reports of our pullback brought only "cries of anguish and charges of betrayal" in Seoul. One ranking official there stated: "As far as we are concerned, the international situation is at exactly the same point it was 20 years ago." He noted that his people could not change the geographic fact that on the Asian continent were two giant Communist nations hostile to his government. His country's only chance of survival was the assistance it received from the United States. This official opposed withdrawal specifically and the new Nixon Doctrine in general.[17]

Also South Korean officials could not forget, and now quickly recalled for us, continued Shabecoff, the consequences of Dean Acheson's unfortunate announcement in 1950 of our intention to omit South Korea from our defense perimeter in Southeastern Asia. As that statement, so they believed, speeded the invasion and attempt to subjugate South Korea by a Soviet trained and equipped North Korean army, now they feared the Nixon Doctrine—which really told the world our forces were pulling out of Asia—would simply invite renewed aggression. The expansion of Communist activities in Laos, Cambodia, and Thailand in the coming months appeared to substantiate their fears. Such concern of Southeast Asians revealed that the thin applause for the Nixon Doctrine scarcely concealed their anxieties. Many officials bluntly accused us of impatience. Even Philippine officials, when talking about a reduced American presence and a return of our bases to the Philippine government, stated that they did not mean we should yield all of them. One of them said, "Let's face it. . . . Without your military presence we are vulnerable." Shabecoff concluded: "In general, the Asians' attitude toward the Nixon doctrine is satisfaction at its emphasis on responsibility and self-reliance. But no one wants to rush the process—in fact, the slower the better."[18]

During the president's brief trip to Saigon on July 30, 1969, Nixon and Thieu, in further statements, proclaimed that progress was being made toward pacification, more effective local administration, greater popular participation in government, and the ARVN's capacity to replace our forces. In a review of their late efforts to achieve a reasonable peace, Nixon recalled Saigon's March 25 offer to talk with the NLF without preconditions and Thieu's six-point offer of April 6, which included the proposal that "those opposed to the Government would be welcomed as full members of the national community." Nixon recalled his own eight-point proposal, "which could lead to the withdrawal of all non-South Vietnamese forces, a cease-fire, and elections under international supervision." Also there was Thieu's very recent (July 11) attempt to expand and execute his six-point plan,

through which all the people of South Vietnam could exercise their right of self-determination through internationally supervised elections, in which they can genuinely express their choice, free from fear and coercion. An electoral commission in which all political parties would be represented would assure equal opportunities to all candidates.

The G.V.N. (Government of Vietnam) has offered to abide by the results of the elections whatever they may be.

. . . . . .

On July 20, President Thieu made the offer to North Vietnam for direct discussions toward reunification through free and internationally supervised elections.[19]

Thieu declared upon his return from Midway in June that "Everything is negotiable." Nixon, therefore, noted in his Saigon statement:

We have gone as far as we can or should go in opening the door to negotiations which will bring peace. It is now time for the other side to sit down with us and talk seriously about ways to stop the killing, to put an end to this tragic war, which has brought so great destruction to friend and foe alike.

We have put forward constructive proposals to bring an end to the conflict. We are ready to talk with the other side about their proposals.[20]

Nixon felt we had made most generous offers of peace, and in the brief time he had held office he had made clear to the world "which side has gone the extra mile in behalf of peace." He truly felt we could go no further:

We have stopped the bombing of North Vietnam. We have withdrawn 25,000 American troops. They have been replaced by South Vietnamese. We have made, and you have made a peace offer which is as generous as any ever made in the history of warfare.[21]

Whatever the president might do, for his critics it was never enough. They told him that ending the war required more than unilateral declarations of policy. He should end the stalemate in the war, accept the status quo politically and militarily, and realize that the first order of business now was to achieve a standstill cease-fire for all South Vietnam. Some proposed we now needed to recognize

the existing leopard-spot partition of South Vietnam into regions controlled either by the Communists or by Saigon and to work out a *modus vivendi* in trade, transport, currency, etc., that would permit those regions to live together in peace. Neither side has anything to lose and both have peace to gain by settling for the *status quo* as the preliminary to free elections and a permanent political settlement.[22]

In these continuing peace efforts accompanying our withdrawal, there was much juggling, balancing, and politicking. The president was accused of a two-faced approach. He had to satisfy the demands of national and world politics. He proclaimed publicly that we had gone the last mile and made the last concession, while he told Saigon privately more withdrawals were soon forthcoming. He reassured the American people we were demanding that Asians do more for themselves, while he told Asian leaders we would be on their side in times of crisis. He sought to balance the desire of our military leaders for victory while meeting the wishes of the people at home for peace. Like all politicians he liked to please everybody; but, as James B. Reston noted, "His rhetoric is bold but his policy is weak."[23] If the enemy continued his stubborn refusal to talk seriously and his military effort to win a victory on the battlefields of South Vietnam, if he proved by his actions that there was no peace possible except by our humiliation, would the American people then support a harder line toward the enemy, a continuation of the war in hopes of eventually finding an honorable and just peace?

Chalmers M. Roberts of the *Washington Post* observed that in the summer of 1969 our policy consisted of the Vietnamization of the war, meaning we began to pull out our troops fast enough to satisfy public opinion at home "but not so fast that the South Vietnamese will panic and their own troops will collapse." Our battlefield tactics changed from the Westmoreland massive "search-and-destroy" operations to the Abrams "protective reaction" policy. This latter policy, as revealed by Defense Secretary Laird, sought to uncover pre-positioned enemy caches of weapons and food, prevent major attacks on our forces, and reduce our casualties. In telling the Communists on July 30 that we had gone as far as we could go, we told the enemy we had put our last bargaining card on the table publicly—until the Communists began to negotiate seriously. The implication seemed clear that if the enemy began serious talks, Nixon might pressure Saigon for additional compromises. The offer of elections, therefore, was not the last word.[24]

Home from his Asian trip, the president told key congressmen that we meant to keep our "commitments in Asia but not to expand them"; we would give economic and military aid when the need arose and it appeared justified. To allay concern over Thailand, he declared that the Thailand government had not asked for ground troops and "there would be no commitment of ground forces," but he admitted the possibility that our air force might aid in the defense of Thailand. His audience apparently approved his doctrine, as did the American people, overwhelmingly. Cutbacks in defense expenditures, expectations of further troop withdrawals, reductions in the staffs of our various but extensive nonmilitary agencies in South Vietnam were announced at the same time the president reported on his trip.[25] The nation had already begun its retreat from Asia, from "our war" back to "their war," from the Johnson aberration to the older, even nineteenth-century, view of Asia.

In late summer and fall of 1969 a bitter debate raged in Congress and among the public over the means of extrication from the war. Few then openly favored a wider war. Fears and hopes, denunciations and defense filled the press, forum, and all communication facilities. At no place was there more public discussion of the war than on the campuses of American colleges and universities. Although Nixon declared the time had come to end the war and made major efforts to do so, his critics faulted his every step and began calling it "Nixon's War." On September 16, he announced a scheduled reduction of our forces in Vietnam to 484,000 men by December 15. This meant that a minimum of 60,000 troops in all would be withdrawn by that date. He then ticked off his efforts to end the war:

> We have renounced an imposed military solution.
> We have proposed free elections, organized by joint commissions under international supervision.
> We have offered the withdrawal of U.S. and Allied forces over a 12-month period.
> We have declared that we would retain no military bases.
> We have offered to negotiate supervised cease-fires—under international supervision—to facilitate the process of mutual withdrawal.
> We have made clear that we would settle for the *de facto* removal of North Vietnamese forces, so long as there are guarantees against their return.
> We and the Government of South Vietnam have announced that we are prepared to accept any political outcome which is arrived at through free elections.
> We are prepared to discuss the 10-point program of the other side, together with plans put forward by the other parties.
> In short, the only item which is not negotiable is the right of the people of South Vietnam to determine their own future, free of outside interference.
> I reiterate all these proposals today.
> The withdrawal of 60,000 troops is a significant step.
> The time for meaningful negotiations has therefore arrived.[26]

This was our signal to Hanoi that we had gone as far as we could go; it was time for them to make some moves for peace. Hanoi could not expect us to keep making concessions without some sort of reciprocity, but that was precisely what it did expect and believe would succeed due to our war weariness and impatience. It stubbornly stuck to this position from 1969 to 1972.

Henry A. Kissinger, Nixon's special adviser on foreign policy, who exercised more power than did the secretary of state, was sorely disappointed in the enemy response to these gestures. He then believed prospects of an honorable peace were dim indeed. Both Nixon and Kissinger had thought our troop withdrawals would bring serious bargaining with Hanoi. Kissinger "had left a broad trail of hints in various foreign capitals that the United States no longer considered a coalition government that included Communists to be harmful to American national interests—so long as the coalition was not imposed."[27] Nixon's statement just quoted above announced that Washington and Saigon were prepared to accept any political settlement reached through free elections. Implied hereafter by omission would be a series of surrenders by us of previously held positions, which some might deem tantamount to abandonment. Talk was heard that Kissinger would accept a mere "decent interval" between our going and Communist takeover of all Indochina.

That Hanoi was disturbed by Nixon's announcement was doubtful, especially since on October 18 the president revealed plans to cut our military budget for the next five years by $4 billion to $6 billion. This action told the world and the enemy that we meant to reduce our troops, costs, responsibilities, and commitments over the globe. Two National Security decision memorandums laid down basic guidelines for a more austere and limited defense outlay. These recognized that with smaller forces we would run greater risks in facing world commitments unless we could reduce them. The guidelines assumed that the Vietnam War would soon be over and the size of the army could be cut back. However, the plan was to retain sufficient strategic weapons to destroy our enemies if they initiated nuclear warfare.

When the president refused to set a fixed timetable for withdrawal, the critics roared louder. Our disengagement was debated more emotionally than our initial involvement had been. While the enemy kept on hitting and running with his costly surprise attacks, Nixon pleaded for unity and time. How much time? asked his critics. He replied that the greater his popular support, the less time it would take. When cynics asked why the delay, they were told it was to obtain a settlement that would assure for South Vietnam "self-determination" through supervised free elections. When they noted that the enemy refused to negotiate, they received the oft-reiterated reply that his incentive to negotiate was destroyed by American impatience and dissension. This in turn brought from the critics the further question that disturbed ever more people: Was not Saigon's incentive to negotiate destroyed by our very presence? The hawks in return feared that our programmed cutback relieved all pressure upon the enemy to negotiate any compromise solution. Leaving or staying, our leverage upon Saigon was weak. Our official position was that since the Saigon government was the product of an election, of due constitutional process which we had encouraged and supported, it should have our support until the people had another election and changed it.

If the enemy still refused to bargain, if all our proposals were rejected quite summarily—as they were—with the usual demand for our total pullout and abandonment of the existing Saigon regime, then what? Nixon was already turning to Vietnamization. This was the key to peace and our extrication; this was Nixon's secret plan of escape, the purpose and inner meaning of the Nixon Doctrine. By this plan we would gradually turn the war over to the Saigon regime and let South Vietnamese youth do the fighting while we gave material, financial, and logistic support—with possibly a brief transitional period of continued air attacks. Our pace of withdrawal would be slow enough, as in the Korean War, to prevent a Communist takeover and frustrate Hanoi's obvious intent to win by exhausting our patience. Thus developed the debate over the withdrawal, its speed, its duration, whether by negotiation or Vietnamization. As the debate proceeded, Vietnamization, which some initially assumed was a cover for retreat and swift withdrawal, won much popular support even among the critics of the war. Later the critics, seeing it as an excuse to justify a sizable and indefinite American involvement, viciously denounced it. Increasing in numbers, they wanted us out completely, with no strings or commitments attached to our departure. They wanted no "Korean solution" this time.

Recriminations between the administration and its critics continued; distrust arose again; accusations of a credibility gap between campaign promises and lagging performance charged the atmosphere of official Washington. Had not Johnson's retirement, Humphrey's defeat, and Nixon's victory in 1968 been a popular mandate to get out of the war? The critics thought, Yes. Louder now were the denunciations of the Saigon regime. Senator Charles Goodell of New York stirred great popular interest for his proposal to prohibit the use of our troops in Vietnam after December 1, 1970. Fulbright promised a new round of hearings by his Foreign Relations Committee, and the Democratic critics of the war, including many liberals and moderates, planned to make the most of the war issue. Antiwar students scheduled demonstrations for October 15. Some threatened to revive the 1968 "dump-Johnson" organization to force an immediate troop withdrawal. Many congressmen reported that surprisingly large numbers of their constituents sympathized with these efforts.

In news conferences and private appeals Nixon fought back. He obtained Rockefeller's support in denouncing Senator Goodell and sought the end of defeatism. He charged that his critics, although perhaps well intentioned, were undermining his plans for ending the war. He felt that the efforts he had made, the troop cutbacks already accomplished, and the announced plans for further reductions did not justify the rising accusations about "Nixon's War." Nevertheless, the critics still carped about his timetable, his tactics, and his long-run objectives, which he kept deliberately ambiguous. The president felt no need to reveal all his options to the enemy before negotiations began.

Even one of Nixon's closest friends and long-time political associates, Robert H. Finch, Secretary of Health, Education, and Welfare, declared that Vietnamization was not a satisfactory long-run solution and noted further the contradiction of trying to force the enemy to talk while persuading the American people to wait. Others noticed with rising anger Saigon's continued refusal to use the time given it by our presence and aid since 1954 to broaden its political base and demonstrate its capacity to replace us. Its sabotage of the cease-fire we sought during Ho's funeral (1969) revealed little desire for any compromise. Few expected any favorable response from Hanoi to any reasonable peace efforts. Some doves observed a slight reduction of Hanoi's rate of infiltration and hoped that some alteration in policy might follow Ho's death.

However, few inside the Nixon administration saw anything to be gained by more concessions. October 12, on NBC's "Meet the Press" television broadcast, Secretary Rogers stated emphatically that there had been no progress in Paris for the last two or three months and would be none unless it was clear that the president's policy was supported by the American public. That appeared to him most unlikely at that moment "because there is so much dissent here and there are so many voices being heard that I think they (North Vietnamese) must have the feeling that the President doesn't have the amount of support that's necessary to carry on for a long time." The secretary of state did not object to the Moratorium planned for October 15 if its spirit was to be constructive and helpful to the president, but if it said " 'You either accept our decision, Mr. President, or else,' if it's coercive, then it could be very disruptive." In fact, the president, he added, was de-escalating the war, and, he noted, so was the enemy.[28]

Very disturbing to the youthful critics of the war and to other Americans was the president's statement to a press conference, September 26, concerning the coming march on Washington. Although he could not control it, he startled many when he said: "As far as this kind of activity is concerned, we expect it. However, under no circumstances will I be affected whatever by it."[29] Shortly after saying this he received a letter from a Georgetown University student suggesting respectfully that the president of the United States should take note of the will of the people and reconsider his prejudgment. In reply, the president advised the young man to consider several points. First, there was a clear distinction between public opinion and public demonstrations. To listen to public opinion was one thing; to be swayed by public demonstrations was another. A demonstration, he noted, was an organized expression of one particular set of opinions, likely of a small minority, which was not shared at all by the majority of the people. For a president to be swayed by such a minority would betray the rest of the people. To allow public policy to be made in the streets by mob actions would destroy the democratic process. Power to the people? Yes, but to the people constitutionally and democratically organized.

In the streets, under mob rule, power would belong not to the majority but to those with the loudest voices and the biggest fists. Anarchy would reign, the ballot would be lost, and every group would then test its strength through confrontation in the streets. No march on Washington was necessary to tell the people or its government that Americans were deeply disturbed by the war, that some deemed the war immoral and wanted our troops out immediately and unconditionally. Millions who would not march believed these things. Therefore, there was nothing new to be learned from such a demonstration. He was already doing the best that he and the wisest men he could gather to advise him, men who had studied exhaustively the whole subject, could devise. To abandon a course long fixed and decided because of a public demonstration would be an act of gross irresponsibility upon the president's part. When asked how to get out of Vietnam, some might flippantly answer: "By sea." They could with equal flippancy ignore the consequences of such an act, but the president said he could not ignore the results both in human and international terms. The death of a nation, the murder of thousands, the decades of coming despotism under slavery, the disappointed hopes of millions in Southeast Asia, and much more lay back of that considered judgment.[30]

By this time our government had reasserted in strong terms the conviction that the war involved larger stakes than just the fate of South Vietnam. The television appearance of Secretary Rogers spelled out the possible results of an American pullout. It would mean, he feared, a tremendous massacre of the South Vietnamese population. This fear the war critics denied, pointing to the survival of Catholics in North Vietnam since 1954. Others insisted that the crimes of Saigon regimes plus our bombing attacks upon helpless civilians were already imposing extensive and unpardonable cruelty upon these people. A sudden pullout, Rogers dreaded, would also bring a general instability to Asia that could endanger the whole world. It would thus be a breach of promise not only to the people of South Vietnam but to all Southeast Asia. Such considerations, the president and his advisers feared, were lost in the public discussion then raging.

Peace proposals filled the air. The planners of the October Vietnam Moratorium and their friends called for an "immediate" withdrawal of all our troops. Some congressmen favored a deadline for withdrawal over the coming year, 1970. Some sought a phased or scheduled withdrawal, with an accelerated cutback of at least all combat troops—estimated to be more than half of the half million men left in Vietnam. Some would protect where possible the South Vietnamese who had allied with us and would also give financial aid to nearby nations that might feel threatened by our retirement. Most called for the speediest possible withdrawal compatible with the safety of our troops, but they shrank from any admission of defeat or failure. Rather they preferred somehow to shift the blame for this upon Saigon. To many it appeared that this was one among many reasons for the much acclaimed Vietnamization program. It was about the easiest and most dignified retreat we could find, but some already called it more correctly "disguised defeat." Although the administration would not admit defeat, it did admit its abandonment of the goal of "military victory." However, regardless of the wisdom of the initial intervention, it still felt a responsibility for achieving an orderly political change. Nothing was to be gained from a debate of that issue. Apparently Nixon agreed with Johnson's belief that defeat in this war would increase the risk of other wars.

There was an extensive and lively debate among Nixon's inner advisers over the tactics of getting us out of Vietnam. Laird favored the speediest possible transfer of the fighting to the South Vietnamese and opposed any delay based on expectations of progress in negotiations. Rogers read more significance than the others into battlefield lulls, signs of enemy restraints or "winding down" the war without positive agreement. Kissinger was given credit for the merger of these approaches and for making our withdrawals rest upon three conditions: improvement in the ARVN's capacity to fight, the reduced level of enemy warfare, and the progress of the peace talks at Paris. Without a full test on the battlefield and without the support of our presence, could we ever know the ARVN's real capacity? None of them favored quick withdrawal without regard for any actions of Hanoi or the wishes of Saigon. Kissinger reportedly contended that if we did withdraw, Europeans and Asians would lose faith in all American pledges, and he feared what the reaction of domestic hawks might be.

Nixon's announcement of the retirement of sixty thousand forces in December had many objectives: to pacify a restless American public, impatient with the dragged-out retreat; to spur Saigon to make a greater effort in its own behalf; to persuade Hanoi that unless it promptly agreed to serious negotiations, we would continue our presence there for some time to come; to build up the ARVN to the stage where it could better defend the nation; and, we hoped, to afford the enemy even less chance of attaining his objectives from Saigon than from Washington. The deceleration also aimed to save as much as possible of our original objectives in going into the war. We were not yet ready to abandon everything just to get out of the war. The Nixon administration was ready to concede to the Communists a share of power in return for peace, but would not grant to them the dominant role, which they seemed incessantly to demand. As early as May 1969, we admitted again that we had ruled out any attempt to impose a purely military solution on the battlefield, but we had also refused to accept a unilateral withdrawal or acceptance of terms at Paris that amounted to a disguised American defeat.[31] Yet, to many, our efforts seemed designed more to speed peace at any price and hardly disguised the fact of defeat.

The Nixon speech of May 14, 1969, came at a time when he felt Hanoi was moving toward serious negotiations. Later in the summer, however, the enemy ceased his efforts and Ho's death possibly brought further delay if not total abandonment of the effort. Official Washington believed Hanoi had lost interest in negotiations long before the fall protest movement against the war gathered momentum over the country. Nevertheless, Nixon wanted to secure the greatest public support for his peace efforts. Another objective of the planned and announced cutback was to defuse the rising protests. Nixon's announcement on October 10, 1969, that the unpopular Selective Service Director, Lieutenant General Lewis B. Hershey, was to take a new post as adviser to the president on manpower mobilization and his promise to make the draft less burdensome to the youth of the land also advanced this purpose. These steps toward peace received the most welcome endorsement of former Vice-President Hubert Humphrey. At this stage some asked how Nixon's pledges to effect more withdrawals could be reconciled with his vows not to be the first president to "lose" a war. Disturbing doubts remained.

While Nixon prepared his highly publicized speech of November 3, 1969, the debate over the war and the means of ending it continued, and the lines hardened between the defenders and critics of Nixon's peace efforts. A larger number of Congressmen and Americans were coming to favor unilateral disengagement. Resolutions to end the war, to fix specific time limits for our total pullout, and others to endorse official efforts without pressure or protest were introduced or being planned for introduction. The basic issue then under discussion was

whether a negotiated settlement could be achieved through a policy of firmness at home and pressure on North Vietnam through the threat of an extended military presence in South Vietnam (as proposed by the Administration), or whether a solution could be achieved through unilateral steps by the United States. These steps would include an accelerated withdrawal of combat troops, a cease-fire, or pressure on South Vietnam to accept a coalition government.[32]

In behalf of the White House, Senator Robert J. Dole of Kansas introduced a resolution endorsing the Nixon approach; it was widely known as the White House Resolution. The president told Dole just before he offered the resolution to the Senate that it pleased him that there was only one reason we did not have peace in Vietnam—"the intransigence of North Vietnam." In support of his motion Dole said that it asked the enemy to show at the Paris talks the same flexibility and desire for compromise we had long demonstrated, and it clearly stated that we would not retreat from our basic objective of "peace with self-determination for the South Vietnamese people." Senator Hugh Scott of Pennsylvania hoped that the students coming to Washington to protest the war that week would "direct some of their energies toward the enemy who stands in the way of peace."

From the ranks of the doves and some former hawks turning dove came further expressions of impatience with official policies. Senators McIntyre of New Hampshire and Moss of Utah—both Democrats—said they could no longer support Nixon's war policies. They concluded that the current plan of combining peace talks in Paris, Vietnamization on the battlefield, and the gradual if limited withdrawal of our troops would not bring the desired peace. Rather they and others now wanted an immediate end to all offensive military action except what might be essential to save the lives of our troops. They declared the time had come for Saigon to chart its own course without our troops and for us to get out of Vietnam with all due speed. In short, we must now save our own nation first because dissension over the war was tearing it apart. Tempers flared over the plans of a small bipartisan group to keep the House of Representatives open all night in support of the Vietnam Moratorium. Representative Wayne L. Hays, Democrat of Ohio, announced that he might abandon a planned trip to Brussels and stay in Washington so he could "single-handedly break up the designs of a few self-appointed emissaries of Hanoi to keep the House in session and make it appear the House is on the side of Hanoi." When asked by Representative Abner J. Mikva, Democrat of Illinois, planning to join the all-night discussion, if he was accusing him of being an emissary of Hanoi, Mr. Hays replied: "No, I think you're just an unwitting tool, just loaning yourself to their designs."[33]

In a major policy shift, but reinforcing a long-held belief of black people, Whitney Young, head of the Urban League, bitterly denounced the war and called for its quick end. As if speaking for the whole black population and all other groups who had not yet achieved the living standard of the world's most advanced nation, he "criticized the war as a 'moral and spiritual drain' that diverted the nation from 'the urban and racial crisis—at the very time that the crisis is at a flash point' "; announced his support for the Moratorium; declared his conviction that the war had an extra dimension for black people, who suffered doubly and died abroad for freedoms denied them at home; said blacks and other poor people lost more from the war than all other groups; and added that if the nation wished to win credibility before the world as a democracy, it must get out of the war. The war had twisted America's soul and created a disastrous drain upon our resources:

Millions go to bed hungry in America every night. Our black ghettos are wastelands. The urgent needs of our rural black people remain shamefully neglected. Our young people—black and white—are in revolt.

We must turn away from Vietnam. We must terminate this war as soon as possible. We must pour our vital resources back into our own land, our own cities, our own people.[34]

Although a few optimists felt at this time the enemy was on the run, pacification was progressing, and Saigon would soon be able to take over the war and prevent a Communist victory, a swelling number of pessimists, cynics, and war critics urged the United States government to cut its losses and turn the burden of the fighting over to Saigon immediately but without causing a collapse of the morale of South Vietnam and its army. However, whether optimist or pessimist, few supported the unilateral cease-fire proposals which a minority of lawmakers of both parties favored in mid-October 1969.

The most extreme and persistent critics of the war advanced several arguments for such a one-sided cease-fire. They argued that since we had officially admitted already that we no longer pressed for a military victory, as such a victory was not feasible, a cease-fire would reduce our casualties. It might bring reciprocal action from the enemy, who just might accept a de facto cease-fire while actually refusing to negotiate a formal one. If the enemy failed to respond to our concession, he would then bear the blame for continuing the war, and this would greatly enhance our moral position before the world. In any case, it could always be terminated if it failed to affect enemy tactics or if it put our forces at a serious disadvantage. At least it was worth taking the gamble.

The opposition to such a unilateral cease-fire came from the Pentagon, the White House, and a wide variety of hawks. The White House echoed the common view that while we ceased the enemy would fire—as he had already demonstrated on so many occasions, the best-known being the 1968 Tet surprise offensive in the midst of a suspension proclaimed by both sides. The general objection to unilateral action was that if Hanoi and the Vietcong troops used, as many believed they would, the cease-fire as a cover to launch a nationwide offensive, they might create such tragic results as to break the spirit of South Vietnam and lead to a clamor inside the United States for an immediate pullout as quickly as possible. Even should the enemy fail to mount an all-out offensive, a series of small hit-and-run attacks could sharply increase our casualty rates. If such raids were insignificant enough, however frequent and destructive they might be, a case might be made that perhaps Hanoi could not control the actions of so many small and local Vietcong units, indigenous to South Vietnam. Hence the blame for ending the cease-fire might then fall upon the United States rather than Hanoi.

On the other hand, should the enemy respect the cease-fire with the Americans and then concentrate the full weight of his assaults upon ARVN units which did not feel bound by ties to the United States and its self-restraint, it might drive a wedge between the allies and undermine Saigon's will to fight. This could destroy all possibility of making a success of our rising strategy of Vietnamization of the war and entirely erase the ARVN's morale. In any case, most military men felt that South Vietnam was not yet able to take over the full burden of the war. They welcomed any reduction in the level of the war that might lower our losses and increase Saigon's chances of gaining control of the countryside. They had long ago abandoned the search-and-destroy principle in favor of the policy of protective reaction.

By midsummer 1970 Nixon's and Kissinger's proposal for a cease-fire in place was adopted policy. This meant we had dropped our demand that Hanoi withdraw its forces from South Vietnam.[35] It was a significant switch in American policy, which hitherto had called for mutual withdrawal, and it was another step in our retreat. Asked to explain the switch, Kissinger seemed evasive. He said he was not abandoning the principle of mutual withdrawal, but then noted that "a lot depends on how you define 'mutuality.'" Such an answer failed to hide the fact that we had yielded a long and strongly held position. Even such a retreat as this, however, failed at that time to impress North Vietnam. Although enemy troops could obviously remain in the South while ours left, Hanoi insisted that Washington guarantee its political victory in the South before it would permit us to withdraw "with honor."[36] As late as May 1972, Le Duc Tho was still pushing for the maximum—that is for American help in ousting Thieu and in organizing a coalition government that would exclude Thieu. Kissinger described this proposal as "the imposition, under the thinnest veneer, of a Communist government." That we would never do.[37]

The distinguished Citizens Committee for Peace with Freedom in Vietnam declared disengagement was feasible only if accompanied by Saigon's demonstrated capacity to defend itself and if it were not forced prematurely by a war-weary American public opinion. Its founders in 1967 included ex-presidents Truman and Eisenhower, and its chairman was former Senator Paul H. Douglas of Illinois. It had a most distinguished membership. The committee declared that any abrupt pullout of our forces by any specific early date or a unilateral cease-fire such as Clark Clifford, Arthur Goldberg, Senators Mansfield, Muskie, and Scott proposed would be a windfall for the enemy and give him full possession of positions he now occupied only fitfully by terror; it would represent a sellout and encourage the victors to undertake additional Vietnams and other similar wars of "liberation."

Anticipating presidential arguments to come, the distinguished Citizens Committee for Peace declared that either a premature withdrawal or cease-fire would put us on the road to defeat with disastrous results:

South Vietnam would be taken over by the Communist North. A blood bath would follow and, based on Hanoi's past performance, hundreds of thousands of South Vietnamese who have fought at our side would be slaughtered.

America's word and leadership would be sharply devalued throughout the world. Every treaty that we have made, every agreement and commitment that we have entered into would be looked upon with suspicion by those countries who have counted on them.

The development of freedom and democracy would be reversed in Southeast Asia, and slowed in Africa and even Latin America. Peaceful methods of social and economic change would be downgraded and violent methods encouraged. A huge part of the world would be increasingly vulnerable to Communist subversion and control.

The effectiveness of the new "wars of liberation" would be confirmed. An open invitation to expanded use of the guerrilla technique of conquest would be extended to those contemplating aggression against their neighbors and ideological competitors.

India, Japan and even Australia would be under increasing pressure to develop nuclear weapons for their own protection. With the proliferation of these weapons, the risks of miscalculation would grow and the chances of a third world war would increase.

. . . There would be bitter recriminations here in the United States once the full significance of our defeat had been perceived. Prejudice, scapegoat-seeking and intolerance would flourish. And the lesson of the success of violent guerrilla tactics to bring about change would not be lost on those who seek to use violence to effect social change here at home.[38]

The committee further hoped we might reverse our regrettable practice of putting our worst foot forward and present a more balanced view of the war. In the past we had showed the destructive capacity of our own weapons and the tragic incidents of the war inflicted by our side only, but had devoted too little attention to the sufferings and deaths of our allies caused by the Communists, who had committed the most inhuman practices, not only against our soldiers, but inexcusably against civilians—old and young.[39] Battle deaths did not compare with the senseless murder of thousands of helpless civilians.

On October 13, 1969, the president took the unusual step of announcing that he would speak to the nation November 3 in an effort to convince the people he was determined to withdraw from Vietnam, but he noted that he would not fix a timetable or set an exact deadline, which more and more Americans were demanding. Only by setting such a date, they declared, could he quiet the opposition and gain popular support for his peace program, secure Russian assistance for his peace efforts in Hanoi, and put the necessary pressure upon Saigon to do more in its own behalf.[40] Although the refusal to reveal a departure date kept from the enemy any information about our intentions, it had its negative implications. Those favoring an open withdrawal date declared that nondisclosure lulled the South Vietnamese into a false sense of security. Saigon politicians would not press for reforms, broaden their political base, seek compromises for peace or do anything much as long as they could count on our continued presence and protection. Their generals believed that at least two hundred and fifty thousand American troops would remain there for several years. That number would be required to preserve a "balance of forces," without which South Vietnam could not last long against any major enemy effort. Nothing would put the heat on these militarists as much as our setting a definite and final departure date, the sooner the better. Both Thieu and Ky still talked of the imprudence and impossibility of total withdrawal of all American forces in 1970 or soon thereafter.

Also the lack of a definite date would fail to persuade Americans in Vietnam and people everywhere that we sincerely meant to withdraw. To those in Vietnam withdrawal seemed far away and unreal. Terence Smith of the *New York Times* reported that they refused to begin planning a return home, "to work themselves out of a job," to reduce efforts and personnel. Even our highest ranking officials, who understood retreat was inevitable, found the situation more bearable as long as there was no definite date of departure. Some may have retained hopes of a reversal, a possible ultimate victory or a Korean solution. Too many anticipated a long drawn-out process of footdragging rather than a quick response to the popular impulse to pull out. The policy of nondisclosure, many declared, fostered the illusion that there was no urgent need to speed our departure or for South Vietnam to do anything—now.[41]

On October 18, 1969, Kissinger privately returned to Harvard Square to seek the advice of his old colleagues, perhaps to reestablish rapport with a distinguished group he greatly esteemed. It was painful for the rising diplomat, Marvin and Bernard Kalb wrote. His university friends had given Nixon the "six months" Kissinger had requested and more to achieve a peace, an extrication with honor, but the war had continued with no end still in sight. They made clear in positive terms their great disappointment. And some gave him the greatest insult possible when they compared his role with Nixon to that of Walt Rostow with Johnson. One colleague called the war "immoral," to which Kissinger snapped in anger, advising his friends "not to oppose the technicians of power by becoming technicians of morality." They urged him virtually unanimously to persuade Nixon to devise concrete peace proposals and as a minimum to reveal a fixed timetable for our total withdrawal. It was all in vain.[42]

Nixon's advisers thought the case against a fixed and publicized withdrawal more persuasive. Let the enemy worry and run some risks. A timetable, designed to satisfy impatient critics here, would seriously undermine the South Vietnamese government. If drawn out too long or long enough to reassure Saigon, it would only provoke additional or continued attacks here. A massive withdrawal announcement would both impair the morale of our forces in Vietnam and most certainly erase any incentive Hanoi might have to negotiate seriously at all. Also Nixon's three conditions for withdrawal rested upon factors that were not precisely predictable: the level of enemy action, the progress of the Paris peace talks, and the rate of improvement of the ARVN's capacity to replace us. These were the same reasons why Nixon in the spring of 1969 had decided to order troop withdrawals only one step at a time and committed himself to no more than three months ahead. The Pentagon had contingency plans that went well beyond that and scheduled withdrawals of possibly two hundred and fifty thousand men over the next year to eighteen months. The president wished to leave the timing flexible and ambiguous in order to be able to take periodic account of Hanoi's conduct, its attitude toward negotiations, its actions on the battlefield, the ARVN's capacity for self-defense, and the likely need to keep feeding an impatient American public's desire to disengage rapidly. This policy, initially decided upon in the spring of 1969 when higher hopes of successful negotiation prevailed, seemed no longer adequate to quell popular restlessness. The November speech was designed in part to help achieve that result.[43]

On the eve of his speech a survey of world opinion revealed that anti-United States feeling abroad was declining, that our beginning of a phased withdrawal and the feeling that the war was ending had taken the issue out of the headlines. In fact, public opinion surveys showed a growing indifference to the war. Not for years had a president been so free from harsh criticism abroad, though plagued by it at home. Although friendly and neutral governments and peoples wished to see the war ended as soon as possible, there was no pressure for a "bug out"; rather there was an obvious desire for an orderly disengagement that would prevent any sudden disruption of international patterns. Our foreign friends believed that instead of being hurt by an early withdrawal, as so many officials in the United States feared, our prestige would be enhanced by it. Although the countries nearest to China and North Vietnam strongly opposed any hasty retreat, any crash withdrawals that would spread panic over vast regions, those more distant, like Japan and Indonesia, had little fear of a gradual withdrawal.

The Japanese, a Tokyo correspondent wrote, did not believe in the domino theory and would feel no alarm if we left Vietnam; rather, they would deem it a correction of "a well-intentioned but dangerous mistake." India wanted all hostilities ended immediately, all foreign forces withdrawn and a popular coalition government established. However, India hoped the United States would continue to make its presence felt in Asia—perhaps within some Asian security system.

With Mansfield prodding him to enter a cease-fire and the Pentagon more strongly opposing it; with the student Moratorium protest against the war ringing in his ears, however much he attempted to close them while watching a football game; with the bitter debate raging between hawks and doves everywhere and the rising antiwar protest over the nation, Nixon wrote his speech for November 3. His early announcement on October 13 of his intention to make the speech led many to believe it was an attempt to disarm the protesters and defuse the effect of the Vietnam Moratorium. Others said the timing of the message so close to some state and local elections indicated a Republican desire to calm the fears among the voters and contribute to a political victory in the election. Perhaps even more important, the speech may have been scheduled to give the president a chance to answer or upstage Fulbright's Vietnam hearings. The White House may have wanted the last word. Rogers and Laird had an excuse to request a delay in their appearance before the committee. Thus, Mansfield, Aiken, and Fulbright decided to postpone the hearings altogether until the president could redefine, possibly change, his policy.

In his November 3 speech the president sought to spell out in full and sharp detail his peace policies and to erase the popular confusion, doubt, and uncertainty over his objectives and tactics. He reviewed the situation he faced on inauguration day January 20, 1969. The war had by then lasted four years; thirty-one thousand Americans had been killed in battle; the ARVN training program was behind schedule; five hundred and forty thousand Americans were in Vietnam; no progress had been made at Paris; and no comprehensive peace proposal had even been suggested by us.[44] He was well aware of the choices before him and of the wide dissension in the country, whichever option he might select.

Politically, immediate and total withdrawal would have been a popular and easy course to take. His predecessor had taken us into the war: "I could blame the defeat which would be the result of my action on him and come out the peacemaker." This ignored actions of Truman, Eisenhower, and Kennedy. Some quite bluntly told him this was the only way to avoid allowing "Johnson's War" to become "Nixon's War," but he said that he had a greater obligation than to the politics of the next election. Rather he had to think of the effects of his decision on future generations and the peace of the world. The question at issue was not whether some wanted peace and others war. The real question was: "How can we win America's peace?"[45]

In a brief reference to the origins of the war and his former association with Eisenhower, he admitted that he could not deny political and even personal responsibility for his support of decisions then taken, but that was not the question before us now. The only question to be answered was: What is the best way to end the involvement? To him, our hasty pullout would be a disaster for the South Vietnamese, the United States, and the cause of peace. For South Vietnam it would inevitably permit the Communists to repeat the massacres which accompanied their takeover in 1954, when they "murdered more than fifty thousand people and hundreds of thousands more died in slave labor camps." As further evidence, he cited the enemy massacres at Hue in the Tet offensive of 1968, when during "a bloody reign of terror three thousand civilians were clubbed, shot to death, and buried in mass graves." Our sudden collapse would see the pattern followed over all South Vietnam, and especially for the "million and a half Catholic refugees who fled to South Vietnam when the Communists took over in the North."[46]

For the United States a pullout would destroy all confidence in our leadership everywhere, he maintained. Three former presidents had "recognized the great stakes involved in Vietnam and understood what had to be done." Kennedy had sought a stable government. Nixon also believed strongly in that. In his opinion, for us to withdraw would mean collapse in South Vietnam and in Southeast Asia. It was the domino theory once again, and just as Truman said of Korea, Eisenhower and Kennedy of South Vietnam, and Kennedy of Berlin, Nixon now said, "We're going to stay there." Johnson had taken the same view. For the future of world peace, any "precipitate withdrawal would be a disaster of immense magnitude." No nation could remain great if it betrayed its allies and disappointed its friends. Our defeat and humiliation would promote recklessness among the great powers still bent on world conquest; most likely it would also spark violence against our interests in Berlin, the Middle East, and eventually "even in the Western Hemisphere." Ultimately this would cost far more lives. It would bring not peace, but more war.[47]

The Munich analogy still echoed; aggression has a voracious appetite which inevitably grows until stopped by superior and determined force. Although he initiated a pursuit of peace on many fronts, he later repeated earlier warnings that the consequences of a precipitous withdrawal would mean a loss of allied confidence in us, and, even worse, would lead us to lose confidence in ourselves:

Oh, the immediate reaction would be a sense of relief that our men were coming home. But as we saw the consequences of what we had done, inevitable remorse and divisive recrimination would scar our spirit as a people.[48]

In a review of his steps to date, he recalled his television speech of May 14, another before the United Nations, and his statements on other occasions in which he had outlined our peace efforts. We had, he declared, "offered the complete withdrawal of all outside force within 1 year"; proposed "a cease-fire under international supervision"; suggested "free elections under international supervision" with Communists sharing in the formation and conduct of the elections. Saigon had "pledged to accept the result of the election." We had not made our proposals on a take-it-or-leave-it basis. We would willingly discuss other plans. In fact, anything was negotiable but the right of the people to self-determination. At Paris, Ambassador Lodge had shown "our flexibility and good faith in 40 public meetings," but Hanoi had refused even to discuss our offers: "They demand our unconditional acceptance of their terms, which are that we withdraw all American forces immediately and unconditionally and that we overthrow the Government of South Vietnam as we leave." Nor had we limited our peace efforts to public forums and public statements, which he had for some time realized were not best suited for the settlement of this war. He had "explored every possible private avenue that might lead to a settlement."[49]

Now he proposed to disclose some of these other secret efforts for peace. He had made two private offers of a speedy and comprehensive solution, but Hanoi's replies called for "our surrender before negotiations." Since Russia supplied most of the military aid to the enemy, on many occasions he had sought Soviet assistance in launching serious negotiations. Also we had tried similar efforts with other governments having diplomatic relations with North Vietnam. A personal letter to Ho reiterating our serious desire for peace, three days before his death, brought the usual Hanoi demands. Other attempts through secret channels were not revealed because of possible future use. The effect of all our efforts since the bombing halt and since he came into office could be summed up in one sentence: "No progress whatever has been made except agreement on the shape of the bargaining table." Who was at fault? Certainly it was not the United States; nor was it the South Vietnamese government: "The obstacle is the other side's absolute refusal to show the least willingness to join us in seeking a just peace."[50]

Why this refusal? Hanoi would not negotiate while it was convinced that all it had to do was to wait for us to make one concession after another, until it won everything it wanted. Further progress waited only Hanoi's decision to talk seriously. Meanwhile, since diplomacy had failed and further efforts down that road seemed totally futile, he offered another plan "which will bring the war to an end regardless of what happens on the negotiating front." Since negotiation had failed, he now sought the Vietnamization of the war. This was his major peace plan, carefully kept secret from the public since his campaign statements of 1968. His hopes of ending the war with honor and justice rested upon the people of South Vietnam. In this way we hoped to find a successful retreat with honor to ourselves and victory for Saigon. Vietnamization, Nixon declared, more truly conformed to the shift in our foreign policy outlined at Guam on July 25, 1969, and since described generally as the Nixon Doctrine. Asian and other nations were to rely upon themselves, not upon us. Our material aid we would give, but not our combat forces.[51]

Again he declared that his doctrine was an essential element in his program to prevent future Vietnams. In explanation, he noted that we were impatient people, who preferred doing something ourselves instead of teaching others to do it. Unfortunately we had carried this trait over into our foreign policy. In both Korea and Vietnam we had supplied most of the money and materiel as well as considerable manpower to help these people preserve their freedom from Communist aggression. However, the defense of freedom was everyone's business, not just ours; but it was especially the responsibility of those peoples whose freedom was in jeopardy. Then he stated a basic principle of his future program:

In the previous administration, we Americanized the war in Vietnam. In this administration, we are Vietnamizing the search for peace.

The policy of the previous administration not only resulted in our assuming the primary responsibility for fighting the war, but even more significantly did not adequately stress the goal of strengthening the South Vietnamese so that they could defend themselves when we left.[52]

The president noted that Vietnamization began after Secretary Laird's visit to Vietnam in March, when he first ordered a substantial increase in the training and equipment of the ARVN. When the president visited General Abrams in July, new orders were drawn to accord with the new program. Now the primary purpose of our troops was to enable the ARVN to assume "full responsibility for the security of South Vietnam." Our air operations were cut by more than 20 percent. After five years of sending more men into Vietnam, we had started bringing them home. Although many retained serious doubts about the success of the Guam Doctrine, Nixon felt the ARVN had continued to make progress, shown ability to assume the burdens we had abandoned, and promised greater successes for the future. Enemy infiltration, so essential to renewed major attacks, was less than 20 percent of what it had been a year earlier. Most important to his immediate audience was his report that our casualties over the last two months had declined to the lowest point in three years.[53]

For the future, he noted, he had adopted a plan worked out in cooperation with the South Vietnamese for the complete withdrawal of all our combat troops and their replacement by ARVN forces on an orderly timetable. As Vietnamese forces became stronger our withdrawal rate could increase, but he would set no precise timetable for the obvious reason that it would remove completely enemy incentive to negotiate. He would refuse to concede anything; he would simply wait until we left and move in. So again, Nixon merely stood on his three points: progress in the Paris talks, the level of enemy activity, and the advancement of the ARVN training program. Some success was noted for the last two conditions, none for the first. Hence our chances of withdrawal were now greater than in June when we made our first estimates. This fact revealed that it was not wise to freeze our schedule of cutbacks; rather it was better to retain the flexibility of withdrawal according to changing circumstances.[54]

Again the president firmly asserted that the enemy should be warned that if he increased his actions significantly we might have to adjust accordingly our timetable as well as our response. He recalled the enemy's confusion over the bombing halt in 1968 about an understanding between us that "if we stopped the bombing of North Vietnam they would stop the shelling of cities in South Vietnam." Now he wanted to be sure the enemy did not misunderstand our withdrawal program. The reduction of our forces depended partially on the lowering of enemy activities and our casualties. He had just noted the reduced rate of infiltration, but he added a clear warning, which many chose to forget later when the April 1970 invasion of Cambodia occurred:

If the level of infiltration or our casualties increase while we are trying to scale down the fighting, it will be the result of a conscious decision by the enemy.

Hanoi could make no greater mistake than to assume that an increase in violence will be to its advantage.

This was not a threat; but he declared he would meet his responsibility for protecting our fighting men wherever they might be.[55]

In rejection of a quick and easy way out, he declared that our destiny as a great nation did not permit us to escape our responsibility:

Any hope the world has for the survival of peace and freedom will be determined by whether the American people have the moral stamina and the courage to meet the challenge of free world leadership.

Let historians not record that when America was the most powerful nation in the world we passed on the other side of the road and allowed the last hopes for peace and freedom of millions of people to be suffocated by the forces of totalitarianism.

And so tonight—to you, the great silent majority of my fellow Americans—I ask for your support.

I pledged in my campaign for the Presidency to end the war in a way that we could win the peace. I have initiated a plan of action which will enable me to keep that pledge.

The more support I can have from the American people, the sooner that pledge can be redeemed; for the more divided we are at home, the less likely the enemy is to negotiate in Paris.

Let us be united for peace. Let us also be united against defeat. Because let us understand: North Vietnam cannot defeat or humiliate the United States. Only Americans can do that.[56]

On December 15, 1969, the president felt his policy of Vietnamization was proceeding well enough to justify his announcement of a further troop cutback by April 15, 1970, of 50,000 more men—which would be a total reduction of our forces of 115,000 men. At this time he repeated his earlier warnings and told Hanoi that if its infiltration rate increased enough to endanger our forces, it would be running a serious risk. He had to report, however, that there had been no progress at all on the negotiation front. The enemy still insisted that we must withdraw all our forces immediately and abandon the Saigon government of Thieu and Ky. That humiliation the United States would not accept.[57]

At this time he announced that Ambassador Lodge had for personal reasons resigned his position as the chief of our Paris peace delegation and been temporarily replaced by his ranking subordinate, Philip Habib.[58] This step the Communists regarded as a deliberate downgrading of the Paris talks, and they soon withdrew their leading delegate and accused the United States of a shameful effort to sabotage the peace entirely. Not until July 1970 did the president replace Lodge with one of our most experienced diplomats, David K. E. Bruce, a Democrat.

In his December 15 speech announcing the troop cutback, the president revealed he had consulted Sir Robert Thompson, the British expert on guerrilla warfare. Described as one of the architects of victory over the Communist guerrillas in Malaya in the 1950s and author of the book *No Exit from Vietnam,* Sir Robert expressed considerable pessimism about our conduct of the war. Especially he denounced our failure to prepare the South Vietnamese to assume responsibility for their own defense. The president secretly sent Sir Robert to Vietnam to make a firsthand and confidential report on the war; after five weeks of intensive study, he had made, said the president, "several very constructive recommendations. . . ."[59]

Although for security reasons he refused to reveal the suggestions, he did note some of Sir Robert's conclusions. Sir Robert had found the military and political situation much advanced since his last visit, especially in the area of security. He noted that we had achieved a position that would enable us to obtain a just peace whether negotiated or not, and to maintain "an independent, non-Communist South Vietnam. . . ." He added: "We are in a psychological period where the greatest need is confidence. A steady application of the 'do it yourself' concept with continuing U.S. support in the background will increase the confidence already shown by many South Vietnamese leaders."[60]

The president found this advice in line with his own attitude and with reports received from others. One disturbing new development was the report of increased enemy infiltration; this explained his earlier warning but, he believed, was not enough to justify the postponement of further cutbacks. Finally, he expressed his personal appreciation for the popular approval of his peace policy and especially the approval of the House of Representatives, in which both Democrats and Republicans had noted their support by an overwhelming majority of 334 to 55.[61]

In the months ahead the Nixon administration repeated frequently its offer of peace through negotiation or turned to its rising reliance upon Vietnamization. In his annual State of the Union Message to Congress of January 22, 1970, Nixon declared our policies were now based on the world

as it is, not as it was 25 years ago at the conclusion of World War II. Many of the policies which were necessary and right then are obsolete today.

Then, because of America's overwhelming military and economic strength, because of the weakness of other major free world powers and the inability of scores of newly independent nations to defend, or even govern, themselves, America had to assume the major burden for the defense of freedom in the world.[62]

On February 18, 1970, in the first issue of an annual foreign affairs message to Congress, President Nixon broadly expanded this theme and offered his peace program for the whole world under the title, "United States Foreign Policy for the 1970's: A New Strategy for Peace."[63] He began by quoting from his Air Force Academy commencement speech of June 4, 1969:

A Nation needs many qualities, but it needs faith and confidence above all. Skeptics do not build societies; the idealists are the builders. Only societies that believe in themselves can rise to their challenges. Let us not, then, pose a false choice between meeting our responsibilities abroad and meeting the needs of our people at home. We shall meet both or we shall meet neither.

He believed we had entered a new era; the postwar period in world relations had ended.

He continued:

Then, we were the only great power whose society and economy had escaped World War II's massive destruction. Today, the ravages of that war have been overcome. Western Europe and Japan have recovered their economic strength, their political vitality, and their national self-confidence. . . .

Then, new nations were being born, often in turmoil and uncertainty. Today, these nations have a new spirit and a growing strength of independence. Once, many feared that they would become simply a battleground of cold-war rivalry and fertile ground for Communist penetration. But this fear misjudged their pride in their national identities and their determination to preserve their newly won sovereignty.

Then, we were confronted by a monolithic Communist world. Today, the nature of that world has changed—the power of individual Communist nations has grown, but international Communist unity has been shattered. Once a unified bloc, its solidarity has been broken by the powerful forces of nationalism. The Soviet Union and Communist China, once bound by an alliance of friendship, had become bitter adversaries by the mid-1960's. The only times the Soviet Union has used the Red Army since World War II have been against its own allies—in East Germany in 1953, in Hungary in 1956, and in Czechoslovakia in 1968. The Marxist dream of international Communist unity has disintegrated.

Then, the United States had a monopoly or overwhelming superiority of nuclear weapons. Today, a revolution in the technology of war has altered the nature of the military balance of power. New types of weapons present new dangers. Communist China has acquired thermonuclear weapons. Both the Soviet Union and the United States have acquired the ability to inflict unacceptable damage on the other, no matter which strikes first. . . .

Then, the slogans formed in the past century were the ideological accessories of the intellectual debate. Today, the "isms" have lost their vitality—indeed the restlessness of youth on both sides of the dividing line testifies to the need for a new idealism and deeper purposes.[64]

These changes wrought by time and circumstances demanded response that differed from that of the initial postwar years. Now we must find a framework for a durable peace that did not rely so much upon a unilateral effort by the United States. The report declared that a lasting peace rested upon three basic principles:

Peace requires *partnership*. Its obligations, like its benefits, must be shared. . . .

Peace requires *strength*. So long as there are those who would threaten our vital interests and those of our allies with military force, we must be strong. American weakness could tempt would-be aggressors to make dangerous miscalculations. . . .

Peace requires a *willingness to negotiate*.[65]

Since 1945 we had in our impatience been too much inclined to do too much for others rather than to teach them to do for themselves. Under our guidance, leadership, and contributions of men and money we had undertaken to lead the world ever upward toward greater peace and prosperity. We had conceived and managed the programs, devised the strategies, and proposed them to our allies. Now the situation, much changed, left us facing a world of stronger allies, a rising community of independent nations, able and ready to deal with local disputes which once might have required our help. We no longer needed to meddle so much in the affairs of other nations.[66]

However, a more responsible participation by our friends in their own defense and progress was, he believed, a better way toward our mutual goals. Preservation of peace required us to keep our commitments, which he intended to do, but a more balanced and realistic American role was essential. For us to insist that others play a part was not a retreat from responsibility; better for us to share than dictate or single-handedly protect the rest of the world. To the whole world, we would now seek to apply these principles and policies.[67] Once more he offered all his earlier peace proposals; however, he declared we would not let Hanoi's refusal to negotiate block our path to peace through withdrawal. Although we were ready for serious peace talks, if they should fail, we would push forward with Vietnamization:

> To seek a just peace, we pursued two distinct but mutually supporting courses of action: Negotiations and Vietnamization. We want to achieve an early and fair settlement through negotiations. But if the other side refuses, we shall proceed to strengthen the South Vietnamese forces. This will allow us to replace our troops on an orderly timetable. We hope that as Vietnamization proceeds the Government of North Vietnam will realize that it has more to gain in negotiations than in continued fighting.[68]

Meanwhile all previous proposals still stood. The key to peace lay in Hanoi. We had taken the three major steps which—the war critics had assured the president—would lead to serious negotiations:

> We stopped the bombing of North Vietnam; we began the withdrawal of U.S. forces from Vietnam; and we agreed to negotiate with the National Liberation Front as one of the parties to the negotiation. But none of those moves brought about the response or the reaction which their advocates claimed.[69]

Vietnamization, he observed, was a program to strengthen the ability of the South Vietnamese government and people to defend themselves:

> It emphasizes progress in providing physical security for the Vietnamese people and in extending the authority of the South Vietnamese Government throughout the countryside.
> Vietnamization is not a substitute for negotiations, but a spur to negotiations. In strengthening the capability of the Government and the people of South Vietnam to defend themselves, we provide Hanoi with an authentic incentive to negotiate seriously now. Confronted by Vietnamization, Hanoi's

alternative to a reasonable settlement is to continue its costly sacrifices while its bargaining power diminishes.

Vietnamization has two principal components. The first is the strengthening of the armed forces of the South Vietnamese in numbers, equipment, leadership and combat skills, and overall capability. The second component is the extension of the pacification program in South Vietnam.[70]

Under this program, the report claimed, we had reversed the trend of our involvement, begun our disengagement, and witnessed an extension of the ARVN's role and capacity to defend the nation. As Saigon increased its share of the fighting and our role declined in numbers and costs, the Vietnamese would need assistance to meet the strains upon their economy. Our economic outlays might increase as our military role declined. The program anticipated sizable expansion of the pacification program. A careful evaluation of needs by a study group concluded that:

The most meaningful criteria for South Vietnamese Government success in the countryside are the establishment in each hamlet of (1) an adequate defense, and (2) a fully functioning government resident in the hamlet 24 hours a day. If the Government can achieve these two objectives, it can prevent the enemy from subverting and terrorizing the population or mobilizing it for its own purposes. The enemy will be denied any but the most limited and furtive access to the people, and will encounter increasing hostility or indifference as they seek the assistance they formerly enjoyed. The enemy forces will be isolated and forced to fight as a conventional expeditionary force, being dependent on external sources of supply and reinforcement.

This is very important: Enemy main force activities have in the past relied on active assistance from the population in the countryside for intelligence, food, money and manpower. This has enabled the enemy to use the countryside as a springboard from which to strike at key Vietnamese cities and installations. If they are forced to fight as a conventional army, with their support provided from their own resources rather than from the population, the enemy will lose momentum as they move forward because their supply lines will lengthen and they will encounter increasing opposition.

To date, the pacification program is succeeding.[71]

For Hanoi peace posed serious and complicated problems. Although not overly hopeful of success, the Nixon staff felt that allied military pressures, strains inside North Vietnam, the uncertainties of its international support, the decline of domestic and foreign anti-American sentiment, and the strengthening of the Saigon government favored a settlement. We remained fully aware, on the other hand, that Communist mistrust of our intentions before and after a settlement, their belief that continued domestic dissension and pressures would force us to withdraw ever more rapidly or make further concessions, their reliance upon political instability to bring collapse in South Vietnam, their emotional dedication to a cause they had struggled so long to achieve, and their own political weakness in the South lessened their will to negotiate. Whatever the enemy's choice, Nixon promised, we would still try to persuade Hanoi that its genuine interest lay in negotiation, and we pledged that "we shall be flexible and generous when serious negotiations start at last."[72]

The president found it continually necessary to explain and defend his Vietnam policies. The debate went on and in April 1970 increased sharply in emotional intensity when he felt it necessary suddenly and without consultation with members of Congress and others within even his own administration, to invade Cambodia at various points along its eastern border up to the imposed limit of twenty-one miles, without prior request from the new government of that little country. He defended the attack on the basis that it was needed to protect our forces while attempting to withdraw from the country. Also he noted that Hanoi's forces had been occupying border zones of Cambodia and Laos across from the Vietnamese boundaries for five years and had constantly raided Vietnam from these sanctuaries and at points were within forty-odd miles from Saigon. He claimed he had not thereby widened the war; he just officially recognized it had been a wider war all along. It had never ceased being an Indochinese war.

Unknown then was the fact that "Operation Menu," a military code name for the secret bombing of Cambodia, or precisely of North Vietnamese troop concentrations along a ten-mile-wide strip of Cambodia near South Vietnam, had been going on, Marvin and Bernard Kalb wrote, since March 18, 1969. Some thirty-six hundred B-52 sorties had been flown against enemy positions here. This had been kept secret from the American public and most members of Congress. Of course it was well known to the enemy.[73] This illegal bombing of Cambodia was one of the initial articles of impeachment drafted by the House Judiciary Committee in the summer of 1974. It was voted down.

For three years we kept bombing Cambodia, but in mid-August of 1973, after half a million tons of bombs—over twice as much as we dropped on North Vietnam during the entire Nixon administration—had been dropped, Congress forced the president to stop the bombing.[74] The enemy had jammed virtually every infiltration route southward for years and he kept it up during and after we stopped the bombing. Nixon claimed it was necessary to protect our soldiers in their withdrawal.[75] This somewhat secret and sudden attack stirred the war critics, students, and millions of Americans to new heights of frustration, anger, and bitterness and led to tragic incidents. In Ohio, national guardsmen at Kent State University fired upon student mobs who were harassing them with insults, rocks, and other weapons with the result that four students were killed and others wounded. State police fired upon students at Jackson State College in Mississippi with more deaths.

These events inspired among many a nearly total loss of faith in the sincerity of the president's search for peace and, some feared, brought the nation near to revolution and a collapse of governmental authority. The president pledged to bring our forces out of Cambodia by July 1, 1970, and made good on it, but his arguments and the fulfillment did not allay his critics. Nevertheless, he continued to justify his policies since coming to office. To rising demands that he quickly pull out of Vietnam, he answered for him it would be the easiest course; he could simply blame the whole involvement on the previous administration. Although he might survive the rest of his term of office, a pullout would have disastrous effects. Beyond the loss of 17 million people to Communist takeover and the over forty thousand American casualties, it would have almost unimaginable consequences. Then in a July 2, 1970, television interview, returning to an ancient doctrine, he said:

Now I know there are those that say well, the domino theory is obsolete. They haven't talked to the dominoes. They should talk to the Thais, Malaysians, to Singapore, to Indonesia, to the Philippines, to the Japanese and the rest. And if the United States leaves Vietnam in a way that we are humiliated or defeated not simply speaking in what are called jingoistic terms but in very practical terms this will be immensely discouraging to the 300 million people from Japan, clear around to Thailand in free Asia. And even more important, it will be ominously encouraging to the leaders of Communist China and the Soviet Union who are supporting the North Vietnamese. It will encourage them in their expansionist policies in other areas. . . .

The president doubted that in any free election the people of South Vietnam would ever accept communism, noted that people had nowhere done so, but then added that if they did so we would accept the results and that he believed the government of Thieu and Ky of Saigon would also.[76] In this lengthy and drawn-out fashion President Nixon finally announced his peace program. It was subject to the most severe examination and sharp denunciation.

The search for peace droned on without even the slightest appearance of progress through the rest of 1970. Efforts to get the talks moving in Paris repeatedly bumped against the stonewall Communist refusal to bend at all from their demand that we set an exact date—not later than mid-1971—for our total military withdrawal from South Vietnam and before leaving oust the regime of Thieu and Ky and impose a coalition government upon South Vietnam prior to any elections. We wished a political solution of the war before agreeing to such terms, but sought as soon as possible a cease-fire to be followed by serious efforts at negotiation. By mid-1970, Nixon believed our military position in South Vietnam assured us control of most of the nation in case a cease-fire could be arranged, followed by a possible partition of the country on the basis of areas then held by each side. However, we would not accept enemy terms that we oust Thieu and impose a Communist-dominated government. The Communists wanted enough time and power inside a coalition regime to permit their ultimate takeover of power through the rigging of any future elections to guarantee their victory at the polls, even with international supervision.

The alternative to these diverse proposals was continuation of the war along with our efforts at Vietnamization, which promised a prolonged war—probably renewed guerrilla style—with vastly reduced United States combat participation but with our continued support of Saigon. At Paris there remained the central problem of who should govern South Vietnam. Nixon would not pressure Thieu to agree to the enemy demand that he step aside and let a Communist-managed coalition government take over. The enemy refused to accept the Nixon-Thieu proposal to settle the issue by elections which he could not manage. Also he would not accept a cease-fire, discuss mutual withdrawal, or do anything else desired by Washington and Saigon until an agreeable political solution was in sight. Hanoi rejected a standstill cease-fire that would have left it little or no territory to govern. Thieu declared in July 1970 he was ready to discuss a "standstill cease-fire" of a temporary character, that differed from a coalition government or a permanent "leopard spot" partition of the country, but he also repeatedly declared that he would accept no coalition government with the Communists. He set three conditions for a cease-fire: its terms must be fully discussed and accepted before taking effect; it must be efficiently supervised everywhere to prevent further enemy gains; and it must be promptly followed by serious discussions directed at a final settlement. After this Saigon offer of July, proposals for a cease-fire spread. We wanted a cease-fire first and discussion later without any preconditions; the enemy would reverse that order. He still preferred to talk while fighting, in the hope that we would grow weary of the effort, further reduce our forces, and ultimately give him a victory through negotiation that he could not win by fighting.

In mid-September 1970 the Vietcong proposed: a cease-fire to be carried out after an agreement on all other points to end the war; the total withdrawal of United States and all other allied troops by June 30, 1971, with no Vietcong attacks during the withdrawal; the immediate discussion of the release of prisoners of war; the creation of a new interim provisional government, but with the immediate ouster of Thieu and the subsequent formation of a new Saigon government representative of all factions—Communist and non-Communist; that all citizens should participate under the supervision of the provisional government in forthcoming elections; ultimate reunification of North and South Vietnam to be achieved step by step, through peaceful means, without foreign interference; and full respect for the sovereignty of Cambodia and Laos. The main demands of the enemy were that there be an "end to what they termed American aggression by complete troop withdrawal and an end to the 'puppet' government in Saigon."[77]

By comparison, Nixon's 1969 proposals had suggested that an international body acceptable to both sides could supervise any cease-fires. He also recommended the gradual withdrawal of most United States and North Vietnamese forces over a twelve-month period following agreement on mutual withdrawals. Any remaining forces were not to engage in combat, and United States and allied forces were to be completely withdrawn as Hanoi's forces left South Vietnam, Cambodia, and Laos. Also we continued our efforts to obtain the earliest possible release of all prisoners of war. In 1969 and 1970 Nixon most strongly favored the fullest participation in the government of South Vietnam of all political elements that did not seek forcefully to impose any form of government. In 1969 the Vietcong favored a coalition of all "political tendencies" that stood for peace, independence, and neutrality. Nixon then and thereafter favored elections open to all who renounced the use of force, but under international supervision. On the other hand, the Vietcong had long demanded that there be no foreign interference or supervision at all and the complete freedom of the South Vietnamese themselves to manage all elections and determine their future. Nixon had no objection to eventual reunification or any decision if it truly reflected the free choice of the people of South Vietnam. His peace plans required that all Indochina—Vietnam, Cambodia, and Laos—be included in any ultimate settlement, but he declared that the neutralization of the whole region would be suitable to him if the people freely chose it.

Thus far had both sides come toward a peaceful solution by October 1970, when Nixon felt a further clarification of his objectives was necessary. On October 7th, in a much-publicized speech described—justifiably, said a *New York Times* editorial—well in advance of delivery, as a "major new initiative" for peace, he presented a far-reaching five-point peace plan.[78] It was an answer to the mid-September Vietcong eight-point plan and perhaps aimed to defuse the peaceniks and campus dissenters and hopefully help the GOP ticket in the mid-term elections of November. It sought also to take advantage of our presumed advantageous military situation in South Vietnam. The belief was widespread that our military posture was then more favorable to us than it had ever been because we thought we held vast portions of the country. The president obtained the approval of his proposals from the officials of South Vietnam, Laos, and Cambodia, he believed, because of the "remarkable success of the Vietnamization policy over the past 18 months."[79]

In this brief but significant speech he outlined his peace plan. First, he sought a cease-fire "in place" in all Indochina—meaning that all armed forces in the region would cease firing their weapons and remain in the positions they then held. It would not end the conflict, but it would happily end the killing. It would be most difficult to establish and maintain a cease-fire in such a war of guerrillas, of no front or rear lines, but he noted that an "unconventional war may require an unconventional truce." Although he put forth his proposals for a cease-fire without preconditions, he laid down certain principles that should govern it. It "must be effectively supervised by international observers, as well as by the parties themselves." Neither side should use it to increase its strength anywhere in Indochina. Rather it should cause an end to all sorts of warfare, including bombing and acts of terror as well as combat. It should also encompass the fighting not only in Vietnam but in all Indochina, inasmuch as the conflicts in the whole area were related. Nixon sought to widen the peace, not the war. Finally, the cease-fire, though it would be most difficult to maintain, should be part of the move to end the war in Indochina.[80]

Nixon proposed an international conference to deal with the three states of Indochina, since the war was of one piece and could not be settled by treating only one area. To him the essential elements of the Geneva Accords of 1954 and 1962 remained valid as the basis for a solution. While we sought such a conference, we would continue the Paris negotiations, which he declared would remain our primary forum for reaching a solution of the war until a broader international conference produced serious negotiations. The third item concerned our further troop withdrawals. He reviewed past cutbacks and anticipated further reductions in 1971 to bring the decline to about one-half the figure when he took office, and then he added significantly:

We are ready now to negotiate an agreed timetable for complete withdrawals as part of an overall settlement. We are prepared to withdraw all our forces as part of a settlement based on the principles I spelled out previously and the proposals I am making tonight.[81]

The president sought a solution that truly met the hopes of all South Vietnamese, declaring his support for three principles:

We seek a political solution that reflects the will of the South Vietnamese people.
A fair political solution should reflect the existing relationship of political forces in South Vietnam.
And we will abide by the outcome of the political process agreed upon.
Let there be no mistake about one essential point: The other side is not merely objecting to a few personalities in the South Vietnamese Government. They want to dismantle the organized non-Communist parties and insure the takeover by their party. They demand the right to exclude whomever they wish from government.
This patently unreasonable demand is totally unacceptable.
As my proposals today indicate, we are prepared to be flexible on many matters. But we stand firm for the right of all the South Vietnamese people to determine for themselves the kind of government they want.[82]

He declared we had no intention of seeking any solution other than one which fairly met the reasonable concerns of both sides, because when the conflict ended, both sides would still be there and the only settlement that would endure would be one which both sides had an interest to preserve. Finally, as a simple act of humanity, he sought an "immediate and unconditional release of all prisoners of war held by both sides," without exception or condition. He felt these proposals held great hope for mankind and might end the cycle of wars that had plagued the world since 1945 and begin a "generation of peace." He proclaimed that the search for peace was his basic objective.[83] It seems the Nixon administration here quietly dropped our long demand that Hanoi withdraw its forces from South Vietnam in reciprocity for our evacuation.

In his recent talks with world leaders, although he discovered men who did not agree with all our policies, he found no world leaders who feared we would use our "power to dominate another country or destroy its independence. We can be proud that this is the cornerstone of America's foreign policy." The finest legacy we could leave from this era when we were the strongest nation on earth would be that "our power was used to defend freedom, not to destroy it; to preserve the peace, not to break the peace." Finally, he asked Hanoi to respond to his plan in the same spirit: "Let us give our children what we have not had during this century, a chance to enjoy a generation of peace."[84]

Thus ended another public exchange of peace proposals between Hanoi and Washington. It seemed another exercise in futility. If we accepted Hanoi's latest offer, eventually communism would rule everywhere in Indochina. The enemy bluntly rejected our entire package in the belief that time was on their side; no concessions were necessary; our withdrawal would proceed in any case; and their acceptance would prolong and complicate their chances of takeover. Most Americans and their allies and friends everywhere praised the "new offer," termed it a far-reaching effort for peace. The cease-fire offer showed a willingness to accept the status quo and a coalition regime on the basis of a standstill at present positions. This was realistic, since any compromise solution would have to reflect the existing political forces. Implied clearly was a fixed timetable for our total withdrawal, probably within one year of the agreement. Nor did Nixon insist upon the winner-take-all elections, required by earlier proposals, but rather stressed the importance of a negotiated solution by a return to a Geneva-type world conference. This was deemed proof of a flexible and realistic approach. Although we did not exclude a measure of Communist participation and eventual total withdrawal, we bluntly rejected enemy proposals that we immediately dump the three top leaders of Saigon and withdraw all our forces and the allied forces from South Vietnam. In fact, beyond popular self-determination, there were no preconditions in the plan; the steps to be taken, the methods used, and all else remained to be negotiated freely. The insurmountable problem was that the enemy demanded our total surrender to his program before the beginning of negotiations.

Observers expressed serious doubts about the possible success of any leopard-spot division of the country. Both sides claimed control of the same sections—one by day, the other by night. Control of disputed areas would certainly be a major problem for negotiation. Such a jigsaw puzzle, one United States official declared, became more complicated the closer you looked at it. Would a standstill cease-fire mean that enemy units could keep the areas they occupied? Could they fly their flag there? Would all enemy forces, including underground leaders, have to emerge and be identified? Would Hanoi's regulars, whose presence in the South the North Vietnamese officials had never admitted, be allowed to receive supplies from the North, or would Saigon have to feed and supply them? Would Hanoi be held responsible for terrorist attacks that might violate the cease-fire? Did it have the power or would it really try to exercise control over the often stubborn and independent Vietcong? Would the regime of Thieu and Ky, which had so often pledged not to cede an "inch of South Vietnamese territory to the Communists," accept any leopard-spot solution which would allow the enemy forces permanently to control the areas they occupied at the time of any agreement? If a cease-fire were declared, who held what and where? By the latest figures, challenged by critics, 92.8 percent of South Vietnam's 18 million people lived in hamlets deemed to be under secure government control. This figure was the highest one claimed since we entered the war in 1965. Only 6.5 percent of the people lived under hamlets controlled by or easily accessible to the enemy. The enemy held more ground than population, but it was in desolate mountain and forest areas.[85] Also, would not such an arbitrary acceptance of such a division of land, people, and power, without popular consent, violate the oft-proclaimed principle of self-determination?

Nixon's advisers and aides declared that the military situation, not the November elections, spurred the peace offer. No matter that the enemy professed quite falsely and dangerously to believe the disappointing election returns repudiated Nixon and his policies, in truth the nation backed Nixon's peace proposal and his planned withdrawal from the war overwhelmingly. Our military situation, his aides declared, now justified our offers:

They contend that this is the first time in the long history of the war in Indochina that the United States could safely accept the risk of a standstill cease fire in the war zone. By this they mean that the American and South Vietnamese forces have finally gained the upper hand in the most important and populated sectors of South Vietnam and that a cease-fire, according to all their studies, would enable them to retain, and perhaps even extend, that position.[86]

Prolonged studies of the previous six months revealed, so officials in Washington and Saigon believed, that the southern half of South Vietnam could be effectively managed by allied forces without major battles against enemy forces. A cease-fire had many advantages. It would prevent an enemy reconstruction of its disrupted bases in Cambodia; it would deny him the right to infiltrate new men and supplies; it would block the further use of his forces against regions anywhere, especially near those areas where he was strongest; it would, of course, end the shooting, and that would greatly enhance Nixon's image as a peacemaker here and abroad; it would give Saigon the lion's share of military and political power over the populated regions of South Vietnam, without any sacrifice of its present governmental personnel; and it would not require our withdrawal prior to political settlement, nor would it bring the dumping of Thieu and Ky, unless by popular desire through negotiation or some election.[87] It did not really offer the enemy much, in view of his long effort to obtain full control of the country, and the only alternative held out was the continuation of the war through the further progress of the program of Vietnamization. Both Russia and Hanoi promptly declared the Nixon plan totally unacceptable.

In spite of such a rejection, doves pretended to see progress toward peace in the exchanges of September and October 1970. They believed both schemes concealed more than they revealed about the kind of deal either side would entertain to end the war. They noted optimistically that while heretofore neither side had been willing to propose or discuss a cease-fire, now both sides proposed formally to negotiate the issue. However, gaps prevented serious and meaningful diplomacy. The enemy continued to seek a settlement that amounted to total defeat of the United States and its allies in a war he certainly had not won. Hanoi wanted our acceptance of its proposals even before negotiations or a cease-fire could begin. It declared we must end our "aggression" against Vietnam by complete troop withdrawal and also put an end to the "puppet" government in Saigon, before negotiations could start. There was no give-and-take in its peace program; it was the surrender, not a peace of compromise, position it demanded from the first moment it came to Paris. Hanoi insisted that a cease-fire and subsequent negotiations must follow the establishment of a coalition regime in South Vietnam, while Nixon still felt a cease-fire should come first, and the nature of the Saigon government should be later determined by free elections under international supervision. Washington realized that Hanoi confronted the ugly problem of whether to risk acceptance of elections, which by Washington's estimate would find the Communists controlling but 15 percent of the eligible voters.

Thus the peace talks in Paris, even at a snail's pace, had reduced the negotiations nominally to two issues, and substantially to but one. The United States decision to withdraw was irrevocable, and in the Nixon five-point plan—so Washington officials believed—withdrawal would be possible within one year. That Communist demand was certainly no longer a major roadblock, but the real roadblock was the enemy demand that Washington impose a new coalition government upon Saigon and set in motion a scheme as old as Communist history by which all power would eventually gravitate into Communist hands. That asked too much of Washington. Washington let it be known that we would not do Hanoi's dirty work. Once in supporting Diem we had intervened with disastrous results. Hanoi now hoped to destroy the Thieu regime, then use the method of proportional representation in elections which it could not dominate but by rigging which it could surely obtain an influential enough minority to claim key ministerial posts. From these positions in time it could undermine the Saigon regime and seize all power. No matter what the enemy plan or hopes were, Nixon flatly refused to betray the Saigon regime. If by popular elections democratically conducted such an unwanted result might eventually follow, we would regretfully accept it, but we would not ourselves guarantee it before negotiations or a cease-fire could be obtained.

The stalemate appeared doomed to continue—no one knew how long—but there were some futile expectations that possibly Saigon's scheduled elections for mid-1971 might produce a post-Thieu government acceptable to Communist negotiators. Little hope was expressed that outside powers such as Russia, England, or France could persuade Hanoi to accept private talks. However, Saigon's increasing efficiency in replacing American soldiers, demonstrated in the Cambodian venture and later, revealed that Vietnamization might work. Communist military victory after our departure was not a certainty. Washington hoped Saigon could create a structure strong enough to prevent defeat before we finally withdrew, and Hanoi apparently sought to hold off any settlement until it had one more military crack at smashing the Saigon system.

Hanoi's emphatic rejection, within twenty-four hours, of the Nixon peace plan jolted the hopes of millions. Enemy denunciation came even before the American people had a chance to react to the offer. Although any leopard-spot cease-fire posed great difficulties for Hanoi, such a response was puzzling. The offer and such a quick rejection certainly weakened the domestic opposition to the Nixon war effort. Since the American people generally praised the proposal as the best one possible, the war was scarcely a factor in the November elections. Both parties approved the official proposals, and Hanoi's reaction was disappointing to most Americans. James B. Reston suggested that perhaps the refusal could be explained on grounds that the enemy had fought so long against foreign invaders that he could not distinguish Americans from former Chinese, French, and Japanese conquerors. Few Communists could understand why Americans would sacrifice so much and then offer to give it all up for virtually nothing but peace. The Vietcong surely wondered how a guerrilla army, dispersed over broad areas and fed by terrorizing the local population, could be kept together for a long time without new supplies. How could Nixon's plan for a fair political solution, that reflected "the existing relationship of political forces" in South Vietnam, be possible under the Thieu regime?[88]

However, the enemy might have realized that Nixon and vast numbers of hawks inside the United States had long believed that an American base in Vietnam was essential to the security of the Pacific, surely a need not reduced by the fact that the British base at Singapore was vanishing, powerful forces were pressing us to evacuate bases in Japan, Okinawa and the Philippines, and our retreat from empire had been steadily progressing since 1945. Yet, in spite of urgent demands upon the president to retain some fifty thousand men in Vietnam, maintain the great base at Camranh Bay and the air base at Danang, Washington nevertheless offered withdrawal of all troops and the possibility of an eventual acceptance of a coalition government representative of all political elements in South Vietnam. Further rejection of such an offer and continued attempts to humiliate the United States revealed Hanoi's ignorance of the American people and risked for the Communists a prolonged hostile presence in their country. This was a situation the Vietnamese for a thousand years had sought and fought to evade.[89]

In response to changing reality, which had first led Johnson to halt the bombing, retire from politics, and dedicate his last year in office to the search for peace, Nixon's withdrawal, negotiation, and Vietnamization efforts— whatever else they might be called—were in substance the beginning of a retreat from the high position of global responsibility which we had assumed after 1945. The American people and their government here backed away from total commitment and found a policy for transition that gave priority to a narrow rather than broad definition of vital United States interests. Here we scaled down our ambitions to match our capacities, not to promote a new isolationism, but to prevent it. Nixon meant no random disengagement, but rather a more credible, selective, and acceptable commitment. The key line, Max Frankel of the *New York Times* astutely observed, was: "We are not involved in the world because we have commitments; we have commitments because we are involved. Our interests must shape our commitments, rather than the other way around."[90] Nixon sought to find a way to step back from Johnson's automatic and unqualified claims of unavoidable commitment as in Vietnam and the Dominican Republic and also took a "long stride back" from Kennedy's efforts to save freedom on earth, to " 'pay any price, bear any burden, meet any hardship, support any friend, oppose any foe to assure the survival and the success of liberty'—anywhere around the world."

He sought to retire with honor some maxims we had cherished since 1945, some which even he had once defended, such as the belief that global and monolithic communism menaced the world and could be frustrated only by the military and economic power of the United States. Although we abhorred tyranny, aggression, poverty, and racism, we could not be the policeman, fireman, protector "against every injustice everywhere." We would have to focus our efforts on protecting our greatest interests, especially peace among the great powers, while other countries must shoulder their share of the burden. Our help would not require us to keep telling our friends what to do or to do it the American way. We would not offer our formulas for union in Western Europe nor our blueprint for democracy in South Vietnam. In fact, he did not even mention the SEATO and CENTO treaties, which the last Republican administration had launched.

CHAPTER SIX

NIXON'S DILEMMA:
COMPROMISE OR SURRENDER,
1971-1972

In the election campaign of 1968, President Nixon stated he had a plan to end the war and pledged to the American people that if elected he would achieve this objective. He admitted that if he failed to do it, he would quite properly be ousted in the election of 1972. From the very beginning of his administration he worked harder than the public knew to reach his goal. Privately and publicly he tested the enemy's sincerity and offered to discuss virtually every possible road to peace. All his gestures met rebuff, but his critics incessantly attacked him for not making concessions, which he had sometimes already offered only to have them rejected with added insult. He sought compromise while both our ally and enemy demanded a total victory. That was one of his many dilemmas.

Antiwar forces inside the United States and the enemy continually pressed Nixon to withdraw, stop the bombing, set a fixed time for withdrawal, totally cut off all economic and military aid to the Thieu regime, and accept a coalition government—all of which spelled certain defeat for Saigon and humiliation for the United States. Hanoi and the Vietcong had not won the war but they expected us to stop Vietnamization, deny aid to Saigon, and—to get back our POWs—impose, before we left, a Communist government upon South Vietnam. The enemy asked us to do what he alone could not soon or easily do. The advice of the critics was: accept defeat and appease a most evil force. The result would invite unforeseen troubles for us and the world. Nixon could reduce our involvement and the casualties and costs, but he could not, except by diplomacy, secure the return of the POWs. He could not satisfy his critics and defeatists at home without abandoning an ally and writing off nearly fifty thousand lives, billions of dollars, and commitments and interests which millions of Americans had long defended as essential. He could not have a peace or honest compromise by negotiation with an enemy whose vital interests in victory were immensely greater than ours and whose leaders were determined to win, at no matter what the cost. He could not win the war in any military sense without the grave risk of total world war and a tremendous escalation of our involvement with men, materiel, and nuclear weapons, which the American public and world opinion would find too horrible to contemplate. Nixon had few options. Compromise seemed impossible. Full force was unacceptable. An uncertain Vietnamization was about all he had left, except surrender, which he vowed never to accept. So after years of public and private effort the future in 1969 appeared to offer only more of the same: limited war to stave off defeat; continued aid—material, naval, and aerial—without combat ground forces; and Vietnamization of the war—in other words, protracted warfare, which the enemy might not accept as he resorted to a more conventional war in 1972.

Hopes of negotiation were dim, but our diplomatic efforts continued. In his coming trips to Communist capitals in 1972, the president welcomed any assistance he could get from Peking and Moscow, but did not count on it. The Communists, he noted in his press conference of November 12, 1971, were unwilling to separate the issue of the return of our war prisoners from the many other problems, but he pressed especially for a negotiated release of prisoners because that was the only way we could ever get them back. Meanwhile, pending a final solution of these and other problems, we would have to retain a residual force, numbers not specified, primarily to use as leverage for the release of the prisoners and to prevent a Communist takeover of South Vietnam. Both of these objectives, he hoped, could be obtained by negotiation; but if that was not possible, we would take another route, not then made known. Further withdrawals would depend upon the three conditions announced earlier: enemy activity, especially increased infiltration, that might endanger our shrinking forces; advance in the Vietnamization program; and any progress made on the release of our prisoners of war. He ignored the third factor frequently offered before—the progress of the Paris peace talks. When asked if he planned to keep a residual force of approximately fifty thousand troops in Vietnam until the prisoners of war issue was settled, the president stated that a negotiated settlement would mean a total withdrawal of our forces, the end of our air strikes, and the withdrawal of our forces stationed elsewhere in Asia in support of the combat forces in Vietnam. A negotiated settlement would allow us to leave and presumably would end all need for our further military aid to South Vietnam.[1]

Throughout the Vietnam involvement there were problems of freedom and national self-determination. Westerners have fairly standardized concepts of these terms. Therefore, when official Washington so frequently asserted that we were fighting to establish and preserve the right of self-determination for the people of that little country, Americans naturally assumed that we were trying to establish our system there. When that proved difficult, if not impossible in any immediate sense—and this fact finally hit us—we suffered a sense of deception and sharp disillusionment with the whole adventure. The war thus lost for many all morality and became a defenseless fraud.

Although Western freedom had never existed in the Orient, somehow we trusted—and some believed—that out of our vast investment major strides toward freedom were being made. Previous presidents wanted to contain communism and strengthen freedom everywhere. However, while they urged liberal reform, they never fixed any timetable for achieving it, nor had they really expected South Vietnam literally to copy us. Rather it seems that they sought to establish the right of the people to establish whatever forms they wished. Any system finally established that met their approval would be acceptable to us. We sought primarily national self-determination, the right of these people to establish and preserve their own national institutions. We hoped to defend their right to be a free nation rather than a puppet. We did not seek to impose ours or any system upon them. What we sought was to save them from having any system imposed upon them against their wishes. These are vital distinctions, and if Americans had understood them and been more charitable in their hopes and expectations, they might have understood the war and our role in it better.

Our indignation swelled over the manipulated election Thieu arranged for October 3, 1971. In spite of our leverage and hopes, General Thieu simply managed the election with little regard to popular wishes. The evident corruption, intimidation, and repression of this Thieu-staged farce nearly erased all defense of our professed war aims. Nixon and his official family felt hard pressed to justify or explain this action. The president admitted that he had wished an open contested election, but when Ky and General Minh refused to run in an election they deemed unfair to them because it was rigged by Thieu, he admitted that we could not "get people to run when they do not want to run."[2] That was hardly an answer. Why should anyone seek to lend any respectability to make fraud credible?

In further observations about the election, the president declared we should not ignore how well the democratic process worked in other ways, for example the congressional elections, the elections to the National Assembly, in which 80 percent of the people voted, compared to but 60 percent in the United States congressional election of 1970. Thieu was elected by over 90 percent of the voters in his farcical one-man election. Nixon regarded Thieu's election as a sort of national vote of confidence.[3] Could that not have been far more accurate had a free election been held? What genuine confidence was there in a referendum which Thieu personally staged for his exclusive benefit while he threatened his opponents? The elected officials were largely handpicked by him. The president warned us to keep our eye on the main objective, which was to end the war quickly, get our soldiers and prisoners home, and prevent a Communist takeover. But what value was that to us or the South Vietnamese if the people were still bound to the will of Thieu and his generals?

Nixon admitted that our objective of a democratic system was not met by the election. It would take perhaps generations to come, but he advised us to understand how difficult the democratic process was and how long it took to initiate it in the West. It had taken Britain about five hundred years to reach its present state, and democracy did not spring up overnight in the United States. He recalled that in the election of 1800 between Jefferson and John Adams only 150,000 people could vote in a population then numbering four and a quarter million. We could not expect our style of democracy to apply there and elsewhere, where no traditions or experience with it existed. However, he felt they were on the road toward it.[4]

Governor Ronald Reagan of California, on a visit to South Vietnam shortly after Thieu's managed election, referred to the "fantastic progress" South Vietnam had made in the last fifteen years and added that he could not understand why so many people, especially the communications media, were so disturbed by this one-man election. Reagan referred to it as a "referendum" and noted that if we wanted to criticize the one-man ballot, we should start with a whole list of nations like Russia, North Vietnam, and Czechoslovakia. Somehow he believed that Thieu's election was comparable to Washington's great unanimous victories of 1788 and 1792.[5] But Washington had not rigged the rules or ousted, imprisoned, and repressed the opposition. And as for Russian and other totalitarian-style elections, we were not fighting and dying for their systems, as we were for that of South Vietnam. The California governor believed we were still justly fighting for freedom and the dignity of man, not totalitarianism.

The critics declared we still had only a dictatorship in Saigon. The 90 percent turnout for Thieu destroyed all illusions of political freedom for the people of South Vietnam; undermined hope for a negotiated solution; tied us for another four years to a man whose four *no*'s—no coalition government, no neutralism, no Communist participation in politics, no loss of territory—meant no peace. From such intransigence only enduring war would follow. Under Thieu there would be no concessions to his internal enemies, no reforms, no broad-based popular support, nothing but continued military confrontation and more casualties. And from Washington, under Nixon, there would be no aid cutoff. There would be continued troop withdrawals, but at a rate paced to the ARVN's capacity to save South Vietnam from defeat. To the critics, that was a program for unending involvement. Senate doves, including Edward W. Brooke and Adlai E. Stevenson, III, believed Thieu's controlled one-man election had erased all argument for the continuation of military aid to South Vietnam. It destroyed, said harsher critics, the "self-determination" factor as a defense of our involvement. The opposition within South Vietnam rebuked Thieu for his dictatorial manipulation of his own election, which, they said, aggravated internal dissension, threatened the survival of the country, and ignored the popular will. One South Vietnamese senator bluntly declared that Nixon could support Thieu, but he could not force the Vietnamese people to support him. Still another South Vietnamese senator declared that Thieu could in any referendum manage any number he wished, be it 60 or 70 percent or more of the election count.[6]

Nixon faced many dilemmas. If he cut off aid, South Vietnam would collapse. If he did not use his leverage, the case for the war was undermined. If he continued to condone Thieu's blunders, popular opposition inside the United States would swell. Continued involvement would risk political defeat, further demonstrations and violence on college and university campuses, and likely additional marches on Washington and other centers. Had an open and fair election occurred, and had Thieu been defeated, that would have removed one of the major obstacles to a diplomatic solution of the war—Hanoi's repeated demand that Thieu must be abandoned. Nixon's acquiescence in this rigged election destroyed the credibility of our frequently offered suggestion to the Communists that elections were the correct route to any just political settlement in South Vietnam. It made much more difficult any hope of peace, except by victory or defeat in battle. And that was no hope at all in terms of the emotions and realities in 1971 and 1972.

In late 1971 and during most of 1972 Nixon sought to buy time: to strengthen the ARVN, improve anti-Communist positions in Laos and Cambodia, and permit the success of Vietnamization. In an interview of January 2, 1972, with Dan Rather of CBS, the president implied that South Vietnam was not yet secure enough for him to feel free to set an early deadline for our total and final withdrawal and offer this in exchange for the return of our war prisoners. Hanoi would have a chance to answer such a proposition when the time had come for our own withdrawal. He set no date for such a deal, but he implied the possibility of a pullout of all our combat troops later in the year and a cessation of all aerial activity in return for the safe return of our prisoners. This would allow a few more months for periodic bombings to keep the enemy off balance. He still refused to pull out our troops while the enemy kept our prisoners, but indicated that our gradual force reductions would continue. He expected that only thirty-five thousand would still be left there by summer. That would be enough to satisfy the American public that he had done everything possible to settle with the "international outlaws" in Hanoi.

George McGovern immediately and falsely charged that Nixon was actually delaying the release of the prisoners in order to postpone the disengagement. In July 1, 1971, we believed Hanoi offered to return the prisoners if we would set a date for our total withdrawal in 1971—meaning the removal of all our troops, cessation of all ground and air attacks, and the dismantling of all bases. Secondly, the enemy then proposed that for Thieu we substitute a coalition regime. McGovern subsequently contended that in discussions with him Hanoi and the Vietcong had agreed that the withdrawal in exchange for the prisoners could be dealt with separately, and the issue of a political solution for South Vietnam could be decided later.

Nixon said the offer had been explored and nothing had come of it. Although he was not ready to withdraw until Saigon was stronger, he strongly suspected that even if we withdrew the troops and ceased the bombing, the enemy would keep the prisoners as hostages until we stopped all military and political aid. The prisoners could be used indefinitely for blackmail. Late in 1971, Hanoi's spokesmen stiffened their posture by indicating to us that their two-pronged proposal was not separable into military and political segments. They set their own price for the return of the prisoners: abandon Thieu and leave. Nixon revealed in the Rather interview that a straight swap—withdrawal for the prisoners—had been publicly rejected. McGovern continued to defend his belief that a truly total withdrawal of military aid would satisfy Hanoi, and on that basis he charged that the president was using the prisoner issue as a pretext to avoid withdrawal, with the further implication that he did it to save Thieu.[7] In any case, Nixon continued to refuse to offer a pullout date or a total withdrawal just for the return of the prisoners. He would not abandon Thieu, cut off aid, cease the bombing, abandon Laos and Cambodia altogether, or abandon South Vietnam and those territories unless Hanoi also withdrew its forces from those areas. In short, the prisoner question could not be settled until the aggression ended. We sought not just the return of the prisoners, but the pullout of all enemy forces from these areas while they sought our total withdrawal before they would return the prisoners. Both still sought essentially to win the war, and neither was ready for compromise. In truth little room was left for real compromise.

In the CBS interview Nixon blundered in saying that the fate of the prisoners was the "one circumstance" standing in the way of our total withdrawal. It did not take long for White House spokesmen to knock that hope down by emphasizing that official policy still insisted that the South Vietnamese have the right to determine their own future. This appeared to justify our keeping a residual force present in South Vietnam and our continuation of the air warfare against the North.[8] Critics charged that this merely sought more time to save Thieu's rotten regime and to achieve the ever elusive military victory. They also feared that out of the failure of negotiations most likely would come another trial at arms. Administration officials admitted that our delegation at Paris had never proposed a date for total withdrawal in exchange for the prisoners, but had merely sought "clarifications" from the enemy of his July proposal. This was to see if he would accept a partial acceptance (the swap the president referred to above) or insist upon the whole package—total withdrawal and abandonment of Thieu. He demanded the whole package. When the chief negotiator for Hanoi said that the two points were indeed linked, our spokesman replied that our withdrawal would have to be accompanied not only by a release of our prisoners but also by a matching withdrawal of North Vietnamese and Vietcong troops from South Vietnam, Cambodia, and Laos. Both sides were still playing to win; they were not seeking ways to end or negotiate an end to the war.[9] While the enemy wanted to destroy the Vietnamization program, Nixon wanted to establish it permanently.

Meanwhile, Nixon continued to reduce our force levels. Already announced were planned reductions to the level of sixty-nine thousand by May 1, 1972, but nevertheless evidence revealed that the enemy, backed by sizable material assistance from Peking and Moscow, was building reserves and getting ready to launch offensives through Laos and Cambodia against South Vietnam and our dwindling forces. Thus arose a major dilemma. The more we withdrew, the more the enemy sought to take advantage of it; and the more he sought to exploit this advantage by gathering supplies, the more we ordered our bombers to attack the trails and prevent the concentrations of men and forces before they reached our troops and our allies. Into this trap both sides fell in early 1972.

While Nixon faced this dilemma, his domestic critics charged that the problem could be solved if only the president would set a date for total withdrawal; but they did not understand that the enemy demanded not only our withdrawal but our imposition of a Communist regime upon South Vietnam. He wanted us to give him what he had not won himself. He said to us: You cannot have the prisoners or end the war with honor or justice at all unless you dishonor yourself and your friends. That generally misread the character of Americans. We wanted compromise, not humiliation. We wanted to get out of South Vietnam, but we would not betray our friends. Thus Nixon could not satisfy his critics without appeasing his enemy and abandoning South Vietnam; but he could not save his ally without more warfare. Larger war seemed the only option. Hanoi could not mount a major military offensive without being bombed on a rising scale, but we could not increase the bombing—expand the war—without greatly embittering the enemy.[10] And that would mean presidential failure to end the war as pledged in 1968.

On January 4, 1972, the *New York Times* in a cable to Hanoi sought to get an official confirmation of McGovern's assertion that Hanoi would recognize the announcement of our firm withdrawal date as representing the end of our support for Saigon and release, without further delay or demands, the nearly four hundred prisoners it was believed to hold. Nixon had maintained that Hanoi wanted us not only to end our support for Thieu, but also to accept its whole seven-point "all or nothing" program. The *Times* asked Hanoi to answer the questions: If the United States set a firm troop withdrawal date, would you release the American prisoners under your control? Would you negotiate on military withdrawals and the release of the prisoners completely apart from questions concerning the political future of Vietnam? On January 6, before the *Times* received a reply, Hanoi's spokesman at Paris, Xuan Thuy, said publicly that if the United States wished to disengage from the war and get back its prisoners, it should "give up aggression, stop the Vietnamization of the war, pull out from South Vietnam all the troops, stop backing the Nguyen Van Thieu bellicose puppet group." Hanoi never directly answered the *Times*'s question, but another channel, the Foreign Broadcast Information Service, a bureau of the Central Intelligence Agency, supplied the answer: United States withdrawal and prisoner release could not be separated from a political settlement in South Vietnam.[11] George McGovern continued to hold his belief that he could get a settlement by simple and total withdrawal. In his acceptance of the nomination speech, he promised more than he could deliver. More than likely he meant simply to abandon the whole effort to Communist control, and, if necessary, he would go to Hanoi and beg the enemy to return the prisoners.

For almost thirty months, Nixon and Kissinger secretly carried on negotiations with the enemy. In an administration plagued by leaks, this was surely one of its best kept secrets. The president long suffered attacks for his apparent refusal to seek rational solutions and compromises. He knew, although his critics did not, that the enemy had already refused many times virtually every concession we could offer short of our total surrender—which he meant never to accept. Twelve times Kissinger had crossed the Atlantic to Paris to confer with the highest-ranking officials about every possible avenue to a negotiated settlement. In late January 1972, first Nixon, then Kissinger, and finally Rogers revealed the story and launched a full-scale diplomatic and political offensive on the whole Vietnam settlement issue. Why did Nixon tell the story of negotiations supposed to be secret and still proceeding, thereby risking a break in negotiations, renewed hostilities, and greater difficulty ahead? Speculation suggested that Nixon desired to "steal the thunder from his domestic critics," who had intensified their attacks, and close the divisions among the American public over his war policy that served Hanoi and stiffened enemy resistance. Disclosure would shift the blame for the stalemate at Paris to the Communists, who for months had publicly accused Washington of failing to reply to their July proposals. For Nixon, it was hoped, it would create a climate here and abroad willing to condone "stiff retaliatory attacks to any North Vietnamese offensive in the coming weeks." It would help set the stage for his coming trips to China and Russia. By revealing his prolonged peace efforts, by publicly proclaiming again his willingness to withdraw all our troops in exchange for a return of our prisoners and a cease-fire everywhere in Indochina, he might help make it possible for China to avoid "accusations that they are betraying their Indochinese allies by dealing with an American President."[12]

In a speech on January 25, 1972, the president in detail once again spelled out his peace proposals for the world to see—"to make public a plan for peace that can end the war in Vietnam." If approved by Saigon, the plan could end the war "now." Again he reviewed the record by reminding his vast audience that when he took office, there were five hundred and fifty thousand Americans in Vietnam; the casualties in action were running as high as three hundred a week; there were no plans to bring the troops home; and the only thing settled at the Paris talks was the shape of the conference table. Since then he had moved to redeem his pledge to bring peace for us and Southeast Asia by the only two honorable means open to us: negotiation, which we had been unable to complete, and Vietnamization, while we steadily withdrew our forces as South Vietnam grew able to defend itself. This second path, he believed, had been successful.[13]

He felt the American people deserved an accounting of his peace efforts. While he recounted the failures, he stated his firm intention to try again to break the deadlock in the negotiations. The record, as he reviewed it, included a series of public proposals to end the war alongside a long-secret attempt to find a solution. His critics knew only of the public efforts, which they had found defective; they knew nothing except by speculation of the other, prolonged secret talks. The president explained that after ten months of no progress in the Paris talks in the early part of his administration, he decided to explore the private channels to see what could be done. Thus after consultation with Rogers, Lodge, Bunker, and Thieu, he decided to send Kissinger to Paris to begin secret negotiations. He said private talks permitted more flexibility in offering new approaches and allowed both sides to talk frankly and take positions free from the pressures of public debate. With so much at stake, he felt, he could not ignore any steps to peace. Thus for thirty months, when he or his chief aides were asked about secret negotiations, they had said only that they were pursuing every possible channel in their search for peace. And, because he determined not to endanger the negotiations—which until recently showed some signs of progress—there was never a leak. Now he felt it necessary to speak publicly because nothing was served by further silence, when the other side exploited our good faith, tried to split the American people, simultaneously avoided serious negotiations, and misled some Americans into accusing their government of failing to do what it had already done. Also, nothing was served by silence when it enabled the enemy to imply publicly the possibility of solutions which he had already privately rejected. Thus it was time to lay the record on the table. Public disclosure might help break the secret deadlock.[14]

Those who had believed the enemy's charge that we had not seriously sought to negotiate could now see that just the opposite was true. The president noted the questions raised by his domestic critics: Why had we not proposed a deadline for the withdrawal of our forces in exchange for a cease-fire and the return of our prisoners? Why had we not discussed the enemy seven-point proposal of July 1971? And why had we not submitted new plans of our own to get the negotiations off dead center? The record would reveal that in fact we had tried all these steps and more only to be rebuffed by the other side. On May 31, 1971, at Paris we secretly offered to accept a deadline for withdrawal for a release of the prisoners and a cease-fire. On June 26, 1971, Hanoi rejected that offer, and proposed instead its own secret nine-point plan, which insisted "that we overthrow the Government of South Vietnam." Five days later on July 1, the enemy at Paris publicly offered a different package of proposals—the seven-point Vietcong plan. That posed the problem: Which package would we answer, the public or the private plan, the seven- or nine-point plan? On July 12, Kissinger inquired of the enemy: Which plan should we deal with? He was told to work with the nine-point plan because it covered all Indochina, while the Vietcong plan dealt only with Vietnam. That was the course we followed. On August 16, we offered complete withdrawal of United States and allied forces within nine months after an overall agreement.[15]

On September 13, Hanoi rejected that proposal and again insisted "that we overthrow the South Vietnamese Government." In short, we had replied to the enemy plan and made proposals of our own, yet the enemy publicly had berated us for failing to respond to his proposals, which he well knew we had already privately done. Domestic critics had picked up the enemy line and attacked Nixon for the same reasons. In October, Nixon tried again to get Hanoi to meet secretly, but although the enemy managed to set a time, he finally canceled the meeting—because, he said, of the illness of Le Duc Tho. Two months then passed after the meeting was called off. The president noted: "The only reply to our plan has been an increase in troop infiltration from North Vietnam and Communist military offensives in Laos and Cambodia. Our proposal for peace was answered by a step-up in the war on their part."[16]

Nixon now instructed Ambassador Porter to present publicly our plan and offer alternatives at the January 27 session of the Paris talks. Then Nixon revealed his plan, which he hoped would prove beyond doubt "which side has made every effort to make these negotiations succeed. It will show unmistakably that Hanoi—not Washington or Saigon—has made the war go on." In this January 25, 1972, address, Nixon announced his new peace proposal.[17] Within six months of an agreement, our troops would be withdrawn, all prisoners of war would be exchanged, and there would be a cease-fire throughout Indochina. In South Vietnam there would be new presidential elections, under international supervision and organized by an independent body that represented all political forces in South Vietnam, including the National Liberation Front. Thieu and his vice-president, Tran Van Huong, would resign one month before the new election. The United States would remain completely neutral in the election and would abide by its results, as long as they were "shaped by the South Vietnamese people themselves." We still supported the right of popular self-determination for South Vietnam, "free from outside interference." Also we proposed that both sides respect the 1954 Geneva Agreements on Indochina and those of 1962 on Laos. There should be no further infiltration of outside forces into Indochina after the cease-fire. All armed forces of Indochinese countries should remain within their national frontiers.[18]

The president noted that there were other proposals in the new peace plan. On July 26, 1971, he had offered privately to undertake a major reconstruction program throughout Indochina, including North Vietnam. Other approaches we would gladly and speedily pursue. We remained willing to settle only the military issues and leave the political issues for the Vietnamese alone to settle. Under his plan there would be a straight swap: withdrawal for a cease-fire over all Indochina and the release of all war prisoners. Hanoi could have its choice, any or all of these proposals. He thought his offers were fair to all and deserved the approval of all nations and the united support of all Americans. He stressed that this offer, made over three months ago, had not been rejected; it had been ignored. He repeated the peace offer, but he observed that there was one thing the United States would never do—"join our enemy to overthrow our ally." If the enemy wanted peace, he would "have to recognize the important difference between settlement and surrender."[19]

The president noted in conclusion that no one could now say "we have not gone the extra mile." If the enemy refused the offer, we would "continue our program of ending American involvement in the war by withdrawing our forces" as South Vietnam developed its defensive capacity. Then he declared ominously: "If the enemy's answer to our peace offer is to step up their military attacks, I shall fully meet my responsibility as Commander in Chief of our Armed Forces to protect our remaining troops." He wished to end the war and believed his plan could do it, but with a mixture of sadness and anger he noted:

Some of our citizens have become accustomed to thinking that whatever our Government says must be false, and whatever our enemies say must be true, as far as this war is concerned. Well, the record I have revealed tonight proves the contrary. We can now demonstrate publicly what we have long been demonstrating privately—that America has taken the initiative not only to end our participation in this war, but to end the war itself for all concerned.[20]

William Safire revealed that Nixon and Kissinger betrayed no diplomatic trust when they told about the previously secret negotiations and cited Kissinger's statement to justify their revelation:

Look, we kept it secret as long as the secret channel was in tandem with the public channel. . . . They gave us a nine-point secret proposal a week before they made their seven-point proposal; we asked which they wanted us to respond to, and they said the nine-point secret one. Even so, we responded to both.[21]

Kissinger was angry at Hanoi's efforts to swing Washington doves against their own government's foreign policy. Many war critics, including members of Congress, believed the enemy propaganda more readily than official statements of Nixon's administration. Thus Kissinger declared: "For the first time, they've used the secret talks to create confusion, and we cannot permit that."[22] Hanoi had succeeded too long and too easily in making the doves believe Nixon as well as Johnson had rejected "fair offers." The truth would sharply discredit that dovish affirmation.

After Nixon's disclosure, Hanoi felt compelled to reveal its secret nine-point plan of June 6, 1971. The North Vietnamese government wanted us out of all Indochina by the end of 1971. All military men and civilians captured in the war would be released at the same time our troops left the country. The United States should cease its support of the Thieu regime in order to permit the establishment in Saigon of a new administration. This new Provisional Revolutionary Government of the Republic of South Vietnam would then enter into talks with the Thieu regime to settle the "affairs of South Vietnam and to achieve national concord." The United States would have to assume responsibility for the damages caused by us to all Vietnam. It would be expected hereafter to respect the 1954 Geneva Agreements and those of 1962 on Laos and cease its aggression and intervention in those countries. Indochina should be free to settle its own affairs. There should be international supervision of the execution of the agreement and international guarantees for the basic rights of the Indochinese people.[23]

Then at Paris on July 1, 1971, the Communists offered their seven-point or Vietcong plan. It was more demanding of us than the nine-point or Hanoi proposal. It required us to remove all our troops and weapons by a fixed date, dismantle our bases, and halt the Vietnamization program. Simultaneously with our withdrawals they would release our prisoners of war. They would accept a cease-fire with United States forces as "soon as agreement is reached on withdrawal." Also the United States must renounce its support of Thieu's "puppet" regime and support the formation of a coalition government, which would hold power until general elections could be held. Only after the new government was created would a cease-fire with South Vietnam take effect. Further problems must be settled by the people of South Vietnam alone, and the two parts of the country would arrange the eventual reunion of all Vietnam. The United States would have to bear "full responsibility" for war damages to both North and South Vietnam. All Vietnam would finally agree on the "kind of international guarantees needed to keep the peace."[24]

Nowhere in these enemy proposals was there a requirement that we take direct action to oust Thieu and his government. Rather, by ceasing further aid to him and supporting the proposal for a coalition, Thieu and his regime would have to take their chances in a future election. The Nixon charge that the enemy sought to humiliate us by insisting that we forcefully oust him and impose a coalition regime was not quite accurate. Nixon was not asked to do for the Communists what they could not do for themselves. He was asked to withdraw our forces and permit a coalition of all native elements to seek a settlement of their own problems. The people of South Vietnam would be able to make their own political arrangements and under appropriate international supervision. Obviously, the Communists would not permit Thieu to rig any more elections in his own favor. Nixon had to agree finally to a solution by which neither side could rely upon or permit the United States to impose any settlement upon South Vietnam.

In a most rare news conference, Henry Kissinger, the president's most trusted adviser in foreign affairs, told more of the story of these secret talks.[25] With surprising emotion, at times amounting almost to tears, this surely brilliant man detailed his efforts for peace. Throughout 1971 we had shown a willingness to consider all proposals in good faith and hoped the enemy would reciprocate. We offered no plans on a take-it-or-leave-it basis. While we exchanged ideas on the peace, we told the other side "it is expected that both sides will refrain from bringing pressure from public statements which can only serve to complicate the situation." This was to avoid having public and private proposals simultaneously. But that was not to be. In detailing the story, he ignored as no longer relevant to the immediate problem the six private meetings of 1969 and 1970, but described the six private meetings of 1971 on May 31, June 26, July 12, July 26, August 16, and September 13.

On May 31, 1971, he noted, we proposed withdrawal of our forces and agreed to set a deadline in return for a cease-fire and the exchange of prisoners. This was the first time we had shown a willingness to set a date unilaterally, without an equivalent assurance of withdrawal from the other side. Hanoi did not specifically reject this or that point as unacceptable. It did not say, "Cease-fire is difficult for us." It did say that any proposal that did not include political elements could not be negotiated, "so our attempt to negotiate the military issue separately was simply rejected."

To those who thought Nixon's plan was too complex and asked why we did not put forward a simplified proposal, he replied that we had already advocated a simplified plan, which the enemy found not negotiable. The North Vietnamese, Kissinger repeated, thus insisted that the only possible proposal was one that included the political elements: "I may say that this is the one position, or one of the positions, which they have never altered, on which they have never shown the slightest give." On June 26, the enemy introduced his nine-point proposal, which linked the political and military issues. To preserve the confidentiality of these negotations Kissinger did not then identify the enemy plan. He described the difficulty presented by the enemy publication of Hanoi's seven-point proposal. Both the critics and the enemy denounced us for not responding to Hanoi's plans, but to which one should we respond, the public or secret proposal? Asked the difference between the two plans, Kissinger said the nine points were less ambiguous, but on the political solution and on the cease-fire the nine points were more detailed. The seven points suggested a truce with the American forces while they withdrew. The nine points called for a cease-fire to be concluded as part of an overall settlement. The principle of a cease-fire was not in itself the issue. The nine points covered some elements not contained in the seven points, such as international supervision, respect for the Geneva Accords of 1954 and 1962, and a general statement about the problem of Indochina.

Kissinger explained that "at the June 26 meeting we agreed, contrary to our May 31 proposal, that we would lump the political and military issues together." Thereafter, we would accept the nine points as the basis for negotiation. Then why did our plan of negotiation include eight and theirs nine? The answer was that one of their nine points was "a demand for reparations as part of a settlement," as it was in the seven-point plan. Our position was that "we could not, in honor, make a peace settlement in which we would be obligated under the terms of the peace settlement to pay reparations." We did tell the other side that although we would not include reparations as part of the peace settlement, we would undertake a voluntary and massive reconstruction program for all of Indochina, which would include North Vietnam. Hanoi's share would likely amount to several billions. This revealed that we had tried to go the extra mile.

Over the next few months we discussed the North Vietnamese proposals in depth and tried in vain to reach some agreement at least in principle. By August 16 we proposed to set a date for withdrawal within nine months after an agreement was signed. If an understanding were reached by November 1, 1971, our withdrawal could come by August 1, 1972. The plan included specific proposals for American neutrality in the forthcoming South Vietnamese elections, and for the first time it introduced other political provisions, such as an American declaration of its "willingness to limit our aid to South Vietnam if North Vietnam would agree to a limitation." Further, we agreed "to the principle of nonalignment for South Vietnam as long as all other countries of Indo-China agreed to the principle of nonalignment." The enemy rejected our proposals September 13, 1971, saying "the withdrawal date was too long" and we had not been clear as to the meaning of total withdrawal. Would any forces remain in an individual capacity? Also the North Vietnamese asserted a simple declaration of our neutrality while the present Thieu government "stayed in office would not overcome the advantage of the existing Government in running and being in office."

Kissinger said we had reviewed these enemy objections and submitted on October 11 essentially the proposal Nixon had publicly announced the previous day, January 25, 1972. We privately told the enemy in October 1971 that we meant the total withdrawal of our own and all allied forces. Also we shortened the deadline. "We gave a precise description of how the political process might operate." We introduced the concept of an electoral commission and revealed that Thieu had agreed to resign prior to the election. We then said we were prepared, once the agreement was signed in principle, "to begin implementing the withdrawal and prisoner-exchange portions, even while the other elements were still being ironed out, provided that final agreement would be reached within the six-month period in which the withdrawals were running." Kissinger thought these public commitments of the United States and South Vietnam added a new element "of profound significance to the political evolution of South Vietnam." Of the nine points, he declared, seven had "been narrowed to manageable proportions," but there were two others that blocked the peace: withdrawal and political evolution.

On withdrawal, there was an ambiguity about the expression "date certain." Hanoi said we should set a date and implement it, regardless of what else happened, "regardless of whether there is a prisoner exchange, regardless of how they negotiate their own proposal. In other words, that we should get out unilaterally." North Vietnam also defined withdrawal to mean not just the evacuation of our armed forces, "but the withdrawal of all American equipment, all economic aid, all military aid, which is, in considering the fact that they receive from 800 million dollars to 1 billion dollars' worth of aid from their allies, a prescription for a unilateral term." On political evolution, our basic principle, Kissinger said, was "that we were not committed to any one political structure or government in South Vietnam." Rather we wanted "a political evolution that gives the people of South Vietnam a genuine opportunity to express their preferences." We had searched our souls trying to find a solution, which seemed fair to us, that would have a commission, including the people who wished to overthrow present Saigon governments and manage an election, under international supervision, while the existing government resigned a month before it occurred. This proposal was not, as the enemy termed it, trivial.

However, it was not enough for Hanoi. The Communists wanted us "to agree with them, first, on replacing the existing Government, and, secondly, on a structure in which the probability of their taking over is close to certainty." They wanted us to do in politics the same thing they asked us to do in the war—surrender and negotiate "the terms of the turnover to them, regardless of what the people may think." The North Vietnamese had repeatedly said they wished "a government composed of people who stood for peace, neutrality, and independence." We could not disagree with that, but further inquiry revealed that they were the only ones who knew who stood for peace, neutrality, and independence or could define the meaning of these terms. He added: "Whenever in these negotiations we have said: 'All right, you don't like Thieu. How about this fellow, or that fellow, or that fellow?' there is almost no one that we know who they believe stands for peace, neutrality and independence."

Kissinger said we were prepared seriously to negotiate immediately with them any scheme that any reasonable person could say left open the political future of South Vietnam to the people of the country, but we were not "prepared to withdraw without knowing anything at all of what is going to happen next. So we are not prepared to end this war by turning over the Government of South Vietnam as part of a political deal." We were ready to support a political process that would give them a chance of winning, but which was not "loaded in any direction." We had said repeatedly that we would abide by the outcome of any political process in South Vietnam, that we were not committed to any particular government, but we would not impose a Communist regime upon South Vietnam. That was the way it stood then and throughout 1972. He noted finally that the only response to the most sweeping offer we had ever made was a massive step-up in their infiltration and a move toward a military solution. It was not our bombing that brought the refusal and the cessation of the secret talks in November. Our increased bombing came late in December 1971, five weeks after the talks were halted.[26]

The enemy did not make clear all his reasons, but it was quickly made obvious that Nixon's January 25 proposal was as unacceptable then as it had been in the previous October. Concerning this plan and the later one of May 8, 1972, it was evident that Hanoi did not recognize the basic distinction between settlement and surrender. Its rejection left Nixon only the options of impossible surrender, escalation of the air warfare and naval attacks, blockades, and mining the waters of North Vietnam or continuation of the Vietnamization program. He chose the last two. The enemy chose to continue his effort for final and total military victory. Expert speculation, supported by enemy statements, about why Hanoi refused our peace offers suggested that the enemy was convinced he was winning the war and total victory would come simply as a matter of time.[27]

When Johnson stopped the escalation of the war in 1968, and Nixon scheduled the withdrawals alongside the Vietnamization program, the enemy no longer was under enough pressure to persuade him to negotiate. Ho's estimate that our impatience would give him victory in the end seemed a sure thing. Hanoi knew that Saigon would soon lose the immense aid of United States combat ground forces. The small residual force we may have planned for South Vietnam until the prisoners were returned posed little threat. Hanoi counted on American public opinion and congressional opposition to force Nixon to make a deal on its terms and especially felt it could count on our rising concern for the return of the prisoners. Further, both Russia and China pledged to continue supplying all necessary war materiel and food for a prolonged war. The enemy had no reason to fear any possible antiwar sentiments within North Vietnam. Although the enemy had lost possibly 790,000 men killed in battle, out of a population then estimated at 21 million, he could easily keep his ranks filled from among the 200,000 youths reaching draft age each year. Also Hanoi's rulers were very patient; they could wait for years and decades; and they appeared ready to accept even total annihilation before they would abandon their efforts to defeat the South and reunite the nation under communism. They truly believed that antiwar sentiment in the United States would soon give them the victory their forces had not won.[28] In that sense Nixon was quite correct when he repeatedly stated in 1971 and 1972 that antiwar elements undermined his peace efforts.

In the immediate sense Hanoi and the Vietcong found Nixon's peace offer objectionable on many grounds: it refused to stop the Vietnamization of the war; it would not immediately pull out the troops, advisers, armaments, and war materials of our armed forces and those of our allies, dismantle our bases and cease all air and naval activities in both zones of Vietnam. They said Nixon persisted in his support of Thieu's system, refused to engage in serious negotiation, expanded the war to include all of Indochina, and spoke of a sham peace while he made real war. They denounced his unilateral publication of the secret negotiations after he had pledged to keep them secret and said it testified to his "perfidious maneuver to deceive the American electorate in an election year." The Vietcong added that it was a deceptive attempt to conceal his policy of prolonging and widening the war. Rather, he still pursued the policy of Vietnamization of the war, which merely aimed at "changing the color of the skin of the corpses" while spreading American aggression. It was nothing but a plan aimed at prolonging the American commitment in South Vietnam and at imposing a neocolonialist yoke on its people.[29] The proposal for elections would merely allow the Thieu regime to keep "intact all of the military administrative and police apparatus as well as the whole system of concentration camps and prisons, . . . including the 'tiger cages.' "[30] In this fashion and for these reasons Hanoi and the Vietcong summarily rejected the first new proposal for a general settlement submitted by the United States since October 8, 1969.[31]

Thus there was still no give from the enemy. In his *Vantage Point,* Johnson listed seventy-two separate initiatives for peace made during his administration and counted fourteen complete or partial bombing halts between May 1965 and March 1968 designed to bring the enemy to the conference table. On March 31, 1968, he had halted all bombing north of the 20th parallel and announced his retirement from politics before Hanoi finally agreed to talk. The talks began in Paris May 13, 1968, but the enemy stalled until all bombing was stopped on October 31, 1968. Now Nixon had put forth an enormous effort to end the war, only to have the enemy demand our surrender.

On February 3, 1972, the Vietcong presented revised proposals at the Vietnam peace talks in Paris. This latest revision considerably hardened the position of the enemy; it made no mention of a cease-fire, as did the original seven-point Vietcong and Hanoi nine-point plans. It did not specify the parallel liberation of the war prisoners as troops were withdrawn, as had previous proposals. The point on a political solution differed also from previous offers. The earlier Vietcong plan anticipated a new administration favoring peace, independence, neutrality, and democracy through which a provisional revolutionary government might negotiate with Saigon. The idea of a political settlement without or before an election and without any outside supervision or interference began to appear possible in 1972. The new proposal in addition called for the resignation of Thieu and declared the Saigon administration must end its belligerent policy, abolish its repressive machinery, end the policy of pacification, dissolve the concentration camps, liberate political prisoners, and guarantee the democratic freedoms provided by the Geneva Accords of 1954. An enemy spokesman declared that what the Communists wanted was the destruction of the legality and the legitimacy of the regime and person of President Thieu.[32] A further explanation by Xuan Thuy of Hanoi emphasized that the military and political issues had been separable in the previous July but were no longer so. That contradicted the Kissinger-Nixon version, which strongly insisted that there had never been any give in the total enemy demand for both.[33]

The Hanoi delegate at Paris explained that during the secret talks of 1971 he had suggested to Kissinger that if Nixon encouraged Thieu not to run for reelection, that would create a favorable opportunity for settling the war without involving the United States further in South Vietnamese politics. Thuy also asserted in his Paris interview of February 5, 1972, that had the United States set a precise date for withdrawal before the Vietnamese presidential election of October 3, 1971, Thieu would not have been reelected. Thus he maintained that an overall settlement would have been possible by withdrawal alone, without the need for an overt political move on Washington's part.[34] Even this, however, would have been only a clever cover for Nixon's retreat, another way of ousting Thieu and easing the Communists into control. The other terms for total dismantling of bases, withdrawal of all aid and even residual forces, cessation of all material and military aid, while the other side kept supporting the Communists, would have assured victory for the enemy. Little wonder Thieu did not wish a cease-fire.

However, there was little to justify Nixon's support for the farcical one-man election, which indicated beyond doubt that the United States intended to stay in Vietnam, and reinforced the enemy opinion that Nixon did not want peace, but wanted victory rather than compromise. The United States, he declared, could have gotten out with honor, without betraying an ally then, but it did not seize the opportunity.[35] Perhaps an opportunity was missed here. As we did not trust the enemy, he did not trust Nixon.

Thuy then added that conditions were no longer favorable for ending the war by means of a complete military withdrawal alone. Now the United States must give a "credible sign" that it was prepared to disengage politically from South Vietnam, and that could be done "only by withdrawing support from President Thieu."[36] The enemy could trust no elections which could ever be held under Thieu or any of his agents; with his resignation but one month before such an election, leaving his henchmen in control of the machinery that ran it, the election would more certainly be rigged against the Communists than it had been against his internal and non-Communist opponents during the previous October. Thieu had for years advocated his four *no*'s, which meant no peace except on his terms. Yet, this was the man Nixon accepted, one who rigged his own reelection and silenced all opposition. This destroyed all illusion that any election could be a truly fair election for anyone, certainly not for the Communists.

Nixon, too, by this action, abandoned our major war aim, the right of self-determination for the whole people of South Vietnam. In this case, to refuse to use our leverage, at least, to cut off all aid in order to prevent a fraudulent election, was to sanction the fraud itself. By late 1971 it was more than evident that Vietnamization may have meant many things, but it surely meant prolonging the war, and with Thieu manipulating his reelection it meant prolonging Thieu, who offered no concessions and no compromises. Thus the enemy could not trust Washington assurances as long as we reinforced such a regime. We said they left us no choice but to fight on, and they said Washington left them to face only an indefinite future of more Thieus.

Thuy also said the United States had never offered to set a definite date for the complete withdrawal of American troops merely in return for the release of all the prisoners, but had always based the offer on the unacceptable conditions of the eight-point American proposal. Nixon and Kissinger had previously disclosed that they had offered to set a deadline for withdrawal in exchange for a cease-fire throughout Indochina and the return of the prisoners, and they said it was the first time we had shown a willingness to do it unilaterally, without "an equivalent assurance of withdrawal of the other side." But, Kissinger and Nixon declared, the offer had been spurned. Thuy said Nixon's policy was "to talk peace and make war," to maintain a "subservient Saigon administration" in power indefinitely, and to keep a residual American force but somehow get back the prisoners.[37]

The enemy could not believe that we lacked the power to force Thieu to do anything we wished him to do; therefore, when we failed to use the leverage they believed we had, the North Vietnamese believed it was because Thieu did what we wished him to do. They saw collusion, not conflict, between Thieu and Nixon. This is not to say that had Thieu been eased out of the way, things might have gone better for the United States; but we might have taken the more consistent path of demanding genuinely open and fair elections and seeing where that path might have taken us. At least it would have offered a more justifiable and flexible approach; as it was, the deadlock, the stalemate, and the war would merely continue. In all these negotiations, at any time we found it necessary, we could have returned and resumed the bombing and other measures if the other side betrayed any agreement. Nixon did not need to make it so easy for both the enemy and his antiwar forces at home to attack his policy on Vietnam.

Privately and publicly, said the Nixon administration, every reasonable effort had been made; but the enemy, confident of victory, backed by American appeasers was no more inclined to make peace with Nixon than with Johnson.[38] Thieu found unacceptable the two points of the revised Vietcong peace plan—that he resign and the United States fix a deadline for troop withdrawals without any preconditions. He said the enemy's aim was not peace but the domination of South Vietnam. He would never accept the two points, because they meant surrender. He felt no more concessions could be made to the enemy, and he expressed concern that Washington might make some commitment without the consent of his government. He resented Secretary of State William B. Rogers's statement of February 3, 1972, that the timing of Thieu's resignation as part of an agreement with Hanoi would be "flexible."[39]

In his press conference of February 10, 1972, President Nixon noted that every proposal we had made at Paris had been a joint proposal by Saigon and Washington and had been offered only after joint consultations. Thieu's offer to resign one month before any election, presented on October 11, 1971, was Thieu's own idea, and, Nixon believed, demonstrated his sincere desire to break the deadlock in the negotiations. Nixon added that he and Saigon were ready to negotiate on the offer just made, but under no circumstances would we make any further proposals without the consultation and agreement of the government of South Vietnam, particularly on political issues, "because the political issues are primarily theirs to decide rather than ours."[40]

He then added:

And I would say also, that under no circumstances are we going to negotiate with our enemy in a way that undercuts our ally.

We are not going to negotiate over the heads of our ally with our enemies to overthrow our ally. As I said in my speech on January 25, we are ready to negotiate a settlement, but we are not going to negotiate a surrender either for the United States, nor are we going to negotiate the surrender of 15 million people of South Vietnam to the Communists.

He hoped this further statement would help allay any ruffled feelings in Saigon.[41]

Domestic attacks upon the Nixon peace plan were sharp and prompt. The then leading candidate for the nomination of the Democratic Party, Senator Edmund S. Muskie, on February 2, 1972, declared it was apparent the enemy would reject the plan and noted that Hanoi had found it unacceptable. Muskie declared the whole involvement was immoral; we had "no right to kill, wound, or displace over 100,000 civilians a month" with our bombs. We had no right "to send young Americans to Vietnam as bargaining chips for the freedom of prisoners of war who would be free if those young Americans were not sent at all." He charged that Nixon's plan had three specific defects: it did not set a certain date for our withdrawal—the offer to withdraw within six months of a general settlement did not meet that necessary prescription. Thieu's retirement but one month before elections would still leave Thieu's "hand-picked agents" in control of the government machinery. "What opponent then would risk his liberty or even his life in open opposition? . . . How could anyone call such elections free?" Third, Nixon created a "stumbling block" in his call for a cease-fire, because that would ask North Vietnam to "concede Saigon's control over most of the countryside." No longer should we ask our sons to fight and die, "not for a cause but for a mistake."[42]

Nixon's plan could only mean the continuation of the killing, and Muskie suggested that we set a firm date for withdrawal of all our "troops, ships and bombers in return for the safety of the withdrawing forces and the release of American prisoners of war." Muskie did not insist, as Nixon did, "on a cease-fire or an agreement in principle on an over-all peace plan as a precondition." Secondly, he said we should make it clear to Saigon that it "must seek a political accommodation with the Communists or lose even indirect United States military support after American forces withdrew." He charged that Nixon's proposals were no more than an attempt "to win at the conference table what we have not won and cannot win on the battlefield."[43] This and other attacks, even before the enemy had time to give a full answer, several officials including Nixon himself felt compelled to denounce.

Secretary Rogers expressed his dismay that such a prominent politician rejected our official proposals even before the enemy had and declared Muskie was beating a dead horse with his suggestion of a negotiated solution of the military issue alone. Rogers did not propose that there be a moratorium on the discussion of the peace issue, but he did believe that a leading opponent should be most careful in expressing opinions in such critical areas.[44] A few days later a White House aide, H. R. Haldeman, was much less polite than Rogers. In a statement in a televised interview, he charged that Nixon's critics were "consciously aiding and abetting the enemy of the United States." He revealed that the president was naturally concerned by the kind of criticism that could get in the way of what he was trying to do and termed it "unfair criticism." Haldeman noted that even before Nixon announced and revealed his eight-point plan his critics were unconsciously echoing the enemy line of attack. He observed that Nixon's plan made all the points the critics sought, except one—turning South Vietnam over to the Communists by putting them in charge of South Vietnam. Therefore, he noted that the only conclusion one could draw was that the critics favored just that and insisted it be done. Here, he said, the critics were consciously aiding the enemy. The antiwar forces regarded these statements as highly counterproductive and unjust, and the critics everywhere renewed their attack on Washington officialdom: the old Nixon was once again emerging; Haldeman's remarks were irresponsible; it helped nothing to accuse critics of a lack of patriotism; and the official accusations were but moth-eaten charges used by past administrations trying to make the criticism of the war the issue rather than the cause.[45]

When asked his view of the critics and his defense by Rogers and especially by Haldeman, Nixon defended his aides. He reminded his critics that although he did not question their patriotism, he recalled that he had once disagreed with official policies but had refrained from open attack when they might jeopardize the peace talks. Although he had criticized the policies and actions that brought the assassination of Diem and the succession of coups which then helped bring further conflict and the conduct of the war before and after he was a candidate, he declared that:

once when President Johnson announced he would no longer be a candidate and the peace talks began, I said then that, as far as I was concerned, as a man seeking the Presidency, I would say nothing that would, in any way, jeopardize those peace talks.

So there is . . . a very great difference between criticizing policies that got us into war and criticizing the conduct of war and criticisms by a Presidential candidate of a policy to end the war and to bring peace.

What we have here is a situation . . . where, within one week after a very forthcoming peace proposal has been made, various Presidential candidates sought to propose another settlement which went beyond that.

My own candid judgment is that that kind of action has the effect . . . or having the Government in Hanoi consider at least that they might be well-advised to wait until after the election rather than negotiate.[46]

Like Johnson, Nixon believed others seriously hurt his own peace offers when they promised more generous terms than he did. We should unite if negotiations were to succeed. It would seem obvious that in such a situation we could not wisely afford more than one quarterback; we had but one president.

These combined executive charges against the antiwar forces came close to charging them with treason. Some felt that was going too far and noted the administration was trying to silence the opposition; it was trying to equate dissent from Nixon's peace terms with being unpatriotic; and it was seeking to prove that such opposition itself prevented the success of official peace efforts. No one could exactly prove that the domestic opposition to the war inspired Hanoi to resist our peace efforts and prolong its own efforts in the hopes or getting a better deal later from a change of leadership in the next election, but many Americans believed the critics achieved that very result, whether they wished it or not.

The net result of all this flurry of diplomacy seemed negative. It changed few opinions about the war, but it temporarily eased the attacks upon the president. It offered only the prospects of more war, greater offensives, which would likely require a massive aerial and naval response. Through scheduled withdrawals, it eased our relations with China and Russia. Possibly through stalling, it gave Vietnamization additional time to succeed. It gave bite to the rising partisanship over the war and the McGovern faction within the Democratic party. It also seemed undeniably true that the dissent stirred by the issue encouraged the enemy to persevere in his belief that a victory by the doves in the election of 1972 would give him his final victory. Naturally, the enemy would hold out for the most favorable terms he could get.

Thieu's future was not decided; North Vietnam was no longer—if it ever had been—prepared to free our prisoners in return for a specific withdrawal date and the halt of further military activities. Hanoi demanded a political solution that amounted to our virtual surrender. That hardened the line considerably. Washington argued without success that we were not defending Thieu but the South Vietnamese right to self-determination, but Hanoi replied that our acquiescence in the fraudulent election of October 1971 proved we were not really interested in a fair settlement. The enemy also insisted that our proposal for an Indochina cease-fire was a trap, unless we first quit the war. The issue now had come down to the core: to get peace by negotiation we must abandon Thieu and stop all aid to Saigon—men, money, and materiel. We had to get out completely and leave all Indochina alone to settle its own problems. Hanoi wanted total victory right then. We were to withdraw without any preconditions. Only our agreement to these terms would probably be accepted by the antiwar forces as "going the last extra mile." Furthermore, the enemy obviously believed, Why settle for less when you can get it all? The exchange gave more hope to the enemy than to Washington: it probably signified a weakening of will in the United States and held out great hopes of further concessions, especially in the event of an election victory by the doves in 1972. One danger was that the enemy might become impatient and take rash actions that would invite stern counterattacks. There remained our great air power and naval strength, both of which could bring vast damage to the enemy.

The enemy took a greater risk than even he may have known March 31, 1972, when he launched another surprise attack across the DMZ upon South Vietnam. Never before, not even in the Tet offensive of 1968, had he risked so much. In this bold, if puzzling, strategy he sent his last twelve trained divisions into the war and left behind to defend North Vietnam only two untrained units. This massive invasion directly across the DMZ now made it plain that Hanoi's regulars were involved. Such a bold defiance risked strong counterattack. If the effort failed, the enemy could seek peace on the most unfavorable terms or lick his wounds as he retreated northward to prepare for another assault perhaps years later. Now, however, he had little chance of success due to the massive intervention of United States air power.

No outsider could really know why Giap chose this move. The weather favored the offense, but at any rate the United States expeditionary forces were leaving on a fixed schedule. They were to be reduced to sixty-nine thousand by May 1, to below fifty thousand a month later, and with election pressure would most likely be almost all withdrawn by November. United States ground combat forces numbered but six thousand when the invasion began. Giap probably wanted to demonstrate that he could defeat South Vietnam and American air power, reveal that Vietnamization was a failure, and achieve ultimate victory by war. Military action might deny time for Vietnamization to succeed, take advantage of American retreat, shake up the American voter, and bring additional pressure upon Nixon to make further concessions, if not abandon his efforts to save the Saigon regime and President Thieu. Communist success would weaken Nixon's diplomatic efforts to reach accommodation with China and Russia. It surely seemed to the enemy that our military retreat reduced our ability any longer to dictate policy in Indochina, and it gave him a chance to succeed. Yet, to have waited until the United States was totally disengaged might have been wiser. Once we had left, reengagement would have been most difficult. Could the enemy have believed Saigon and Thieu under Vietnamization were growing stronger and in time might become able to defend a non-Communist regime? A preventive strike might avoid greater future trouble.

Nixon refused to accept the Communist demand that he impose a coalition regime, which would be a giant step toward ultimate enemy control. Some observers noted that Hanoi sought to humiliate both Nixon and the United States by these actions. To get our POWs back, the enemy felt, we would concede his every demand.

Initially, the enemy once again appeared on the verge of success. He moved southward, seized territory, and temporarily captured one provincial capital and threatened others. He misread the American public, if he thought the antiwar forces, the pressure to secure the return of the prisoners of war, American impatience, and psychological exhaustion with this prolonged war would win for him what he could not gain by warfare alone. He surely erred if he thought we had lost both the will and the capacity to retaliate. The enemy thus seemed about as ignorant of our nature and character as we had often been of his. A closer reading of events might have shown the enemy that the prowar forces had not yet vanished. Congressional efforts to curb the president's war powers continued to fail, if by thinner and thinner margins. Nixon warned Russia and China that even great powers bore a "special responsibility" to discourage their client states from attacking their neighbors—an argument which the president pressed home during his visit to Moscow and which later events revealed to have had some influence. Hints also came that our withdrawal program might .be temporarily stopped or delayed. Although on April 1, 1972, Nixon offered to resume the then suspended Paris peace talks, he demanded that Hanoi first call off the offensive launched the previous day. Nixon was not about to go to Moscow in the wake of military defeat and have his leverage thus weakened. With Communists you bargain only from strength, not weakness. One official noted at the time when enemy success loomed: "If Hué falls, Moscow is out."[47]

Our withdrawal rested upon the assumption that it would be matched by a lowered level of aid to the other side by Russia and China. It did not signal appeasement or surrender. Always possible was a resumption of the fighting, the bombing, and any other measures deemed necessary. Nixon never lost all his options. Fearing the enemy would achieve a surprise and sudden military victory, the president resumed the bombing by air and by sea and expanded our attacks to include the mining of the harbors and waters of North Vietnam. Hanoi, pressing us to negotiate, stepped up the war, openly invaded the South, and declared that the DMZ was not a border; hence crossing it was not an invasion but the defense of its own country. Our response was to run some very grave risks, which once again brought the antiwar forces out howling.

The Nixon administration justified this renewed and intensified warfare of spring 1972 by a review of its efforts for peace and the enemy response to those efforts. Republicans loved to repeat the story of our withdrawals over the past year as evidence of fulfillment of the Nixon pledge to extricate us from the war. On April 26, 1972, the president gave a broadcast speech in which he again stated that our every peace effort had been met by the North Vietnamese with a blunt rejection and a massive escalation of their military effort to win. We had waited patiently through hundreds of sessions at the Paris talks in hopes of a diplomatic solution, but all in vain, because they sought a military victory—"a victory they cannot be allowed to win."[48] William Safire, who helped Nixon write this war speech warning the enemy of the consequences of his offensive, later wrote:

> In a six-week span, Nixon rose to the final challenge of his Vietnam Policy by a foe that never wanted to negotiate and always wanted to win; he reacted with the application of enough power to counter that bid for victory, but with enough coolness in its presentation to the American public to be accepted without another Kent State.[49]

Nixon noted with seeming pride that this massive attack had been resisted on the ground solely "by South Vietnamese forces, and in one area by South Korean forces," and pledged that none of our ground forces would become involved; but to support the ARVN, he had "ordered attacks on enemy military targets in both North and South Vietnam by the air and naval forces of the United States." This he believed, on assurances by General Abrams, would prevent defeat. He also believed this proved that Vietnamization was succeeding, and as proof he announced that our troop withdrawals would proceed on schedule. By July 1972 our force levels would be down to forty-nine thousand. In spite of wide demands that he stop the bombing and return to the Paris talks, he would not repeat the story of 1968. Already he had sharply reduced the level of our participation in the war, but in diplomacy he failed to get from the enemy anything but the demand that we oust the Saigon government and impose a Communist dictatorship in its place. He recalled his frequent warnings that if the enemy responded to our peace efforts by stepping up the war, he would react to meet the attack for three reasons: to protect our remaining troops, facilitate our withdrawal program, and "prevent the imposition of a Communist regime on the people of South Vietnam against their will, with the inevitable bloodbath that would follow for hundreds of thousands who have dared to oppose Communist aggression." Our recent strikes were aimed to achieve these goals, were directed only against military targets, and would not end until the invasion stopped. He believed enemy efforts revealed his failure to win over the people of South Vietnam politically and militarily. Nixon then added his oft-repeated conviction: "Their one remaining hope is to win in the Congress of the United States and among the people of the United States the victory they cannot win among the people of South Vietnam or on the battlefield in South Vietnam."[50]

The president still thought the stakes were great in this war, for us and all mankind, because if one country, armed with the most modern weapons by other countries, could invade another nation and subjugate it, "other countries would be encouraged to do the same," anywhere. If the Communists won in Vietnam, the risk of war elsewhere would be enormously increased. Again he declared we were not trying to conquer North Vietnam or anyone. We sought no bases; rather we had offered most generous peace terms—with honor for both sides: "But, we will not be defeated, and we will never surrender our friends to Communist aggression." He reflected that in his travels to Peking on his historic "journey for peace" early in 1972 and in his coming trip to Moscow in May he had found and hoped to find great respect for the office of president of the United States. Then he observed:

If the United States betrays the millions of people who have relied on us in Vietnam, the President of the United States, whoever he is, will not deserve nor receive the respect which is essential if the United States is to continue to play the great role we are destined to play of helping to build a new structure of peace in the world. It would amount to a renunciation of our morality, an abdication of our leadership among nations, and an invitation for the mighty to prey upon the weak all around the world. It would be to deny peace the chance peace deserves to have. This we shall never do.[51]

The same defense of our resort to further bombing and naval attacks was given by Secretary Rogers. Rogers told Fulbright's Senate Foreign Relations Committee the invasion now fully revealed the cruel hoax which Hanoi had long sought to foist on the American people, that somehow the Vietnam war was a civil war.

"Now, it is quite clear—and I don't believe anyone can deny it—that this is a major invasion, offensive action by the North Vietnamese in South Vietnam."[52] Rogers noted that South Vietnamese pilots were flying many of these tactical missions, but added that if we removed all our forces, the result most probably would be a bloodbath and the destabilization of the entire area. Other nations with whom we had treaties would try other options. He felt it a waste of time to engage in further useless talks with North Vietnam as long as the enemy used them merely for a propaganda forum. To him, negotiations were quite different from talks; they sought seriously to resolve difficulties. He also believed the situation now differed greatly from that which Johnson faced in 1968 and promised greater success than had been achieved then. Now we did not have five hundred and thirty-five thousand Americans in South Vietnam. Now we had trained and equipped the South Vietnamese to defend themselves. Also the enemy had never before committed all his forces outside his own country. Rather, there had been a sort of limited guerrilla warfare. There were infiltration efforts and sapper tactics, but now there was a major invasion that required vast reinforcements and supplies of gasoline and oil and all the rest that accompanies conventional warfare. With our additional help in this crisis, time would be available for Saigon to advance further and faster to the stage in which it could defend itself by air and by land without our military presence. Rogers declared we would continue to use our air power to prevent a Communist takeover and added that, while we would do many things he would not reveal, there were two things we would not do:

We are not going to reintroduce American ground combat troops to South Vietnam and we are not going to use nuclear weapons in South Vietnam or in

North Vietnam. But short of that, we are not going to make any announcements of what we are going to do or not going to do.[53]

Secretary Laird, long opposed to resuming the bombing and an advocate of restraint on Vietnam ever since he took his cabinet post, advised the White House that the Hanoi and Haiphong areas contained vast petroleum stocks and truck and tank parks of great significance, but added that even if they were destroyed, little effect would be felt on the battlefield for weeks, possibly months.[54] However, on April 18, 1972, he told Fulbright's committee that the raids could go on if the enemy kept up the invasion. In fact, he did not rule out the possibility of a blockade or mining of the port of Haiphong. We might have to "impose a naval quarantine on Haiphong to stop the entry of ships carrying military equipment, or alternatively mine the channel leading into the harbor." Also it might be necessary to protect our troops and permit their withdrawal. However, he clearly indicated that one purpose of the bombing was to emphasize "the need for military restraint upon both North Vietnam and the Soviet Union." Russia had given Hanoi the equipment without which the invasion would have been most unlikely. Vietnamization had assumed that South Vietnam might hope to defend itself against the local Vietcong, but not against Hanoi's regulars equipped with the most modern weapons by Peking and Moscow. "The United States, he said, had been 'very careful' to provide South Vietnam only the military equipment that would give it an 'in-country capability' of defending its security." By contrast, Russia had "imposed 'no restraints' on the type of equipment provided North Vietnam, with the result that there are now '12 North Vietnamese divisions marauding all over the countryside in Southeast Asia." Laird suspected Russia desired to continue the war and our costly involvement. This gave her time to modernize her own armies while helping to effect the defeat of Vietnamization, which she saw was working.[55]

With the end of our ground combat operations, the only means left President Nixon was the use of air and naval power. The bombing and the naval attacks would continue and would expand. Reasons offered were many and diverse. The attacks would notify Hanoi that we still had the means and the will to respond to its continued aggression. They would prevent the defeat and subversion of South Vietnam and defend the ancient principle of self-determination. Commitments still must be honored if our role as a great power was to be upheld and other nations were to continue to respect us. If global stability were to be achieved and preserved, we had no other choice left. The enemy had stepped up his attacks over all Indochina and still sought a military victory. Our forces must be protected while disengaging. We must not be humiliated. The only way we could prevent humiliation for ourselves and our allies from further and worsening tactics of terrorism, stealth, and a suicidal dedication was by the use of our advanced equipment, especially our air power. To fail to respond to such blatant aggression in open defiance of the 1968 agreements and understandings could only show a weakening of will, with what tragic consequences no one could foresee. We had stopped the bombing of North Vietnam in 1968 with the understanding that the enemy would not fire at our reconnaissance planes, cross the demilitarized zone, and attack the cities of South Vietnam.

Hanoi strongly objected to our interpretation of the "understandings of 1968," denying they ever existed. In its view we agreed to halt the bombing and all other acts of war against North Vietnam without "reciprocity," after which peace talks would begin.[56] It quoted Ambassador Harriman as agreeing to this, but our State Department emphatically declared that such "understandings" did exist. Hanoi sought to give its version of the events leading to the bombing halt and make Washington appear the transgressor. The State Department resisted all pressure to make public the documents clarifying the story; a departmental spokesman reiterated that "understandings" existed, but "important diplomatic considerations" prevented official disclosure of the full story. One senior official of the State Department said such considerations consisted mainly of a desire not to embarrass Russia, which played a major role in satisfying Johnson in 1968 that Hanoi grasped the terms of the understanding. Cyrus R. Vance, the deputy American negotiator during the Paris talks of 1968, said Hanoi's denials were "just silly." He noted that Hanoi's version was "a selective summary which is only a partial version and leaves out very substantial parts of the discussions between us." In his *Vantage Point,* Johnson described how he had sought through channels from Russia double reassurance that Hanoi comprehended the "understandings" and had received confirmation that it did.[57]

Johnson agreed to halt the bombing on the condition that prompt and serious talks would follow; Hanoi would not take advantage of the cessation by attacks across the DMZ and endanger the lives of our men stationed in northern South Vietnam; the enemy would not carry out large-scale attacks against South Vietnam's major cities such as Saigon, Hue or Danang; and he would permit aerial reconnaissance over North Vietnam. It was made clear in all the negotiations leading to the halt that if these terms were violated by the enemy, we would resume the bombing and take what other measures we might deem necessary. Hence, whatever response Nixon wished to make after he came to office was implied in the "understandings" of 1968. The enemy just refused to admit the agreement of 1968 and chose to make whatever propaganda value out of his denial he could. Truth was he never lived up to the agreement. From the refusal to engage in serious talks down to the blunt and direct invasion by his regulars across the DMZ in 1972, and to a less extent before that, the enemy proved again he was bound by no pledges.

Also, President Nixon had frequently stated since 1969 his own conditions. These had been directly challenged, and the whole Communist world had expanded its efforts to defeat and humiliate the United States. Bombing was no more inhuman a method of warfare than a knife, a bullet, an artillery shell, a booby trap, or grenade. Although accidents occurred, our bombing was not directed against noncombatants as were enemy terror attacks. Washington believed that had we not responded to the enemy attacks, our failure would have affected the attitude of China and Russia toward us nullifying official efforts to achieve global stabilization. Our bombing was about the only means left us of playing the grim game of power politics. It was a game we could not avoid playing, and we had to play it well if we wished to survive.

Hawks in and out of the Pentagon stubbornly held to their faith in force—if we meant to achieve our objectives in the war. They saw the options clearly: get out of Vietnam; continue the stalemate; escalate the war; or pursue Vietnamization. Few had any faith at all in diplomacy—then or later. Their view was that our various military ventures—the Cambodian venture, the mining of enemy waters in the spring of 1972, the expanded aerial attacks of the summer of 1972, and the massive bombing of late December 1972—brought the enemy to reason and to negotiate seriously. Doves might berate these ventures and mourn the tragedies for helpless civilians victimized by them, but hawks thought of preventing enslavement, of victory for posterity, as well as of the living generations.

Mark W. Clark, the retired World War II general, urged the president to get tough. His experience in the Korean War justified that policy. The general saw important similarities between the two wars in the Orient. In both, we fought the same enemy. The enemy was the aggressor. He conformed to no recognized international rules of warfare, "both as to the killing of innocent civilians and the treatment of prisoners of war." He respected "strength and forceful action" and despised and exploited "weakness and appeasement." Finally, when he was severely punished and could not obtain his battlefield objectives, he was quick to run to the conference table, where, from experience, he discovered he could get more concessions through diplomacy.[58]

Clark said that when he himself faced a similar situation with Korea in 1953, the message he got from the enemy was: "Turn on the heat, let the despicable enemy have it." And that he did. He stopped the talking, which had been one prolonged insult, and stepped up the air and naval attacks all over North Korea. Kim Il Sung, the Communist boss of North Korea, got the message fast, and after a six-month steady barrage, called Clark in the middle of the night and proposed full resumption of the talks. After that, the armistice came quickly. Clark believed "we could have obtained better truce terms quicker, shortened the war, and saved lives if we had got tough faster." Now in 1972 he told the president we did not get tough fast enough in Vietnam. There was no mileage in Johnson's policy of bombing one day and stopping the next, in such a "no-win policy." He believed Nixon showed great courage and wisdom when he increased the pressure upon the enemy.[59]

Nixon's expansion of our air warfare was aimed at Moscow and the American public, as well as at the enemy. A careful assessment of his mood at the time revealed he was deeply disturbed by the indirect but nonetheless vital Soviet support for these enemy attacks. The timing of the enemy offensive made it appear that the United States was weak and failing in Vietnam at the very time Nixon was heading toward Russia to settle outstanding problems with that major world power. He refused to be embarrassed by Hanoi's tactics. If Russia meant to give maximum support to its ally in North Vietnam, Nixon could afford to do no less for his friend in South Vietnam. Extensive bombing might chill the mood of the coming negotiations in Moscow, but if it disrupted the flow of war supplies southward and the reinforcement of Hanoi's regulars, thereby warning Hanoi that its continued expansion of the aggression would face mounting raids in the North, it might also persuade Russia to use its influence to moderate enemy demands and seek a peaceful solution. He also feared that if he did not respond to the enemy offensive, there would be an angry domestic reaction to any agreements he might reach with Russia on arms control, trade expansion, and other hoped-for settlements. Hanoi should not be left unpunished for its aggressions. It needed a firm reminder that our withdrawal and disillusionment with the war gave them no immunity from punishment. The raids upon Hanoi and Haiphong and the mining of the waters were meant to notify Hanoi and Russia that even if we were retreating and reducing our level of action we would still exact a heavy price for military offensives.

To save the summit conference with Russia, Kissinger in a visit to Moscow in mid-summer 1972 discussed with Brezhnev the link between "Russia's need for grain and credits and America's desire to see the Vietnam war ended." Both men wanted detente to succeed. However, his aide, Alexander Haig, and others maintained that Hanoi had begun to change its hardline policy, cease its demand for our ouster of Thieu, and consent to two contending factions in South Vietnam, not because of any possible Soviet pressure but because of the damaging effects of our mining and bombing inside North Vietnam. At this point observers noted that Hanoi was abandoning its former unyielding positions and pledging its willingness to accept a political process in which neither side would seek to eliminate the other or to "impose" itself on the other.[60]

Kissinger by that time believed Nixon's great gamble of force against Hanoi had worked, because Brezhnev

needed tranquility in his volatile East European backyard; he needed Western technology to transform and modernize Russia's backward economy; he needed a summit with Nixon to offset the American opening to China. In short, he needed so much that he swallowed the humiliation of the mining and prepared to welcome Nixon.[61]

That reassuring thought erased Kissinger's fears and removed his earlier doubts concerning the risks.

Laird noted that one purpose of the bombing was to impress upon both North Vietnam and the Soviet Union the need for military restraint. While we had been very careful to keep ourselves in check, our restraint, he observed, had been answered by an invasion across the DMZ in violation of the agreement of 1968. This must be dealt with as a very serious matter, which our government could not take lightly. Russia should see the necessity of limiting Hanoi's use of the equipment sent from Moscow. Obviously, the invasion by conventional tactics and weapons was made possible by the means that could have been supplied only by Moscow.[62]

Our raids upon the North, like the invasions of Cambodia and Laos in 1970 and 1971, had been for the same common purpose. They would give a psychological support to the people of South Vietnam. They would certainly gain time for further progress in Vietnamization and for improvements in the ARVN's military capability—on land and in the air. Massive bombing had always been our last available weapon. Nixon had warned that it might be used.[63] It caused the least loss of life for American forces and was therefore most acceptable to American public opinion, however damaging or inhuman it might seem to the enemy or the antiwar forces elsewhere. Nevertheless, in Washington one keen observer, Max Frankel of the *New York Times,* wrote:

It is thought here that Mr. Nixon's primary purpose in bombing Hanoi and Haiphong was to serve notice that he would not go to Moscow without somehow balancing the challenge to his Vietnamese ally. White House officials acknowledged that it was too late to force a recall of the North Vietnamese armies and their Soviet missiles and tanks, but the hope is that at least the war's psychological impact on the Moscow meetings has been blunted.[64]

The Nixon administration was aware also that we had made major gains in the Vietnamization and pacification programs that profoundly changed the situation that existed when Johnson halted the bombing in 1968. Such changes the war critics somehow missed, wrote Steve Young to the editor of the *New York Times.* The landlord class had been crippled by land reform; the National Liberation Front had been sharply weakened due to village security and democracy. One observer noted there had been thirty-five hundred village and hamlet elections since 1967. Prosperity had returned to rural areas, thanks to the improved security and a measure of stability, and a viable political structure had emerged. In 1968, however, the Communists could attack virtually every city in South Vietnam at once, even with the presence of five hundred thousand American troops, but in 1972, with our troops gone, they could muster mainly a North Vietnamese invasion over the DMZ with minor thrusts across the South Vietnamese border with Cambodia and Laos. It was time we paid more attention to South Vietnam and its people and not so much just to Thieu and his puppets.[65]

The spring offensive of the enemy did not reveal that Vietnamization was a total failure, but it did show that without American air power South Vietnam was not yet able to preserve its independence. It did not prove either that a limited use of air power could win for Saigon. It did seem to demonstrate that the enemy could not win as long as we were willing to use fully our air and naval power. It suggested that a diplomatic rather than a military solution was most apt to succeed. Certainly, for the moment, the resort to air power was a policy for getting us more deeply into the war rather than out of it; but hindsight suggested, in view of the enemy's willingness in October and November of 1972 and January 1973 to engage in serious negotiations, that its use had been not a minor factor in bringing that more peaceful tactic into use. The massive bombing and mining undoubtedly helped to persuade the enemy to negotiate his desires.

In resuming the bombing and mining of the waters of North Vietnam, Nixon took considerable risk—greater than Johnson was willing to take. He risked the possibility of Chinese and Russian intervention, the collapse of his efforts to achieve a detente with those powers, and a renewed, if not greater, outburst inside the United States from the antiwar forces, who seemed above all to think that the only task left us was to surrender the struggle in order to secure the return of our prisoners of war and missing in action.

The critics yelled that our use of air power to save Thieu every time he ran into a crisis trapped us and our air force endlessly into a war directed by Hanoi and Saigon. All Saigon had to do when in trouble was to demonstrate its inability to defend itself, and we would come running to its assistance. Whatever the case against our use of air power, Nixon was determined not to lose the war, the election, or his long-planned diplomatic victories in China and the Soviet Union. In fact, the hawks believed that had we used our air power fully in 1964 and 1965 we might have long ago achieved even a military victory, but the doves continued to contend that the war demonstrated decisively that bombing could never achieve either a military or diplomatic victory. At least, this enemy "go for broke" effort surely pointed the way toward the desperate need to look earnestly for a diplomatic solution.

However, while we searched for a diplomatic solution, we sharply expanded the war. Nixon declared that all we had risked hung in the balance, and added that we would not be defeated and would never surrender our friends to Communist aggression. These threatening words were the tip-off that a critical point had been reached. The enemy's spring offensive gravely endangered our entire Vietnamization program and risked upsetting the president's whole scheme of global detente with China and Russia. The Paris talks were stalled and diplomacy seemed stalemated, but our losses in battle continued. The reasons for the invasion of Cambodia in 1970 and the continued heavy bombing of Vietnam had been to provide time for South Vietnam to defend itself. If after our making serious efforts for peace and sharply reducing the numbers of our troops involved and the level of our actions, the enemy tried to achieve a quick military solution, Nixon felt our back was to the wall and retaliation was imperative. The risks of expansion of the air war were high, but he deemed the situation required the venture.

The antiwar critics denounced the president's tough speech of April 26 and his stance thereafter. Fulbright could feel only severe depression and sadness for the nation. After all the destruction of life and property, there was still no end to the tragedy. McGovern denounced the whole Nixon thesis: "The President says we bomb to prevent a bloodbath. But his immoral and outrageous bombardment is the bloodbath." The critics had a field day denouncing official failures in both Saigon and Washington. They observed that Vietnamization had been more than a total failure; without our air power all would have been quickly lost; and withdrawal had ceased in favor of deceptive uses of naval and air strikes from outside and offshore from South Vietnam. Such an expansion of the scale of the war and the rhetoric condemning it guaranteed that the war would be a major issue in the coming election campaign, but somehow the violence, the demonstrations, and turbulence that had generally met the Cambodian venture and other actions of previous years failed to erupt this year.

Too many Americans agreed with the president and believed he had done about all honor and fairness required to withdraw from the war. In fact, they were growing tired of the critics and others who incessantly attacked the nation and its system. Although some feared we had probably underestimated Hanoi's capacities for "sustained challenge" in South Vietnam, and field commanders believed the offensive might endure for quite awhile, Nixon tried to put the public at ease by saying the North Vietnamese had absolutely failed to rally the South Vietnamese to their side and still controlled less than 10 percent of South Vietnam's population. Others countered with the observation that while the president had noted in 1971 that the South Vietnamese by themselves could "hack it," in his recent speech he admitted that if we halted our naval and air warfare and quit Vietnam, it would mean, of course, a Communist takeover.[66]

At the Texas ranch of secretary of the treasury, John Connally, April 30, the president met with a group of prominent Texans of both political parties. There, for more than an hour, he made further observations to justify his intensified warfare. Again he noted that despite the enemy invasion, over 90 percent of the people of South Vietnam were still under the control of Saigon. He reiterated the vital importance of our expanded efforts. Sixty-nine thousand Americans were still there; the consequences of inaction could not be ignored; and a bloodbath for hundreds of thousands would follow a Communist takeover. He recalled the tragedy of 1954 and afterwards, when Communists took over North Vietnam. The Catholic bishop of Da Nang estimated that at this time at least five hundred thousand people who had opposed the Communists "were either murdered or starved to death in slave labor camps." He remembered a trip to South Vietnam in 1956 when he and Mrs. Nixon visited refugee camps housing over a million North Vietnamese who had fled from Communist tyranny. Now he feared what would happen to these people if the enemy seized all South Vietnam. He wanted to end the war, yes, but only in a way that would prevent a recurrence now or shortly hereafter of those tragic events.[67]

Americans and others wondered what Nixon would do if the enemy kept coming, our ally kept crumbling, the Russians kept stalling, and the political and other risks kept mounting. Nixon's answer was:

We are prepared to use our military and naval strength against military targets throughout North Vietnam, and we believe that the North Vietnamese are taking a very great risk if they continue their offensive in the South. I will just leave it there, and they can make their own choice.[68]

That was an ominous threat. However, before taking drastic action, Washington sought to try other options. For a few more days, Nixon fought back hard with the means available—supply Saigon, keep open the channels of diplomacy, and remind the Russians of their complicity and responsibility for aiding Hanoi's aggressions. Ruled out only were the reintroduction of our ground forces and the use of nuclear weapons. Hope persisted that the ARVN could hold out, that the enemy operated on a very long supply line in weather that would not be favorable for very long. Desperate options, said observers, did not appear attractive. Washington could order systematic destruction of the enemy population, but that was too horrible for consideration. It could land marines in North Vietnam to destroy key installations, depots, harbors, and possibly liberate some war prisoners. It could challenge Russia more directly and possibly force North Vietnam into negotiations by attacks on its supply ships and by closing Haiphong Harbor by mining or blockade. Of course, we could also break the diplomatic stalemate by secret and significant concessions to the enemy that would spare him the appearance of defeat and humiliation while we engaged in forceful military action. Both Russia and the United States without confrontation could agree to end or reduce their arms shipments to the two Vietnams. Both could favor a prisoner exchange and supervise a general settlement to save face for all.

Nixon faced a difficult choice, but the pressure to avoid failure at this late date was great. C. L. Sulzberger of the *New York Times* noted that the more the Vietnamese front disintegrated, the more Nixon's whole Asian and global strategy weakened and Soviet prestige increased. Giap's offensive had to be blunted. No matter whether we should have initially intervened there, history would judge us by our power and determination to succeed.[69] In perspective it was quite a gamble for Nixon, who had pulled out his ground forces to please his domestic critics, believed he could count on the South Vietnamese backed by our air and naval power to smash any invasion, and calculated that if that failed, he could force the enemy to negotiate a compromise solution by bombing Hanoi and mining Haiphong Harbor.

In a nationwide television and radio speech of May 8, 1972, Nixon explained "his new course" in Indochina. Again he recounted past public and private efforts to negotiate a solution and declared he had offered "the maximum" any president could offer: a de-escalation of the fighting, a cease-fire with a fixed deadline for our total withdrawal, and new elections under international supervision with Communist participation "in the supervisory body and in the elections themselves." Thieu had even "offered to resign one month before the elections." We had offered to swap prisoners of war in a ratio of ten North Vietnamese to every American. All these offers the enemy had rejected with insolence. His answer to every peace offer was escalation of the war. Even within the past two weeks alone, since Nixon had offered to resume · negotiations, Hanoi had launched new offensives in South Vietnam: "In those 2 weeks the risk that a Communist government may be imposed on the 17 million people of South Vietnam has increased, and the Communist offensive has now reached the point that it gravely threatens the lives of 60,000 American troops who are still in Vietnam." This left us only two issues: in the face of massive attack, could we do nothing and endanger the lives of our troops and leave to South Vietnam "a long night of terror?" Obviously not. Secondly, in the face of total intransigence by the enemy at the peace talks, could we join him to impose his despotism upon South Vietnam? Obviously not: "We will not cross the line from generosity to treachery." Three clear hard choices remained: prompt and total withdrawal, continued diplomatic efforts, and "decisive military action to end the war." The bloodbath terror and enduring despotism made the first utterly unacceptable. It was preferable to try negotiation again even though it took two to negotiate. Now. "as throughout the past 4 years, the North Vietnamese arrogantly refuse to negotiate anything but an imposition, an ultimatum that the United States impose a Communist regime on 17 million people in South Vietnam who do not want a Communist government."[70]

That was no choice at all. In this tragic war the killing must stop, but by our simply getting out we would only worsen the bloodshed. Interminable negotiations rewarded stubbornness by allowing aggression and war to continue. The only way to stop the war was to keep the weapons of war out of the hands of the international outlaws of North Vietnam. While throughout the long struggle we had exercised restraint unprecedented in history—the responsibility of a great nation—the enemy had abandoned all restraint, sent his entire army against his neighbor, refused to negotiate, threatened the lives of our soldiers being withdrawn, and shown every intention of seeking solely a military victory. Hanoi must be denied the tools of further war. Therefore, as he spoke the president had ordered these measures:

All entrances to North Vietnamese ports will be mined to prevent access to these ports and North Vietnamese naval operations from these ports. United States forces have been directed to take appropriate measures within the internal and claimed territorial waters of North Vietnam to interdict the delivery of any supplies. Rail and all other communications will be cut off to the maximum extent possible. Air and naval strikes against military targets in North Vietnam will continue.[71]

He declared these acts were not directed against any other nation; other countries with ships then in North Vietnamese ports had been notified that their ships would have "three daylight periods to leave safely." After that time the mines would be activated and ships would then leave only at their own risk. Then he added significantly:

These actions I have ordered will cease when the following conditions are met:
First, all American prisoners of war must be returned.
Second, there must be an internationally supervised cease-fire throughout Indochina.
Once prisoners of war are released, once the internationally supervised cease-fire has begun, we will stop all acts of force throughout Indochina, and at that time we will proceed with a complete withdrawal of all American forces from Vietnam within 4 months.[72]

He thought these terms generous. They did not demand the surrender and humiliation of anybody; they would let us withdraw with honor; they would end the killing, bring our war prisoners home, and permit the Vietnamese people to settle their own political affairs; and above all they would permit all the nations of Indochina to turn to peace and reconstruction. To Hanoi he said: "Your people have already suffered too much in your pursuit of conquest. Do not compound their agony with continued arrogance; choose instead the path of peace that redeems your sacrifices, guarantees true independence for your country, and ushers in an era of reconciliation." To South Vietnam he pledged continued support against aggression and declared: "Your spirit . . . will determine the outcome of the battle. . . . Your will . . . will shape the future of your country." To other nations, especially those allied with North Vietnam, he declared the actions he had taken were not directed against them, but aimed solely to protect the lives of sixty thousand Americans if the Communist offensive continued to roll southward and to protect 17 million people of South Vietnam from brutal aggression.[73]

To Russia, a great nation which he expected soon to visit, he directed special comments. He said: We respect you as a great power; we recognize your right to defend your interests when threatened; and in return you must recognize our right to defend ours. Your soldiers were not in danger; ours were. While you help your allies, you must expect us to help ours:

But let us, and let all great powers, help our allies only for the purpose of their defense, not for the purpose of launching invasions against their neighbors.

Otherwise the cause of peace, the cause in which we both have so great a stake, will be seriously jeopardized.

Our two nations have made significant progress in our negotiations in recent months. We are near major agreements on nuclear arms limitation, on trade, on a host of other issues.

Let us not slide back toward the dark shadows of a previous age. We do not ask you to sacrifice your principles, or your friends, but neither should you permit Hanoi's intransigence to blot out the prospects we together have so patiently prepared.

He added that both nations were on the threshold of a new relationship that could serve all mankind and noted that we were ready to build on this relationship; but, he observed, "The responsibility is yours if we fail to do so."[74]

On May 9, 1972, a day after the president's dramatic announcement, Henry Kissinger fleshed out part of the background events and factors.[75] He recalled that Hanoi had canceled a private meeting scheduled for November 20 when Le Duc Tho suddenly became ill; but, as the president had noted January 25, 1972, we offered to resume the talks when he recovered. We had insisted upon a representative from Hanoi because without its political leadership the Paris delegation simply lacked "sufficient authority to make these private talks useful. We never received a reply to this message of Nov. 19." On January 26, the day after Nixon's speech, we informed Hanoi we were ready to resume private talks, and, on February 14, received a reply suggesting March 15 or any time thereafter. The North Vietnamese haggled a bit more about the date. We set a date; they could not agree. They agreed to another and then postponed it. We suspended the Paris talks March 27, and four days later Hanoi agreed on April 24, provided we returned to the Paris negotiations. Then we sent Ambassador Porter back to Paris, told the enemy we were ready to resume the plenary sessions on April 13 and confirmed the meeting of April 24. However, when that last message was drafted, March 31, "we were not aware of the fact that a major offensive had in fact started at the demilitarized zone, and therefore, some of the press reports that we were tying the resumption of the plenaries to the end of the offensive are totally wrong." Kissinger declared we had told Hanoi this offensive was inconsistent with peace negotiations, that we were exercising great restraint in our response to it "to give the negotiations every chance to succeed." When the letter was delivered April 2, Kissinger revealed he was not sure the offensive was full-scale until Easter Sunday.

Kissinger continued that Washington knew during March that a military buildup was under way, but showed great restraint in face of the fact. We authorized only the normal protective reaction strikes, nothing against supply installations or missile sites "because of our concern for our relationships that had been established in Peking and that we were trying to develop in Moscow." Then followed further messages—six in all—in April concerning private talks before Kissinger went to Moscow, where he discussed at great length the problem of Vietnam. He told the Soviet leader about

the extraordinary complexity that was posed for us by a massive invasion of the entire North Vietnamese field army against South Vietnam, an invasion that if it achieved its objective was bound to jeopardize the security of 60,000 Americans, and the impact that such developments had to have on our attempts to move forward on a broad front.

Russian leaders "felt that every effort should be made to resume negotiations," and we agreed to return to the Paris talks if we received a firm assurance that a private meeting would rapidly follow. We would consider almost any reasonable approach that would reduce the violence and advance a solution of the difficulties, but with one proviso: "We would not impose a Communist government on Saigon; we wanted a genuine political solution."[76]

Then came two plenary sessions at Paris and a private session, in which "we again went through every conceivable approach for ending the military situation," but then only to have read to our delegates the long-published statement of the Communist position. Kissinger continued: "It had taken us six months to set up the meeting and innumerable exchanges and when we got there, what we heard could have been clipped from a newspaper and sent to us in the mail. This was the situation we confronted last week."

What did the enemy then demand of us that we had rejected? Prior to any cease-fire, the following steps must be taken:

The President of South Vietnam must resign. What is called [sic] the other side "the machinery of oppression" of the government must be disbanded.

Pacification must be stopped. Vietnamization must be stopped, which means the end of American military and economic aid. All persons who have been arrested on political grounds should be set free. Then a government should be formed which is composed of all those who favor peace, independence, neutrality and democracy, presumably, by definition, including the Communists.

In that government, in other words, the Communists would be the only organized force, since all the organized non-Communist forces would have been disbanded by definition.

All of this is prior to a cease-fire. Then this government is supposed to negotiate with the Communists a final solution. In other words, this is only the thinnest veneer; this government, which already contains the Communists, is then supposed to negotiate with the provincial revolutionary government, which at that moment will be the only force in the country which has an army, which is backed by the North Vietnamese Army. It will be the only force in the country that has any physical strength, and it is supposed to negotiate with them a final settlement. And all of this . . . is before a cease-fire.[77]

This was what Nixon had rejected. Little wonder the nation overwhelmingly voted in November to defeat George McGovern, a man who sought to make it appear that Nixon had stubbornly refused to accept peace terms, honorable and just. Nixon rejected such a thin veneer, such an imposition of a Communist victory. To end our aid and disband the Saigon regime as a prelude to negotiation were the only issues on which the negotiations broke down. All our concessions were totally ignored or refused. This was what Nixon faced in May 1972. The enemy had mounted a major offensive which he would stop only on terms no president could accept. Only with great pain and reluctance was the president forced to act. For two years we had negotiated with Russia on a broad range of issues and were on the verge of success, of new relationships that could benefit humanity. Surely Russia could not be oblivious to the impact of the actions of one of its friends, "particularly when those friends are armed with the weapons of this country." He asked his audience to consider what it would think,

in the months before a summit meeting, if an American ally, armed with American weapons, attacked a Soviet ally and put into jeopardy the tens of thousands of Soviet troops, whether you would not ask yourself whether we should have exercised some restraint.

We could not go on attempting to negotiate while the enemy mounted attacks when it suited his objectives. Our terms, Kissinger believed, were most reasonable. They would leave the determination of the political future to the Vietnamese and would let us withdraw with honor and end the fighting. Hence it was wrong to say we had embarked upon a course designed to impose our solution.[78]

Renewal and expansion of the bombing again stirred wide debate and bitter denunciation. Air power had its advocates and detractors throughout the war, yet with advancing troop withdrawals it was about all we had left to retard enemy actions. War critics cited the revelation of the *Pentagon Papers* that the bombing had been futile, and they made public a secret Nixon administration study of 1969 by Henry Kissinger and his National Security Council staff with other government agencies which reached similar conclusions. Significantly the first Kissinger National Security study memorandum showed that nearly four years of our bombing destroyed $500 million to $770 million of capital stock, military facilities, and current production in North Vietnam, but in the same period the enemy received from other Communist countries aid to the amount of $3 billion—four to six times as much as we destroyed. In fact, North Vietnam was better off in 1969 than it was in 1965. Aid from Russia, China, and other Communist nations averaged about $115 million a year during the war years prior to 1965, but rose when the bombing began in 1965, reaching about $1 billion a year by 1968. After the bombing halt in 1968, Communist aid to Hanoi again declined. It did not prevent enemy ability to supply its armed forces, but it did impose vast hardships on the people of North Vietnam. Larger warfare had been the general response to failure of diplomacy to find a solution.[79]

The reactions to these decisions by Nixon and Kissinger were not as abrasive as some expected. Spurred by Fulbright, Senate Democrats passed by a vote of 29 to 14 a resolution against the escalation of the war, and dovish members of Congress sought to include Nixon's peace offer in a proposed congressional mandate to end the war. Long ago, lines on the war issue had hardened. The expected denunciations and defense of executive actions poured forth, but the turbulence of earlier protests was missing. Bitterly disappointing to Washington was the failure of Russia to restrain Hanoi's action. In spite of all our diplomatic effort, public and private, Hanoi's demands remained the same, and Soviet hints that she might be able to induce the enemy to talk seriously proved empty.

The latest peace terms reduced the time for United States withdrawal from six to four months and pledged to cease all acts of force throughout Indochina, to relieve Hanoi of fears that our planes from Thailand and aircraft carriers might continue their attacks. No mention was made, however, of the possibility of air and naval attacks by the United States if the enemy broke his cease-fire or other agreements. There was no demand that North Vietnamese soldiers should leave South Vietnam. Nothing was said specifically about Thieu's resignation one month before elections, about any elections at all or about our ancient pledge of national self-determination for Vietnam. All political issues were now to be left to the people of all Vietnam to settle among themselves. Neither Thieu nor his "Four No's" would delay any longer our withdrawal. Political solutions were left to the natives. Vietnamization—meaning the South Vietnamese people alone—would have to protect South Vietnam. If our withdrawal led ultimately to a Communist takeover, it would be by the failure of South Vietnam not by our imposition of a Communist regime prior to departure or as a price of peaceful extrication. That would save our face with some honor. Nothing was said or implied as to what we would do once we were gone and violations of the cease-fire—so widely expected—erupted over South Vietnam. Nothing was said about further material aid by the United States.

Nixon's blockade posed especially hard choices for Russia. Brezhnev and his associates now had to decide whether they wished global peace with the United States or continued rivalry in Vietnam and elsewhere. Washington wanted no confrontation with Russia; however, it did not hesitate to challenge Moscow's expansionist designs, making it clear to Russia that she could not expect to negotiate mutual agreements and achieve better relations with us while simultaneously threatening our interests elsewhere—as by arming Hanoi to kill American soldiers. Confrontation with the United States over Vietnam would seriously risk the Russian policy of accommodation with the West, but if the Soviet leaders saved their policy of improved relations with America by choking off aid to Hanoi, they would weaken their bargaining leverage. Russia, one of the greatest violators of international law in history, protested the blockade but did not cancel the pending Moscow summit conference with Nixon. By this sober decision a showdown was avoided, and the world breathed easier.

Nevertheless, Russian aid to Hanoi continued. The blockade made more difficult, but not impossible, further deliveries. Although we did not accuse Russia of promoting the invasion, we did charge that she supplied Hanoi in early 1972 with some very advanced weapons in the knowledge that they would be used for just such a military operation as the spring offensive. That risky action brought an American challenge and rejection. The president could not fail to read the meaning of Soviet strategy over the past year which led to the showdown. In May 1971 the Russians had signed a treaty in Egypt that strengthened their base in the Middle East and thwarted our efforts to solve the Arab-Israeli conflict. In August, they signed a treaty that gave a green light for India to fight Pakistan and establish an independent Bangladesh, which ultimately enhanced Russian prestige and power in the Indian subcontinent. And in April 1972 they signed a treaty with Iraq that would most likely increase tension between Iran and Iraq and advance Russian influence in that turbulent region. And now came the North Vietnamese spring offensive backed by Soviet weaponry. Nixon could not ignore these events; rather he felt compelled to challenge Soviet expansion. Thus one journalist concluded: "The Kremlin was confronted with a fundamental contradiction in its policy: the belief that it could pose threats to vital U.S. interests without jeopardizing its attempt to work out a new relationship with America."[80]

Kissinger and others admitted that the decision to blockade North Vietnam risked a showdown with Russia, but painful as it was for them and for us, "no honorable alternative was available."[81] Kissinger did not think the risk was unacceptable. Rather he believed no showdown was likely and declared administration plans for the summit meeting in Moscow were proceeding. We wished better relations with Moscow and urged Russian officials to make the vital decision to give priority to the ties with the United States over any gains it might make by unrestrained support of such countries as North Vietnam. He declared:

We recognize that the decisions we have taken present some short-term difficulties to the Soviet leaders, but we also believe that the situation that they permitted to evolve presented massive difficulties for us, and both sides have faced the problem throughout of making some real choices; that is to say, if one wants a genuine improvement in relations, as we do, one cannot also at the same time maximize the pressures all around the periphery.[82]

He did not pretend to know what the Russian answer would be; he could only affirm for us the belief that a new era in East-West relations was possible and our determination to continue our search for improvement of them. He had just returned from a trip to Moscow, where he had discussed Vietnam at great length and had stressed our deep concern about the North Vietnamese offensive. He had not there discussed any precise actions planned by us, because we had not then decided upon them, but he noted:

I do not believe that there could be any doubt in the minds of the Soviet leaders of the gravity with which we would view an unchecked continuation of a major North Vietnamese offensive and of an attempt by the North Vietnamese to put everything on the military scales.[83]

However, he noted with some rancor that after he returned from Russia and we had agreed, at Soviet urging, to both private and public talks with North Vietnam, Hanoi had launched three major attacks. He did not believe Russia had a deliberate plan to humiliate the United States in Vietnam; but, he added,

any thoughtful national leader looking at the masses of offensive equipment might have considered the consequences and, prior to a meeting that had, and still has such high prospects, one should ask oneself whether it can be in the interest of either party to impose a major setback on the other.[84]

Nixon's strategy was designed in part to put pressure on Moscow. After three years of stalled diplomatic and military action, he decided to take a new approach through Russia and retreat further from the terms formerly demanded of Hanoi. He now chose to blame the Communist superpowers for his failure to end the war and the frustration of his program of Vietnamization. Since Moscow had supplied the weapons for his failure, it must be pressured to help him find an escape. While Nixon retreated from the terms demanded of Hanoi, he raised a challenge to a new adversary, Russia. He wished to make Russia share some of the same frustrations. If his ally had to face greater troubles because of less United States aid, so should Hanoi due to declining Soviet assistance. He wished Russia to suffer as much from setbacks to Hanoi as we did from those to Saigon. The blockade therefore meant that Russia should share our Vietnam agony "as the price of progress on arms control, tempting trade arrangements and other agreements that had been prepared for the Moscow meeting this month."[85]

Nixon here switched from a war he was not winning to a confrontation which offered us a better chance. With a "low level of military risk," he gained time for diplomatic maneuver. He could pressure Russia to share the burden of finding a settlement by pinning part of the blame for the problem upon her. He hoped to establish a "linkage" of the East-West issue. There would be no settlement of European and Western problems with Russia until we could get a solution to the problems of the East. Out of this, Washington hoped at least to secure an agreement covering military actions, while the political future of Vietnam remained for Hanoi and Saigon to iron out in the future. In this fashion, we retreated from a tight settlement that would fix the political arrangements to one that would simply permit us a decent interval for extrication.[86]

This revealed our despair at gaining the full settlement we once sought—that is, exchanging a total withdrawal and bombing halt for a return of the prisoners, a cease-fire, and the withdrawal of North Vietnamese regulars from Laos, Cambodia, and South Vietnam. "Hanoi had always demanded also a halt in American military aid to the Saigon Government and help in deposing its head, President Nguyen Van Thieu." Nixon would now settle apparently for a peaceful withdrawal and cease-fire without mention of Saigon, Thieu, or the further aid issue. In essence, what that seemed to mean was: Let us out with honor and you can later settle your problems without our intervention. He did not here insist upon Hanoi's withdrawal of its forces from South Vietnam. This meant first partition, followed in a short while by Communist seizure of South Vietnam, unless good fortune demonstrated that Vietnamization was a success. Obviously, Nixon was advancing the concept that if Hanoi demanded that we cease all further supplies to South Vietnam, we would demand that all outside powers, especially both Russia and the United States cease supplying offensive weapons to rival Vietnamese governments.[87] Meanwhile, Washington could again take the road of greater military pressure. It had almost exhausted the route of diplomacy.

In further defense of our expansion of the war and the risks taken by the blockade, Kissinger asked: What is it that we ask of North Vietnam? What was there in our offer that a country could not with honor accept? We had told the enemy: If you return our prisoners and if there is an end to the fighting, we will withdraw all our forces and stop all acts of force throughout all Indochina. That was no attempt to impose our solution. Our good faith should not be challenged. For months we had offered many possible roads to peace, but had failed to stir even a discussion of our proposals. The other side had rejected all our efforts and staked all on a purely military solution. This had brought the moment of crisis, which some compared then to the Cuban missile crisis of 1962. Kissinger thought the two situations had some important differences:

> We do not view this as a confrontation between us and the Soviet Union. We are not attempting by these actions to impose a one-sided solution. We are trying to work out some principles of international conduct and an end to a conflict which threatens, alike, our interests as well as the interests of other countries that have a stake in the preservation of peace.[88]

Theodore Sorensen, aide to President Kennedy, strongly protested that there was little or no comparison between the risks taken by him in 1962 and those taken by Nixon in the 1972 blockade. Both attempted to cut off Soviet shipping and risked the nightmare of nuclear war, but there all resemblance ended. Briefly, he insisted that the "sudden secret delivery of long-range nuclear weapons only ninety miles from our shores" was a far greater danger to us than the "open delivery of conventional weapons nearly 9,000 miles away." The 1962 Soviet effort sought to transform Cuba into a strategic nuclear base with Russian combat units "capable of attacking any city in the United States and the Western Hemisphere," while in 1972 Soviet equipment with almost no personnel in Indochina had "no mission beyond those borders." The Kremlin falsified and tried to keep secret their missile shipments to Cuba, while it openly acknowledged its determination to supply its allies in Indochina. Kennedy "obtained a unanimous vote in the Organization of American States authorizing his action and the participation of Latin-American vessels in the barricade." He also "invoked the Treaty of Rio as well as a new and specific joint resolution of Congress." Nixon preferred to act alone, without authorization or participation by allies or Congress.[89]

Although both presidents were criticized for their actions, Kennedy was denounced for not going far enough, Nixon for going too far. Kennedy sought to maintain a measure of discretion and flexibility which Nixon's action did not allow. Military developments in the Caribbean were then far more subject to our control than events in far-off Indochina. Our picket ships, unlike mines, could be instructed from Washington to let certain ships pass. Prohibited ships were to be turned around or seized, not blown up, and the ban was "applied only to those ships carrying offensive weapons." Kennedy's quarantine was selective; it did not cut off food and other civilian supplies. Nixon's did. Kennedy's blockade would last only until the missiles were removed, but Nixon's blockade would end only when the invasion ended. By a more careful limit of his objectives and holding his fire, Kennedy used his quarantine to clear the way for an early negotiation of the missile crisis, but mines that would sink all ships entering and leaving North Vietnam waters would most likely bring confrontation—the very thing presumably Nixon wished most to avoid. Although in 1962 we had reason to be fearful of Russian strength, the Soviets were far more powerful and potentially dangerous in 1972 in both naval and especially nuclear power. Nor was world opinion in 1972 arrayed behind the United States as it had been in 1962.[90]

North Vietnam promptly replied that she would never accept Nixon's "ultimatum." Hanoi termed the mining of its harbors and waters the gravest step yet in escalating the war, "an insolent challenge to the Vietnamese people." It directed a barrage of propaganda at Washington, calling it a "colonialist aggressor," which the Vietnamese people would forever fight to defeat. Le Duc Tho, Hanoi's chief negotiator, said the negotiations to end the war had been stalled for four years because Nixon wished to Vietnamize the war rather than negotiate seriously. He accused the president of sticking stubbornly to his eight points which kept Thieu in power. It was Nixon, not the Communists, who sought to impose a regime upon the people of South Vietnam. As for the bloodbath theory, Hanoi's agent declared it was Nixon who drowned the South

Vietnamese in a bloodbath. He strongly denied any intention to humiliate the United States or anyone and wished only to negotiate seriously on the problem of respect for the basic rights of the Vietnamese people as expressed in the 1954 Geneva Agreements.[91]

He noted that Nixon had missed a good chance for peace when he rejected Hanoi's nine-point peace offer of the summer of 1971. He clearly objected to Nixon's latest peace proposals because a cease-fire without a political settlement would permit the United States to continue arming and supplying Saigon, and if a cease-fire broke down during the negotiations for a political settlement, Nixon might order a resumption of air and naval attacks, a possibility which Secretary of Defense Melvin Laird had already announced. Such questions would have to be settled if the United States were to get a military settlement before a political solution and if the establishment of a coalition government were to be arranged.[92]

The East European Communist bloc condemned the blockade, saying it revealed Nixon's refusal to admit the total failure of his Vietnamization program; they judged it a violation of international law. North Korea called it an extremely dangerous criminal act. The blockade stirred high hopes in South Vietnam, but on second thought it feared it would be unable to cut off all supplies while the current offensive could run for weeks or longer with supplies already in place. With the exception of Great Britain, European nations were cool to Nixon's action; they feared it meant a wider war with unforeseeable consequences. To some it seemed the war was feeding and growing upon itself.[93]

The one basic issue of the war, the central stumbling block of all its diplomacy, the ever recurring theme from 1954 on was: Who would finally govern South Vietnam? In the crisis of 1972 the Communists loudly denied that they wished to impose a Communist or socialist government in Saigon, while official Washington and the South Vietnamese government flatly said they did. An American diplomat bluntly observed: "I don't believe them."[94] This basic disagreement lay behind the inability of the negotiators to establish a coalition regime for South Vietnam. The Communists would not accept Thieu and his system, and Thieu would not accept any solution that denied his legality, his control over all South Vietnam, and the sovereignty of South Vietnam as a separate state. We could live possibly with a compromise; they could not. Hanoi said what it wanted in South Vietnam was a three-part coalition government that reflected reality—Thieu and his group, the Communists, and a third faction not closely united to the other two. This would be a rather mushy, uncertain, and disorganized identity. Washington and Saigon believed the Communist third essentially sought a veto on all actions inside the coalition and eventual takeover—after a decent interval for American withdrawal. The Communists denied any such intention, but during the whole course of the war their oft-proclaimed intention was to establish their power first in the South and then to reunite all Vietnam, if not all Indochina, under Communist rule.

In May 1972, the Communists sought to assure everyone their objectives were independence, neutrality, and peace. Even Kissinger observed that the White House simply did not believe the Communists' promises, because they would be the only really organized and disciplined force left after Thieu's organization had been disbanded. If his leadership and organization were destroyed, his followers and the neutral third, never adequately disciplined and organized, would be left exposed to the ruthless and highly disciplined Vietcong and the Communists. Thus in insisting that Washington help impose such a coalition system, the enemy was really demanding that we help him destroy Saigon and establish a Communist despotism over all Vietnam.[95] That was our fear in mid-1972. Any replacement of Thieu's regime acceptable to the enemy could then lead only to Communist despotism. Neither Saigon nor Washington trusted any enemy pledges or guarantees.

However, during the remainder of 1972, Washington sought to reduce our combat role to the use of air and naval power alongside further efforts to negotiate a settlement by reduction of our demands. This combination of a policy of withdrawal, concession, and expanded use of air power—if Washington could pull it off and if Saigon could be persuaded to accept it—would have been quite an achievement. The enemy might have gone along with it, if its purpose had been merely to save face and permit an honorable cover for American retreat; but if it seriously expected to achieve victory over Saigon, that was another and impossible thing to expect. The Nixon offer to quit Vietnam within four months and stop all military activity there if the enemy would accept a cease-fire, return our prisoners of war, and account for all our missing in action would satisfy most Americans. At least we would escape the dishonor and humiliation of having to help Hanoi impose a Communist government upon the South Vietnamese people. However, that escape for us would not guarantee self-determination for South Vietnam—our major war aim.

On June 29, 1972, Nixon reiterated in a press conference his terms of May and repeated his explanation of the blockade and expanded air attacks. Again he declared that their purpose was to prevent Communist aggression from succeeding, protect our remaining forty thousand troops, and retain some bargaining leverage for securing the return of our war prisoners. He still felt when diplomacy failed that the only way to get anything from the enemy was to do something to him. That meant:

hitting military targets in North Vietnam, retaining a residual force in South Vietnam, and continuing the mining of the harbors of North Vietnam.
  Only by having that kind of activity go forward will they have any incentive to return our POW's rather than not account for them as was the case when the French got out of Vietnam in 1954 and 15,000 French were never accounted for after that.
  I shall never let that happen to the brave men who are POW's.[96]

By the end of June 1972, the president felt that the spectre of defeat which Saigon had faced earlier in the spring had been turned around. South Vietnam was now on the offensive, and although the attack had not been hurled back everywhere, Saigon's ability to defend itself on the ground had been demonstrated—but, he admitted, not without the support of our air power.

Again in June he said he would not negotiate with the enemy the creation of a coalition government in South Vietnam. He thought his offer left to all factions in South Vietnam a fair chance to achieve their reasonable goals without our further intervention. What he still wanted, he added, was an internationally supervised cease-fire, a total withdrawal of our forces, and cessation of all bombing. However, he felt forced to observe that over the past three years

> we have tried every device possible . . . to get negotiations going. We have withdrawn forces, we have made very forthcoming offers, we have wound down combat activities on our part, and the result has been simply an ever increasing intransigence on the part of the enemy.
>
> Believe me, it was only as a last resort that I made the very difficult decision of May 8, knowing how much rode on that decision. . . .[97]

He still thought his decision was wise. The fact that his summit diplomacy went ahead, in spite of it, confirmed his judgment.

As the 1972 political campaign began to heat up and the doves, led by George McGovern, pressed for congressional resolutions to end the war on virtually any terms that would bring the war prisoners home—as though that were the only issue in the war—the president had further reflections. In his news conference of July 27, 1972, he observed that if he followed the advice of the Senate doves, it would mean that "there would be visited upon South Vietnam the same atrocities that were visited upon North Vietnam, with perhaps at least one million marked for assassination because they had fought against North Vietnamese attempts to conquer South Vietnam." And again defending his efforts to negotiate, he declared that we had made fair offers in exchange for the return of our war prisoners and the unaccounted-for missing in action:

> But having done this, there is one thing that we have not offered—and this is one hangup in the settlement today—and that is the demand of the enemy indirectly or directly to do what they cannot accomplish themselves: impose a Communist government in South Vietnam. That would be the height of immorality, to impose on the 17 million people of South Vietnam a Communist government with the bloodbath that would follow.[98]

It would be the height of immorality to let such a tragedy ensue in South Vietnam as that which hit North Vietnam from 1954 through 1956. In mid-1972 the enemy charged Washington with going all-out to win through a deliberate effort to bomb the dikes in North Vietnam and bring great disaster to the people along the Red River. The war critics around the world raised a great outcry at this and seemed to accept for truth enemy propaganda and accusations. Whatever hits were made upon these dikes Washington claimed were unintentional and, if they occurred at all, were accidental and never extensive. It believed the critics were the victims of clever enemy propaganda. In Nixon's view the charge was a deliberate attempt by the enemy to create an extraneous issue, to divert attention

from one of the most barbaric invasions in history, compounded by a violation of all concepts of international law in handling prisoners of war. For them, with their policy of deliberate murder and assassination and otherwise attacks on civilians for the purpose of killing civilians, for them to try to seize on this and divert attention from them, first, to me it is a patent propaganda effort, and it is one that I think needs to be answered.[99]

To those who charged us with immorality for the bombing, Nixon recalled an earlier discussion with President Eisenhower, who talked about a tough decision he had to make in World War II. When people then raised the moral issue of bombing German cities, which obviously killed thousands of civilians, Ike admitted it was a terrible decision to have to make. But then he said that on the question of its morality we had to answer the fundamental problem of perhaps the whole war: "The height of immorality would be to allow Hitler to rule Europe."

President Nixon then observed:

Now, in our case we have not gone that far. We are not going to bomb civilian targets in the North. We are not using the great power that could finish off North Vietnam in an afternoon, and we will not. But it would be the height of immorality for the United States at this point to leave Vietnam, and in leaving, to turn over to the North Vietnamese the fate of 17 million South Vietnamese who do not want a Communist government, to turn it over to them.

That is what this is about. That is the only issue that is left. Those who say "End the war" really should name their resolution "Prolong the war." They should name it "Prolong the war," not because they deliberately want to. They want to end the war just as I do, but we have to face this fact: We have only one President at a time, as I said in 1968.[100]

Washington, having survived and pushed back the greatest attack Hanoi could mount now or in the distant future, asked Hanoi to negotiate while Nixon needed help or risk having to deal with him during his second term when he would be in a much stronger position. It seemed to Nixon that in his diplomacy with the Communist superpowers he had been able to persuade them that they had "much larger fish to fry in the world than Indochina and the Chinese feel confident of Hanoi's long-term success in any case."[101] In this interpretation— and the full story will not likely soon be known—Nixon all along had wanted the two Communist giants to help him get out of Vietnam with almost nothing but a sense of honor in retreat. The question was: Could Hanoi forget 1954, when it was persuaded to settle for less than total victory? Did Nixon's repeated efforts to negotiate and the gradual reduction of his former demands—although accompanied by renewed military efforts of the moment—hold out the promise of a final victory after all? Why concede anything when he was withdrawing and his political base seemed totally unlikely to support ever again escalation of the war? Washington, too, seemed more interested in detente with Russia and reaching an understanding with China than in continuing its pursuit of a winless war and a thin hope of genuine freedom for centuries to come in South Vietnam. Ho's gamble on American impatience seemed increasingly a sure thing. Hanoi could struggle on a while longer. The illusion of peace—at best but a decent interval for our withdrawal—held out in October and November 1972 would suggest confirmation of these enemy hopes. Former hopes of frustrating wars of national liberation, meeting the Red Peril, guaranteeing to the South Vietnamese people the right of national self-determination, and preserving and establishing freedom for the people of South Vietnam—all these and other noble goals which took us into the war—were now forgotten. Our peace plans sought only a quick exit for our forces—and that was about all the enemy would permit—but Saigon and Washington would stall a while longer in the illusion that something could be salvaged from all the effort.

CHAPTER SEVEN

"PEACE IS AT HAND," 1972

On October 26, 1972, Hanoi broke the silence on peace negotiations secretly continued since July and revealed that on October 8 North Vietnam had made an offer deemed serious by Washington. This possible breakthrough ended a prolonged stalemate and brought a sense of urgency and speed to the peace talks. So promising seemed the enemy proposal that Kissinger stated on the same day, October 26, "Peace is at hand." Thus began a round of talks that virtually all observers genuinely believed promised an early end of the tragedy. Hopes were high almost everywhere, except in Saigon, where Thieu and his advisers cried, "betrayal," "abandonment," and "sellout," declaring that the United States could not decide for South Vietnam the question of peace. Most experts agreed that the nine-point agreement announced October 26 was a major concession to the United States and a minor concession to Saigon. Many factors explained the change of direction. The Nixon diplomatic efforts to achieve detente with Moscow and Peking had some influence. Great powers had interests that transcended the value of a minor scrap over some limited Asian rice lands, which the United States was already abandoning. Washington officials believed that rising awareness of these greater interests helped to persuade Russia and China to tolerate Nixon's massive bombing and mining activities, which hurt Hanoi.

The failure of Moscow and Peking to challenge the United States and their advice to Hanoi to accept Nixon's peace offer of May 8 were signals Hanoi could not ignore. In that offer, the president gave up most of our former demands. For the return of our prisoners and an internationally supervised cease-fire, he offered to stop all acts of force throughout Indochina and pull out all American forces within sixty days. That yielded our former demand for the evacuation of all enemy troops from South Vietnam, but it ignored political solutions, the principle of national self-determination, and all commitment to General Thieu. Such an offer suggested to the enemy that if he would give us a decent amount of time and a face-saving formula for withdrawal, we would, in leaving, give him a very good chance to get virtually everything he wished. Of course, prior to departure we would not do his dirty work for him. For the enemy this was better than continued warfare. That peace offer went far toward convincing Hanoi that more could be won by diplomacy than war, especially when the Easter offensive began to stall. Some believed Nixon's double response to the offensive—power and compromise—broke the Communist offensive and led Hanoi to try for peace.

The Communists were in better military shape in South Vietnam than they had been since 1969. With possibly one hundred and forty-five thousand North Vietnamese troops then in South Vietnam—Saigon put the figure at around three hundred thousand—the Communists controlled from one-third to one-half of the territory of South Vietnam. These rural areas contained about 10 percent of South Vietnam's 17 million people. Also the Communists controlled considerable portions of territory and people in the "Saigon-controlled" areas. The enemy plausibly decided that the situation offered an opportunity to end the military conflict and expand its political gains. As one captured enemy document revealed, Hanoi said the cease-fire would silence the big guns, but the small guns would stay active. Each side—Washington and Hanoi—saw in the same events ample justification of its actions and proposals. By talking they might reduce the war while they consolidated and strengthened their forward positions and prepared for future advances.

The enemy could reason that without further United States active military support, Thieu's strength would weaken if not vanish. Our air support had prevented his defeat in the spring offensive. Without our continued aerial assistance, Thieu's army would fall apart from corruption, defection, and flight, and in a fairly short time through a coalition government or subversion the Communists would simply take power. Thieu's stubborn opposition to the arrangement confirmed these enemy assumptions. Nor could the enemy be unaware of the election in the United States. The timing of the breakthrough, if that was what it was to become, may have been influenced by Hanoi's awareness that George McGovern had little chance of victory. Hanoi realized there would be no immediate, unconditional, and total unilateral American withdrawal as the dovish McGovern had pledged. By October 8 Hanoi had accepted the argument, which official Washington had suggested, that a settlement before the election might be preferable to one made after Nixon was assured of four more years of power. Undoubtedly, a settlement before the election day would have enhanced Nixon's chances of success. Never again would he need a settlement of the war so badly. It would be a fulfillment of his 1968 pledge to end the war in his first term. The enemy may also have pondered the possibility that four more years of American material aid, backed by air and naval power off shore, in Thailand and Guam, and the Vietnamization program would have greatly strengthened whatever government existed in Saigon.[1]

The diplomats with Hanoi contacts, wrote Ted Szulc of the New York Times, advised Washington not to regard the enemy shift from war to peace negotiations as a sign of weakness. In their careful assessment, the key element in Hanoi's decision to negotiate seriously was Nixon's massive bombing and mining program. That persuaded the Communists that they could not decisively defeat the South Vietnamese armed forces. For the moment the best they could expect was to prolong a very costly and bloody stalemate. They could fight on indefinitely, but the effort would likely bring "diminishing returns." Although their great allies, China and Russia, kept supplying their war needs, the North Vietnamese wondered if they would continue their assistance as they "moved toward better relations with Washington." The bombing damage after six months outweighed the advantages of a return to the "protracted warfare" of the early years of the war, let alone any more major offensives such as those in 1968 and 1972. Virtually all observers, Communist and non-Communist, saw in Hanoi's decision to try for peace a shift in strategy rather than a concession of weakness or admission of defeat. They declared that those tough men of Hanoi, dedicated followers of Ho, had not fought for a generation just to give up all their aspirations.[2]

As early as 1969 Kissinger had expressed the belief openly that Vietnam was a poor place for the exercise of our power. He had said the United States could not "win" over a stubborn nationalist force; we could only destroy a people. Rather we should get out as honorably as possible. Both Nixon and Kissinger sought the most honorable method of extrication. They wished to preserve our credibility as a world power, faith among our allies, and respect even from our enemies, and to obtain a peace with honor. Therefore we sought from the Communists assurance of a "decent interval" after our departure before they tried to seize power. The problem was to get Thieu's support and to persuade the Communists to be reasonable and patient.

The continuing hostility toward the war, the enduring domestic problems still unsolved, and the fears stirred by our repeated interventions and surprise escalations of bombing and mining kept our friends in Europe on edge and raised the likelihood of the collapse of our hoped-for gains with China and Russia. All these circumstances pressed us to seek a way out with or without honor. Some noticed the rising danger to our economy inherent in the continuing unfavorable balance of payments in the public and private sectors. It seemed that the continued decline of our assets in relation to our liabilities could bring only worse troubles. The argument for further war made less and less sense. Few could see how our extrication from this distant and minor theater could really endanger the national security of the United States. Virtually every American wanted the killing stopped at once. The whole antiwar movement, although not as militant in 1972 as in 1968, still endured.

Many Americans, led by George McGovern in 1972, seemed to believe that the only issue left was the return of our war prisoners. All else they would sacrifice to this objective. By the fall of 1972 it appeared that the best deal possible was the return of our prisoners and missing in action in exchange for our withdrawal and leaving South Vietnam to settle its own problems. There was little hope of enduring peace. Both sides expected civil war, perhaps at a lower pace, to resume at any time, and both actively prepared for it. Diplomacy between Hanoi and Washington could not settle vital political problems; only the parties involved in South Vietnam, Communists and anti-Communists, could finally do that. The American people no longer had faith in Thieu or his government; none had any hopes of establishing democracy or freedom in any foreseeable future for South Vietnam. The one thing they would not do was to impose communism upon South Vietnam. Nor did they any longer wish to impose Thieu upon that country. And they now seemed to believe that the risks of peace were more acceptable than the risks of further expanded air warfare.

Although Nixon had never said in the 1968 campaign that he had a secret plan or any specific plan to end the war, he had pledged in New Hampshire in early March that his leadership would "end the war" in Vietnam. To Nixon critics it was of no consequence whether he had a plan, for if he thought he could end the war, he must have one in mind; but they could never get him to spell it out in precise detail. Many wondered how he could pledge to bring peace if he didn't have a plan. William Safire, special assistant to the president, wrote that he meant only to pledge that he would use fully our economic, diplomatic, and political leadership to speed the peace. He once declared that if he had a gimmick, a magic formula for peace, he would tell LBJ.[3]

When asked at his news conference of October 5, 1972, if he saw signs of peace before the election, Nixon answered that peace would come just as quickly as he could get the right settlement, one that would prevent the imposition of a Communist regime upon Saigon and get our prisoners returned. He stressed, however, that under no circumstances would the timing of any settlement be determined by the fact of the coming election. If we could get the right settlement before the election, we would do it; if not, we certainly would not accept less than that before or after the election. He recalled that well-intentioned men in 1968 had made "a very, very great mistake in stopping the bombing without adequate agreements from the other side." He would not now repeat that error. Told that Hanoi might be waiting until after the election to make a settlement in the belief that if a Democrat won, it would get a better deal, he declared that was possible and noted that some Americans in 1968 favored a bombing halt before the election in the belief that it would help defeat him in the election that year. Then, taking a shot at his critics, who denounced his every peace plan as totally inadequate and promised better in 1972 to both the enemy and the doves, he said:

I must say that both Senator Humphrey and I, I think, were quite responsible in that election campaign in refusing to comment on what were then only preliminary negotiations, recognizing that any comment by one who might be President might jeopardize the success of the negotiations.[4]

Hanoi might put its eggs in that basket and believe the dovish Democrats might win. Possibly it might conclude from his statements about a peace with honor and his refusal to agree to a settlement which would impose a Communist regime on South Vietnam that it would get a better deal from the other side. However, he would continue to try to convince the enemy that waiting until after the election would not gain for him anything.[5] Later, when the election had been won and the Paris agreement of January 1973 had been signed, White House aides openly referred to doves who had attacked Nixon's peace efforts as members of the "sellout brigade" of appeasement, retreat, and surrender.

Senator George McGovern styled himself as the peace candidate, made that his major campaign plank, and apparently expected that issue to put him in the White House. To win the election, he promised that immediately after the inaugural oath he would stop all bombing and acts of force in all Indochina, end all further shipment of military supplies, begin our troop withdrawal, and bring out all usable materiel from Indochina, without any prior concessions by the enemy. After he had done this he would notify Hanoi and tell the North Vietnamese he expected them to return our prisoners and missing in action as they had pledged in their seven-point proposal of 1971. Then he would tell all parties that we would no longer interfere in their internal politics and they could work out their own settlement, but that we would cooperate with them to see that any settlement, including a coalition government, gained international recognition. He would bring home our men from Laos and Cambodia and close our bases in Thailand. Then as the people of Vietnam sought to rebuild their country we would join others in helping repair the wreckage left by war.

When Nixon refused to sign immediately the October draft, Hanoi accused him of "vile deception." Nixon had said he would not be "tricked or treated" into rushing into Hanoi's self-proclaimed deadline of October 31 for signing the agreement. The date passed. Kissinger's previous announcement that peace was at hand appeared destined for disappointment. When no further progress was evident, McGovern and others charged that Kissinger's presentation was only a campaign maneuver to steal the peace issue away from McGovern.

In his first television broadcast of the campaign, Nixon broke his earlier pledge not to make the peace settlement an election issue. In March 1971 Nixon declared Vietnam would not be a good political issue in 1972.[6] Later he told the nation and the world that people everywhere would watch the election results and added: "The leaders in Hanoi will be watching. They will be watching for the answer of the American people—for your answer—to this question: Shall we have peace with honor or peace with surrender?"[7] Angered by that statement, McGovern accused the president of a "cruel political deception." Then he gave his version of the recent negotiations. As he told it, Kissinger made the deal in Paris, took it to Saigon where Thieu bluntly rejected it, then brought it back to Nixon who said no in agreement with Thieu. Thus, McGovern said, we must painfully conclude that the events of recent weeks "were not a path to peace but a detour around Election Day."[8]

McGovern derided Nixon's policy of ending the war with honor. He said the president by his bombing had descended to a new low of barbarism and this just to save his own face and prop up Thieu's corrupt regime. Also he said that Nixon's reelection would give Thieu open hunting rights against the Vietnamese people. Nixon was a man who would make draft dodgers the scapegoats for his own murderous and barbaric policies in Southeast Asia. (This from a critic whose party had originally taken us into the bog.) Nixon willingly surrendered, he said, the most precious ideals and values of the country by bombing and napalming defenseless people, including thousands of little children. Even after the election, McGovern still yowled, wrote a Nixon defender, about Nixon's "sinister plots," "massive crimes," and "murderous . . . barbaric policies" in Asia. Sargent Shriver, the Democratic vice-presidential candidate, also referred to the president as the number one warmaker and the number one bomber of all time.[9] However, the war was not in the election campaign of 1972 the vital and emotional issue it was in 1968. Nixon had defused it by his withdrawals and especially by the sharp reduction of our casualties and wounded. Most foreign nations and Americans agreed with the president when he said we should not end the war foolishly by appeasement, but with honor. Observers believed that both Saigon and Hanoi, weeks before the election, discounted McGovern's chances and calculated only their chances before and after Nixon's election. Apparently Thieu felt his position would be stronger after a Nixon victory than before, especially if he made no major concession to Nixon to facilitate such a triumph.

In conclusion, it was obvious that Kissinger's blunt statement that peace was at hand helped Nixon. It was to most Americans the first genuine light at the end of the long tunnel. Most Americans believed it; they believed Kissinger almost more than they did the president. They felt that somehow McGovern would rashly yield all for nothing and humiliate the United States by begging a Communist aggressor, who had committed about every crime imaginable, to forgive us and let us out of the war. They could not ignore that this man, a great humanitarian and Christian, somehow could never quite see or admit the awesome crimes of the enemy, the enemy's great massacres from 1954 on against totally helpless persons, not just accidents of war, but calculated atrocities to terrorize his fellow countrymen into a long night of endless despotism. McGovern made us ashamed of our country when he put the worst possible interpretation upon our involvement—which, in spite of what its many critics said—did have a certain nobility of aim and purpose. McGovern himself, not the war, became the main issue of the campaign; with or without the war, he never had a chance. The election victory certainly reinforced Nixon's belief that the people backed his efforts for peace, and it seems reasonable to conclude that the majority of those who voted for Nixon wanted the war ended just as much as those who voted against him. In truth, most Americans long before the election concluded that they agreed with the president's approach to peace and feared McGovern's method would humiliate the nation, abandon an ally, and bring peace with dishonor. Thus, if peace was an issue in the campaign, it helped Nixon more than McGovern.

Nixon felt he had reached the stage where at least he might obtain a fair compromise. The former turbulence, demonstrations, and public denunciation, domestic and foreign, had sharply declined. His successful diplomacy, concessions to Peking, arms limitation and parity with Russia, and trade concessions that benefitted the two greatest superpowers had seemingly persuaded China and Russia to urge a peaceful solution upon Hanoi and the Vietcong. Some observers believed that the dangerous confrontation of 1962 over the missile crisis had left the Communist giants in a cold chill at any possible nuclear war; therefore in this latest hope of avoiding another, they sought every reasonable chance to use their influence for peace. In short, the belief was that the Cuban crisis of 1962 made the Vietnam crisis manageable in 1972 and 1973. Vietnamization promised future success. McGovern had called our peace gestures, such as Kissinger's journeys, a "publicity stunt." A sincere try for peace might stop that partisan attack and enhance Nixon's election chances. Certainly Hanoi and the Vietcong could profit from a rest, from a policy of reasonable compromise that held out a fair to excellent chance of ultimate victory. In this situation, Washington was cautiously hopeful and welcomed Hanoi's surprise draft offer of October 8.

Thus rumors of peace filled the air and journalists and commentators, usually cautious, were reporting the possibility of a rapid settlement when an unexpected broadcast from Hanoi on October 26 proclaimed—as though it was finally settled—the secret terms of a United States-North Vietnam peace agreement and accused Washington of stalling in carrying it out. Hanoi revealed the terms of the proposed agreement and gave its interpretation of events leading to it. This gave it the first chance to break the silence, and that served to even the score with Nixon and Kissinger, who had in 1971 broken the silence and revealed lengthy but futile secret negotiations at that time. The enemy broadcast revealed that secret negotiations since July had been searching for a solution, and in late September Kissinger and Le Duc Tho had met in Paris without much success and then again for five days beginning October 8, when both sides agreed with the words of Hanoi that "a new, extremely important initiative" in the form of a draft agreement had been presented by Hanoi. This agreement was very close to Nixon's May 8 proposal and seemed to merit a most serious discussion.

In early October 1972 Kissinger felt most optimistic about the prospects of peace; he believed the situation at that moment was uniquely right. One of his aides asked:

How many times in the future are we going to have the Soviet Union in a condition of near-famine, China absolutely terrified about what the Soviets might do along their border, and a conservative President so sure of his reelection that he can afford to be more receptive to a settlement?[10]

They agreed that Kissinger was hell-bent to get out before the election. Asked if he was not now backing a bankrupt policy in Vietnam, Kissinger snapped that we had accepted a moral obligation to give South Vietnam a chance, but "we have *no* moral obligation to stay there for all eternity. . . ." He asked rhetorically: "What did de Gaulle do for France in Algeria?" and answered, "He wanted to leave in such a way that the departure seemed an act of policy so that France could keep some of its dignity. . . . That was his great achievement, not the precise outcome of the war." The problem for both France and for us was to leave with honor. Withdrawal itself was not the problem. If we just left, Hanoi would not return our prisoners, but would likely make further demands—for example, that we cease all aid to Saigon, and other things that would surely humiliate us. He admitted the war was going to be deemed a misfortune for the United States: "All we've got left to get out of the war is a shred of dignity, and hopefully—if we settle it by an act of policy other than by just running—a chance of restoring some sense of unity to our discussions again, across the board."[11]

Hanoi hoped to have the agreement signed by mid-October and noted that even the American negotiators called the draft "an important and very fundamental document which opened up the way to an early settlement." After several days of negotiations, the enemy account said that by October 17, the two sides had reached agreement on almost all the problems, except two which posed no insuperable obstacles. The Hanoi statement noted that Nixon had on October 10 officially expressed to the North Vietnamese premier his appreciation of his goodwill and his offer but had raised a number of "complex points" which required further consideration and explanation. Hanoi declared it had clearly explained its views on all these points and had received from the president on October 22 a second message expressing his "satisfaction with the explanations" offered. Thus, declared Hanoi by October 22, 1972, the "formulation of the agreement was complete."[12]

The nine-point draft agreement announced by Hanoi, and not disputed by the United States, included these provisions. In summary, the United States respected "the independence, sovereignty, unity and territorial integrity of Vietnam as recognized by the 1954 Geneva Agreements." Twenty-four hours after the agreement was signed a cease-fire should be observed in South Vietnam and the United States would stop all military activities and end the bombing in North Vietnam. Within sixty days the United States and all foreign nations would withdraw their forces from South Vietnam, and the two South Vietnamese parties, Saigon and the Vietcong, should receive no troops, advisers, military personnel, armaments, or war materiel in South Vietnam. However, they should be allowed "to make periodical replacements of armaments, munitions and war material that have been worn out or damaged after the ceasefire, on the basis of piece for piece of similar characteristics and properties." The United States would "not continue its military involvement or intervene in the internal affairs of South Vietnam." All captured and detained personnel of the parties were to be returned simultaneously with the United States troops' withdrawal. The people of South Vietnam should decide for themselves their political future "through genuinely free and democratic general elections under international supervision." The United States was "not committed to any political tendency or to any personality in South Vietnam" and did "not seek to impose a pro-American regime in Saigon." National reconciliation and concord would be achieved, and the democratic liberties of the people would be insured. An administrative structure called the National Council of National Reconciliation and Concord, made up of three equal segments, would be established to implement the signed agreements made by the Provisional Revolutionary Government of the Republic of South Vietnam and the Government of the Republic of Vietnam and to organize the general elections. The two South Vietnamese parties would consult about the formation of lower-level councils. They would also fix the armed forces in South Vietnam "in a spirit of national reconciliation and concord, equality and mutual respect, without foreign interference." They would seek to reduce the numbers of troops on both sides and to settle internal matters as soon as possible. They would do their utmost to reach a settlement within three months after the cease-fire came into effect. The reunification of Vietnam should be achieved through peaceful methods.[13]

Also a four-party joint military commission and a joint military commission of the two South Vietnamese parties would be formed. An international commission of control and supervision should be established and an international guarantee conference on Vietnam would be convened within thirty days of the signing of the agreement. The signatory powers promised to respect the fundamental rights of the peoples of Laos and Cambodia as recognized by the Geneva Agreements of 1954 and the 1962 Geneva Agreements on Laos. This meant respecting their "independence, sovereignty, unity and territorial integrity." They agreed to respect the neutrality of Cambodia and Laos, to refrain from using their territories "to encroach on the sovereignty and security of other countries." Foreign countries would also withdraw from and cease reintroducing troops and war materiel into these countries. With the end of the war and the coming of peace, conditions for creating a new, equal, and mutually beneficial relationship between North Vietnam and the United States would be created. The United States would "contribute to healing the wounds of war and to postwar reconstruction" of North Vietnam and all Indochina. The agreement would come into force when signed and would "be strictly implemented by all the parties concerned."[14]

The Hanoi broadcast stated, and this Washington later disputed, that the two parties had also agreed on a schedule for signing the agreement. The enemy said we agreed on October 9 that we would stop the bombing and mining in North Vietnam on October 18, both parties would initial the text of the agreement in Hanoi on October 19, and the foreign ministers of the two countries would formally sign the agreement in Paris on October 26. But Hanoi went on to say that on October 11 the United States sought to change the schedule to read thus: on October 21, the United States would cease the bombing and mining; on October 22, the two parties would initial the text in Hanoi; and on October 30, they would formally sign it in Paris. But then on October 20, "under the pretext that there still remained a number of unagreed points," the United States again sought a change in schedule; and so it went, they said, as we suggested change after change. Finally, they contended that both sides had agreed to a definite date for signing the agreement on October 31, 1972.[15] However, that date passed without any further action. Hanoi wished to rush the signing because it seemed to believe it would be better to secure a settlement before the election.

Kissinger and Le Duc Tho had reached only a tentative understanding and agreement on most of the above provisions and expressed the hope that a fixed schedule desirable to both sides could be met, but no hard pledges or agreements had been made to do so. On October 12, Kissinger had returned to Washington to brief the president, while in Saigon, Thieu, already aware of the secret Paris talks, declared his opposition to any coalition with the Communists. Back in Paris, Kissinger, according to Hanoi's statement, had reached agreement "on almost all problems." Hanoi said only two unspecified points of disagreement remained. From October 18 to October 23 Kissinger had lengthy talks in Saigon with Thieu, whom he found more stubborn than Hanoi. In fact, the day after Kissinger left Saigon, Thieu declared the proposals drafted at Paris were unacceptable. Thus Saigon, backed apparently by some Nixon second thoughts, brought a delay, a demand for further clarification, for tying together some "loose ends." These developments brought from Hanoi the charge that Washington's behavior jeopardized the whole agreement, that the so-called difficulties with Saigon were a mere pretext to delay the implementation of the United States commitment. In Hanoi's view the Thieu government was clearly a puppet of the United States and simply could not sabotage any settlement which we really desired. Thus the enemy declared that Nixon was not negotiating in good faith, but was rather dragging out the war to deceive American public opinion and to cover his scheme to maintain a puppet in Saigon.[16]

Hanoi's unexpected broadcast, Nixon felt, could not be ignored; it had to be answered and promptly. Within a few hours, on October 26, 1972, Kissinger gave the official reply.[17] From an administration which for a month had said almost nothing about the peace talks, this 11 A.M. news conference in the small White House briefing room, before five hundred newsmen, conducted by one of the nation's most brilliant performers was possibly one of the most dramatic moments of the whole war. Friends and critics termed Kissinger's presentation without notes or prompting as a truly virtuoso performance. In this presentation, which will probably be remembered longest for one statement which the world had longed to hear, he said, "We believe peace is at hand." Unfortunately for him, just a few moments later in the same speech he said it should be relatively easy to complete the agreement within a few days—to tie up some "loose ends." In this presentation he gave the official version of events, and most likely it will be decades before the full story can be told. He noted that private negotiations had been under way with Hanoi for nearly four years and had resumed July 19, but he added that heretofore they had always foundered on Hanoi's insistence that a political settlement must precede any military solution and must in substance really predetermine the political outcome in its favor. In short, the enemy meant that before we could get our prisoners back and achieve a cease-fire we must impose a Communist government upon South Vietnam.

We had in these private meetings believed progress toward peace could come only if the political and military issues were separated—that is, if the enemy would settle with us the methods to end the war, and if the political solution was left to the various parties of South Vietnam to discuss among themselves, that would be true self-determination. For years Hanoi had refused to budge from its position, but on October 8, for the first time, North Vietnam proposed what we had long suggested, that the two issues be separated. This made it possible for us to negotiate concretely. Here the North Vietnamese suggested that the United States and North Vietnam between themselves settle the military aspects of the war and agree upon some very general principles within which the South Vietnamese parties could determine the political future of South Vietnam and all Vietnam. Thus, they dropped their demands for a coalition government and a veto over the personalities and the form of any future government. They also agreed for the first time to a formula which permitted discussions of a settlement for Laos and Cambodia.[18]

On these points we could begin serious talks. The essential goodwill seemed to prevail then for days and laid the basis for rather rapid progress which promised an early and final solution. Kissinger readily admitted that he had no complaint with Hanoi's description of the events, except to note the seeds of one particular misunderstanding. Hanoi erred in its statement that we had promised to sign the draft agreement October 31, 1972. They constantly insisted that we commit ourselves to that date, but he said we had not invented or proposed those exact dates. His instructions from the president, he noted, were to "make a settlement that was right, independent of any arbitrary deadlines." Rather we had agreed to "make a major effort to conclude the negotiations by Oct. 31," and at times had given schedules by which "this might be accomplished."[19] With Communists, from James Byrnes on, our statesmen had learned that "mights" become "woulds." It never paid even to think outloud about possibilities when negotiating with Communists, for even the mildest hints or suggestions they took for certainties. The statement that we would try did not imply a definite pledge that we would. However, when the date passed and we had not signed, the enemy and the antiwar forces again had a round of denunciations and recriminations.

In further defense and in awareness of the rising charge that Saigon had a veto upon any solution, Kissinger stated that the South Vietnamese had suffered, and their government—our ally, which would remain after our departure—had every right to share in making its own peace, to have its views heard and taken extremely seriously; but we also had to "preserve our own freedom of judgment" and make our own decisions on how long to continue the war. He declared that Hanoi had, however, erred all along in thinking that we could simply impose any solution upon Saigon. Many issues remained yet to be settled, and Saigon had obviously expressed its views with its customary forcefulness. We agreed with some, not with others, a position he had made clear to Saigon. Also he had conferred with other countries in Southeast Asia and had found certain concerns and ambiguities that required modification and improvement. He believed one more brief session would suffice, because "what remains to be done is the smallest part of what has already been accomplished. . . ." Then he gave his condensed version of the terms just announced.[20]

What were the obstacles to a final settlement? The main reason for the delay was that in a negotiation stalemated for five years—one which did not achieve a breakthrough until October 8—many general principles were clearly understood even before the breakthrough, but a detailed study of the text revealed many "nuances on which the implementation will ultimately depend," and they were of great importance. Much had to be specified in precise language which both sides clearly understood. Loose ends had to be tied together. For example, both sides desired a cease-fire in the abstract, but neither side was precise, as it had to be, about the timing and spacing within a country of no clear front lines. A cease-fire might be accompanied by last-minute efforts to seize as much territory as possible, perhaps even to extend operations long enough to establish political control over various areas. This was a fear well founded indeed, because during the days after the possibility of peace, both sides speeded their reinforcements and efforts to get as much as possible while they could.

Kissinger wanted to avoid the danger of further loss of life and possible further massacres. He felt additional discussion of methods necessary by which the international supervisory body could be put in place at the same time the cease-fire was announced. Arranging a cease-fire in this situation of great variety among three different countries with very sticky problems of language was an exceedingly complex matter. He noted differences of view and interpretation of the text of the draft agreement which required clarification. For example, he wanted Hanoi to understand that the National Council of National Reconciliation and Concord was "an administrative structure," not in any way to be construed as comparable to a coalition government.[21] This had been a major objection of General Thieu. Nor was it clear to either side precisely what was meant by the reference to the Geneva Accords of 1954. Did that mean to make all Vietnam one country, to erase the DMZ and the partition at the 18th parallel, and therefore to justify the presence of North Vietnamese regulars in South Vietnam? Was all Vietnam now one country again, or, as Saigon insisted, was the temporary partition of 1954 still in effect? In short, the lengthy discussion of these disturbing questions of unity and sovereignty revealed that the basic issues of the war had not been settled. Thieu was then telling his people that no agreement which his government did not approve was acceptable. Kissinger suggested that each side, North Vietnam and the United States, could decide whether the agreement should be a four-power, three- or two-power deal, which the major partners and their allies could decide as they wished. He also believed Saigon would finally accept the time schedule Washington desired.

In the question-and-answer period, when asked the obvious question, which McGovern and many others soon raised in the election campaign, why this program could not have been achieved four to eight years earlier, Kissinger said there was no possibility four years ago of such an agreement, simply because the enemy had demanded our total withdrawal without any conditions and consistently refused to discuss the separation of the political and military issues. The North Vietnamese always insisted they had first to settle the political issues with us before there was a cease-fire, and we had to impose for them or with them a solution which would "predetermine the future of South Vietnam."

Now, for the first time, they had given up both those demands. Now the military issues could be settled first and by themselves, and somewhat later the people of South Vietnam could fix their political future without any one group inside or outside South Vietnam having a veto or able to dictate a settlement. In this way Washington could withdraw from the war with honor and truthfully say it had given South Vietnam a chance to exercise the great principle of national self-determination, which since 1965 we had said was our objective in the war. Of course, we had hoped the South Vietnamese in a genuinely free election would choose the greatest possible measure of freedom, personal and political; but if they chose communism or any other system, we would accept it as long as it was their decision.

Kissinger's news conference raised high mankind's hopes of an early peace settlement. Strange, but this brilliant scholar and dedicated servant of peace was believed by people who would have doubted either Johnson or Nixon. Although he confirmed Hanoi's announcement of the draft and its details and denied Hanoi's contention that he had consented, as a condition of the agreement, to sign the accords by October 31, the people paid more attention to that statement of his belief that peace was at hand. He greatly minimized the differences that remained for solution. He sought to conciliate and reconcile all factions, including Hanoi, Saigon, and all mankind. He appreciated the enemy offer, remembered Saigon's long suffering and the hopes of virtually everyone, but he did say firmly that we would not be stampeded into an agreement until its provisions were right, nor deflected from one when its provisions were right—undoubtedly slanted toward Saigon and Thieu. Anxiously he sought to persuade Hanoi not to make a major issue of the failure to get the agreement signed by October 31. North Vietnam, he revealed, had been told that he would meet with Le Duc Tho virtually anywhere (except in Hanoi) whenever Le Duc Tho wished to complete the talks, which he hoped could be soon. Most surely he wanted to convince his audience that the agreement was a great achievement for the United States. He singled out for special notice that the enemy had made major concessions by dropping his demand for a coalition government, which would quickly absorb all power, and his demand for a veto over the personalities and the structure of the existing government.

Kissinger revealed that although Saigon could not veto our actions, the president would not deal with Hanoi without consulting his ally. This meant that Thieu could no longer prevent our withdrawal. It also was a commitment to Hanoi that sealed the bargain before it was signed. Kissinger stated that "we cannot fail and we will not fail over what still remains to be accomplished."[22] That statement endorsed the settlement and sought to assure Hanoi that it was not being swindled by our refusal to sign on October 31. Rather it was a reiteration of the private efforts made earlier in the month. With its eyes on the election of November 7, Hanoi offered a climactic week of peace headlines for the president and sought assurances that no objections in Saigon and no second thoughts in Washington would upset the agreement. While Kissinger talked with the president in Washington and visited Saigon, the enemy jumped the gun and published prematurely the terms of the agreement because we had sought three delays within two weeks. Thus the North Vietnamese gave way to a decade of mistrust and suspected the worst; their broadcast and the record of the delays, they hoped, might either provoke a presidential reaffirmation or create for him two weeks of the most troublesome and embarrassing publicity. Thus, Kissinger's conference, in its profession of a determination to win a peace without a Saigon veto, constituted for Hanoi a victory. It brought both a pledge that the agreement stood and provoked a new wave of pressure upon President Thieu to acquiesce.

On a difficult issue, Kissinger declared that South Vietnamese civilians, prisoners, likely Vietcong agents held prisoner in South Vietnam, would be released through negotiations between Saigon and the Vietcong. For us that meant that our prisoners would not be detained until all Vietcong were returned.[23] For the enemy it posed the disturbing possibility of lengthy troubles between the two sides in South Vietnam. Obviously, the cease-fire could be broken by either side and expanded warfare resumed. Although we promised withdrawal and cessation of all acts of force during the cease-fire, our air power remained stationed in Thailand, Guam, and on offshore aircraft carriers. Hanoi's regulars were also to remain in the South and could be supplied from the North.

The vagueness of the original draft could cause endless trouble. Yet it was about the best possible under the circumstances. Thieu would be free to use his forces peacefully to win the contest for the future political control of South Vietnam, but, like Hanoi, he, too, would not be allowed to rig the rules to guarantee his own victory as both sides had been doing in their divided country. Nixon's key concession to Hanoi was, with great hesitation, his willingness to allow one hundred and forty-five thousand North Vietnamese troops to remain in South Vietnam in fairly clearly defined and legal enclaves to support a Vietcong political effort that experience had always shown to be far more skillful than that of their adversary. Our air power would remain nearby, but once we had withdrawn and ceased all acts of force it would be unlikely that we would return. However, the president could reason that at least he had not by his own action imposed a Communist regime upon South Vietnam. Rather he could say for the United States that since 1954 we had, by expanded material and financial aid and great loss of life, tried to give South Vietnam a fair chance to build freedom. Surely eighteen years of aid and the sacrifice of fifty-six thousand lives were enough. If freedom failed there, the fault would have to lie with the people of South Vietnam. Aid and men we could give for a limited time, but the will we could never supply.

That the president sent such a distinguished delegation to Saigon to negotiate the final details of the peace settlement revealed Nixon's high hopes of diplomatic and political success. With Kissinger in the lead, there was an unusually large and high-powered team of aides, including General Creighton Abrams, Army Chief of Staff, former military commander of United States forces in South Vietnam, whom Thieu trusted. It also included "William Sullivan, the State Department's top Southeast Asia expert, and U.S. ambassador to South Korea, and Philip Habib, who helped write South Vietnam's constitution and could guide Saigon on the changes necessary to legalize a coalition government with Communist participation."[24]

The hope, the expectation, and the plan was that Thieu could be persuaded to accept the terms without too much delay or difficulty and Kissinger could then go on to Hanoi to initial the settlement and then back to Paris for the formal signing with Le Duc Tho by October 31. But Nixon seemed to change his mind. Washington sought further clarifications, specific terms to spell out the details to avoid future troubles. Thieu wanted guarantees unacceptable to Hanoi. In short, problems piled up which Kissinger could not settle with either Thieu or Hanoi. Many critics began to yell betrayal, deception, and election maneuver by Tricky Dick, another try for victory, and it all meant that the war was to go on and on. Hanoi's spokesman, Xuan Thuy, regarded our delays and refusal to sign the agreement as very serious and declared that the whole arrangement was jeopardized.[25]

From Thieu in Saigon to his agents in Paris, South Vietnamese officials made promptly known their objections to the draft agreement. It was known openly by then that Thieu and Kissinger had basic and possibly sharp differences when they had recently met to discuss the peace terms. Kissinger had a tough time explaining to Saigon officials what he meant by

the "administrative structure," the "three Indochinese states," the omission of any reference to a withdrawal of North Vietnamese forces from the south, the right of self-determination, the use of Cambodia and Laos for the routing of troops and supplies, and finally the reestablishment of a firm demilitarized zone between the two Vietnams.[26]

Of special significance was our quiet abandonment of the major war aim of the United States—the right of national self-determination of the South Vietnamese people. Kissinger declared "the three Indochinese states" was a mere typographical error. Saigon saw these omissions as a basic surrender to the Communists, and some of its leaders declared Kissinger had fantastic brains but no heart.[27]

Without Saigon's signature no agreement would be legitimate. Thieu told the nation that self-determination could not come from secret meetings. Although the Americans were friends, they could settle nothing for the people of South Vietnam. The Vietnamese problem must be solved by the Vietnamese. The cease-fire had not been accepted by the parties involved. The key condition essential for peace was the complete withdrawal of North Vietnamese troops and full recognition by Hanoi of South Vietnam's full sovereignty and control of its own territory. The South Vietnamese people were urged to buy and display the yellow and red national flags, then being sold at the cost of 50 cents to $1.25. The Saigon government also reminded the nation that to be a Communist, to work for a Communist, or display a Communist flag was a crime punishable by death.[28] In short, Saigon wanted the war to go on with our aid and direct participation until full and final victory was won. Nixon discovered that while Hanoi wanted his aid to impose communism upon South Vietnam and Thieu wanted it to save his dictatorship, neither one sought freedom.

Saigon saw the draft agreement simply as a maneuver for Communist takeover. Although the Communists paid lip service to national self-determination, their political solution was directed not to that noble goal but to the question of power, "more precisely, with how you wish to have power put in your hands, something which to date you have failed to acquire by the force of arms and for which you lack popular support." Saigon declared the Communists had proposed a political solution that would disrupt the existing government of South Vietnam and neutralize the political forces that might obstruct Communist measures. To Hanoi's recent statement that "any solution to the conflict must reflect the realities of the situation," Saigon's Paris agent sharply replied: What realities gave you the right to demand the imposition of a three-segment government upon South Vietnam? What gave you the right to acquire power to participate in the government of the nation before the people had an opportunity to consent to it? What justified your claiming the right to divide authority between this or that group or to fix the percentages?[29] Of course, the answer to such questions, which Saigon could not admit, was by right of arms, of military success, by right of Saigon's failure to defend its own system. That was the great reality of their situation and of the whole world in this tragic age.

Thieu bitterly opposed the draft agreement, he wanted to fight on until full victory over the Communists was won, and he would not grant the Communists even de facto territorial sovereignty over the areas they then occupied. All sovereign power should belong exclusively to the people of South Vietnam, and his government was then the only rightful one. General Thieu complained in September 1972 that his government had permitted the people too much democracy too soon. Popular disorder and dissension invited Communist penetration. Thus he decreed by executive order the end of elections at the hamlet level. These elections for local officials in the country's 10,775 hamlets were the most cherished and democratic of all elections.[30] Now virtually all the nation's administrative officials would be appointive. Add this to the national election system which Thieu had rigged to allow only one man—himself—to run for the presidency, plus a tightly censored press and other media, and the result was almost a defiance of the only excuse we ever had for intervention—the freedom, national and personal, of South Vietnam and its people. With Nixon seemingly assured of victory and in spite of the coming withdrawal of the United States, Thieu felt his White House benefactor would save him no matter what he did. His arrogance was a burden too much to bear for his people and for the American nation as well. Now he could return to Oriental despotism which was the custom long best understood. That was his way of Vietnamizing democracy.

Thieu was bitter at any agreement that left North Vietnamese troops camped on South Vietnamese soil. But his greatest concern sprang from the cease-fire, which would bring great political unrest. Surely the many groups—politicians, journalists, opponents, dissidents—he had silenced, fined, and imprisoned would now make trouble for him. The cease-fire with all enemy and contending forces left in place in itself violated the national sovereignty of

South Vietnam and was the major wedge by which communism could eventually take over all South Vietnam. Although Nixon did not impose that result, he permitted the initiation of the sequence that might affect it. As the "loose ends" piled up with further study of the draft agreement, Thieu's demands for clarification and favorable settlement posed great difficulties for Washington. The man of the four *no*'s stuck to his beliefs. He continued to demand enemy troop withdrawal—at least that Hanoi tacitly pledge their eventual withdrawal.

Try as Kissinger did to persuade Hanoi to make some concessions, he failed because North Vietnam would never publicly and officially admit it had sent forces South and so could not admit repatriating them. Also of great importance for Hanoi and its pledge of ultimate reunification was its right to influence and intervene in the South. Any pledge to withdraw would be a renunciation of that basic right, an abandonment of its Vietcong ally, an acceptance of Saigon's claim to sovereignty, and an admission that South Vietnam was legally a separate state. To Hanoi, this would make North Vietnam the aggressor in its own country. Also the political significance of the cease-fire would rest upon the ability of each party to show its dominance of any given region, and when the Vietcong surfaced to claim authority they would need support, especially in the populous Mekong River Delta and around big cities. Should Hanoi pull out its forces, its ally would be greatly weakened in such key areas.

Thieu wanted a cease-fire at the same time throughout all Indochina. If the Communists retained even for a short time their stranglehold on key areas in Laos and Cambodia, they could not only dominate those countries but slip illegal assistance into South Vietnam in violation of the cease-fire. Also Thieu demanded that the DMZ be explicitly recognized in the cease-fire agreement. This was important to South Vietnam since the DMZ was the one legal basis for a border between South and North Vietnam. Any cease-fire in a situation of no clear territorial lines was full of pitfalls. A standstill cease-fire would thus not likely end hostilities; rather it would probably shift the nature of the war from set battles between major units to the former small units of guerrillas and counterguerrillas, terrorists and police, assassination teams and psychological warfare squads on both sides seeking mastery of the country. Intelligence intercepts revealed Communist plans to delay compliance with a cease-fire to gain further advantage, and Saigon had similar schemes. Kissinger knew both sides posed great difficulties for an honest enforcement of the cease-fire. Both sides never ceased efforts to get ready, not for peace, but for continued warfare.[31] Thieu entertained grave doubts as to his capacity to counter this certain Communist strategy without the continued assistance of United States air power and material aid. He wanted to keep his big crutch as long as possible.

Thieu viciously denounced the proposed National Council of National Reconciliation and Concord, which was to help maintain the cease-fire and build the new political order. Although the United States regarded this body as a mere "administrative structure," Thieu saw it simply as a coalition government and was sure the Communists so deemed it. Under cover of this maneuver they meant to grab total power over South Vietnam. Kissinger seemed not to think of it so seriously, but Nixon appeared to have some sober second thoughts about it that agreed more with Thieu. In a three-segment commission of Saigon loyalists, Communists, and neutralists, Thieu was well aware that for him it was a stacked deck, which made his chances of survival dim indeed. He strongly declared he would "never accept a government of three components," and over Saigon's military radio came "a thinly veiled threat" that the South Vietnamese army would oppose any American attempt "to impose a tripartite coalition government" on the people of South Vietnam.[32]

Thieu demanded a referendum to determine whether his people wished to change the constitution to permit Communist participation in the government. Of course such an election, rigged by Thieu, would reject the draft proposal and Hanoi in turn would reject such an election. In such fashion Thieu put Nixon in the embarrassing position of appearing to do what he said he would never do—impose a coalition on Saigon. Even Nixon was losing some of his options. One observer noted: "We should never have given Thieu such unqualified support. It was stupid, and now the chickens are coming home to roost." Of course the president retained very powerful leverage. He could stop material aid, financial support, cease paying the salaries of the ARVN, and withdraw all air support; but that would doom South Vietnam, bring wide defections from the ARVN, and invite "military coup and massive bloodshed," which Washington sought to avoid.[33] Thieu was dependent, but he was no puppet. From the first, he threatened to obstruct the whole process of peace, refused to sign any deal he did not approve, and posed for Nixon the risk and challenge of imposing a doubtful peace upon an ally or leaving him to face grave dangers alone.

In long talks with Thieu, Kissinger took a more hopeful view of the possibilities. He told Thieu that he still had a million-man army, a police force of one hundred and twenty thousand men, and the promise of continued American aid during the period of reconciliation—in short, he had a fighting chance. In the tough debates between Thieu and Kissinger, Nixon's advisers at the scene contended that the major portion of the country and its population centers would be under Thieu and his forces as then deployed. The various commissions established to work out the new political system and the elections would all be designed to reflect the strength of the rival forces. His army and police force greatly outnumbered the Vietcong and even Thieu's estimate of North Vietnamese regulars still in South Vietnam. The Vietcong had been badly mauled and decimated and would take years to reorganize if it could do so at all. United States war planes would remain in Thailand, Guam, and offshore for an indefinite period ready to retaliate in case massive violation of the agreement occurred. Nixon's agents held out the belief that both Peking and Moscow wanted peace and would stand with Washington in efforts to support the rules and to deprive both sides of the supplies essential to major aggressive war. Kissinger and Bunker told Thieu that the bargain made at Paris gave him a good chance to win control over much of South Vietnam.

Unhappy as Thieu was with the agreement, they told him that he would scarcely be any better off; the enemy would likely be no easier to handle after another round of resupply, infiltration, and offensive action. They observed that Hanoi's willingness to let Thieu administer territories then under his control was a major concession, which in previous negotiations had proved insurmountable. Formerly, the enemy had demanded the total ouster of Thieu and his ruling clique. No matter how long the fighting continued, Thieu could never be assured of durable political victory. All Washington could do was give him a reasonable chance to avoid Communist takeover.

How much pressure Nixon's delegation sought to apply was not made known, but they made it plain to Thieu that Nixon would not spend another year of military effort and domestic dissension to extend Saigon's territorial or population control by a small percentage. They also told the general bluntly that Hanoi would never end a war which had cost them so much without some hope that its Vietcong ally could gradually obtain political influence in South Vietnam. Most unlikely would it be that Thieu could ever hope to win the total victory so dear to his own heart. If Thieu sought to delay the cease-fire too long, the possibility existed, and he was made aware of it, that Washington might publicly break with Thieu and curtail all further aid. That would of course irreparably damage Thieu, South Vietnam, and the whole cause of peace.

After a study of the draft agreement, war critics, led by George McGovern, promptly asked: "Why, Mr. Nixon, did you take another four years to put an end to this tragic war?" Their belief was that peace could have come much sooner on the terms just announced. McGovern and his followers thought Thieu's regime was so corrupt, the war so immoral, the cost in lives and in national spirit so debilitating, that instant and unilateral withdrawal without any conditions but the return of our prisoners was justifiable long ago. Whatever the ultimate explanation one answer would have to be because Nixon stubbornly rejected unilateral withdrawal and refused to abandon an ally and dishonor both a sacred pledge and our great sacrifices in blood. He sought a fair chance for victory through Vietnamization and our air power, or through a face-saving negotiated peace with honor. And for four years he had tried both. Enemy offensives had twice shown the failure of Vietnamization; only our air power and ground forces had finally saved our ally from defeat. The current proposal could not have been possible earlier, as Kissinger stated, because the enemy demanded a political solution simultaneously with a military settlement that predetermined the political outcome in Hanoi's favor. Now he abandoned that formula and dropped his demand for the ouster of Thieu. At least Thieu had a chance of survival, and the Communists had a chance of takeover. Nixon now seemed to consent to a procedure by which Communists could seize power, but it could be reasoned that he himself did not impose it upon South Vietnam.

The enemy had not been willing to accept these terms earlier. In 1968, if not sooner, he had few if any compelling reasons to seek or accept a cease-fire, but now the situation had changed. South Vietnam had a million men under arms, and with time its position would greatly improve. Laird officially declared that Vietnamization had sharply changed the circumstances of earlier years; its success had enabled us to bring out our military forces and leave the South Vietnamese with the capability for their in-country security. The land attacks, although launched with great suddenness and surprise had failed of their objectives, had really been fought to a standstill on the ground by the ARVN. Nixon had used air power against Hanoi and Haiphong in a way vastly different from the self-imposed restrictions of the Johnson era. Furthermore, Sino-Soviet attitudes toward the war had changed; Russia and China seemed to have tired of the war, its costs, its hindrance to other programs and objectives now more urgent. Pressure for peace, absent earlier, came from Hanoi's great friends. Kissinger had tried for years also to persuade the enemy to separate the military and political settlement of the war, to provide a means by which we could quit the war and obtain the release of our POWs and missing in action without imposing a Communist regime upon South Vietnam. This new offer solved that dilemma. These factors, official Washington felt, explained why the October draft could not have been possible earlier. At least we now had found a means by which the South Vietnamese could determine their political future. At least we could say we had given South Vietnam a fair chance at national self-determination—perhaps our major objective in being there. The circumstances which permitted this had not previously existed.

Nixon would never accept the humiliation which Hanoi seemed anxious to impose upon the United States by its incessant demand that we quit the war totally without any preconditions on its part and in going use our leverage to impose a Communist regime upon South Vietnam. If we had refused to use our full pressure for freedom in South Vietnam's internal politics, we would certainly never use it or even try to do so for Communist despotism. The president could have withdrawn from the war totally in 1969 had he been willing to accept Communist terms. Such a "bugout" or "cop-out" would have been dishonorable and would have betrayed our friends and allies everywhere. He declared in February 1973 that the trust, confidence, and assurance of our allies in our dependability was essential to world peace, and added:

Had we taken the easy way out, which we could have done years ago, certainly when I came into office in 1969, our failure there would have eroded and possibly destroyed their confidence in the United States and, of course, enormously encouraged those who might have aggressive intentions toward us.[34]

Nixon's critics noted that he gave more than he got, had in effect ratified Hanoi's conquest of large portions of South Vietnam, allowed Hanoi's regulars to stay on to preserve their conquests, had overturned in fact the South Vietnamese constitution without any local consent by approving a process of rewriting it and replacing it with another. In brief, he gave Thieu's enemies an equal chance to shape the future of South Vietnam. Thieu might well question the value of such an ally, for his chance of survival was quite limited. Many did not think the draft agreement brought the peace with honor Nixon said he had in mind.[35] It was more like the peace with dishonor that he declared was the program of George McGovern, his major political opponent. McGovern would appear to have been more honest with himself and the American people in this respect. Hanoi gained so much by the October agreement that for many it was hard to believe it would not have been accepted years ago. We had suggested that the military and political issues be settled separately, but the North Vietnamese had stubbornly rejected that. We had never before offered them such an easy chance to grab power, if indirectly, over South Vietnam.

After the election of November 7, Nixon sent Kissinger back to Paris to seek further clarification and tie up the "loose ends." Saigon's objections and Nixon's sober second thoughts seemed to justify further effort to spell out in detail the precise terms and implications of the October draft. Secret talks thus resumed, but difficulties arose, and on December 13, 1972, Kissinger came back to Washington to report failure to get an agreement. Evidently Kissinger could not then persuade Le Duc Tho to accept the modifications sought by Thieu and Nixon. He could not get from Hanoi a formal, precise, and unequivocal statement that the Saigon government was the sole sovereign authority over South Vietnam. He could not get from Hanoi the slightest indication of any willingness by hint, deed, or word to withdraw its troops in part or whole, at any time, from South Vietnam. Hanoi would neither admit the presence of its troops nor deny its legal right to be in South Vietnam before, during, or after a cease-fire. And even should Hanoi agree to such terms, it was widely believed, the Vietcong would not, and the fight would continue. Did Nixon and Kissinger believe that the initial draft of October 8 could possibly operate without perilously weakening Saigon's position? If so, they too were guilty of a great deception. Its essential ambiguity, which permitted both sides to anticipate possible victory, alone made possible its acceptance. When Saigon demanded, with Washington's support, further concessions to clarify and strengthen its position, obviously Hanoi then sought amendments in its behalf. In truth, there was little room left for genuine compromise.

In the secret talks with Hanoi and Saigon, Kissinger and his deputy, General Alexander Haig, ran like errand boys to and fro desperately searching for a formula to satisfy both sides. To some they acted more like mediators than participants. It was not possible to get pledges from one sufficient to reassure the other. Fears were too great, demands too sharp, and memories too long and vivid. Deny as they did all likelihood of future bloodbaths, both the Vietcong and the Saigon supporters feared the worst after our withdrawal. They prepared for further war, not durable peace. They talked cease-fire, but to Saigon the proposed political settlement was a coalition government, which Thieu repeatedly rejected in the belief that it would lead promptly to a Communist takeover. Hanoi refused equally any solution that totally denied to it a chance to win. Any deal that evacuated all American forces and ended our aerial assistance while it left Hanoi's regulars on its soil in addition to the hard-core Vietcong posed for Saigon unacceptable peril. Washington could not pledge permanent aerial assistance such as had saved Saigon from likely defeat in the spring and summer offensive of 1972.

Thieu and Saigon were genuine obstacles to peace. Ambiguities in the

October draft could not be cleared up without upsetting the whole proposal. Kissinger had wisely sought to avoid the lawyer's trap of a delusive certainty. The fundamental issue of sovereignty had to be obscured, and some hope had to be left for each side. Kissinger had sought a means by which Washington could escape responsibility for allotting political power in South Vietnam. Acceptance of any such responsibility had been a major mistake of the whole intervention. We certainly had no obligation to maintain any particular regime in Saigon. Once we had fought—so many believed—for national and personal freedom for South Vietnam, but the war, the corruption, and the despotism of all the Saigon governments had made a myth of that objective. Now our two decades of aid and ten years of direct war had really been too much. Extrication was defensible. If Vietnamization had not succeeded by 1973, it should have.

At the secret talks, suddenly suspended in December 1972, Washington had specific objectives. We sought a closer link between the end of the fighting—the cease-fire in South Vietnam—and the end of the war in Laos and Cambodia. We wanted a final accord, a durable peace, not just another armistice. Also we sought some tangible evidence from Hanoi of a willingness to pull back its troops before we signed the agreement and some declaration of intent, partial evacuation or similar demonstration of intent to withdraw from Laos and Cambodia. Again we wished to make clear that the National Council of Reconciliation and Concord was understood to be only an administrative structure, not a coalition government. Optimistically, we asked Hanoi to accept separate nationhood, some sovereignty for South Vietnam. Not for Thieu, but for South Vietnam. It would help if we could get an agreement to restore and honor the DMZ established by the Geneva Accords of 1954.

When the diplomats finally began to discuss the real issues, they discovered that differences still remained for future resolution. Accusations were mutual. In a press conference of December 16, 1972, Kissinger gave our official version of why the talks stalled.[36] For a brief period, once again both sides discussed the issues, presented proposals, accepted some, rejected others, and made real progress. It seemed "we were within a day or two of completing the arrangements." Then for unknown causes, he said, Hanoi began to stall, the atmosphere changed, and "the negotiations have had the character where a settlement was always just within our reach, and was always pulled just beyond our reach when we attempted to grasp it." He did not know what decisions were made in Hanoi, but, after the first three days, he declared, the negotiations turned sour.

In short, the enemy haggled, stalled, and reneged. As soon as one issue was settled a new one was raised. It was tempting, Kissinger said, to keep trying in a matter so dear to the hearts of so many people, but he added "the President decided that we could nôt engage in a charade with the American people." Once again he felt compelled to state our basic attitude. In such a situation where peace could be very near, he said, if we could get an agreement the president deemed just we would proceed with it. Our basic objective was to get something more than an armistice. We wanted to move from hostilities to normalization, to cooperation.

But we will not make a settlement which is a disguised form of continued warfare and which brings about by indirection what we have always said we would not tolerate.

We have always stated that a fair solution cannot possibly give either side everything that it wants. We have—we are not continuing a war in order to give total victory to our allies. We want to give them a reasonable opportunity to participate in a political settlement. But we also will not make a settlement which is a disguised form of victory for the other side.[37]

However, we could not deal in good faith with one who every day one issue was settled raised a new one, and when that was resolved raised it again in a different form and at another step or phase of the negotiations. While millions prayed and anguished for peace, it became unbearable to negotiate on one frivolous issue after another. As we broke off the talks, we declared we would resume our efforts again at some future date if and when the enemy was ready for serious negotiations. Kissinger still believed the spirit of the negotiations begun in October was the right one.[38]

He would neither speculate upon the motives of the enemy nor divulge more information about the secret talks. With Le Duc Tho he had pledged secrecy in hope of an early resumption of the negotiations, and they had agreed to keep open the lines of secret communication. Although he had just said he did not wish to speculate upon enemy motives, he thought it possible that the North Vietnamese found it easier to face the risks of further war than the uncertainties of peace. They might be waiting for a worsening of relations between us and Saigon, for more public pressures on us; and possibly they simply could not make up their own minds.[39] Parenthetically, he might have suggested also that by delay and obstruction since 1968 they had won more by diplomacy than by war. Why make any concessions to a retreating enemy? Possibly Hanoi thought that Nixon only wanted a decent face-saving interval for our withdrawal, or that he would be relieved to obtain a charade of extrication with honor, while it won final victory.

While Kissinger denied that North Vietnam had the right to intervene constantly in the South, he also recalled the numerous cease-fire proposals made since 1970 without objection by Saigon, although those proposals had not required North Vietnamese withdrawal. Therefore, we no longer demanded enemy withdrawal; nor did we support Thieu's demand for it. Kissinger still insisted that the text of the October agreement was 99 percent complete.[40] That figure he should have lowered considerably, if truth and realism had intervened in the judgment; and a little later he admitted his troubles with exact figures. After that overdramatic preelection statement that peace was at hand, that remaining problems could be easily settled within two or three days, caution would have been much wiser.

A bit later in the question-and-answer session, he came back to a point he deemed fundamental. When asked, Did not our insistence that the two parts of

Vietnam should live in peace with each other constitute the fundamental disagreement? He answered: "I can't consider it an extremely onerous demand to say that the parties of a peace settlement should live in peace with one another and we cannot make a settlement which brings peace to North Vietnam and maintains the war in South Vietnam."[41] That summed up the dilemma of Nixon and Kissinger. How could we quit and call something a peace which left open the possibility of war? Our air power had been the balancing factor, which offset the enemy presence in South Vietnam. It was a sort of equivalent of a land invasion of the North, which limited warfare and fear of a wider war with China and Russia had long checked.

Respected observers believed the vital issue at stake was South Vietnam's insistence that Hanoi acknowledge in writing that there were two separate Vietnams, North and South, and that the Saigon government was sovereign over all of South Vietnam. After sober review, possibly against Kissinger's better judgment, Nixon ordered Kissinger to push for this concession. That was a vital change in the October draft which Washington, not Hanoi, sought. Thieu had correctly read the initial draft, which implied that there was only one Vietnam. Article I of the Hanoi broadcast version, which Washington affirmed was correct, stated: "The United States respects the independence, sovereignty, unity and territorial integrity of Vietnam as recognized by the 1954 Geneva agreements."[42] The original Geneva Agreements regarded Vietnam as one country, but divided by a temporary military line. It did not establish a permanent partition of the nation. The word *unity* was the key. In this and possibly other respects Washington, as well as Hanoi, was responsible for the collapse of the talks. Generally in negotiations when one side demands a change of previously accepted positions, that permits the other side to make similar demands in its own behalf.

Washington's acceptance of Thieu's demand for a return to the DMZ and recognition of some sort of South Vietnamese legality would seem to give Thieu a limited veto upon our action, erase any role for the Vietcong, and appear to Hanoi as evidence of insincerity on our part. Nixon could have contended that enemy acceptance of a three-part National Council of National Reconciliation and Concord which would include Communists, non-Communists, and neutrals provided sufficient recognition of the legality of the South Vietnamese government. Kissinger noted that North Vietnam could not be allowed to have local peace while its forces constantly intervened in the South, but that ignored the impact of our air force upon North Vietnam and the capacity of the United States to resupply Saigon's armies.

Kissinger and others believed that during a recess in the peace talks between November 25 and December 4, the Hanoi politburo, swinging toward the hawks who had denounced the concessions of the October 8 draft, decided not to sign an agreement but to stall. By feigning interest in a deal through a succession of new proposals and pressured by the Vietcong who strongly opposed any arrangement that left Thieu in office or any recognition of two Vietnams, which would make illegal their claim to participation in the government of South Vietnam or Hanoi's right to keep troops in South Vietnam, they hoped antiwar pressure inside the United States and the Western world would ultimately give them victory without any concessions at all.

In short, the enemy—like Nixon—had second thoughts. Informed observers and responsible American officials in Paris believed the talks collapsed because of the Nixon demand for a change in the draft agreement calling for a recognition of the DMZ as a temporary political border. Kissinger had not stressed this in the negotiations of October. Hanoi would not accept a deal that implied recognition of the Thieu government's sovereignty over all South Vietnam. That was a basic issue of the war. Without a military victory neither side could demand a settlement of this question in its favor. Should either side persist in this claim the war would have to continue. We could not obtain certain victory for Thieu; at best all we could hope for was to get our troops, prisoners, and missing in action out, and leave it to the people and forces of Vietnam to find their own solution. Thieu was so incensed at Kissinger's concessions to Hanoi that he sent a special envoy to Washington to talk directly with Nixon. His request for a personal summit Nixon rejected. Marvin and Bernard Kalb wrote: "It was only after the Paris talks were suspended and Kissinger had flown back to the President's side that Duc got the message that he would be welcome in Washington." Spurred by the possibility of an early return of our prisoners of war, Nixon bluntly told Thieu's emissary that he would sign an agreement with Hanoi when he deemed it the right one, "with or without you." He added that if Thieu chose to continue the war on his own, he would risk losing our aid, without which South Vietnam could not survive.[43]

In early October we seemed willing to ignore the DMZ issue, but Thieu made it a sticking point, and Nixon ordered Kissinger to try for it. Then Hanoi, pressured by the Vietcong, bristled and reversed direction. Kissinger could not get the tighter agreement Presidents Nixon and Thieu wished.[44] While permanent peace was our major objective, Saigon, the Vietcong, and Hanoi wanted victory. Hanoi worked on the assumption that any cease-fire would be lightly supervised, if at all, and last just long enough for Giap to prepare his forces for another drive for total victory and for United States withdrawal. Enemy leaders, tough men disciplined by a dynamic leader and dedicated philosophy, mindful of a generation of constant struggle, could not abandon hope of victory when once again it seemed so near. The issue of "sovereignty" of the two Vietnams was too much for them. Their dream was of Communist control of all Indochina.[45]

Pressured by Thieu and frustrated by Hanoi's refusal to compromise, Nixon ordered resumption of air and naval warfare against Hanoi and Haiphong on December 18. Our attack had been suspended in late October as a demonstration of goodwill when the talks seemed serious and hopeful. Now, however, after more than four years of negotiation, we relearned something we should never have forgotten—that Hanoi was as determined as ever one day to dominate all Indochina. Washington now believed the enemy's diplomatic stall sought to gain time for another massive buildup of its military forces. Hanoi, it now seemed clear, would accept a cease-fire only in its own time and on its own terms. After Kissinger's latest press conference blaming Hanoi for the collapse, Hanoi countered with the accusation that Washington sought 126 separate changes in the draft treaty of October 8, 1972, and declared that Nixon resumed the bombing to force acceptance of his terms. The president adopted a carrot and stick policy, but he held open the possibility of renewed peace negotiations. He wanted a rapid settlement, but his spokesman declared: "We're not going to allow the peace talks to be used as a cover for another offensive."[46]

The morality of the bombing, at this Christmas time as well as at many other times, was a question that disturbed millions. Talk of revenge by Communists, after the war wherever they won power, never ceased. Kissinger denied that we engaged in indiscriminate bombing. Although it was widely rumored that he strongly opposed this attack, which brought possibly thirteen hundred civilian deaths in two weeks, he denied it.[47] He agreed with Nixon that throughout the war our bombing had been directed against military, not civilian targets. What did that awesome devastation of late 1972 and the war itself mean to achieve in the large sense? A series of Nixon notes cited by William Safire revealed the president's reasons for the bombings. Nixon believed that the bombing brought the enemy to the conference table, persuaded him to yield hardened positions, make concessions on issues, such as the return of the war prisoners and the violations of the DMZ, and shortened the war.

Concerning the essential morality of bombing and the use of power, he agreed with Eisenhower's former comments about the immorality of allowing Hitler to enslave Europeans for generations to come. Eisenhower felt that the enormous air attacks of World War II had been justified to stop Hitler. Nixon thought the heavy sacrifices of the moment might effect the liberation of millions yet unborn. Obviously, all killing was immoral, but to allow the Communists to conquer untold numbers of South Vietnamese was also immoral. To prevent Communist tyranny anywhere Nixon deemed a noble mission. To protect Americans, civilians and soldiers, and to obtain the release of the war prisoners and the missing in action were most worthy objectives.[48] Such reasons did not satisfy the critics, who could see only the tragedies of the ever present warfare. To stop such catastrophes and achieve other objectives, as Nixon had earlier observed in defense of his previous spring attacks upon Hanoi and Haiphong, "Strength means nothing, . . . unless there is a will to use it. . ."[49] Was it immoral not to use it against evil? If so, how valid was the thesis of limited warfare?

The antiwar critics vigorously denounced Nixon's renewed air action and could find no evidence of another enemy buildup. Allied intelligence, however, reported that traffic had tripled on the land routes from China, and Hanoi had stockpiled near the DMZ enough new equipment to permit another assault wave. Nor had Russia and China refused further supplies. A Defense Department spokesman explained the decision to resume the air warfare:

Hanoi had built up a military potential that had the threat of surprising and embarrassing U.S. negotiators in Paris. Because there was no sign that Hanoi was sincere in trying to overcome remaining issues, the President was left with unpleasant alternatives. He chose to put more pressure on Hanoi to negotiate sincerely, and to spoil North Vietnam's growing military capability before it was unleashed.[50]

In short, Hanoi was not going to be left free to intervene in South Vietnam while immune from punishment at home. Nixon here told Hanoi: Come back to Paris and help us find a just and permanent peace or continue to suffer massive destruction of your homeland.

Kissinger spoke more in sorrow than anger when he referred to Hanoi's diplomatic tactics. Possibly he believed Hanoi was not entirely to blame for the collapse of the talks; more likely he thought Saigon was responsible. Thus, instead of directing all our fury at North Vietnam, pressure might have been also applied on Thieu. Saigon's demand that its sovereignty over all South Vietnam be written into the deal caused Hanoi to balk. When Kissinger spoke glowingly about peace at hand both he and the president were surely well aware of the sovereignty issue and apparently found the draft then acceptable. The brilliant diplomat found it acceptable, but the lawyer president pressed by Thieu wanted a clarification that required a major enemy concession. Thus the hopes of October collapsed, and the bombing resumed.

Nor had Kissinger found the DMZ clarification essential, because the cease-fire agreement which would leave North Vietnamese regulars and Vietcong forces widely scattered all over South Vietnam really minimized the issue. Also other pledges to let the people of South Vietnam settle political questions, including ultimate reunification made such DMZ zones, sovereignty questions, and two Vietnams really none of our business. To Kissinger, the insistence upon recognition of the DMZ seemed relatively unimportant in view of these other provisions. In his October 26 statement, he showed no special concern for the DMZ and seemed to feel the settlement a good one even though it took no special note of the DMZ. The cease-fire, if enforced, included safeguards to prevent a major enemy attack. He noted that the nine-point draft barred any replacement for enemy forces in the South. Attrition would reduce their numbers. Thus if Hanoi obeyed the terms of the draft, it could not reinforce its troops. If it chose to violate the agreement, the DMZ provision certainly would not stand in the way in the future any more than it had in the past. Against the argument that the zone was needed to divide the two zones, Kissinger reasoned that all political arrangements would have to be decided by the Vietnamese after we left. Repeatedly, he said all we wanted was a solution that did not impose a Communist government on Saigon, one that gave Saigon a good chance of defending itself. Of course, Thieu really wished the exact opposite: a solution that would impose his regime on South Vietnam.

However, in his December 16 press statement, Kissinger said he had sought from Hanoi some language, however vague, that would "make clear that the two parts of Vietnam would live in peace with each other and that neither side would impose its solution on the other by force."[51] Briefly, he sought from Hanoi some sort of acknowledgment that the Saigon government had a right to exist. Yet he knew that when Hanoi agreed to recognize Thieu and his Saigon government as one equal part of a three-segment National Council of National Reconciliation and Concord, it had accepted Thieu as an equal in the organization that would settle the political future of South Vietnam. That was the very heart of the draft agreement, the basic compromise which he had long sought, the only arrangement that gave both sides any hope of gaining anything from all the long struggle. That was the compromise procedure, the ultimate solution, by which no one could predetermine the future of Indochina. However, without formal recognition by Hanoi of two Vietnams, the DMZ, and Saigon's sovereign control of South Vietnam, Thieu would not sign the agreement. Although Washington said it would not let a Saigon veto obstruct a settlement, in essence that is what it seemed to be doing in December 1972. When Hanoi refused to accept such a compromise Nixon ended the talks and resumed the bombing.[52]

James Reston wrote that it was probably true that Kissinger, as well as Secretary Rogers, and most senior officers in the State Department opposed the bombing offensive and would have been more willing than the president to take a chance on signing the ambiguous terms of October 26. However, there was no chance of a break between the president and his brilliant adviser. Both wanted to get the war behind them and get on to more pressing problems elsewhere, of arms control, world trade, monetary reform, peace in the Middle East, reconciliation between the races, and endless domestic problems.[53]

However, some weight should be given to the view that Nixon went to China and Russia seeking help for a solution of the Vietnam question along the lines of the Korean and German formula of one nation and two states. Unification ultimately might be achieved, but not in such a way as to disturb the relations of great powers or destroy a new world balance of power. The United States said that it would never let Saigon veto a peace it deemed just; it expected Russia and China to pressure Hanoi to reciprocate. Our threat of a fund cutoff and a total retreat would quickly force Thieu and Saigon to accept a cease-fire.

The great powers had difficulty in persuading their client states to accept the October solution; North Vietnam had perhaps as great difficulty as did Saigon in accepting that arrangement. Hanoi did receive important concessions such as the right to have its troops in South Vietnam and the right of the Vietcong to exercise control over broad areas, but it also virtually gave up its basic war aim—unification of the whole country under Hanoi. Legally it would recognize Saigon, accept its control over the vast majority of the land area and population, confront the possibility of suffering itself a bloodbath from Thieu's persecutions, and finally face a South Vietnamese army and police force that vastly outnumbered within the country its own forces. Saigon had similar fears. In spite of Thieu's incessant *no*'s, he began preparations for the acceptance of a cease-fire and showed a willingness to try to live with the agreement, whether he signed it or not.

CHAPTER EIGHT

THE VIETNAM ACCORDS, 1973

President Nixon decided in mid-December 1972 that he had had enough of Hanoi's stalling pattern in the peace talks at Paris. The enemy had made too many frivolous demands and tentative agreements only to renege, evade, and then increase them again. Hanoi denied any stall and accused Washington of backing down on its own previous agreements. Washington declared the enemy too often falsely assumed we had agreed to many provisions, when we had only talked about them. Although he declared that it was most promising and brought us close to peace, Kissinger did not sign the October agreement. At that time he certainly expected the "loose ends" to be quickly settled and thus to sign the final draft.

Thieu's objections, supported by Nixon, required further talks to reach a tighter and better agreement. When Hanoi did not get exactly what it wished, it began to be evasive. Thus the December talks collapsed. Nixon called Kissinger home and on December 18 ordered the resumption of the bombing of North Vietnam north of the 20th parallel. For the next twelve days there followed a pattern or carpet bombing more destructive than in the whole war to date. Over the enemy heartland we unleashed our B-52 bombers and faced the most heavily defended piece of real estate in the history of warfare. Our losses were heavy, but our bombing was devastating. Our aim was to paralyze Hanoi and Haiphong, the two largest cities of North Vietnam. This meant the destruction of their power plants, industrial installations, military bases, transportation, railroad yards, and port facilities, which we had already mined and blockaded. Unfortunately, civilians, hospitals, and homes were also hit.

The aerial attacks caused critics everywhere to have a thorough go at Nixon and the war. One defender of the official policy noted that the "sellout brigade" of defeat, appeasement, and surrender like a pack of dogs kept nipping at Nixon's heels all the way to the final peace. Before mankind our image appeared dark and ominous indeed. Our aerial destruction of the highly populated region of Hanoi and Haiphong brought global denunciation. Our Canadian friends in their House of Commons found it deplorable and voted unanimously to condemn it. A highly respected French newspaper, *Le Monde*, called the raids an abomination, comparable to Nazi bombing attacks. Japan's major paper called us a "blinded giant," and a Buenos Aires report called the attacks "genocide."

The United Nations Secretary General Kurt Waldheim voiced his concern, and Pope Paul VI expressed his profound bitterness over the excessive number of victims of this war. Olaf Palme, Prime Minister of Sweden, compared Nixon's blitz against North Vietnam with the Nazi massacres of World War II, for which Nixon suspended full diplomatic relations with Sweden. Even the new labor prime minister of Australia, Gough Whitlam, joined the pack against us. Chancellor Willy Brandt of West Germany remained diplomatically silent, but his friends quoted him as saying the bombing was disgusting and unfathomable. Great Britain's generally cautious and restrained Labor Party leader, Roy Jenkins, called the aerial assault one of the most cold-blooded actions in recent history. Some said it was "back to the stone age" for North Vietnam. Nobel Prize winner in Physics, De Leon N. Cooper of Brown University, just returned from Europe, reported that over there we were becoming the twentieth century Huns. To many Americans, it seemed that what Kissinger had described as a 99 percent agreement had become an Orwellian nightmare. Senator William B. Saxbe, Republican of Ohio, was incredulous and desperate; he felt Nixon had lost his mind on this issue. Mass demonstrations against our raids appeared in front of our embassies abroad, and the Communist and non-Communist enemies of the United States had a field day, matched only by the despair of too many American liberals and friends here and elsewhere who failed lamentably to see the necessity of official efforts to force a peace of no surrender. Many Congressmen asked for a cutoff of all funds for this "unholy and unwanted war" if such an "inexcusable" massive attack did not soon cease.

Had we won a quick victory in 1965-1967, such vicious attacks would most likely not have been heard. Prolonged frustration, devastation, loss of lives, and no sight of ultimate victory frayed nerves and brought bitter resentments and recriminations. But the president faced bitter choices when Hanoi refused all entreaties for an honorable peace. He could abandon his ally to the enemy, let the suffering drag on interminably, or use our massive air power to destroy Hanoi's capacity for further aggressive actions. Since public opinion here made any other escalation of the war unacceptable, he could use only this blitz to achieve his long-sought just peace.

Hawks defended the bombing, the mining, and all the efforts to effect such a peace on these grounds. If at this late date we simply managed a thin cover for our total surrender to enemy terms, the consequences for us would be catastrophic. A false and illusory peace that permitted the enemy to make a mockery of our long and painful effort would be insufferable. Russia and other nations would interpret our action as a sign of weakness and raise their price around the world for any and all settlements of questions. They would likely challenge us at endless points as they did once in Cuba in 1962. Surrender of South Vietnam on any installment or gradual plan would lead our remaining allies to lose confidence in us and in our willingness to meet our many treaty commitments elsewhere. Furthermore, when the enemy soon flooded into Saigon and elsewhere in Indochina and beyond—the domino theory had not yet died—Americans would experience great remorse and possibly lose faith in themselves. The war critics seemed to have forgotten the long years of guerrilla terror and the countless thousands of South Vietnamese killed by a most fanatical and ruthless enemy. Nor could they envision the endless ages of despotism to which a Communist victory would doom the living and yet unborn millions of South Vietnamese. If the bombing should succeed—and no one could then prove that it did not—in speeding the just peace Nixon sought, it would seem to have been truly justified.[1]

Nixon sought to bomb the enemy back to Paris and to reason. Students may long debate whether his strategy worked. When asked about it, Kissinger would only observe that after twelve days of massive attacks, the enemy agreed to resume the talks in early January and within a few days accepted a settlement that brought a cease-fire and some promise of an enduring peace. Hanoi denied that the bombing had any influence at all. Nixon halted the bombing north of the 20th parallel on December 29, and, after the talks resumed in January and gave promise of success, he announced on January 15 the cessation of all military operations over North Vietnam. The mines were not to be deactivated until after the treaty had been signed January 27, 1973. Without any reciprocal offer from the enemy here ended for the first time since 1968 all military activities in enemy territory. This was a unilateral action by the United States, but was in agreement with policies announced by Nixon long before.

On May 8, 1972, the president had announced the plan to bomb North Vietnam and mine its harbors, but at the same time he also said he would end this policy when Hanoi agreed to return our war prisoners and accept an internationally controlled cease-fire throughout all Indochina. Hanoi had also been told that once there was progress in the peace talks we would take unilateral steps to advance the efforts. By this gesture we signaled Hanoi our appreciation and Saigon, especially President Thieu, our belief that the enemy was being reasonable and that no further objections from Saigon would be acceptable. Thus when the Paris talks were resumed in January, all acts of war against North Vietnam ended as soon as a settlement was reached.

Pressured by our bombing and possibly by Russia and China, Hanoi in late December 1972 had shown signs of readiness to resume talks, sent Le Duc Tho back to Paris, dropped its extreme demands, and within a few days worked out the final settlement with Kissinger, whom Nixon had ordered back to France. The rapid pace of events in January seemed to support Kissinger's October statement that peace was at hand with but a few more days of consultation. However, the first several days of the resumed talks were chilly indeed. Kissinger found himself standing outside the enemy residence waiting in vain for someone to open the door for him. Finally he opened it himself and walked in to begin the talks. Soon the ice thawed, and the hard talk of genuine diplomacy arose.

After the bombing halted, the antiwar critics eased up on their attacks.

Senators Mansfield and Scott applauded the cessation. Even Senator Henry Jackson, the hawk from Washington state, found it helpful. Plans to cut off funds for further war were delayed pending word from Paris. Senate doves on the other hand had their doubts; they had been disappointed before. Some suggested waiting at least until January 20, Nixon's inauguration day. If by then peace had not come, Congress could cut off the funds and stop the war. Meanwhile, Secretary Laird stated that Saigon was ready to defend South Vietnam and Vietnamization was now so successful that even if the peace talks failed, Saigon and the ARVN could survive. He suggested that we seek with Russia and China to impose an arms embargo upon both sides in the event of any future warfare between Hanoi and Saigon or between the Vietcong and the non-Communists of South Vietnam. In that way we might together force the belligerents into peace—or at least into much reduced warfare.

To summarize, the peace talks resumed and agreement came quickly in January 1973 because of nearly universal fatigue and weariness with the prolonged war. Millions wanted to get on with the solution of other problems long pressing upon mankind. Although the enemy strongly denied it, the carpet bombing of late December told the enemy what he might have to face in the future if he stubbornly refused to yield his unreasonable demands. At his news conference on January 24, 1973, Kissinger would say only

that there was a deadlock . . . in the middle of December, and there was a rapid movement when negotiations resumed on the technical level on Jan. 3, and on the substantive level on Jan. 8. These facts have to be analyzed by each person for himself.[2]

Enemy losses were awesome. Precise figures are unavailable, but our intelligence sources estimated that from five to ten thousand enemy soldiers may have been lost in the raids. In Hanoi alone North Vietnam probably lost over thirteen hundred killed and close to the same number wounded. It was not so much the number of human losses, our military leaders believed, but the destruction of his industrial installations and the promise of more to come that forced the enemy to come to terms.

Aerial photography revealed that 80 percent of North Vietnam's electrical-power capacity was destroyed, 25 percent of its petroleum and gasoline supply was lost, every major military installation in the North was struck at least once, and some stubborn targets were bombed repeatedly until finally destroyed. Vast supplies moving from China across the country were "cut sharply by attacks on a dozen vital rail yards and bridges." Although we lost twenty-eight planes—including fifteen B-52 Stratofortresses, knocked out largely by Communist surface-to-air missiles—the loss was bearable at least for a short-run object lesson. The air force also contended that the objective was not civilian lives, but enemy installations. Compared to the fire-bomb raids of World War II, which killed hundreds of thousands, these raids destroyed property, but very few lives. To the military mind, all the dovish talk about enemy morale being stiffened by air attacks was so much nonsense. If you destroyed his military capability, you did not care what his morale was because he would now wage war less effectively.[3]

Observers believed that Sino-Russian pressure upon Hanoi and the Vietcong persuaded them to return to the path of diplomacy. China and Russia had other and greater interests; Nixon's ping-pong diplomacy had been effective. Also the enemy may have realized now that an unpredictable Nixon might get tougher and impose further punishment upon them without any great loss of domestic support. As long as American casualties were small and the troop withdrawal program continued, there was little chance the doves would prevail against the use of air power alone. The October proposal would at least get our troops out of Vietnam and give the Communists an equal chance to win their objective. Likely both sides saw little to gain by further stalling, haggling, and fighting. That road would bring only further suffering, possible escalation, or continued stalemate. We believed South Vietnam might be able to defend itself, and we officially told ourselves that Vietnamization was finally succeeding. One thing was very clear: since 1968 steady and firm domestic opposition prevented any and all attempts to escalate the war and try for a total and traditional military victory. Nixon had begun his administration with the motto that negotiation was better than confrontation. By the proposed solution we avoided the imposition of a Communist or coalition government upon South Vietnam or of any other predetermined solution. The ultimate political system of Indochina was left to the people themselves whether they were ready for it or not.

After the failure of the 1972 invasion, Hanoi realized it could shift the struggle from the battlefield to diplomacy and seized the chance Nixon offered it to do so. Our intelligence sources believed Hanoi miscalculated in early 1972 when it planned its spring offensive. It had not believed that Nixon could so easily ignore antiwar sentiment in the United States and resume the bombing of the North. Nor had it expected him to risk intervention by Russia or China by mining the harbors and waters of North Vietnam. Possibly most important of all, the enemy leaders had not fully appreciated the awesome power of our B-52's when used tactically against infantry around battlefields such as at Quang Tri, Kontum, and An Loc. When by the end of the summer its offensive stalled and supplies and troops were exhausted, Hanoi decided to try for a negotiated solution. We believed it had planned all along to obtain some sort of a peace by the end of 1972, but now realized it would have to make more concessions than it originally intended. Now it shifted from a military to a political struggle.[4] It did not anticipate the carpet bombing that followed the December stall in the talks. This was probably the clincher.

Nixon's final suspension of all military activities over North Vietnam January 15, 1973, the return of Kissinger to Washington the previous day, and the announcement by the White House that he would return to Paris by Tuesday, January 22, to complete the text of an agreement, and the special mission of General Alexander Haig to Saigon signaled the end of our direct involvement in the war. Saigon could read the signs well and realized that it would not be so easy again to delay or reject a settlement. Thieu still had four objections. One was to the mixed military commission to supervise the cease-fire, composed of the four direct participants in the war: the United States, North Vietnam, South Vietnam, and the National Liberation Front. It was agreed that its headquarters would be in Saigon, but there was a conflict over the location of other units. Thieu wanted units at Da Nang, Pleiku, Bien Hoa, and Can Tho. Hanoi wanted them also at Hue, My Tho, and Phan Thiet. Saigon objected to Hanoi's areas. Thieu noted that those belonged to the Vietcong and were strongholds of the enemy which surrounded Saigon's positions. That was not acceptable. The second conflict was over the prisoners. The protocols were too vague in defining which prisoners were to be released after a cease-fire and seemed to ignore several classes of prisoners then held by the Communists. Thieu wanted the protocols to define the types of prisoners to be released—foreign military and civilian prisoners held outside South Vietnam, including those in Laos, Cambodia, and North Vietnam, and civilian and military prisoners held by the Communists inside South Vietnam.

Furthermore, there was the question of the limitation of movement. Under the proposed agreement, South Vietnamese military and police units would not be allowed to move freely within their own areas or fly over them. Thieu asked: "How can the police keep order if they cannot move around freely? How can we train pilots if we cannot fly?" Finally, there was the constant problem of the demilitarized zone. Saigon wanted it clearly acknowledged that the southern half of the demilitarized zone, then in enemy hands, belonged to South Vietnam. There were other objections to the agreement in South Vietnam, but these four were the major ones. General Haig reported to the president that Thieu generally accepted the agreement and in any case would no longer reject the inevitable.[5]

When it seemed that Thieu might again try to obstruct the settlement, two of the oldest and fiercest hawks in the Senate found it imperative to offer some firm advice. Both Barry Goldwater and John Stennis told Saigon not to create obstacles to the peace and warned that South Vietnam would lose support for any further economic and military assistance if President Thieu prevented a settlement. Stennis declared that Saigon should be aware that there were limits to what the American people were willing to do. Goldwater added that support for Saigon would rapidly diminish if Thieu tried to balk at this late date.[6] Time was running out now. Thieu faced his great moment of truth: Vietnamization was now to be tested. These were dark days for everyone involved, but for none as much as for Thieu and the people of South Vietnam.

On January 23, 1973, Kissinger and Le Duc Tho initialed in Paris the Vietnam Agreement and Protocols.[7] The final draft was made public January 24. On January 26 President Nixon issued a proclamation which told the American people the long ordeal had ended; we had achieved our goal of peace with honor in Vietnam, and he proclaimed 7 P.M., January 27, a national moment of prayer and thanksgiving and the twenty-four-hour period beginning at that hour a national day of prayer and thanksgiving.[8] Then on January 27 the four parties in the war officially signed at the round table in Paris the Vietnam peace pacts, which ended our longest war.

Between this conference of 1973 and that of 1954 were noticeable contrasts. In 1954 we had refused to cooperate and had scarcely spoken to the Chinese or in any way recognized their presence. Now we used every persuasive trick and argument to win the cooperation of both China and Russia. In 1954 both Saigon and Washington had refused to sign the treaty. Now we acknowledged that military victory over the Communists was not realistic and admitted that Communists would play a role in the future of South Vietnam. However this time they could not dictate the peace. A non-Communist South Vietnam was now more powerful and capable of preserving its independence. This time there was a genuine stalemate which made a compromise essential unless the war was to resume, and that route promised no sure victory for either side. The basic peace terms of 1954—which, if executed, would have given victory to the Communists through a coalition government and managed elections—were now abandoned, and provisions were made for a more genuinely democratic election which offered both sides a chance to win. This time because of the promise of trade and world peace, the Chinese fear of Russian attack and encirclement, and Russian desire for peace in Europe, it was easier for the superpowers to compromise.

Final evaluation of these agreements will have to wait, but immediately it was clear that prospects of enduring peace in Indochina were dim. We obtained no real solution of the question of Laos and especially Cambodia and no firm pledges to release the thousands of civilian and military prisoners held by the Vietcong and the government of South Vietnam. That sticky problem was left for a most uncertain solution by those parties themselves, with the hope it could be solved within ninety days. Although our combat forces supposedly would quit Vietnam, our presence would remain because an estimated five to ten thousand noncombat civilian military technicians, aviation mechanics, and others would be needed to help the ARVN.

Obviously, we did not get Hanoi's regulars out of South Vietnam. They not only stayed, but within a month came reports of tanks, supplies, and vast reinforcements spilling southward from North Vietnam along the old trails toward South Vietnam, with the obvious intent of preparation for continued struggle. Would pressure from Russia and China, so desperately sought by Nixon and Kissinger, be sufficient to stay Hanoi's hand and prevent renewed and major warfare, or would we have to resume the bombing to get the enemy back on the track toward peace? Further, the International Control Commission, plagued by the requirement of unanimity, found itself deadlocked between the Communists and non-Communists on virtually every issue of substance. Nor did Thieu's continued and stubborn repression of all opposition and dissent hold out much hope of serious effort to make the peace settlement work.

Saigon obtained much of what it had sought earlier. It won the specific and continued recognition, if but temporarily, of the government and sovereignty of South Vietnam.[9] Kissinger secured the deletion from the agreement of the term *government structure* in the reference to the National

Council of National Reconciliation and Concord. Thieu deemed this most vital to him. By this he presumably avoided all implication of a coalition government. It permitted Washington to reiterate its refusal to impose such a regime. Also, it was a concession to Thieu that all parties pledged to respect the DMZ at the 17th parallel as established in the Geneva Accords of 1954. Nor did the literal wording of the treaty specifically mention the Vietcong or the Provisional Revolutionary Government (although in substance it did, because the four parties signed it). Nowhere did the treaty officially acknowledge Hanoi's right to have troops in South Vietnam. All military activities by non-South Vietnamese forces were to end, and the forces to be reduced and ultimately demobilized; but the cease-fire itself and the leopard spot solution simply accepted the unmentioned fact of their presence. Saigon obtained the most valuable pledge of our continued material aid and assistance in economic reconstruction. It also won an equal chance to survive. In fact, it had a far larger military capacity than did the Vietcong and North Vietnamese regulars in South Vietnam. However, unless Moscow and Peking forced restraint upon Hanoi, perhaps even an arms embargo such as Defense Secretary Laird proposed, reinforcements in violation of the treaty could change this balance. The uncertainty of their pressure to prevent this posed one of the great problems of the peace.

On balance the enemy gained the most, Thieu the least. The enemy won our pledge to withdraw all our armed forces from South Vietnam within sixty days in exchange for the return of our prisoners of war and the accounting for our missing in action. That meant that soon our remaining 23,500 soldiers would quit the country. We pledged no further action against North Vietnam and Hanoi was allowed, without mention of the fact, to keep its troops in South Vietnam. We estimated their number at 145,000. Saigon said it was over 300,000. Thieu then had a million-man army and a large police force, both well supplied by us. Hanoi claimed, with considerable truth, that its ally, the Vietcong, needed protection against Thieu and the ARVN. Whether Hanoi's forces would wither away because of attrition and the prohibition of further reinforcements, no one could know; but anyone could see one big and blunt fact: We left and they stayed. Thus the challenge of guerrilla warfare was not met, and South Vietnam was in essence partitioned into many little areas and groups. It was the old Communist tactic of taking whatever they could get, even if only a piece at a time. By dropping our former insistence upon mutual withdrawal, we gave Hanoi a settlement by which the Vietcong were protected by the presence of North Vietnamese forces and could claim for themselves considerable parts of South Vietnam. That was a partition of South Vietnam, a major victory for the Communists and an even worse defeat for Thieu, Saigon, and the United States. That rewarded aggression. The treaty really won for the Vietcong substantial recognition as a political entity within their own areas of control and an opportunity to achieve power in Saigon. In addition, all Indochina obtained from us a pledge of further sizable aid in reconstruction. Officials in Washington talked of $7.5 billion, with $2.5 billion possibly going eventually to North Vietnam.

For these truly major concessions to an undefeated enemy, we obtained little in return. We arranged our own withdrawal from the war. We secured the return of our prisoners and some of the missing in action. The enemy dropped his demand that we directly impose a Communist regime under the guise of a coalition government upon South Vietnam, but by turning the future of that little country back to the local parties that was what we permitted indirectly by withdrawal. The National Council of National Reconciliation and Concord, which would manage the elections, was, if for that limited purpose, essentially a coalition regime. With the rule of unanimity prevailing it would hardly be likely that the enemy would yield matters of substance to Thieu's clique. Either deadlock or war would follow. This was the most fragile piece of the agreement. The three segments—Thieu, the Vietcong, and the neutral bloc—were not and could not be equal. Firm enough were the Communists and the Thieu clique, but the third element was mush. Whatever it was, either the Communists or Thieu would almost certainly dominate it or ignore it. The two warring factions would have to define and create the neutral faction. Although diplomats said one could not even refer to the council as a government because its whole life and function were keyed to the one task of setting up the elections, that was not the victory Kissinger claimed it was.

Although it was not a coalition government itself, the council had the most vital and decisive function of creating one, since neither side would yield without further struggle. The major United States and Saigon concession—the essential compromise heart of the Vietnam Accord—came right here, when the Communists were given in essence a veto power over the potential members of one-third of the council. The peace settlement called for the council to operate on the "principle of unanimity." That condition would almost certainly prevent all agreement on substantive issues. The role of the neutral third was most vague, and Kissinger did not make clear the uncertainty, when in reply to a question concerning the future role of the neutralists he said:

We have taken the position throughout that the future political evolution of South Vietnam should be left to the greatest extent possible to the South Vietnamese themselves and should not be predetermined by the United States. Therefore, there is no understanding in any detail on the role of any particular force in South Vietnam.[10]

In our view, there could then be no genuinely free Western style elections in South Vietnam because neither Thieu nor the Communists would permit them. The council was not a government itself, but it could certainly prevent the creation of one. That veto was fatal to peace.

Of little value to our peace hopes was the fact that nothing in the treaty restricted or even mentioned our military presence elsewhere in Southeast Asia. Our bombers, a thousand or more, from land and sea, Thailand, Guam, and aircraft carriers were left there to persuade all factions to work seriously for peace. That was about the only real leverage we had left against the enemy, beyond some faint hopes that Russia and China would restrain their allies. Of course, Thieu was wholly dependent upon us for economic and military aid. However, we wanted genuine peace, not unending war in Indochina. The failure to settle the situation in Cambodia kept our bombers busy there long after our forces had left South Vietnam and our war prisoners had returned. In June 1973 Kissinger still was meeting Le Duc Tho in a seemingly ceaseless effort to make the January accords stick.

Observers promptly asked: What did we get in January that we did not have in October, and, whatever it was, was it enough to justify the prolongation of the war and the tragic bombing in late December? Kissinger gave the official version. In spite of his premature "epigrammatic phrases," such as "Peace is at hand," the October draft contained uncertainties which he believed then could be quickly and easily settled. Now in late January he felt the final negotiations had succeeded in doing just that. He noted again that what we had wanted in October, but had not then obtained, we now had won.

We obtained, in addition, a larger International Control Commission police force than the enemy found acceptable in October. We had wanted some 6,000 men stationed widely over South Vietnam, and the Communists had wanted a limit of about 250, with half stationed at fixed positions and the rest free to move only with the permission and transportation supplied by each zone commander. The final draft set the number at 1,160. That was not much gain because if the parties involved wished to evade the treaty it would take tens of thousands—more than we ever sent there—to establish and preserve the peace. We won a clear separation of the prisoner of war issue. No longer did the enemy seek to tie the release of our war prisoners and missing in action to the release by Saigon of its thousands of Communist prisoners—soldiers and civilians. Now between North Vietnam and the United States was but the single issue, not bound by the inner struggles in South Vietnam, the simple swap: we evacuate all our soldiers, they return all our prisoners and missing in action.

Many observers believed these limited gains of late January did not justify the tragic bombing of December and the terrible losses of prolonged warfare. They said the January deal was substantially the same as the October 8 draft. Both Kissinger and Le Duc Tho generally agreed on this. To the war critics the heaviest losses of the war were, therefore, totally unnecessary. Now, if communism should quickly by war or peaceful struggle secure power over South Vietnam and unite it with North Vietnam the whole effort would have been nearly a total tragedy.

However, for Nixon the case was not so easy. From an official view of the settlement, should it be honored by all parties, it offered a thin chance of an honorable peace. The treaty did not establish the right of North Vietnamese troops to be in South Vietnam. If the agreement were honestly executed in time, Hanoi's troops would be reduced, and all foreign forces would quit South Vietnam. The normal attrition of personnel could not be made up by the reinfiltration of any outside forces. The treaty flatly prohibited all such reinforcement. The same prohibition would go for any future solution of Laos and Cambodia. The trails would dry up, and the problems would be left for settlement by the South Vietnamese alone. The agreement forbade any military movement across the DMZ and required full respect for that zone. The treaty further had a provision requiring the reduction and demobilization of forces on both sides. With the rapid withdrawal of all non-Southeast Asian forces, the only other country with troops left there would obviously be North Vietnam. Kissinger then declared:

> Therefore, it is our judgment that there is no way that North Vietnam can live up to that agreement without there being a reduction of the North Vietnamese forces in South Vietnam, without this being explicitly stated.
> Of course, it is not inconceivable that the agreement will not in all respects be lived up to. In that case, adding another clause that will not be lived up to, specifically requiring it, would not change the situation. It is our judgment and our expectation that the agreement will be lived up to. . . .[11]

Therefore if the treaty were honored by all factions Nixon could quite justly say he had finally won his objective of "peace with honor." If the enemy dishonored the agreement, the fault would lie with Hanoi, not Washington. But what a tragedy: in that likely case, all that we would have won from twelve years of war, the longest in our history, would have been that we got out of it. Long before we entered this war we knew a Communist pledge was not reliable. During all the negotiations, before and after the cease-fire, the Communists kept right on fighting for victory.

In all human relations some ambiguity is essential. Face-saving compromises must cover up failures to win once strongly held demands. Defenders of the treaty hoped it might work just because each side could claim it won. For example, for Saigon the DMZ was accepted, but if the deal were successful and the future reunification of the two parts of the country should follow, the line would vanish. So Saigon's victory was but temporary, while Hanoi did not lose the chance and hope of eventual and permanent reunion. South Vietnam's sovereignty and Thieu's own position of power were recognized, but only temporarily pending the full execution of the treaty, which might alter both. The provision for the neutralist third segment of the National Council of National Reconciliation and Concord left at least the chance for both the Communists and the Saigon clique to win its support. Both might have to make concessions to gain that. The ultimate solution of South Vietnam's political system was not predetermined by anything done in the treaty negotiations. That was precisely Washington's objective. Hanoi could claim truly that the treaty offered them a chance to unite all Vietnam again. It did require that this and all other objectives be achieved peacefully. That was the problem for the future, but if militarist cliques like Thieu's had their way, the "temporary" conditions would become permanent. Le Duc Tho left Paris with the blunt statement that Communists would never yield their ultimate goals. The war in one fashion or another would continue until victory was won.

Any evaluation of the treaty could only note that it created more fears than hopes. The cease-fire would be most difficult to enforce. The control commission was too small, and the two parties within South Vietnam faced nearly insurmountable problems of agreement upon area lines, keeping the peace, and managing truly open and free elections. The Vietcong would not likely permit free elections anywhere. The difficulties of governing such a divided country, plagued by sharply contrasting political and economic ideologies, held out only the probability of ceaseless struggle. The National Council of National Reconciliation and Concord could settle no problems of substance because its requirement of unanimity gave each side the veto. Communists keep very few pledges, especially those contrary to their objectives. The basic trust essential to peaceful solutions and genuine compromises was here totally lacking. Instead there was only an enduring and undying hostility between the two factions. For the United States, the treaty meant peace through withdrawal, but neither faction in South Vietnam had that option. For them the war continued; the fear remained.

Possibly the continued presence of North Vietnam regulars was necessary to protect the battered Vietcong forces from Thieu's persecution, but the likelihood amounting almost to a certainty that Hanoi would sharply reinforce its numbers to whatever degree it deemed necessary made a peaceful solution of genuine compromise pure fantasy. Nor was there any real probability, once our forces were totally withdrawn, that they would ever return or that Nixon would long continue such carpet bombing attacks as those of late December 1972. American public opinion would not support a prolonged aerial attack of that intensity—if any. Nor would the Communist giants deny further aid to their friends. The powers concerned with Indochina who met in late February at the Paris conference flatly refused to underwrite or guarantee the peace treaty. They provided no machinery of enforcement, made no pledges of any kind; they merely expressed approval of the peace effort and left any future problems in the hands of the belligerents—mainly in those of Hanoi and Washington. Any chance that Russia and China would impose an arms embargo or seriously caution restraint upon their friends was very dim. In fact, Russia and China had long been competing for influence within the domestic Communist regimes everywhere, and especially in Indochina. If any side denied aid and support, the other would surely win favor; and with the enduring Sino-Soviet split there was little likelihood of any collusion between them.

Saigon won no direct or specific pledge of further United States military assistance. It could rely upon us for further material aid and sufficient military materiel to defend itself, but we would always control the spigot and could turn it off or on to suit our interest. However, in view of past Nixon surprises in the Cambodian invasion, our aerial attacks, and the mining of waters of North Vietnam, the enemy could not be sure as to what the president might do if they violated the cease-fire. The Paris agreement permitted the two South Vietnamese parties to replace armaments, munitions, and war materiel that might be damaged, destroyed, or worn out after the cease-fire on the "basis of piece-for-piece" of the same characteristics and properties, under the supervision of a proposed joint military commission of control and supervision. Kissinger expressed the hope that such a one-for-one replacement would prove unnecessary, that there would be no major flareups of fighting to require it, and that the United States, Russia, and China would all limit future deliveries to the two Vietnams.[12]

As the situation once again changed from "our war" back to "their war" after 1972, "our concern" remained. We continued to give financial and military aid to Saigon, to support Thieu and his government, to ignore the violations by both sides of the pledges made to work for peace. In March 1975, President Ford was again heard warning the nation of the dangers of isolationism and reiterating the validity of the domino theory, as he sought additional sums to save a beleaguered South Vietnam.

On March 26, 1975, when trouble loomed in the Middle East over the collapse of his shuttle diplomacy with the Arabs and Israelis and the disintegration of Indochinese anti-Communist efforts, Kissinger lectured his critics on the nature of the world and our obligations as a great power.[13] He declared that we faced great trouble in many places and that the situation called for a renewed sense of national purpose; then he reiterated a cold war thesis:

> We must understand that peace is indivisible. The United States cannot pursue a policy of selective reliability. We cannot abandon friends in one part of the world without jeopardizing the security of friends everywhere.
> We cannot master our future except as a unified people. Our energies should be directed not at recriminations about the past but toward a vigorous and constructive search for a lasting peace and to this the Administration is dedicated.[14]

We faced the possible collapse of South Vietnam, as well as Cambodia, and the long predicted Communist takeover of all Indochina. Tired of incompetence and corruption in Saigon, pressed by internal problems of recession and inflation, threatened by an energy shortage and rising unemployment, and angered at violations of the Paris agreement by both sides in Vietnam, Congress was on the verge of reducing sharply if not cutting off entirely further aid to South Vietnam then or fixing a terminal date of three years. To forestall such an action, which he deemed fatal, and to lay the blame upon Congress for such a catastrophe, Kissinger said:

> The problem we face in Indochina is an elementary question of what kind of a people we are. For 15 years we have been involved in encouraging the people of Vietnam to defend themselves against what we conceive as external dangers.
> In 1973 we negotiated a settlement in which we withdrew our forces and in return achieved the release of our prisoners. This settlement, it is well to recall now, was—while we were negotiating it—generally criticized for our holding out for stronger terms.
> The fact of the matter is that now that we have withdrawn our forces and have obtained the release of our prisoners, there was never any question that the United States would continue to give economic and military aid to Vietnam. What we face now is whether the United States not just will withdraw its forces,

which we achieved, and not just will stop the end of the loss of American lives, but whether it will deliberately destroy an ally by withholding aid from it in its moment of extremity.[15]

A basic question, he feared, was how other people would view our actions. If we abandoned an ally, others in Israel, West Europe, Greece and Turkey would not likely be assured by our pledges. Although there was after the Paris agreement a wide belief that America had shed enough blood for South Vietnam, which should thereafter defend itself, he declared:

There was never any proposition that the United States would withdraw and cut off aid, and these agreements were negotiated on the assumption that the United States would continue economic and military aid to South Vietnam and also that there would be some possibility of enforcing the agreement, and this is the basic problem with the policy in Vietnam.[16]

Nor did Kissinger accept the administration proposal to end all aid after three more years. The situation was too grave for such a technical compromise or political reconciliation to avoid a domestic confrontation between the Congress and the White House. Rather Kissinger declared:

My own personal conviction, . . . is that the right way is to vote annually what is necessary. There are some problems in the world that simply have no terminal date. In Indochina, as long as the North Vietnamese are determined to attack, it is not responsible to say that there is an absolute date at which an end can be achieved.

. . . . .

I'm saying that as a people we should not destroy our allies and that once we start on that course it will have very serious consequences for us in the world.[17]

He did admit that there was no legal or technical obligation to give such aid, but insisted there was a very strong moral commitment. This he could deduce, it might be observed, from the trend of American history—from Truman's program of aid to Greece and Turkey to the deepening involvement of the Johnson era. This reiteration of the domino theory and revival of cold war rhetoric stirred once again voices of opposition. Americans were still divided over the issue. The disintegration of the South Vietnamese will to fight and the nearly total failure to use our aid—their army turned rabble in flight and abandoned all weapons with scarcely a token defense of province after province—raised necessary and vital questions about its capacity to use any aid, except possibly civilian relief. The evils of corruption and incompetence came home to roost.

On March 15, 1973, at his news conference, Nixon had warned the enemy not to move equipment south. There were reports that three hundred tanks and vast reinforcements beyond mere replacements were proceeding toward South Vietnam. He declared:

That we have informed the North Vietnamese of our concern about this infiltration and what we believe it to be, a violation of the cease-fire, the cease-fire and the peace agreement. Our concern has also been expressed to other interested parties and I would only suggest that based on my actions over the past four years, that the North Vietnamese should not lightly disregard such expressions of concern, when they are made, with regard to a violation.[18]

Observers wondered if Nixon could resume the war on his own authority if the enemy should violate the truce. Many members of Congress believed that once the sixty days had passed and witnessed the withdrawal of our troops and the return of our war prisoners, the war was then legally over. By March 28, 1973, that treaty process would be completed, and any attempt by the president on his own authority to resume the fighting with American personnel would create a first class constitutional crisis. Already Congress had bipartisan legislation ready for floor action forbidding reintroduction of any American forces in Vietnam. In 1970 the Tonkin Gulf Resolution of 1964 had been repealed. After the withdrawal and prisoner release the president could no longer use the argument of necessary protective reaction—that is, he must use whatever force he deemed necessary to protect our troops during withdrawal. It would not be easy for him on his own authority to order a resumption of American combat in Indochina. That truth may have been one reason why the enemy broke the cease-fire, along with the fact that Thieu had done the same. In fact, every knowledgeable observer could only ask: What cease-fire?

United States public opinion was always important in enemy calculations, but he found little public opposition to Nixon's ventures after we sharply reduced our ground forces and our casualties declined. Public opinion would likely support any reasonable effort the president made to prevent the humiliation of the United States or the violation of pledges honorably made. It was soon evident that the success of the agreement would rest primarily upon the United States. We could offer Hanoi economic aid in reconstruction, always providing Congress would allocate the amounts required, or we could resort again to force. If the war were resumed, almost every observer believed, Saigon would soon collapse without our aid, but no one was heard to say we should ever again enter combat action on the ground. Washington retained but a thin hope that the predominant interests of the great powers in trade and the relaxation of tensions in other areas would persuade them to lower their investments in Indochina. By the time the peace was signed, we had already furnished the ARVN with vast overstocks of military supplies of every category, certainly enough for the defense of South Vietnam if its people had the will to unite and fight.

This fragile deal could easily be broken; even the fear of failure could drown its hopes of success, especially if judged by past experience in Indochina. But if anything had been learned by the awesome tragedy of the past forty years, the Paris treaty had a chance. Most observers with inside knowledge of the situation feared the stronger zeal and unity of the Communists would in time prevail. To them, the treaty was but a thin cover for United States retreat, to permit us an honorable escape, after which would come the resumption of the struggle and Communist takeover.

The Paris accord was truly a thin reed of peace. The enemy had not been defeated, had not abandoned his long-run objectives of conquest, and could not be trusted to keep the peace. Nor could Saigon. Both sides willfully broke the cease-fire agreement. The United States tried too hard and too fast to escape all responsibility for preserving the peace. It failed at the postwar conference to shift the burden to others. No real world force was established or existed to enforce the agreement. The United Nations could not act against Communist vetoes. The Four-Nation International Control Commission and Supervision would not take any effective action because it was plagued by the rule of unanimity. Hungary and Poland permitted no investigations of Communist violations of the cease-fire. Neither Thieu nor the Vietcong ordered their troops to cease firing. Although the Communists and non-Communists of Laos signed a cease-fire agreement on February 21, 1973, no durable solution was found for Laos and Cambodia. No political solution was possible for South Vietnam as long as Thieu repressed all opposition, jailed Communists, and censured their actions. In mid-March 1973, Thieu still insisted that no elections would be allowed as long as Hanoi's troops remained in South Vietnam. If they left, it was most doubtful that such elections would be allowed. If he continued to repress the opposition and make impossible any peaceful solution as he did, then the Communists had no choice but to resume the war. That resumption was almost a certainty, especially after the final departure of United States forces.

The International Control Commission could not monitor the peace until there was peace. It could not even begin to function until the Vietcong and Saigon could agree upon the "areas of control," over which the fighting continued. Who could say who governed what? By day Saigon might claim it governed a zone; by night the Communists claimed they did. Zones grabbed at the last minute by both sides and after the signing of the treaty were still in contention. The Communists did not dare to surface and reveal their identity or locations for fear of Thieu's reprisals. Any chance of genuinely free elections to establish the true identity of control and power was lacking. Thieu feared the role of the third segment in the National Council of National Reconciliation and Concord. Nor did Hanoi cease its endless twists and maneuvers to gain an edge in any direction. It sought to hold up the exchange of the prisoners for our withdrawal, to link once again the return of the POWs to the execution of other parts of the accord calling for the return by Saigon of enemy soldiers and civilians. Thieu had stalled his part, and Hanoi claimed the treaty was all of a whole and no one could violate any part of it without giving the other the right to do the same. However, the treaty had provided for the separation of our prisoner return in exchange for our withdrawal from its other parts. There was no linkage between that direct commitment between Hanoi and Washington and the other parts calling for a separate handling of the other issues between the two parties within South Vietnam. Kissinger knew too well the great difficulty of obtaining quick or any solutions of political issues between Saigon and the

Vietcong. To tie the return of our prisoners to that problem would invite a prolonged delay in their return.

Aid to North Vietnam was a most bitterly debated issue. Although earlier the Nixon administration had broadly talked about the possibility of a $7.5 billion aid program for all Indochina and estimated Hanoi's allotment at possibly $2.5 billion, in early 1973 Kissinger said those sums were "not current." The president referred to aid to the enemy as "an investment in peace," which could mean a bribe to behave. Critics called the plan a humiliation, and Hanoi sought to picture it as the payment of reparations by the United States for aggressions against Vietnam, a sort of atonement for our sins against the Vietnamese people. Kissinger made a special journey to Hanoi immediately after the accord was signed and talked broadly there of postwar objectives, including the possibility of American aid. He strongly recommended on his return that such a program would bring the men of Hanoi out of their long-inhabited cells, introduce them to the outside world and persuade them possibly to cooperate in efforts to solve all their problems peacefully.

Asked how big a factor the aid to Hanoi was in persuading the Communists not to break the cease-fire, Kissinger preferred not to put it on that basis. To him the big problem was

whether Indochina can be moved from a condition of guerrilla war—or even open warfare—to a condition in which the energies of the peoples of that region are concentrated on constructive purposes.

. . . . .

It is rather a long-term investment in a structure of peace, and in turning people whose whole experience has been with conflict, with guerrilla war, with hostility toward the outside war [sic], into pursuits with which they are essentially unfamiliar. And this is our interest in the program, and why we are willing to explore a program of reconstruction for all of Indochina.[19]

He believed we should take risks for peace and reconstruction as we had for war. The alternatives to this effort he found even less rewarding and far more dangerous.

When Congress hinted that it would not favor the program, Secretary Rogers would not deny the possibility that the president might use funds already budgeted to execute the plan. He also urged Congress to restrain its opposition to aid for Hanoi at least until all our prisoners were returned and our troops were withdrawn. Congress was in an ugly mood in early 1973 because the president had threatened to impound funds to prevent exceeding the ceiling on the national debt and to prevent further inflation. In the partisan struggle between executive and congressional power, between continued welfare programs and Nixon's desire for economy and reduction, the issue of aid for the late enemy was caught in the center. Certainly aid to Hanoi never had a chance as long as the fighting continued in Indochina.

Some hinted that Nixon sought to make "fat communists" out of the Hanoi politburo, in the belief that economic prosperity would make them softer and more amenable to peaceful relations with the rest of the world. If we could do it with a detente with Moscow, why not with Hanoi? All agreed that no aid would be immediately forthcoming. Only after all our troops had been withdrawn, all prisoners had returned, all southward infiltration of men and materiel had ceased, and the enemy had given every indication of his acceptance of the cease-fire and observance of the treaty—only after the most careful evaluation of these factors and the needs of Hanoi in the context of postwar reconstruction would we consider aid. Certainly Hanoi would receive from us no aid which in any way might facilitate further war against South Vietnam or any other region.

Hardly 50 percent of the American people ever supported foreign aid in the best of times, and then only to keep nations from going Communist. Few could contend we should aid a nation already Communist, especially when it did not by deed renounce its imperial aspirations. Heard over the land was the case against any aid to the undefeated enemy: they killed our boys; they started the war; they committed aggression against their neighbors. Why should we reward an unrepentant aggressor? We should better spend the money at home for housing, health, education, welfare, and endless domestic needs. Surely we should not give such aid to our enemies when we were already cutting back on about a hundred domestic programs in a determined effort to avoid increasing the already excessive national debt. Let Hanoi's Communist friends help rebuild North Vietnam, and especially let any foreign aid for all Indochina come from and through multinational agencies.

Surprisingly many former doves, sharp critics of the war and proponents of peace at almost any price, soured on the proposal for aid for the enemy. Even George McGovern, probably receiving signals from his fellow South Dakotans and anxious for reelection, could no longer favor it. Hubert Humphrey could no longer back the plan. Observers felt such passionate doves had a moral obligation, now that their much desired peace and American extrication had occurred, to support such an aid program. Conservative Americans such as Senator Harry F. Byrd, Jr., of Virginia saw no obligation at all to pour additional billions down a rathole and expressed great concern about the rapidly deteriorating financial position of the nation, the continued devaluation of the dollar, and the incessant deficit spending. Nor did they believe the Communists had abandoned their aggressive designs. Aid was peace with bribery. Such aid was not justifiable, because Indochinese countries lacked stability, were notoriously corrupt, and would waste it on further war. Such a program would be but an effort to build a structure on quicksand.

The critics found no parallels with previous postwar aid programs. We helped those who accepted defeat and surrendered, but we gave no aid to North Korea. George Marshall initially implied aid to Russia in his plan announced at Harvard in 1947, but Russian refusal saved us from a most probable Senate rejection of the plan. A few observers saw aid as a tool to advance our political interests. It might, however, help Thieu win the support of the third segment against the Vietcong, especially if it were channeled through Saigon. The daily violations of the truce on both sides and the intelligence reports of three hundred tanks and vast reinforcements moving southward from North Vietnam made the whole idea of aid very remote. There was also, to many, a contradiction in a plan which would aid a most brutal enemy but deny amnesty to Americans who refused to serve or deserted in Vietnam. They sought to tie an amnesty amendment to any aid for the enemy program. Let Nixon take both or none. Questions arose: Who would administer the aid program? Allocate the funds? Define the functions?

Critics saw further conflict between billions of aid to enemy nations and the ending of REA loans, the impounding of rural environmental funds, and late presidential speeches about bloodbaths and enemy "outlaws and butchers" in Hanoi. It was confusing for some people, who saw Nixon bombing Hanoi at Christmas, to be asked by Easter to support his "investment for peace" to rebuild what he had just caused to be destroyed. On the other hand, some felt the aid must be given, because the treaty implied a commitment to give it. Those who had until January demanded peace at almost any price, now, it would seem, had an obligation to back a program to secure its success. Nixon's administration was prepared, a subordinate hinted, to make "one hell of a fight for the program." It was far better to turn people everywhere toward peaceful pursuits than to leave them totally frustrated and bogged down in ceaseless warfare. Hanoi, too, had to have a stake in the peace. While the costs of peace were great, the costs of war were greater. Nixon said the aid funds could come out of the national security budget—meaning from the area of foreign assistance and defense.[20]

The great peace dividend, meaning savings expected from a shift of funds from war to civilian needs, it was evident long before the peace was signed, would not be available. Inflation, dollar devaluation, rising costs of the volunteer army, and the security costs of our commitments erased that hope. Nor could we trust the hopes of better relations with Russia, China, and other areas. The continued fighting long after the Paris accord was possible only because those countries supplied the materials for the Communist troops and rejected our proposals for restraint and an embargo to lower the level of the fighting. The long anticipated normalization of international relations between Communists and non-Communist societies would certainly not develop easily or quickly. Time only would reveal whether the trust required for it existed. Sino-Soviet pressure upon North Vietnam, our economic aid to Hanoi, the very powerful leverage of our financial and material aid upon Saigon, and the possibility of our renewed bombing were the only bargaining points we had left to preserve the peace.

We called the Vietnam accord a peace with honor, but it was most likely a cover for retreat that left unsolved the problem of Indochina. Some would term the Paris settlement the completion of a cop-out or bugout, finding a pattern of retreat, of no peace and no honor, that reached back to LBJ's great reversal of March 1968. With that decision to cease further escalation, and then Nixon's phased withdrawal (scarcely covered with rosy hopes of successful Vietnamization of the war), statesmanship tried to meet the popular demand to get out of the war. Alongside our evacuation, Nixon's famous doctrine announced at Guam in 1969 downgraded our global role and reduced our commitments by declaring that we would help with money and economic and military supplies those who needed it to prevent Communist conquest, but not with our ground forces. Then through one concession after another we retreated from our former policies and demands. We went from a military policy of search and destroy to protective reaction, even if it took us into Cambodia openly in 1970 and secretly with air attacks before that to cover our retreat. We soon yielded our demand for mutual withdrawal of Hanoi forces alongside our own, and in October 1972 and then January 1973 accepted a cease-fire in place, which obviously left enemy troops from North Vietnam scattered over much of South Vietnam. More significantly, the once glorious rhetoric about our fight for the right of national self-determination for the people of South Vietnam was abandoned when we agreed to accept a three-part council which gave the Communists a veto upon any political settlement with South Vietnam. This gave any Saigon government only a chance to prevail. But long before this we had accepted rigged elections, political repression of all opposition, and terror tactics that made a total mockery of popular self-determination. Thus we withdrew our troops and sought to save our national honor, but in doing so we brought neither peace in Vietnam nor honor to our long avowed war aims.

On March 29, 1973, Nixon declared:

> We have prevented the imposition of a Communist government by force on South Vietnam.
> There are still some problem areas. The provisions of the agreement requiring an accounting for all missing in action in Indo-China, the provisions with regard to Laos and Cambodia, the provisions prohibiting infiltration from North Vietnam into South Vietnam have not been complied with. We have and will continue to comply with the agreement. We shall insist that North Vietnam comply with the agreement. And the leaders of North Vietnam should have no doubt as to the consequences if they fail to comply with the agreement.[21]

This statement plus the treaty agreement that required the cessation of all military activities by the United States against North Vietnam, a cease-fire in South Vietnam, and a limit to replacement of all military weapons to a piece-by-piece basis had vitally significant meaning for Saigon. When the crisis of March-April 1975 arose and the enemy swept southward across the DMZ and began a series of conquests of province after province ever closer to Saigon and threatened the total defeat of that country, there arose a great cry of American betrayal. Nixon may have promised more than he and Kissinger could deliver.

Saigon's Ambassador to Washington, Tran Kim Phuong, declared on April 2, 1975, that Washington had pledged to continue military aid and in the event of a major enemy violation of the treaty to use whatever air and other possible action might be necessary to prevent its success.[22] Nixon's warning to the enemy in late March 1973 certainly implied as much. However, Congress had intervened to restrain any reintroduction of military activities in all Indochina. It had passed a law July 1, 1973, which stated:

> Notwithstanding any other provision of law, on or after Aug. 15, 1973, no funds herein or heretofore appropriated may be obligated or expended to finance directly or indirectly combat activities by United States military forces in or over or from off the shores of North Vietnam, South Vietnam, Laos or Cambodia.

Thus all Indochina was off limits to American military action. Without the support of our air power by land and sea, Saigon's chances of survival against future major offensives were perhaps fatally weakened. No United States president thereafter could risk further action by defying the Congress. The last bombs fell on Cambodia August 14, 1973. Beginning in mid-February 1973 our prisoners of war began returning home; before the year ended, all had been returned, and most of the missing-in-action had been released. However, some people believed some of the latter were still kept by the enemy.

While the four participants signed the treaty of Paris and later proceeded with the effort to secure the peace, the fighting went on within the little country, and our bombers were active over Laos and Cambodia. Both Saigon and the Communist allies within South Vietnam fought on to gain control over the land and people. Neither side defended popular freedom. Both sought the survival of a minority group, a clique of militarists and Communists. We left the war still calling it a war for freedom; but it had never been anything but a struggle between two dictatorships. Freedom was an illusion.

CHAPTER NINE

IN SUMMARY

Certain hard truths about this war and our age must be understood. Peace, so desired by most of mankind, is not pacifism. Men must have the courage to fight with all their might and intelligence for justice and freedom. Neither reason nor pacifistic martyrdom would peacefully persuade totalitarian dictators or ruthless minority elites to cease aggression and permit rational methods of evolution to work. Gandhi's tactics worked against the highly civilized and progressive British because they respected his soul-force, Satyagraha, which means truth and firmness, and deeply moral tactics.[1] Against Hitler, Mao Tse-tung, Stalin, and other modern Caesars, passive resisters invited only extermination. Those who hate war should recall one of Churchill's favorite quotations:

> Pale Ebeneezer thought it wrong to fight
> But ruddy Bill who killed him thought it right.

A hard fact of life in this tragic age was that force was both required and justified. The only question before us was: Should it be in the hands of those dedicated to justice, mercy, freedom, and dignity, or those who imposed enslavement, repression, and brutality?

The world of the middle and late twentieth century required more order if any peace was to exist, but order without liberty was not enough. Unless some system could be devised to secure collective order and liberty, anarchy would continue. We erected mere facades of government—Leagues and United Nations—while genuine world order with liberty for nations and individuals backed by essential powers of enforcement was yet to be created. The risks of such weakness and inaction were far too great. Honorable men tried in Southeast Asia to halt an evil force, and equally honorable men, tired of the cost and the failure, demanded that we cease the effort.

Beyond doubt expanding Communist victory—either monolithic or multinational—would increase our burdens, multiply our dangers, require larger military outlays (not smaller, as the antiwar critics expected), and mean that enemy encirclement might require a sacrifice and discipline most apt to take us nearer to an armed camp society. One does not build safer worlds by abandoning allies and appeasing evil. When dissent accepts anarchy, condones aggression, and brings disobedience and subversion of governments and societies, the consequences will most likely be tighter discipline and greater despotism, or ultimate defeat. In seas of despotism, islands of freedom which retreat from commitment would bring their own destruction in a short time. Advanced nations must help retarded areas in all ways. Love and aid thy neighbor as thyself is the answer to communism and most of the challenges of mankind. As Dean Acheson observed, death is the only disengagement possible for any of us. Solon of Athens once suggested that crime might be abolished "when those who are not wronged feel the same indignation as those who are."

As we faced a dark and ominous future in 1975, some critics of our appeasement tendencies noticed with sadness that although Communist attacks in both Cambodia and South Vietnam brought indescribable human misery—countless refugees running for safety from the almost constant bombardment by Communist guns, millions needlessly starving, suffering from wounds, and dying—few in the Western world protested. Some asked where all those voices were now that roared so loudly in the late 1960s against our air attacks and bombardments and unavoidable injuries against both civilians and soldiers of the Communist-held areas? Communist guns in March 1975 were primarily causing such tragedies, but now no doves marched, picketed, or demonstrated in Washington, gathered around Trafalgar Square in London, or shouted strong denunciations in Sweden and other antiwar countries as they did in the Johnson era. Yet people were still fleeing and dying. Was the defense of freedom less worthy than the advance of Communist despotism?

On leaving office in January 1953, President Truman expressed his fear that if communism should gain abroad, we would have to become an armed fortress at terrific cost. If we expected to be free and prosperous at home, we would have to create strength and prosperity throughout the world. That was the answer to those who loudly demanded during the crisis that we first put our domestic house in order before trying to impose universal peace. We cannot afford to let the outside world bleed and suffer until we perfect our domestic system. Long before that impossible event, anarchy and war will surround and overcome us. Like it or not, we cannot avoid the double burden of working for peace, freedom, and security here and elsewhere simultaneously.

The cry of "No more Vietnams," heard so frequently for years, if obeyed literally, could well hasten more dangerous crises. Little wars limited in purpose and size could prevent the far more dangerous wars between great powers that most probably would come if anarchy, indecision, and lack of will encouraged the likely invasions that would grab off the lands adjacent to such totalitarian aggressors as China and Russia and in time others. Now as never before those who seek to save freedom need the steady ability essential to develop and defend policies with limited objectives. Total efforts for total victory only risk our annihilation. Our success, possibly our bare survival, may now rest upon our ability to live all our lives with unsolved problems, certainly with many problems that cannot be solved quickly or easily. In both Korea and Vietnam we showed a promising capacity to learn this difficult lesson. Extreme hawks and doves did not yet grasp this wise moderation.

Isolationism was unthinkable. Man was too widely involved through communications, technology, trade, travel, economic investment and diplomacy to dream longer of isolation. A great nuclear power such as the United States confronting another such as Russia could not totally abandon either Europe or Asia or any other area. The dovish assumption that Southeast Asia had so little importance that we could afford to ignore it was too risky in its total negligence of this area and, by example here, to other people who carefully watched our deeds more than our words and shaped their policies accordingly. Hawks certainly should not claim—and who among them really had?—that Vietnam was as vital to us as Western Europe, but they did better understand that tossing small parcels of territory and relatively backward peoples to totalitarian hordes was a luxury people dedicated to freedom anywhere could ill afford. Whatever weakened us by ever so little cumulatively strengthened our enemies. The anarchy and vacuums which dovish retreat from responsibility would foster over wide areas of the globe would invite rather than deter aggression and conquest.

In President Nixon's judgment, for us to quit Asia would bring a great wave of isolationism that would press for dangerous cutbacks in our role everywhere, including Israel and Europe. Polls showing a popular desire for retreat from the war and responsibility were not the answer to our world problems. He concluded this point by noting that the day we quit playing a responsible role in the world—in Europe, Asia, and the Middle East—or gave up, or receded from our efforts to maintain an adequate defense force—"on that day this will become a very unsafe world to live in."[2]

Antiwar critics, Communists, and a rising number of Europeans falsely equated our actions in Southeast Asia with those of other imperial powers and failed to distinguish our role from that of France before 1954. France fought to save an empire, for all the reasons historical empires were initially obtained—profits, raw materials, markets, bases, sea power, and national prestige. When these were no longer obtainable, France simply quit. She would not fight on for an illusory freedom for such a backward people. France was never invited in, but was rather driven out by the people and governments of Vietnam. We were officially invited and welcomed into South Vietnam, and we gave years of struggle, billions of dollars and, of far greater value to us, some fifty-six thousand lives and larger numbers of wounded men to the cause of national freedom for the people of South Vietnam. We sought and asked nothing more. Such a war to prevent slavery for millions of people for possibly generations to come was certainly neither obscene nor immoral. In motivation, it may have been, along with the Korean War, one of the most unselfish struggles we ever fought. The whole country was not worth in any monetary estimate the amount it cost us. At worst it was a mistake in judgment, at best it was a limited and local investment in global peace and security designed to reinforce the hopes of nations, large and small, that our pledges would be kept.

Critics of our intervention correctly observed and denounced the fact that we aided Saigon governments that were dictatorial and repressive while supposedly fighting for a greater freedom, and they declared with much truth that there was little or no distinction between the belligerent regimes in South Vietnam. One big difference prevailed, however, between them. Saigon, whatever some of its leaders may have wished, did not invade the North, threatened no outside peoples, made no effort to export its system or impose it upon others, and constituted no danger to its neighbors while we were there. Although for us it was not enough to be anti-Communist when we should have consistently been profreedom, it was better to live in a world, even a dictatorial world, of nations that did not threaten other peoples and systems than one which did. This may seem to many a very thin justification for such a weighty investment of men and materiel, but since our influence was not sufficient to impose our blueprint upon others, it was certainly better than inaction and Communist victory.

The greatest handicap to our effort in Asia sprang from the failure of others to join us in what was truly the common cause of all—the right of all peoples large and small to national and personal self-determination. It was intensely sad that we could not inspire our Western allies, our own people, or even the people of South Vietnam to unite against the aggressors. After generations of stubborn and selfish isolationism, our leaders finally learned the lesson of global responsibility, but too many people, including our former partners, failed us and our common cause. Forced to yield empires, they retreated after 1945 to their homelands and hid behind their nationalism and provincialism. Our mistaken 1918-1941 isolationism did not excuse their abandonment of the struggle for global peace outside Western Europe after 1945. Two wrongs seldom make a right.

Most senseless of these nations was Russia, facing as she did untold dangers southward from China. Russia was both a European and Asian power. Her fears born of past experience and her hopes inspired by her late successes led her into a dangerous policy of imperial expansion around her rim lands westward and southward, thus intimidating Western Europe and even the United States, when Europe was no longer a danger to her and America wanted nothing so much as to return to the normalcy of profits and disarmament. Instead of encouraging subversion of Western institutions, she could more wisely have seized her great opportunity to cooperate with the West and consolidate her strength and national independence. She had nothing to fear any longer from the West—only from the East. Since 1945, the United States, among the major nations, came closest to grasping one of the most fundamental facts of the twentieth century—global interdependence and universal responsibility for human survival in freedom and justice.

Saigon governments, largely manned by military personnel and backed by powerful landlords, refused to execute the reforms essential to winning the peasants and the great masses of their people to their side. South Vietnam was not a nation; it had little sense of community essential to success, no will and understanding required to survive in freedom. Beyond doubt there was a very large and bitterly anti-Communist element in South Vietnam, but it lacked a national program and leadership. However much we may offer people, if they and their leaders do not have the will to create freedom, to sacrifice for it, they will never win it. Such a will, vigilance, and dedication the South Vietnamese did not have.

Long ago in Jamestown and colonial America, we learned that men could not grow corn outside the stockade until they had eliminated or pacified the Indians. Rural and urban pacification was the dream of Washington liberals who wished to extend the Great Society to Asia; it was the "other war" that had to be won—alongside the military victory—which was not winnable until the enemy forces in South Vietnam could be defeated. This victory could not come without the support of the peasants who wanted land reform, village democracy, education, health, and a broad welfare program. While our forces were too small to permit our universal presence and the defense of every village or the entire countryside long enough to establish a sense of security—our troops were here today and gone tomorrow—the enemy built and by terror and promise kept permanently a subversive infrastructure in most of the country and could make life miserable or impossible for those who sought to support Saigon. A war with unseen and unknown guerrillas constituted an enormous problem for Saigon and its allies.

The manpower and will to ferret out the nightly movements and the endless trails of the enemy required sacrifice beyond the capacity of the South Vietnamese. Repeatedly was heard from the native soldiers: Why should we fight and kill our fellow countrymen? The ARVN preferred the limited effort, liked to stay along the roads and in the cities, and too often refused to fight at all. Confused, intimidated by the eternal presence of an unseen enemy, victims of a corrupt and dictatorial government, fleeced by greedy landlords, uncertain of our permanent presence and protection, bitterly divided into dissenting groups, it was certainly not dedicated to a landlord-oriented militarist clique in Saigon. Rather it felt harassed on all sides and was plagued by the rising problem of the refugees, torn from their villages and concentrated in protective hamlets or shelters far away from their lands.

The Vietnamese people had little enthusiasm for the seemingly endless war and were all too happy to welcome our presence, our money, our aid, and to let us do the fighting. People so repressed, so illiterate, and so poverty-ridden and terrified had great difficulty understanding a Communist menace, when they had such urgent and immediate problems of their own to face daily. Furthermore, a Saigon government that refused until very late to draft its own young men, a ruling elite that sought only its own rents and shares, and a people who preferred profits on the black market and thievery from our warehouses and storage lots and really went on a spree during much of our presence were not yet ready to be saved or to save themselves. The few Oriental allies we had fighting with us were virtually hired mercenaries, paid by us and seldom aware of or dedicated to the cause and ideals we sought to promote. Our power both to destroy and build was immense, but to persuade, carry conviction, inspire determination, bridge cultural gaps, and thereby effect essential and speedy changes, it had fatal limits. While the enemy destroyed faster than we could build, fought guerrilla style, outpromised Saigon with land reform and socialist utopia, Saigon would never counter these tactics with the unity and courage required.

In a war in which we were more than an ally and less than a colonizer there was no precedent to guide us. When our involvement grew but failed to prosper, disillusionment began. We never quite found a way to use our vast power effectively against a third-rate enemy force or for our own ally. Much was said of our supposed leverage, but to use it was a most sticky and difficult task. Chester Cooper, a distinguished adviser and member of the State Department, wrote:

> The historical landscape of our involvement in Vietnam is dotted with the burial mounds of carrots, sticks, demarches, aides-mémoire, presidential letters, and ambassadorial confrontations. But our ability to get a South Vietnamese Army unit to advance, a dishonest province chief removed, a minister to move expeditiously on a major economic problem or to move more cautiously on a delicate political matter has been at best marginal. Throughout the years we have been the junior partner in the enterprise. In the last analysis, the only "stick" we had available to influence a troublesome government in Saigon was the threat of total American withdrawal. And as the size of our forces, and therefore the extent of our commitment to our commitment, increased, this sanction became less and less credible. In short, our leverage declined as our involvement deepened.
>   . . . . .
> The American stake in Vietnam has been very high; indeed there have been times . . . when our stake in preserving a non-Communist South Vietnam seemed higher than that of the non-Communist South Vietnamese themselves. But the Diems and Kys and Thieus are not the first nor will they be the last to parlay their weakness into a form of strength. Konrad Adenauer, Chiang Kai-shek, and Syngman Rhee are charter members of the club.
> New nations of Asia and Africa regard terms like "independence" and "sovereignty" seriously, even literally. And while among most of the developing nations Western technology is still held in high esteem, Western political omniscience is no longer taken for granted. Nigerians and Guatemalans and Vietnamese are convinced (and why should they not be?) that they know better than outsiders how to handle their own affairs. This means: Advice, yes; "interference," no! Aid, yes; "strings," no! It means too that a great power's relations with weaker nations tend (even within the Communist orbit) to be conducted on a government-to-government basis, rather than by the old-style metropole-to-colony or master-to-satellite arrangement. Thus the United States must now persuade rather than demand, request rather than insist. It is under such circumstances that the application of "leverage" requires consummate skill.[3]

Apparently we could neither force Saigon to accept our advice by withholding our aid, nor could we use our vast nuclear and air power to effect the defeat of its Communist enemy.

Another disadvantage in this war was that we could not risk an unlimited use of our power; it was so great that its total use would have had only the most dire consequences. Although their total power was far less than ours, the Vietcong and Hanoi might use it all and ultimately prevent our victory, if not win for themselves by exhausting our patience with no-win, limited warfare. For us total or unlimited warfare would risk bringing Russia and China into the war, probably starting World War III, and earn for us the denunciation of most of mankind including our own people. MacArthur's invasion of North Korea had brought the Chinese into the Korean War less than a generation earlier when China was far weaker. It was dangerous to ignore or forget history. Fear of a larger war with China and Russia kept us from invading North Vietnam, using nuclear weapons, total saturation bombing of Hanoi, Haiphong Harbor, and the Red River dikes and any all-out use of our armed forces, at least until May 1972. With all our strength we never went for victory, but with much less strength the enemy did. Ours was a limited war, not his; he aimed for total victory no matter what the length and the cost. It was more difficult if not impossible to obtain peace from an enemy when you limited your effort and he did not, when you sought a compromise settlement and he sought only absolute victory.

On the other hand, unless we risked a massive use of our manpower in conventional war, victory of any rational sort was impossible. However, nuclear weaponry would have annihilated millions of people, and what profit to anyone to liberate a graveyard and call it victory? While humane considerations denied us the full use of our technological supremacy, the lack of manpower to match our potential enemy also made the use of conventional forces against his massive numerical strength most difficult, and really incapable of being fulfilled, especially when he chose to use guerrilla tactics. Yet from the first, Washington mistakenly trained the ARVN to fight conventional rather than guerrilla style warfare. The enemy refused to fight this way, at least until he was near final victory. Neither we nor Saigon had the manpower or the will to fight the enemy on his own terms and with the same method. That would have required a twenty-four-hour day-and-night effort, away from the cities and roads, in the forests, swamps, and hills, to disturb his movements and capture or destroy his supplies. If you fight an alley cat, as one observer said, you must put in a stronger cat of your own and chase him down every alley in the land until he is destroyed or surrenders. It took us too long to grasp this, and when we did, we lacked the will to stay on course or pay the price.

Time lay on the side of the enemy; to us it offered only endless costs and losses. Since he could, backed by powerful friends, match our escalation and, in spite of our air attacks upon his homeland and his trails, manage to supply his forces at any level of war we found acceptable, he could go on indefinitely. In our original combat intervention and our later limited incursions into Cambodia and Laos, we assumed Peking and Moscow would not intervene. Although they did not send troops, they never halted their support. In fact, they always took enough action to maintain the balance between the two contending factions and prevent a Communist defeat. It was far cheaper for them to achieve such a balance than for us to win a victory, and escalation was easier for them than for us. Optimistic hopes of quick victories in Washington, inspired by rosy reports from our Saigon agents, who often lacked accurate information, did not prepare the American people for the ugly realities of this prolonged war. Too long, Washington judged the war by its own limited understanding; it was aggression pure and simple from Hanoi, inspired and aided by Peking and Moscow. In truth, it was also a civil war, first against France and then between Communists and non-Communists in all Indochina, and now in South Vietnam.

Official Washington also assumed that the Vietcong was merely a puppet of Hanoi, and the enemy, on the other hand, that Saigon was only a puppet of the United States. Saigon and the Vietcong were not puppets: both had legitimate interests in the conflict and both refused to be pressured against their will or interests by either Hanoi or Washington. In this manner, Washington miscalculated the nature of the enemy and the war, assuming that Hanoi could alone negotiate a settlement, when even Hanoi could not persuade the Vietcong to do anything it deemed harmful to its own interests. The Vietcong felt that Hanoi had sold it out once before in 1954 at Geneva, when Hanoi settled for a half victory that abandoned the Vietcong. Hence the Vietcong would not likely permit Hanoi or any outside government to determine the final peace for it. Nor could Washington dictate to its ally in Saigon the conditions for a final settlement. Nixon could promise Hanoi in May 1972 he would withdraw all our forces within four months after a cease-fire and the return of our war prisoners, but he could not grant Hanoi's other demand: that he first impose a coalition—really a Communist—government upon South Vietnam. Neither Saigon nor the Vietcong was willing to subordinate its objectives to its friends and supporters.[4]

Washington took for granted that it could bomb Hanoi and the Vietcong to the conference table, but all our aerial attacks could not halt the supply efforts over the many trails. Not bombs and artillery, but enough infantry to occupy territory permanently would bring victory. Our limited efforts only insured a continuing stalemate with an ever costlier escalation and consequent worsening of relations with Russia and widening fears around the globe of an ever more disastrous war. The hawkish view too long in the ascendancy in Washington and Saigon erroneously assumed that in spite of this situation we should obtain a solution in Vietnam that amounted virtually to a victory for our side. Just as we accused the enemy of seeking through negotiation a victory he had not won on the battlefield, so did we continue to ask of him the same. As the stalemate both on the battlefield and at the conference table continued, our patience vanished faster than did the capacity of the enemy to endure further struggle.

Washington sought incessantly to portray the enemy as guilty of massive acts of inhumanity while holding up to the American people a picture of Saigon governments making rapid progress toward constitutional democracy and personal freedom. In this effort a great contrast developed between the picture and the reality, widening the famous credibility gap and brought a nearly total distrust of official Washington pronouncements on the war itself. Never had Americans been so quickly and dramatically informed of a war and all its grisly details. Atrocities, bloodshed, My Lai massacres, body counts, detailed pictures and vivid descriptions shocked a humane-minded nation. To millions of Americans this made the whole war effort a most revolting nightmare. They could not see so vividly Communist murders and atrocities against innocent civilians.

Kennedy and Johnson initially eased us into the war, and the American people had not grasped the significance of those first steps. In truth, too often officials kept too much of our expanding involvement a secret. Later Johnson held out the rosiest hopes and promises of early victory and troop withdrawals while simultaneously and repeatedly asking for just a few thousand more troops. Our officials in both Saigon and Washington gave glowing accounts of victories in battles and rural pacification while our newspaper correspondents, who had been in South Vietnam much longer, were free of political pressure, and often were more objective in their observations, sent out reports of failure and growing tragedy. This set the stage for a rising popular disillusionment with the war, strong enough to explode against whatever government might be in power and bring a reversal of policy and leadership. The truth was that Saigon, the Vietcong, and Hanoi all practiced tyranny. All perverted the democratic process, established concentration camps, persecuted dissidents, silenced speech and the press, and crushed all opposition. Ho erased local self-government, but Diem eliminated elected village government in June 1956. Thus anti-Diem, anti-Thieu, and other opposition groups had a case about as strong against official Saigon as against Hanoi. The official government of neither North nor South Vietnam came near to the system Washington sought.

Before 1968, if ever, Washington did not adequately understand that the war could not be won by military effort alone, that any chance of victory would depend upon political and diplomatic efforts. It did not understand revolutionary warfare. Unless the masses of South Vietnam could receive and believe the promise of a better life, land reform, and political change toward a larger freedom and could experience measurable progress in these directions, Saigon governments would never win enough popular support to achieve victory. Patriotism was too weak to sacrifice lives and property for the establishment of democratic freedom. Hanoi and the Vietcong understood better the requirements of the situation. In the strategy of people's revolutionary war the aim was not to defeat American forces, wrote Sir Robert Thompson, because that would have been beyond the enemy capacity:

The aim of the strategy was to reach a situation in which the North Vietnamese and Vietcong, at a cost which was indefinitely acceptable to themselves, were imposing on the South Vietnamese and Americans a cost which was not indefinitely acceptable to them. At that point they must be winning.

. . . . .

If victory could not be won by a decisive military campaign or battle, what then were Hanoi's possible channels to victory? There were four: a failure of American resolution; a failure of Vietnamese resolution; a failure of the Americans and South Vietnamese to adopt the correct counter-strategy; and a failure of the South Vietnamese to build, with American help, a stable and viable state and government.[5]

All four of these channels to enemy victory still existed in 1973. Vietnamization offered little hope that the ARVN alone could do what both the ARVN and the United States armed forces together could not do before our withdrawal began, and internal political pressure in the United States demanded after 1968 that the United States withdraw from the war at the earliest possible date. Label it defeat or something else, one truth was obvious: We quit the war before victory was won or the war was lost. That was an act the United States never before would have accepted.

With our continued withdrawal, enemy hopes of ultimate victory checked progress in diplomacy and certainly complicated Saigon's chances of victory through its own efforts. This was the result of a war which never threatened the independence of North Vietnam and the continued rule of its Communist government. Hanoi could always fall back on the status quo. It had little to lose and everything to gain by its actions in South Vietnam, Laos, and Cambodia. For Hanoi it was a no-lose policy. It cost Ho far less than it cost Johnson. Thompson wrote:

To put the situation very bluntly, all the people of North Vietnam had to do between 1965 and 1968 was to exist and breed. The United States Air Force could not interrupt either of those activities.
    If the costs were comparatively low and at least acceptable for the North Vietnamese and Vietcong, it was a very different kettle of fish for the South Vietnamese and Americans.[6]

At the height of our involvement the war was costing Russia only about $1 billion a year, while it was costing us nearly $30 billion.[7]

Russia had little interest in ending a struggle so costly to us and so cheap for her. And while her protégé could wait us out in security from invasion or from ultimate defeat, she could virtually guarantee if not our defeat, our inability to win. That was why war critics referred constantly to this unwinnable or no-win war. As long as the Communists could disrupt the countryside and menace the cities, as in the Tet offensive of 1968 and the great offensive of 1972, they could frustrate our efforts at pacification and reform and demonstrate to the people the inability of Saigon backed by the greatest power on earth to guarantee their security. While the Communists did not win popular support by those offensives, they did reveal our glaring inability to protect the people; that denied to us and Saigon the popular support essential to any kind of victory.

The United States had great power after World War II; but that power, however great, had limits. Alone we could not police the world, but we sought to establish worldwide collective security arrangements, which might permit us with others to undertake such a security system. Little wonder John Kennedy complained of our overcommitments. Arthur Schlesinger, Jr., observed that President Kennedy concluded in 1961 that we must recognize the limits of our power:

We must face the fact that the United States is neither omnipotent nor omnisicent—that we are only 6 per cent of the world's population—that we cannot impose our will upon the other 94 per cent—that we cannot right every wrong or reverse each adversity—and that therefore there cannot be an American solution to every world problem.[8]

In mid-March 1975 Senator Mike Mansfield, witnessing the near collapse of the United States-backed Lon Nol regime in Cambodia and the stepped-up attacks of the Communists upon Saigon forces followed by Thieu's abandonment of several provinces of South Vietnam to the Vietcong, saw what he termed the "beginning of an end of an era" of our involvement in the Asian mainland. Now he saw a "shift away from the Asian mainland and a concentration of sorts in islands of the Pacific." He believed the shift would reflect a geopolitical truism, "namely that the United States is not an Asian power but a Pacific power." If this was so, wrote John W. Finney of the *New York Times,* Mansfield would be a "symbolic bridge between the two geopolitical concepts, a man whose career was molded because the United States viewed itself as an 'Asian power' and who came to be a leading critic of American political and military involvement in Asian affairs."[9]

We should have been more selective in our commitments and especially our combat engagements. With limited war, limited power, and limited will we should have chosen areas more vital to our national security and hopeful of achieving genuinely democratic success than the bog of despotism in Vietnam.

In a dangerous and hardly acceptable reading of history, of Munich and appeasement, Washington seemed to assume the danger from this small faraway region to our future was equal to the Axis challenge of the previous generation and forgot to hoard its strength and energy for possibly greater troubles and obligations elsewhere. We assumed our power and will—if and when tested—would prove adequate to our policies, but this was not supported by the united will of the American people, our European allies, and the United Nations.

Johnson exaggerated our commitments and the dangers. Neither the example of Eisenhower, Kennedy, Munich, the Truman Doctrine, nor history exacted any pledge from us to fight in South Vietnam. SEATO permitted us to intervene unilaterally to stop Communists from seizing Indochina, but it contained no specific pledge of combat assistance. We had no treaty obligation; we had only a misinterpretation of the lesson of Munich: no more appeasement of aggression.

Hindsight showed our anti-Communist fears were excessive, continued Schlesinger. In the very days when this hysteria was greatest, 1945-1950, possibly longer, we had an atomic near-monopoly, an undamaged national economy, and broader support in the United Nations and from other nations than any other power on earth. Nationalism remained a greater force in the world than communism or any other internationalism. As Stalin in 1929 decided to communize Russia first before risking destruction in seeking to advance global communism, so Tito and the rest were first nationalists and then Communists. The enmities inside the Communist world, the deviation beginning with Tito, then Mao, most likely even Ho and Castro, the rebellions however limited in Poland, East Germany, Hungary, and Czechoslovakia—all revealed the growth of polycentrism rather than monolithic communism, which scholars and statesmen might have seen earlier than they did. Both Russia and China had suffered for decades enormous losses which left them too weak to challenge seriously the Western world, but since 1950 the United States had devoted its lives and used its resources in struggles far from its home base to contain them.[10]

Since United Nations endorsement of the war to save South Vietnam from defeat could not be won, we should have taken no unilateral action to do so. Western Europe, other Southeast Asian nations, Commonwealth nations, and as many others as possible should have joined the effort. No nation alone can solve the problems of Latin America, Africa, and Asia, where for decades turbulence was likely to prevail. The revolution of rising expectations was not yet over. The "third world" and doubtlessly the satellite world and dissenting elements within Communist nations, not to speak of overpopulation pressures, would not make it easy for China and Russia to move into all the vacuums and weak areas of the globe. If our power was not absolute, neither was theirs. If we could not help people to freedom who did not wish it enough to fight for it, they could not make people puppets and slaves without an enormously costly effort and possibly unbearable burdens.

Whatever actions we took on the world stage should have been in partnership with others, not alone. Nations will seldom do for themselves anything they can so easily get others to do for them. Freedom and security are everybody's business. Nothing could better serve the Communists than for us indefinitely to go on bleeding and dying in faraway places while they were left alone and given the time to develop and consolidate their power. If Communist despots can secure more puppets or allies, by terror or promise, to fight for communism than we, by our vast economic and technical assistance can persuade others to fight for freedom, we are destined to lose. If free men cannot sacrifice and dedicate enough of their time, energy, and resources to establish and defend their freedom to match the efforts and the discipline of totalitarians, freedom is lost. The question remains: Can free men and men who would be free voluntarily drive themselves more efficiently than men not free can be driven by powerful masters? Can persuasion do more than terror and demagogic deception? It takes much longer to fulfill a promise than to make one, to build than destroy a system, to demonstrate self-reliance than demand obedience at the point of a gun.

Financial and technical aid we should have offered South Vietnam, but nothing more. In a protracted and limited war that was initially more a civil war than aggression, the wiser course for us—no direct military involvement—would have forced Saigon to execute the reforms necessary to save itself and avoided for us the burdens and risks of prolonged war. We could have and should have said: Execute the reforms or you receive no aid, and most certainly no combat assistance. It's a rough world, and we should have used that leverage. At least it could have saved us considerable trouble. The failure to use this advantage was one of our greatest mistakes. The first was the unilateral commitment of ground combat forces in an essentially peripheral area, where no vital interests of ours were involved. This omission negated the whole defense of the war made so ceaselessly to the American people. We were told it was a war for freedom, social justice, and democratic ideals. We were also told it was to contain communism and Red China. In truth, we were once again merely reinforcing and backing a reactionary police state, run by militarists, dictators, and elites hardly different from the enemy and possibly more corrupt and callous in their disregard for the masses of people.

Hindsight teaches that Eisenhower should have exacted firm pledges and perhaps have waited for the execution of reforms by Diem in 1954 before giving extensive aid. However, no demonstration of good faith was made or required, but Diem got his aid. Kennedy pressed him to accept a plan to frustrate the enemy by political and military reforms in exchange for our aid. Again there were no reforms, but the aid was given. In 1963, Washington pressed Saigon, then faced with deep dissent and near civil war, to make concessions, even withheld some help and threatened to withdraw some advisers, but Diem and Nhu refused to believe we meant it, and our continued support showed they were correct. Upon coming to power, Johnson had an opportunity to review the whole situation and demand fulfillment of promised reforms, as the price of further assistance, but he failed to use it. A better chance appeared after his overwhelming victory over Goldwater in 1964 and his pledges not to send our boys to fight the wars Asian boys should fight. No action. Before we began bombing the North and put in combat ground forces, frank and blunt talk with Saigon had perhaps its last chance to be effective. Surely when several South Vietnamese provinces rebelled, the threat of our withdrawal might have been used and have been effective. But no real pressure and no reforms remained the story to the bitter end.[11] Without reforms there was no genuine popular support, no answer to enemy promises, and therefore no possible victory.

Only the most sincere effort to establish and secure the broadest freedom for all the people could justify the war. Such an effort was not made by either Saigon or Washington. Only if our involvement bought time for Saigon to become self-reliant and able to move toward individual freedom as well as national independence was it defensible. If Vietnamization could really succeed and finally bring such a freedom, the outcome could be constructive, but in 1973 the reality was depressing, and strong doubts persisted. Had Saigon heeded our advice to execute essential reforms, the situation would surely have been different, but Saigon had failed to use the time our presence afforded to do these necessary things.

Whatever failure there was must in final analysis lie mainly with the people of South Vietnam and their governments. They were badly divided and worse governed; they lacked genuine national unity and patriotism; and they had little grasp of the ultimate consequences of their defeat by the Vietcong. They had no basic experience with freedom and politics of any sort to enable them to guide their own destiny. Our fault was a mistaken judgment that we could with but limited advice, aid, and men quickly help them out of their ignorance, disunity, corruption, and poverty. The more we helped the deeper we ourselves became involved.

As early as 1966, George Ball declared:

> An effective strategy to cut our losses must be so designed as to make it clear: (a) that the United States has fully met its obligations to the South Vietnamese people and to the world, and (b) that it is the South Vietnamese people who have failed, not us.[12]

Consistently during the war he had quietly urged noninvolvement of our ground forces. Even in 1964 he noted that escalation bred escalation. The party which seemed to be losing would always raise the ante. Even though we committed our ground forces, he told Rusk and McNamara in 1966, there was no assurance we could achieve our objectives. Rather would we run the risk of getting bogged down in a conflict of long duration and uncertain result.[13]

Most unfortunate for our war effort was the fact that we were never really convinced that the war was necessary, that our security and national interest were sufficiently involved. We were never sold on this war as we were on the war against Hitler and Tojo. Although reports came after 1959 of Hanoi's infiltration southward, the figures revealed that only a limited local Vietcong, those returned from the North since the exodus of 1954, and a few Hanoi regulars availed to confront the nearly half a million ARVN forces. This was surely no earth-shaking danger to Washington. Despite sophisticated estimates that in guerrilla warfare it required possibly ten to fifteen conventional soldiers to counter one guerrilla, these figures had little meaning for most Americans. Domestic and foreign opinion saw little justification for our rising involvement.[14]

Whatever the future judgments may be, few contemporaries will dispute the enormous cost of this war. It brought the loss of tens of thousands of young men and endless sorrow to their families and friends, the diversion of our resources and energies to destruction when they were so desperately needed for peaceful purposes, the bitter dissent and disunity within our country, and the great strain it put upon our relations with others, including our closest friends. It impeded our efforts to reduce the tensions of the cold war and overinvested our strength in an area of only limited importance to us. It drew upon us worldwide denunciation and caused a national soul-searching equalled only by the Civil War.

We left Vietnam without having achieved our war aims. South Vietnam was not saved for freedom or even independence. China was not contained by us, and if checked at all, that was due to her concern with Russia. We did not find a satisfactory answer to guerrilla warfare or wars of national liberation. Nor was the domino theory proved true, but the continuing menace to Cambodia, Laos, Thailand, and others suggested the possibility of its validity. When governments fail to come to grips with their own social, economic, and political problems, and ruling circles fail to demonstrate a sacrificial patriotism for the common cause and put both their lives and fortunes behind their efforts, ancient regimes and systems may topple. The people of Indonesia demonstrated the courage and capacity to defeat a Communist effort to seize power, as did the people of the Philippines and, with British assistance and after a lengthy effort, of Malaysia.

In Vietnam, the most likely end seemed a Communist victory, although perhaps delayed by "Vietnamization," which was frankly a cover for our withdrawal before tragedy fell upon all Indochina. When we left we did not "Vietnamize" peace; we only "Vietnamized" the war. Washington indicated as early as June 30, 1970, a willingness to accept a coalition government in South Vietnam without national elections, and in May 1972 Nixon offered to leave South Vietnam within four months of a cease-fire under international supervision without any reference at all to the right of self-determination for the South Vietnamese. Thus we finally abandoned our long insistence upon free elections, national self-determination, and the whole democratic process.[15]

It will probably be a very long time before the United States ever again intervenes unilaterally in local wars in such distant areas as Indochina and before another president, without a formal declaration of war and broad popular support, commits our forces as Johnson did in 1965. Local anti-Communist groups will have to rely more upon themselves to do the fighting. The Nixon Doctrine permits economic, financial, and technical aid and advice, but not ground combat forces. In this way, we avoided further overcommitment and returned to an earlier policy of more limited and vital national self-interest. We have avoided direct intervention in Central Europe, however much we may have wished to aid those peoples seeking freedom from Russian subjugation. Nor, as of March 1975, had we intervened directly in Greece, Cuba, Chile, and the Arab-Israeli dispute. Even a great power can and must say no. It cannot settle every dispute, especially not by using its armed might where diplomacy and restraint may be more effective. Negotiation is truly better than confrontation.

However, the nagging question still remains: Who would have helped the South Vietnamese if we had not? Certainly not our historic allies and NATO partners. They lacked the stomach, will, and resources for major efforts outside Europe. Regional organizations were unable to assume such burdens. Nor did the widely popular proposal that in the future we work through the United Nations offer a fair chance of success. That organization did not have the unity essential to action; it was not a government of the world but a forum for disunited nations, for propaganda. In most significant matters, the veto and Russian intransigence nullified its usefulness. Whenever we took the Vietnam problem to the United Nations our efforts faced the veto, angry recriminations, and the stubborn refusal of others to take any action.[16] Both Peking and Hanoi, as nonmembers, refused to participate and publicly rejected United Nations jurisdiction over any part of the Indochinese conflict. Unwilling to risk loss of favor and position in the Communist world, Russia made it clear she would veto any resolutions concerning the dispute.

Still unanswered are the questions: Must the world continue to allow the Communist nations to go on grabbing off one area after another? And must the non-Communist nations wait until dangerously too late to unite to prevent their final and fatal defeat? The warning from this war is that free people and those who seek freedom should unite. No nation, however great and powerful, should have to undertake the defense of freedom and civilization alone. In this respect, not the United States but others, by their neglect and abdication of responsibility, must assume a major responsibility for whatever failure there was to contain totalitarianism in Southeast Asia.

CHAPTER TEN

EPILOGUE, 1975

Little more than two years after the Paris accords of January 1973, and within but a few weeks, the Army of South Vietnam, Thieu's government, and the system we had supported since 1954 collapsed. Thus ended all hope of achieving the objectives we had so long sought. President Ford officially designated and proclaimed May 1, 1975, as the last day of the "Vietnam era."[1] This was to meet the congressional provision which entitled veterans to benefits for services in the armed forces "during the period, beginning August 5, 1964, referred to as the Vietnam era." The president was authorized to determine the last day a person could qualify.

The collapse of our ally and protégé came with unnecessary, unexpected, and stunning suddenness. Although the diplomats who arranged the Paris accords did not expect that arrangement to last, and both sides thereafter violated it, they surely expected South Vietnam to survive longer than it did. With the vast amounts of material we left behind and later supplied, the ARVN should have been able to match its enemies. At Paris a decent interval was designed to prevent our humiliation, to let us escape from the war with some measure of honor, and to give Saigon a chance to salvage something out of its efforts. With our departure, all the chronic weaknesses of this elite regime, revealed throughout this study, suddenly surfaced and destroyed it. A unilateral decision by Thieu and his advisers to abandon outposts in the northwestern highlands of South Vietnam—although deemed by some military observers a strategically wise retreat from too wide exposure—led to panic and then to a massive rout.

As the full impact of the disintegration of Saigon's army and the final abandonment of over $5 billion worth of United States-supplied equipment became evident, a stunned world asked how Communist forces could almost effortlessly accomplish within three weeks what had been beyond their reach for nearly a quarter century.[2] The initial explanation offered was that North Vietnam succeeded not because of overwhelming power, but because in about two-thirds of the country the ARVN lacked the will and the leadership to fight.

The collapse and flight from the highlands, first eastward toward the sea and then southward toward Saigon, still left Thieu with an estimated million-man army, one of the largest air forces in the world, and plenty of ammunition and equipment to continue fighting.

Until the first week of March 1975 there had been little evidence of looming tragedy, but then came reports of fresh enemy divisions moving southward. Enemy troops began overrunning ARVN outposts in the sparsely populated Central Highlands. Such attacks had occurred here before, from 1961 to 1972, and usually the Communists had been turned back; hence there was confidence that Saigon could once again handle the situation. Not so this time. At three A.M. March 10, the enemy attacked Banmethuot, capital of Dar Lac province, 150 miles northeast of Saigon. Within three days this montagnard capital, never before in danger and once strongly befriended by the United States forces, was taken by the Communists with virtually no resistance. In fact, most of the ARVN forces in the town defected to the Communists.

That was the tip-off that nearby provinces were in danger of falling to the enemy. To that point, Thieu strongly insisted his government would never willingly yield any territory but would fight to the death to hold it all and regain what was lost. However, this defeat jolted Thieu, who then isolated himself from his advisers, made decisions on his own, issued orders without explanations, and refused to consult with United States officials on the spot. Here began a crisis of leadership. Meanwhile, it became painfully clear to Thieu that anticipated, even pledged, United States aid—military supplies and direct combat forces—would not be forthcoming. A massive North Vietnamese attack, now under way, would not bring the awesome air attacks that had saved South Vietnam in 1972.[3] A string of visiting United States congressmen had shocked him into the unnerving awareness that but few Americans longer felt any great concern for his fate or that of his country.

On March 13, Thieu decided to abandon the Central Highlands, save what he could of the army and population, and leave behind him a scorched earth and deserted wilderness to the enemy. Soon this decision would be applied to other regions eastward and southward until the enemy formed a ring around Saigon and then waited a few weeks for Theiu to resign and his successors, finally General Duong Van Minh ("Big Minh"), to surrender Saigon without a battle. The tragedy that followed these sad events is almost beyond description and was a surprise to even those who had long anticipated the fall of South Vietnam. Once the news spread of withdrawal, panic spread from the top down through the ranks of the ARVN to the lowest foot soldier. Each group did whatever it could to save itself. Many cast off their uniforms, discarded their arms, abandoned their equipment, burned their homes, and melted into the masses of people fleeing eastward and southward. As they fled to the South China Sea many died for lack of food and water. Exposed to the jungle, the heat, and attacks by the enemy and by their own fellow countrymen in and out of uniform, many more died along the march. Troops and senior officers expressed amazement at the order to abandon so much land and equipment to the enemy without even a show of resistance.

They raced toward Hue, but it was quickly surrounded and captured by the enemy in hot pursuit. In the former imperial capital, panic quickly spread. Both the civil administration and the army quietly, almost secretly, slipped out of the city. By foot, in trucks, buses, cars, bicycles, and even tractors, old and young moved southward, hopefully, for the safety of Da Nang. Part of the enemy had simply by-passed Hue and moved rapidly southward in pursuit. The route was littered with the wreckage of helicopters that simply ran out of fuel. Officers from senior down deserted their units and seized any means of transportation available. Finally they grabbed jeeps and even ambulances. Military vehicles broke down or ran out of fuel and were abandoned. Then all civilian vehicles, including motorcycles, were taken by soldiers overpowered by fear. They sometimes sprayed passing motorcyclists with their guns, kicked the bodies to the side of the road, and mounted the Hondas, only to receive the same fate a few miles further down the road. All authority collapsed. Da Nang became a jungle, wrote one eyewitness, "with every person fighting for his own survival, the armed soldiers naturally holding the advantage."[4]

Wealthy families concealed in ambulances sought to escape in planes. Sometimes spectators saw them spring from their ambulances and fight each other for scarce space on any transport that offered hope of escape. In some instances, civilians were simply pushed off planes to certain death. Two planes crashed on takeoff because of overloading. A third barely managed to take off, but only by tossing overboard virtually anything portable. When that was not enough, the airmen hurled almost one hundred soldiers off the rear cargo ramp at an altitude of between three and four thousand feet. That plane made it out. In short, within the final weeks before the demise of South Vietnam, its armed forces, its leadership, its very civilization appeared almost totally demoralized. The sight of Americans quitting the country, the failure of Congress to reassure Thieu, his resignation and flight, and the desire to prevent the destruction of Saigon by futile last desperate efforts to defend it, left his successors no choice but to seek a peaceful and orderly surrender.[5]

Then Da Nang fell on Easter Sunday. It was conquered by Saigon's troops, not the enemy. It was subjected to a reign of terror by the ARVN, which kept aid from coming in and the fleeing refugees from escaping. Government soldiers threatened with certain death anyone trying to flee. Few escaped. The officer in command of the region helplessly stood by and watched as his "renegade army roared through the dying city, waiting for the North Vietnamese to come in and restore order."[6] While the ARVN melted away, Hanoi's forces rapidly moved southward. South Vietnam hoped to buy time, secure United States aid, and retreat to defensible positions around the capital. Thieu, his critics charged, sought to protect only his clique. His closest advisers and fellow countrymen now demanded his resignation and called for the creation of a broadly based government and immediate negotiations with the Communists for a surrender that would stop the war and the suffering.

As these tragic events unfolded, Washington watched almost helplessly, shocked only by the speed of the collapse, not by its final occurrence. It had long been expected. Referring to the Vietnamese refugees and soldiers trapped by the Communist tidal wave, Vice-president Rockefeller said that it was too late for us to do anything about it, adding, "I guess a lot of them are going to die." At the same time, Secretary of Defense James R. Schlesinger declared that thirty days would determine whether South Vietnam could survive. President Ford let it be known he had no plans or authority to reintroduce our air power. In fact, the War Powers Act of 1973 directly prohibited our involvement in further military action in Indochina, and Ford had no desire to ask Congress for permission to resume air warfare there.

However, since January Ford had sought congressional approval of funds for both military and humanitarian aid to South Vietnam. Congress quickly turned down military aid and haggled over humanitarian aid, which finally came too late to be of any assistance except to the refugees, to facilitate their evacuation and relocation in the United States. Many believed we had a moral obligation to end the slaughter, aid the refugees, and save them from a feared bloodbath, but not to send more guns, especially when what we had sent had scarcely been used—in fact, had largely been abandoned. The belief was overwhelming that further aid was too late. Some believed Ford's request for $722 million in military aid to stop the panic in Saigon was but a charade, designed to keep the executive record straight. Ford could tell Thieu he had tried to fulfill an obligation, while at home he could blame Congress for failure to supply Saigon as generously as Russia and China supplied Hanoi and the Vietcong. Thus he and Thieu could agree that Congress and the American public must share some of the blame for the final tragedy. Virtually no one believed the statement by General Frederick C. Weyand, the army chief of staff, who had just made a hurried trip to Saigon, that further military aid could save the day. How could a few hundred million now do what billions earlier could not do?[7]

Kissinger wanted aid supplied indefinitely, with no terminal date. That would inspire South Vietnam to carry on with confidence, but Congress was in no mood for such policies. It saw no light at the end of any tunnels. Ford probably sought time to arrange the safe evacuation of our personnel and our Vietnamese friends and supporters. To announce emphatically that no further aid was forthcoming would risk attacks by the ARVN and frustrated native Vietnamese upon them. Only by linking aid to the safe return of Americans, the White House thought, was there any chance of getting any military aid at all.[8] In spite of his desire to end all recriminations and get on with the problems that lay ahead, Ford blamed Congress for its refusal to approve emergency funds as the main cause for the collapse of South Vietnam, while Kissinger reportedly thought Thieu should have made the enemy "bleed" during the ARVN's withdrawal from the North.[9]

In a press conference at San Diego, April 3, 1975, Ford declared that North Vietnam had repeatedly violated the Paris accords. It had sent North Vietnamese regular forces into South Vietnam in great numbers—he thought around 150 to 175 thousand. He expressed his frustration at the refusal of

Congress to grant his requests for economic, humanitarian, and military assistance to South Vietnam and angrily regretted the limitations placed upon executive power over the last two years. That, implied his critics, revealed he was still a hawk and wished he could again bomb North Vietnam. He warned others not to lose faith in us. We would remain strong, continue our role as a leader, and stand by our allies. He said, "I specifically warn any adversary they should not under any circumstances feel that the tragedy of Vietnam is an indication that the American people have lost their will or their desire to stand up for freedom any place in the world."[10]

Was he a believer in the domino theory? Yes, came the answer:

I believe that there is a great deal of credibility to the domino theory. I hope it doesn't happen. I hope that other countries in Southeast Asia—Thailand, the Philippines—don't misread the will of the American people and the leadership of this country into believing that we're going to abandon our position in Southeast Asia. We are not.[11]

He declared he had ample power, in spite of the War Powers Act of 1973, to use combat troops if needed to protect the evacuation of our personnel in South Vietnam. He would abide by the act—which, he admitted, did impose certain limits upon his authority; but it did allow him within limits to protect the evacuation by force, and if necessary he would use that law. Asked if the whole war venture was wrong, had been a mistake, and whether any lessons been learned from it, he responded:

Unfortunately, events that were beyond our control as a country have made it appear that that policy [*which four previous presidents had endorsed*] was wrong. I still believe that policy was right if the United States had carried it out as we promised to do at the time of the Paris peace accords, where we promised with the signing of the Paris peace accords that we would make military hardware available to the South Vietnamese Government on a replacement, one-for-one basis.
Unfortunately, we did not carry out that promise.

Did he blame Congress for that? He did not flatly say so, but he noted:

The facts are that in fiscal year 1974 there was a substantial reduction made by the Congress in the amounts of military equipment requested for South Vietnam.
In fiscal year 1975, . . . the Administration asked for $1.4-billion in military assistance for South Vietnam. Congress put a ceiling of $1-billion on it and actually appropriated only $700-million.

Those were the facts, but he would let the American people judge them. The great tragedy of South Vietnam could have been avoided. Was the war, in which we lost over 55,000 lives and spent approximately $150 billion, all a big waste? Not if we had carried out our solemn commitments made at Paris. He refused to admit all was lost and even expressed his belief there was still a chance to salvage the situation.[12]

Ford faced difficult problems. While privately at this point he talked of "a disaster of incredible proportions," he publicly pretended to believe that all was not lost. Any expression of resignation to defeatism or the rejection of further aid would hasten the fall of South Vietnam and possibly complicate the evacuation of our personnel. Critics blamed him for feeding the recriminations he should have avoided and soon denounced.[13] Thieu's power melted away so rapidly over the next two weeks that hope of saving anything faded. Facing that catastrophic probability all Ford could get from Congress was support for the limited use of our forces to evacuate our personnel and limited humanitarian aid for the refugees.[14]

Now began the last chapter for President Nguyen Van Thieu. His exit had long been a demand of the Communists in return for any peaceful solution of the war, and Thieu had just as long insisted he would fight to the bitter end, which he nearly did. As he went, he spoke out angrily against the United States. He charged that his once great benefactor and ally had abandoned his nation and betrayed its sacred pledges of 1972 and 1973 to come to his aid if a serious danger confronted South Vietnam. He said we were not trustworthy, and he blamed us for forcing him to accept a peace in 1973 that left enemy forces on his territory. The United States, he declared, had not respected its promises; it was unfair; it was inhumane; it was not trustworthy; it was not responsible.[15] He declared Nixon had described all accords, including the Paris accords, as mere "pieces of paper" unless executed, and he stated emphatically that Nixon had promised Saigon not only military and economic aid but also "direct and strong United States military intervention" if the Communists broke the agreement. Thieu declared he needed immediately the $722 million Ford had requested. Nixon had once made very serious pledges to him, he revealed, and he would now hold us to them. He also said if we gave him the same aid Russia and China gave the other side, South Vietnam would win. Thieu blamed the United States primarily for his failure, but he also attributed some of the mistakes of word and deed to his generals. Then after ten years in office, he resigned his post on April 21, 1975, and left for Taiwan.

Did Nixon make secret pledges of combat forces in case of major enemy violations of the Paris agreement? The answer is overwhelmingly affirmative. On April 8, 1975, Senator Henry M. Jackson told the Senate that there existed between the governments of the United States and South Vietnam secret agreements which envisioned fateful American decisions, agreements whose very existence had never been acknowledged. This set off a debate about our credibility and responsibility, and Jackson appeared somewhat irresponsible for making such unproved accusations in a very ticklish situation. The White House admitted there had been public warnings by Nixon and private communications which said about the same thing, but its spokesmen added that whatever assurances had been made in 1972 and January 1973 had been nullified by the War Powers Act of 1973. Kissinger talked of moral obligations and admitted on March 26, 1975, that Nixon had told Saigon that if it cooperated with the cease-fire, Congress would probably grant the funds; but Kissinger said no mention was made of any assurances about any reaction of ours to enemy offensives.

Senator Jackson demanded that the administration make public whatever statements or pledges had been made and asked that Kissinger be summoned to testify under oath if necessary. Others also urged an investigation to ascertain the facts. Meanwhile, the White House confirmed that assurances as to our assistance and enforcement of the Paris agreement had been offered clearly and publicly by Nixon, including a promise of vigorous reaction to any major enemy infractions of the treaty. Although Ford learned shortly after taking office that there were such letters by Nixon, he would not then release them to the public. The White House asked anyone who proclaimed there were secret pacts to produce the evidence to prove it. Senator John J. Sparkman, chairman of the Senate Foreign Relations Committee, requested Ford to send his committee all pertinent documents relating to the 1973 Vietnam cease-fire agreement. Ron Nessen, Mr. Ford's press secretary, refined the issue slightly by declaring that private and public exchanges scarcely differed; he contended that the issue was really whether secret commitments had been made about which neither Congress nor the American people were aware. Ford, Kissinger, and General Alexander M. Haig, Jr., Mr. Nixon's former chief of staff, said there never were any.[16]

Reasonable doubts vanished when on May 1, 1975, the *New York Times* published two Nixon letters to Thieu. In the first communication of November 14, 1972, Nixon said:

But far more important than what we say in the agreement on this issue is what we do in the event the enemy renews its aggression. You have my absolute assurance that if Hanoi fails to abide by the terms of this agreement it is my intention to take swift and severe retaliatory action.

He then declared it would be difficult to continue their common effort to work for peace if Thieu failed to agree on the terms being arranged. Nixon would feel forced to consider other options, perhaps go it alone or withdraw further support; hence Thieu should go along. Then for a second time he repeated his

personal assurances to you that the United States will react very strongly and rapidly to any violation of the agreement. But in order to do this effectively it is essential that I have public support and that your government does not emerge as the obstacle to a peace which American public opinion now universally desires.

Finally, a third pledge was made in a second letter from Nixon to Thieu of January 5, 1973. He first warned that the

gravest consequence would then ensue if your government chose to reject the agreement and split off from the United States. As I said in my December 17 letter, "I am convinced that your refusal to join us would be an invitation to disaster—to the loss of all that we together have fought for over the past decade. It would be inexcusable above all because we will have lost a just and honorable alternative."

Then for the third time Nixon declared and pledged:

Should you decide, as I trust you will, to go with us, you have my assurance of continued assistance in the post-settlement period and that we will respond with full force should the settlement be violated by North Vietnam. So once more I conclude with an appeal to you to close ranks with us.[17]

After the publication of the Nixon letters, Ford was urged to make a full disclosure of all private documents bearing on any commitments to Saigon. Ford had observed that there were agreements to offer such aid, and expressed regret that the president's hands had been tied over the past two years by the War Powers Act of 1973. That meant, thought Clark Clifford, that Ford would have used full force to contain the enemy but for that law and would have fulfilled the secret commitment in the way he did on his own by ordering air strikes against Cambodia and landing marines on its soil when a group of its impulsive young officers seized the *Mayaguez*, a United States merchant vessel on the high seas off Cambodia in mid-May 1975.[18] Senator Jackson accused the administration, in failing to disclose the documents, of misleading a foreign government and the United States Congress as to the nature of a commitment to that government. Senator Mike Mansfield joined Jackson in appealing for the release of the material, and said: "It looks like the jacks are coming out of the box and I think the sooner this thing is cleared up the better off we shall all be."[19]

Since Ford was not involved in the "secret agreements," Jackson thought Ford could easily tell all. However, Ford wrote John J. Sparkman, who had requested full information for his Foreign Relations Committee, and denied the request. The president justified his refusal on grounds of "executive privilege, the need to keep diplomatic correspondence secret, and a desire to 'leave the divisive debates over Vietnam behind us.' " A State Department spokesman still declared there was little if any substantial difference between Nixon's private letters and his public statements made at the time.[20] He further asserted that Nixon's promise did not amount to a "commitment" and added that "if we had had any so-called secret commitment we would have used it in the Congressional debate" over the cutoff of our combat activities under the War Powers resolution of 1973. Probably Nixon with all his Watergate troubles had no desire to add others.[21] From the first, it had been obvious that the promises were made to get Thieu to support the Paris treaty, but to have made them public would have risked Hanoi's abrogation of the whole deal.

Little wonder that when Hanoi struck with great force at Banmethuot and elsewhere and no response or aid came from Washington, Thieu was stunned into the realization he must begin a retreat to more defensible areas and hoard his wasting strength. Nixon's promise was nullified by the Congress and the

American public, and to Thieu's government this would surely be deemed the violation of an honorable pledge. This unilateral promise Nixon never, during all the debate about the War Powers Act of 1973, revealed to Congress and the American people. He did not tell Congress its action could lead to the abandonment of an ally. War critics denied there was any moral or other commitment because neither Congress nor the American people knew about it or approved it. In truth, that pledge was made three times in letters signed by a president who had won a popular election in every state except Massachusetts and the District of Columbia in 1972.

It should be repeated, however, that both Thieu and North Vietnam committed major violations of the Paris agreement—which made a shambles of the whole arrangement. Neither side was willing to make any concessions, and in a civil war it seems one side must lose. This failure to execute the treaty suggests that Thieu first broke the secret pledge. However, Washington never condemned Thieu or pressured him to cease his violations of the Paris accords.

Kissinger revealed that Nixon did not publicize the exchange of letters and pledges in 1972-1973 because he felt it would infuriate Hanoi and jeopardize the cease-fire arrangement in Paris. Thieu would not sign any arrangement without such a guarantee of protection, and Hanoi would not have signed any agreement had it known such a pledge existed.[22] Nixon, Kissinger, Congress, and the American public then very badly wanted a settlement that extricated us from the war.

David K. Shipler of the *New York Times,* an experienced observer of South Vietnam's final nineteen months before collapse, declared that Thieu was blinded by the illusion of United States power.[23] He observed that in the summer of 1974 Hanoi began to increase its pressure all over South Vietnam. At this critical moment, he wrote, an American diplomat privately predicted that if Washington kept on arming Saigon without pushing it to compromise politically with the Communists, both Washington and Saigon would lose the war. Thieu's government simply could not face the possibility of real compromise, nor could the Communists. Thieu could not possibly implement the Paris accords, yet he could not possibly win the war. If he had resigned and another regime assumed power and was willing to take the risk, there might have been some hope of preventing a total Communist takeover. Such talk, to our Ambassador Graham A. Martin, was defeatism.

Both sides broke the Paris agreement, but each side ignored its own violations and denounced the other. Hanoi built a most formidable supply system for its troops, including good roads inside South Vietnam, oil pipelines from North to South Vietnam, and improved airstrips. The enemy turned the Ho Chi Minh Trail through Laos into a four-lane highway and sent down fresh troops, new tanks, heavy artillery—all the stuff of modern conventional warfare—but conducted few assaults. Rather he just waited to see what response Saigon and especially Washington might make to such major infractions. Nothing was done.[24] Nixon had other urgent problems—Watergate, the energy crisis, the Arab-Israeli War, and inflation with rising unemployment. Hanoi surely believed there was little risk of further United States combat intervention.

The political solution mandated by the Paris agreement, continued Shipler, was most distasteful to Thieu. It demanded that he grant democratic liberties for the Vietcong to operate openly as a political party, and it called for a Council of National Reconciliation and Concord, composed of three forces—Thieu's regime, the Vietcong, and a third or neutral force. That trio was too risky for Thieu, who thought he was quite safe behind American aid and Nixon's secret pledge. The pledge remained and was strengthened by American jet fighters and highly advanced weaponry. Even when Congress barred further combat aid in 1973, Thieu still felt safe behind Nixon's commitment. Our aid program and the pledge gave Thieu a false sense of security, led him to refuse all efforts at compromise or negotiation with his enemy, and caused him to ignore the Paris agreement. In the first year of its existence, he launched minor offensives, ousted the Communist troops from parts of the Mekong Delta and the central coast, established outposts, resettled some refugees in newly won lands, and even raided Cambodia.[25]

Thieu wanted no political process to succeed that would in any way weaken his authority. Anthony Lewis wrote:

He prohibited movement between zones, reclassified political prisoners as common criminals to keep them in jail and effectively banned all parties but his own. He not only refused to carry out the terms of the Paris agreement; he made it a crime to publish them in South Vietnam. And at the moment the cease-fire was to come into effect, he launched aggressive military operations.[26]

For such infractions, Thieu needed our tacit support and seemingly had it. Washington had given him a quick billion dollar arms shipment just before the truce. Thieu reportedly told an American journalist in early February 1975 that "since the signing in Paris the United States had never put any pressure on him to make political concessions to the Communists—that is, to carry out the peace terms."[27]

Ambassador Martin and the United States, wrote Shipler, did nothing to discourage these ventures, to persuade Thieu to live up to the Paris agreement. The Saigon Assembly was ignorant of the mood of the United States Congress and the American people. We had ceased to be concerned about Vietnam; in fact, with every passing day fewer Americans desired to support any longer Thieu or his regime. No Washington official expected the Communists to abide by the treaty, even if Thieu honestly tried to adhere to it. Saigon feared any liberties extended to the enemy would be abused and accompanied by terrorism, by grenades rather than ballots; but after our withdrawal it had little choice but to take the risks or fight and unite as it never had before. In a policy of drift and inaction time passed, and the Paris deal became for Saigon what Thieu long feared—"a cloak for surrender."[28]

In Thieu's desperate last days of power, amid his accusations and emotional outbursts, Washington remained relatively subdued. Kissinger and Ford sought to escape all responsibility for Thieu's ouster. They requested

Russia and China to restrain Hanoi and sought their aid in getting information of Hanoi's demands, but in spite of detente and "Ping-Pong" diplomacy, their notes were never answered. This brought Kissinger's sharp denunciation of his powerful "friends." He bluntly reminded them that we would continue our efforts to ease tensions, but would insist that the "easing of tensions cannot occur selectively."

"We shall not forget who supplied the arms which North Vietnam used to make a mockery of its signature on the Paris accords." Later he softened that a bit when he declared detente had not yet reached the stage that we could expect Communist countries to cut aid to their allies because the United States reduced aid to its own allies, nor could we blame them "for living up to their commitments in Indochina because the United States did not live up to its own."[29] Washington offered Thieu full and sympathetic consideration of any request he might make for asylum in the United States. Initially, he went to Taiwan. As late as April 21, 1975, Ford still expressed hope that Congress would approve his request for $722 million in emergency military aid and $250 million in humanitarian help.[30]

Almost as if unaware that a national pledge had been broken and an ally abandoned, Ford in New Orleans declared on April 23 that once again America could regain a sense of pride that existed before Vietnam. However, it could not be achieved by refighting a war that was finished. Asking the American people to put on blinders, he said:

> I ask tonight that we stop refighting the battles and recriminations of the past. I ask that we look now at what is right with America, at our possibilities and our potentialities for change, and growth, and achievement, and sharing. I ask that we accept the responsibilities of leadership as a good neighbor to all peoples and the enemy of none.
> . . . . .
> We are saddened, indeed, by events in Indochina. But these events, tragic as they are, portend neither the end of the world nor of America's leadership in the world. Some seem to feel that if we do not succeed in everything, then we have succeeded in nothing anywhere. I reject such polarized thinking. We can and should help others to help themselves. But the fate of responsible men and women everywhere, in the final decision, rests in their own hands.[31]

He also declared that the Indochina war was ended "as far as America is concerned," and he called for a great national reconciliation here at home. On that same day, the Senate backed authority for Ford to use our armed forces to protect the evacuation of our personnel and voted limited humanitarian aid to Saigon.[32]

In late March, frustrated by the failure of their mission, the truce teams of the six hundred members of the International Control Commission and Supervision began packing to leave Saigon. Telephones in many headquarters went unanswered thereafter. In fear for their personal safety and that of their families, large numbers of the South Vietnamese who had worked with the Americans clogged many offices in search of visas to leave for America, then desperately searched for the money and transportation to get out. "If Ford can save us, he will be a very great man. We shall be grateful," they said, but few thought he could really save South Vietnam at this last stage.

When United States army veterans saw the ARVN collapse, abandon billions of dollars worth of equipment, push babies and mothers aside in rushing to save themselves, shove civilians, old and young, off planes, boats, trucks, and buses, seize bicycles and all the property and money of fleeing civilians, and heard eyewitness reports of demoralized Saigon soldiers raping young women and fighting among themselves—they expressed near total disgust at such absence of pride, discipline, honor, courage, and dedication. Whatever illusions had sustained any hope of victory now vanished. Without our air power and combat presence, nothing could be saved.

As the Communists began to tighten the noose around the capital center, all that mattered to the South Vietnamese was how to save their families and themselves by getting out of the city or the country in any way possible, no matter at what cost in lives or money. Whatever people had to sell they sought to exchange for gold, about the only property deemed of universal value. Local currency sank rapidly. Property that could not be moved suffered a disastrous discount. Within two weeks one palatial Saigon villa was reduced in advertised price from approximately $125,000 to one-fourth that amount. Those who could hoarded all the gold they could save or get. For a short time dollars were also deemed valuable. Aside from gold and dollars there was not much they could take with them. Cars, homes, furniture, and savings in banks, which soon closed, were all abandoned.

Families in flight got lost from one another; some made it out safely, others did not. Some offered thousands of dollars in bribes for passage out. Others begged Americans leaving the country to take with them their wives, daughters, and even their babies. Thousands of Vietnamese prepared for flight, jammed highways, streets, airports, embarkation points, any place where helicopters, airplanes, and ships offered even the slightest possibility of escape. Rich and not so rich bought small ships or anything that would float or move out to sea or down rivers in search of United States or other foreign vessels which waited offshore and gave prospect of final escape.

Within those last three weeks before the Communists took over Saigon April 30, 1975, we helped evacuate in all some 6,000 Americans and possibly 130,000 Vietnamese. Even Saigon officials found ways to speed the departure of Vietnamese families of Americans. They cut the usual time-consuming, costly, and painful red tape. Even after the Communists took over Saigon, for a few days thereafter ingenious, desperate, and courageous South Vietnamese obtained small craft and took to sea in search of any ship that would offer help. Our Defense Department did not say how many ships had been left offshore to take them out safely. Asked about the legality of such a rescue effort, a spokesman for the Defense Department declared: "There is no law that says you can't pick up people in distress on the high seas."

As people left, those without hope of exit engaged in an orgy of looting—in virtually every home and business in every city and town. Local police simply ignored it. In Da Nang soldiers of the Saigon army, drunk and angry, indulged in "incredible pillaging." They wandered over the town in all kinds of vehicles, even used armored cars to break down doors and gates in order to steal whatever they could move. Civilians did the same. Observers described the evacuation as "the hours of madness." They blamed it all on the ARVN. Officers and their troops sought to flee the Communists by any means, even though it meant pushing civilians around, beating them, and in some instances even firing upon anyone in their way.[33] The fleeing refugees were more afraid of their own soldiers than of the Communists.

One man who had been stopped seven times by the Communists reported: "They never touched a hair on our heads. . . . They were all very young boys, 16 or 17 years old. They just told us to throw away any guns we had, and said we were stupid to run away. 'Wherever you run, we will be there soon anyway,' they said."[34]

Evacuation was not a simple issue; it had broad implications. From Ford and Kissinger came statements that we had a deep moral obligation to save our friends who had worked with us. Ambassador Graham A. Martin declared from Saigon he would not quit the country until they were safely out, but our officials had a problem: if we began evacuation too quickly, that would tell the world, especially the Communists, that we had given up on Vietnam, further undermine South Vietnam's morale, and bring worse panic. Also the United States Congress refused to give aid or military protection for the evacuation of the Vietnamese alone. Quietly, Martin began to ease our personnel out of the country, but it took considerable pressure from Washington to persuade him to act with the urgency Congress and others felt the situation required.

Ford's authority to use military force to aid the evacuation was both defended and attacked. Legal opinion was divided over whether the War Powers Act and other legislation prohibiting American military involvement in Indochina would permit it. Finally Congress gave limited consent. No more force than was absolutely essential to evacuate our own citizens should be sent. It would be used only for that purpose and no longer than was absolutely essential for it. The clear implication and meaning of Congress was that our forces would be used only to get our personnel out, not the Vietnamese. Any money for military aid would be tied directly to the evacuation effort. In brief, we wanted no wider war.[35] The majority believed there was ample authority for the use of force, but the minority saw a dangerous precedent in letting the president use his inherent powers as commander in chief to do it. Memories of Johnson's use of the Gulf of Tonkin Resolution lingered. Five ships of our navy were soon standing off the coast of South Vietnam, with a marine helicopter squadron. Aircraft carriers moved toward the area.

Evacuation was risky. Congress suspected that Ford's final bid for aid to Saigon was designed to get Americans safely and peacefully out of the country. He feared last minute violence at the hands of native South Vietnamese or possibly from the ARVN itself. It was then clear to any informed person that

South Vietnam had lost its war and any aid we might authorize would be too late. However, Ford felt it necessary to keep asking and pressing for the military and humanitarian aid to prevent any possible native obstruction to evacuation. Defense Secretary James Schlesinger admitted that the purpose of our aid was as much psychological and political as it was military. At best, such aid might keep a Saigon government together until we escaped. Further, not to ask for any aid at all, Ford feared, would have caused the immediate collapse of Saigon and bring the very "panic and probably anti-American rampages that would have jeopardized a safe withdrawal." So the charade went on for several days with the administration pressing Congress for vast sums to provide military and humanitarian aid to a regime it believed had no chance of survival and Congress eventually setting aside funds it believed would never be used. Some said Congress paid a ransom to Saigon to let us go in peace, and Congress began to feel this was a "symbolic price that must be paid to get the Americans out."[36]

Observers believed the Communists tacitly allowed us considerable time finally to evacuate Saigon, but the last hours before they took command of the city were the most terrifying. April 29, 1975, was the day the United States ended virtually two decades of military involvement in Vietnam. It was a tumultuous day. Our fighter planes flew cover for our retreat, and our marines guarded the grounds of the American embassy in Saigon, as eighty-one helicopters from our ships in the South China Sea landed at Tan Son Nhut airport and on the roof of the United States embassy to pick up possibly a thousand remaining Americans and many Vietnamese. These were but a few of the many, possibly hundreds of thousands of Vietnamese, who wanted to leave but found no way to flee. Large airplane transports initially sought to land at the airport. But, as Kissinger said, "We then attempted to land C-130's but found the population at the airport had got out of control and had flooded the runways, and it proved impossible to land any more fixed-wing aircraft."[37] Those eligible to leave were then moved elsewhere and later taken by helicopters to ships in the South China Sea.

The helicopter evacuation took over sixteen hours—unexpectedly long. In the process, two marines were lost when their helicopter crashed into the sea and two other marines guarding an office at the Saigon airport were killed by artillery fire. Our helicopters were under fire and so was the Tan Son Nhut airport. From long-range enemy artillery, shells burst upon parts of the city. Buses raced around Saigon to pick up refugees and searched for points of safety and evacuation. This consumed troubled hours of uncertainty and risked grave danger before the evacuees finally reached the embassy. There, with thousands yelling, begging, and clamoring to get into the embassy, they had to crawl up and be lifted over a ten-foot wall. All around them masses of South Vietnamese, in a desperate attempt to escape a Communist bloodbath, followed close behind and crowded against the embassy walls. A few even crawled to the top and fell over only to be thrown back by marines stationed along the wall to protect the evacuation of Americans. Our marines had to use pistols and rifle butts to dislodge the Vietnamese and prevent them from flooding over the walls and hanging onto the helicopters. Yet they kept coming, and the marines continued to beat them back until the last Americans and select Vietnamese were pulled over the wall. Then, with those outside the wall yelling, "We want to go, too," and hundreds of Vietnamese climbing over the fence about midnight of April 29, "the marines withdrew to the second gate. At 4:30 on the morning of the 30th, the marines formed a line with their rifles out, bayonets fixed and withdrew backward one step at a time until they disappeared into the embassy building."[38] Inside the compound they waited for a helicopter to take them out.

Some eight hundred marines guarded the evacuation process at the Tan Son Nhut air base and the American embassy. Hundreds of South Vietnamese soldiers with weapons converged on the air base trying to escape. Across the street from the American embassy civilians and soldiers looted everything in sight, took abandoned embassy cars, and any removable fixtures from apartments where Americans had lived. Scarcely had the embassy been evacuated when they ravaged that last symbol of American wealth and power. While Communist shells burst over the city, American fighters went into action to protect the refugees from "marauding helicopters" that sought to prevent their flight. Caravans of Vietnamese cars followed the American buses seeking entrance to the embassy and flight out of the city, but most of these failed to gain entrance. As an eyewitness account described it: "Wrecked and burned motorcycles littered the entrance to the compound. Wrecked American cars were in winches, some with windows shot out. One was left with its motor running, lights on and door open."[39] All this, while from Washington Kissinger appealed to Hanoi not to storm Saigon. He believed South Vietnam was by then prepared for a peaceful surrender of the city. The new and last president of the Republic of Vietnam, General Duong Van Minh, shortly afterward offered to surrender the country and the city to the Communist commander, only to be curtly told that he had nothing to surrender. The end left deep bitterness in Saigon. The Communists took over South Vietnam on May 1, 1975. So what Ho Chi Minh had sought in vain to get Wilson to accept in 1919, Gerald Ford finally conceded in 1975.

For the United States there remained the refugee problem. Eventually an estimated 130,000 fled South Vietnam and headed by various means and with several stopovers to the United States. They were mainly orphans and youths, but their coming posed a challenge to our charitable nature. Initially was heard, in opposition to further outlays for a people many felt we had already suffered and paid for long enough, the cry, "Jobs for Americans first." The spring of 1975 was gloomy for too many Americans. Nearly 8.9 percent unemployment and continued inflation amid stagnation of the economy left few priorities for charity.

Proponents sharply reminded us of our tradition of help for the downtrodden and oppressed of all lands and of how others after World War II had done so much more than we had. Switzerland had aided about a million refugees, although it had a small land area and a native population of only four million. Bombed out and barely able to care for its own people, England had aided several million refugees. Others had shown a similar generosity and humanity. When the House initially voted down a bill, including aid to resettle the refugees, Ford declared: "This action does not reflect the values we cherish as a nation of immigrants. It is not worthy of a people which has lived by the philosophy symbolized in the Statue of Liberty." In late May 1975, Congress authorized $405 million to meet that human obligation.

A *New York Times* editorial said that while our country could do little more to influence events in Cambodia or Vietnam,

it can welcome and assist those 150,000 Vietnamese and the handful of Cambodians who escaped to this country.
There can be little doubt now why Vietnamese queued by the thousands to get away, risked their lives to climb aboard American helicopters, sailed undependable craft out on the open ocean to reach waiting American vessels, and at the end clawed frantically up the walls of the American Embassy compound. For them, America was a beacon of hope as the long dark night of tyranny closed over their homeland.[40]

Regrettably the *Times* had not supported the efforts of noble men to prevent that final tragedy.

Why the final collapse of South Vietnam? Answers were diverse and offered by many people. General Westmoreland suggested that when the total history was written it "might show that the use of several small-yield nuclear weapons at some early point conceivably could have put an end to the whole thing and caused less suffering in the short run than subsequently was caused in the long run."[41] Others would support his conclusion that the United States strategy of containment of imperial expansion since World War II had led us to overextend ourselves. The Korean War should have brought a reassessment and possibly retreat. Wise men should have said "Stop!" But Westmoreland declared that the "Kennedy years were the worst."[42]

The ARVN collapsed, he wrote later, for several reasons. Any military force on the offensive has the advantage of the initiative, and Hanoi could mass its forces at points of its own choosing without fear of an attack on its home territory. Also the cease-fire with Communist troops in place all over South Vietnam allowed North Vietnamese troops to outflank the ARVN on every front. Hanoi's violations of the agreement—using the demilitarized zone, Laos, and Cambodia—plus the rapid buildup of forces with their heavy additions of Soviet materiel enhanced its military advantage. "South Vietnam's sole aim," Westmoreland wrote, "was to hold on to its territory and avoid encroachment along the cease-fire line." Its forces were spread out and vulnerable to defeat at "any point that the enemy chose to mass his forces for attack." Thus, when Hanoi tested Saigon and Washington in January 1975 by making a large attack on Phuoc Long province but forty miles north of Saigon and met no military response, that was the tip-off that the time was ripe for further massive efforts. Then, when Thieu finally understood from the visiting congressmen that further

American material support was uncertain, he wisely began to hoard his supplies and conserve manpower and equipment. In anticipation of major enemy offensives he planned withdrawal to concentrate on more vital areas.[43] Although he did not like simplistic answers to the question of who was to blame, Defense Secretary James R. Schlesinger acknowledged that the sharp decline in our military aid to Saigon was a factor in the collapse.[44]

Walt Rostow suggested that South Vietnam might still be saved from collapse if the United States invaded North Vietnam. He declared that one option we still could use was to "put ashore two Marine divisions at some strategic point in North Vietnam and with them hold a perimeter until the North Vietnamese agree to honor the 1973 accords."[45] Many hawks believed the American people simply failed to see their moral obligation to stop the outlaws from Hanoi, but they failed to notice also the violations of the Paris agreement by South Vietnam. The hawks blamed the failure on the whole postwar pattern of "small wars, gradualism, creeping escalation and other partial commitments that were militarily unsound," to use Westmoreland's words. They thought it was highly regrettable that as the final crunch came Ford could not emulate Nixon and order the renewed bombing of North Vietnam and the mining of the waters and harbors of that country. They saw a failure of will in Washington and Saigon. They saw China and Russia constantly resupplying Hanoi and the Vietcong, while Congress in a dovish backlash against the whole involvement reduced and threatened to cut off entirely aid to our side.

Thieu was never willing to accept any political solution unless it preserved his system; but he could not impose it, and we would not do it for him. However, he violated the Paris agreement at several points, and the enemy could certainly notice that he did so without any evident protest from Washington or from Ambassador Martin in Saigon. Ford simply observed that Thieu's unilateral withdrawal decision created a chaotic situation and expressed regret that congressional action had tied the executive's hands for the past two years. Kissinger said:

I believe if it had not been for the moralities of executive authority resulting from Watergate, if the aid levels had been appropriate over the years and we had been freer to conduct foreign policy that was possible under those circumstances—partly for reasons in which the executive shares a responsibility—I believe that certainly the difficulties we face this year could have been avoided for a number of years.

However, he concluded that we should now stop assessing the blame "and ask ourselves where we are going from here."[46]

Anthony Lewis of the *New York Times* declared what happened in Vietnam in late April 1975 was the collapse of a myth—"the myth of an independent, flourishing, nationalist South Vietnam with the will to fight for itself. It is a case not of America 'destroying a country' but of reality destroying an illusion."[47] Truly after 1950, another declared, our unseen problem and task had been not how to get involved but how to avoid involvement. The intervention had been a mistake from the first and could but fail. It was a civil war which only the people directly involved could finally settle. Although but a few South Vietnamese appreciated Westernized liberal values, most of the people we backed—the militarists, bureaucrats, politicians, landowners, businessmen, professionals, intellectuals, clergymen—were guilty of "rampant venality, corruption, and barbarism" and were comparable to a bunch of rapacious warlords. Our intervention sprang from American ignorance and fear. A former State Department East Asia policy aide wrote:

Ill-informed about the indigenous nationalist roots of Vietnamese Communism, fearful of Moscow-run "monolithic Communism" after Mao's China triumph and blackmailed by the French (the price Paris demanded for joining any European defense arrangement), we took the wrong road in early 1950. And kept to it—even after the French went home—because of our enduring fear of communism.[48]

Did he think there existed a sufficient basis for hope to offset that fear?

Observers reflected that this tragic end had come despite the fact that Saigon for years had virtual equality in numbers of men under arms with the Communists, "despite the incalculably greater aid in firepower and technology that the Saigon side received from abroad, and despite nearly seven years of direct participation by American troops, aircraft and warships."[49] It could scarcely be ignored that while Thieu feared the loss of our aid, his army simply refused to fight and abandoned in excess of $5 billion worth of equipment and supplies.

Objective assessments concluded that the collapse originated mainly in the "internal inadequacies of the Saigon regime itself—its inability to inspire; its corrupt, incompetent military leadership; its rigid, unresponsive political structure. No amount of American aid could have made up for these chronic deficiencies as Saigon faced its Vietnamese enemies."[50] Sagging morale alone could not explain the fall; nor could the mistakes of some officers. Malcolm Browne said many Vietnamese believed the fatal flaw of the ARVN was a fondness for military luxury—an appetite they acquired from the United States example. While the ARVN was often far better equipped with modern weapons, fighter bombers, communication equipment, and transport after 1954, the Vietcong and North Vietnam often in crude huts manufactured "grenade casings from scrap aluminum, shotgun cartridges made of brass tubing and of French coins with holes in the centers accommodating percussion caps," and much else required to fight their initial crude concealed style of warfare. General Giap, Browne noted, once said that in the early stages of the war: "The sole source of supply could only be the battlefront—to take the materiel from the enemy and turn it against him." And now in the last stages of the war, although he would have had sufficient supply to defeat the ARVN without it, Browne noted: "Even at this hour Saigon's forces are being hammered by captured American-made howitzers and machine guns and other weapons. The Communists recently captured more than 600 tanks and personnel carriers in Central Vietnam alone—enough to supply a good-sized army."[51]

Even a South Vietnamese officer questioned the wisdom of accustoming an army to a comfortable war, in which men could move around in helicopters and motor transports, rather than walk through swamps, underbrush, hills, and steaming jungles; enjoy unlimited artillery and extensive spray machine gun sweeps over dense brush and the jungle ahead; and have constant air support. Then when you let officers and men get "used to sleeping in bed at night," what happens? The obvious answer was that they grew soft, inert, and lost their chance for any freedom. The Vietnam officer described it very well:

I will tell you what happens. At a certain point neither the troops nor the officers are willing any longer to walk to battle, hacking their way through jungles if necessary. So they stay in their helicopters and get shot down or cut off from American rescue, or they drive along the road, where they get shelled or ambushed, and cut to pieces.

Every officer knows this, but our army has become flabby and lazy over the years, and we owe some of that to the kind of luxury aid you gave us.[52]

In truth, however, anti-Communist forces never had the disciplined determination to win that the Communists developed. Communist strategy throughout the war was to operate even the largest units guerrilla style. Many observers, including Browne, declared:

The secret of the Communists' defense against whatever weapon or force has always been to try to avoid offering a big target and to disperse men and weapons.

Tran Hung Dao, the medieval Vietnamese general who brought guerrilla warfare to a high art against the occupying Chinese, taught his army to assemble only at the point and time of battle, and then in greater numbers than the enemy had. After the fight his troops would disperse again to avoid inevitable enemy reinforcements.

The South Vietnamese soldiers could have used the same tactics, if they had been inspired by a greater will to win and to sacrifice all for their cause.[53] And if they had been given a cause.

One Vietnamese veteran sadly said: "Some of us knew what was wrong. . . . Some of you knew what was wrong. But on the whole both our peoples remained blind, and even now we seem to have learned nothing. Well, it no longer matters."[54]

Our Saigon ally lacked the leadership, the discipline, the unity, and the will to win as compared to his Communist enemy. Because of its desire to save the wealth, rank, and power of a small minority, the administration could never make the concessions essential to broaden its political support, to bring the masses of peasants to its side. After the resignation of Thieu, a Saigon journalist believed that even in a free election, the Communists would win power in South Vietnam.

The war was lost long before the spring of 1975. Although our army was never defeated, it never expelled the Communists from South Vietnam. It simply quit the field, and in doing that our war aims and our foreign policy in Indochina failed. They failed not for lack of strength on our part, but from our lack of will to use our full strength and stay the course until victory was won. Pressured by the American people, the Congress made a political decision to retreat from a war which hindsight revealed it should never have begun. Certainly it should never have started a war unless it had the full approval of the American people—*and other nations.* The future may well record that the free world and the world that would be free should have united to win, that the collapse could be traced to that lack of unity and will.

Final conclusions of the tragedy will be long in debate. Many expressed some hopes out of it all, while louder voices entertained fears. Asians saw the final decision as the end of colonialism and the long era of Western imperial domination; to them it was a victory for nationalism and had been a war of national emancipation. China expected the lowered tension to speed its acquisition of Taiwan; North Korea raised its hopes of a Korea reunited under the Communist banner; Japan, the Philippines, Thailand, and others began a reassessment of their position, one of less reliance upon the United States; Cambodia and Laos quickly came under Communist subjection; North Vietnam—with war materiel of over $5 billion value, now possibly the third greatest military power on earth—anticipated a reunited Vietnam and possibly domination of all Indochina. The Southeast Asian dominoes feared for their future and sought to make their peace with their powerful neighbor in Vietnam.

West Europeans saw the fall of Saigon as a sobering influence and with provincial smugness felt the United States would now wisely turn its attention and invest its strength in areas more vital to its own national security, which were, of course, Western Europe and the Middle East. There was concern in Washington and possibly elsewhere that our failure in Vietnam would weaken the credibility of our multiple commitments in other areas. Doubts existed, and Washington, led by Kissinger and Ford, initiated a policy of "reassurances" by word and deed.

Ford sharply reacted to the Cambodian seizure of the American merchant ship *Mayaguez* on the high seas off the Cambodian coast in May 1975. After a sixty-hour effort to contact the Communist government of Cambodia, he ordered military action, the landing of marines and air strikes to recapture the ship and its thirty-nine crewmen. Seemingly unaware of the enduring congressional denunciation of Johnson's carrying on a war without its approval, Ford now told Congress what he was going to do. He did not ask their advice, he acted; and since he won quickly, few challenged his claim that he acted under his power as commander in chief, and under the limits imposed by the War Powers resolution of 1973.

Ford's action was apparently designed not only to obtain the return of the ship and its crew but also to tell the Communists and the world that we would not be pushed around, as Senator Barry Goldwater declared, by a "half-ass nation." Critics felt this was a risky and greatly exaggerated response that ill became a humane and responsible nation; they wondered what our response would be if in response to the United States's capture of a Russian ship within our claimed territorial waters, Moscow decided to bomb Norfolk? However, Ford's action won great popular favor. Had it brought the destruction of the ship and the murder of its crew, then what? According to the *U.S. News & World Report* of June 2, 1975, as it was, to achieve that result cost "15 killed in the assault on Tang Island, 3 missing and presumed dead and another 23 lives lost in a related helicopter crash in Thailand. Fifty men were wounded." This did not include the total monetary cost, not immediately estimated. Ford seemed to believe that deeds more than words would reassure our allies that we had both the strength and the will to protect both our interests and honor our commitments.

To allay any concerns of a doubting world, other reassurances were offered. Key congressional liberals and moderates dropped their plan to cut defense spending and overseas forces in the coming year. The Vietnam situation changed the picture, said one senator, and made it very important not to signal Russia and others that we were giving up. We must make clear to the world that while Congress had decided against further war in Vietnam, we had not decided to return to isolationism. Mansfield and others who had long favored limited troop withdrawals from Europe shelved their measures. Fifty-one congressmen sponsored a resolution again confirming our treaty commitments, and seventy-six Senators signed a pledge of continued military aid to Israel.

Washington sought to dispel fears of a United States return to isolationism in the aftermath of the Vietnamese disaster by speeches denouncing the idea, by President Ford's visit to Europe in late May 1975 to revive and strengthen NATO, and by Kissinger's warning to Russia that the United States would remember who furnished arms for Hanoi's offensive (which broke the Paris agreement and Russia's pledge of 1973 to support a peaceful conclusion of the war in Indochina). Soviet leaders indicated genuine concern that our Vietnam failure might bring a reaction against too close dealings with Russia, thereby weakening detente. Moscow did not boast of the Communist takeover in South Vietnam and was reportedly urging caution on Portuguese Communists anxious to grab complete power there. However, detente never meant that either we or they would change our character or cease our efforts to advance our interests wherever possible. It did not mean Russia would stop trying to advance communism any more than we should cease trying to advance human freedom. However, the brilliant and articulate Daniel P. Moynihan declared American liberals had shown a failure of nerve, of being concerned not with freedom abroad but only with "freedom from involvement."

After the initial relief of both hawks and doves at the end of the war, there was a round of mutual recrimination. Almost everyone had his explanation for the failure. By mid-April 1975 a Gallup poll revealed that 78 percent of the people opposed any additional military aid to South Vietnam and Cambodia, so observers could blame the majority of the American people. Some begged us not to repeat the "Who lost China?" debate of 1950-1952 with the "Who lost Indochina?" in 1975. Maxwell Taylor expressed regret at the evidence that the conduct of our affairs had seemingly passed to a leaderless Congress, although its young mavericks probably reflected the dovish wishes of their constituents. He feared that such a shackled leadership and weakened national will would invite numerous probes of our strength, possibly in Korea and the Middle East. He concluded that the Vietnam finale "by impairing our reputation for reliability, weakening our alliances, and exposing our internal weaknesses to friend and foe has been highly detrimental to the many forms of national power that contribute to our national security—power derived from unity, self-confidence, allies, reputation, and military strength."[55]

Other nations have suffered a failure of policy without any disastrous or even noticeable loss of strength or credibility. The former theory of a monolithic, single-centered, Moscow-dominated global communism vanished with the defection of Tito and Mao Tse-tung, and the assurance that Castro and others would be likely to take the same national deviationist path. Then Kennedy persuaded Russia to withdraw its missiles from Cuba, and other Soviet probes were challenged; but Russia remains a superpower.

If Russia could not stamp her brand upon the world, neither can the United States remold the world in its own image. We never sought to extend capitalism, republicanism, or our precise system to Indochina; rather we merely sought to help them to develop their own brand of individual and national freedom. We tried, but they were not ready for the effort. Our action may have been quixotic, but it was not evil in motive. Critics noted our failure, and some concluded that the United States had been both unreliable and dishonorable in its abandonment of South Vietnam. Regrettable as the final collapse was and our failure to prevent it, our record since World War II, thought James Reston, was fairly clear. The world should be in no doubt how we would respond to any serious challenge to our vital interests. In a brilliant interpretation, he declared:

Washington reacted to the Soviet threat to Berlin with the airlift; to the Soviet Sputnik challenge in outer space by going to the moon; to the disaster of the Cuban Bay of Pigs with the blockade of Khrushchev's Cuban missiles in the second Cuban crisis; to the Communist threat to Greece and Turkey with the Truman Doctrine; to the economic wreckage of Europe after the last World War with the Marshall Plan; to the Soviet pressure on Japan with a security pact and the most generous and imaginative economic and political settlement ever offered by a victorious nation to a defeated nation.[56]

Neither Russia nor other nations on sober reflection could afford to misread that record and feel they could risk pushing us when our primary interests were challenged. A united America, out of Southeast Asia, could possibly be stronger than an embittered and disunited people wasting its resources fighting peripheral wars of very limited importance to our national security. Speeches by Ford and Kissinger certainly could not reassure our historic friends and allies, if that record did not. And if our retreat from overcommitment, rising out of the Vietnam tragedy, persuaded Americans and others that our power had limits, and warned others that they would have to do more for themselves, that might be a most healthy thing for all concerned. Certainly it would relieve us of the impossible burden of trying to be a lone world policeman. The warning for us all is clear. Free people and those who want freedom must devise means for collective security and defense, must unite or they will ultimately perish. That will require a greater measure of discipline, austerity, and courage than the present national indulgence and suicidal tendencies toward global anarchy can accept. Our motto should be not One for all others, but All for all.

At the end of the tunnel, the Vietnamese people did not find light; they found a dungeon. The. warning is obvious and ominous. First Russia, then the satellite nations, followed by China, Cuba, North Vietnam, all Indochina, and then—who will be the last domino?

APPENDIX I

Nixon's Peace Proposal, January 25, 1972

1. There will be a total withdrawal from South Vietnam of all U.S. forces and other foreign forces allied with the Government of South Vietnam within six months of an agreement.

2. The release of all military men and innocent civilians captured throughout Indochina will be carried out in parallel with the troop withdrawals mentioned in Point 1. Both sides will present a complete list of military men and innocent civilians held throughout Indochina on the day the agreement is signed. The release will begin on the same day as the troop withdrawals and will be completed when they are completed.

One month before the presidential election takes place, the incumbent President and Vice President of South Vietnam will resign. The Chairman of the Senate, as caretaker head of the Government, will assume administrative responsibilities except for those pertaining to the election, which will remain with the independent election body.

The United States, for its part, declares that it:

Will support no candidate and will remain completely neutral in the election.

Will abide by the outcome of this election and any other political processes shaped by the South Vietnamese people themselves.

It is prepared to define its military and economic assistance relationship with any government that exists in South Vietnam.

3. The following principles will govern the political future of South Vietnam:

The political future of South Vietnam will be left for the South Vietnamese people to decide for themselves, free from outside interference.

There will be a free and democratic Presidential election in South Vietnam within six months of an agreement. This election will be organized and run by an independent body representing all political forces in South Vietnam which will assume its responsibilities on the date of the agreement. This body will, among other responsibilities, determine the qualification of candidates. All political forces in South Vietnam can participate in the election and present candidates. There will be international supervision of this election.

Both sides agree that:

South Vietnam, together with the other countries of Indochina, should adopt a foreign policy consistent with the military provisions of the 1954 Geneva accords.

Reunification of Vietnam should be decided on the basis of discussions and agreements between North and South Vietnam without constraint and annexation from either party, and without foreign interference.

4. Both sides will respect the 1954 Geneva agreements on Indochina and those of 1962 on Laos. There will be no foreign intervention in the Indochinese countries and the Indochinese peoples will be left to settle their own affairs by themselves.

5. The problems existing among the Indochinese countries will be settled by the Indochinese parties on the basis of mutual respect for independence, sovereignty, territorial integrity and non-interference in each other's affairs. Among the problems that will be settled is the implementation of the principle that all armed forces of the countries of Indochina must remain within their national frontiers.

6. There will be a general cease-fire throughout Indochina, to begin when the agreement is signed. As part of the cease-fire, there will be no further infiltration of outside forces into any of the countries of Indochina.

7. There will be international supervision of the military aspects of this agreement, including the cease-fire in its provisions, the release of prisoners of war and innocent civilians, the withdrawal of outside forces from Indochina, and the implementation of the principle that all armed forces of the countries of Indochina must remain within their national frontiers.

8. There will be an international guarantee for the fundamental national rights of the Indochinese peoples, the status of all the countries in Indochina, and lasting peace in this region.

Both sides express their willingness to participate in an international conference for this and other appropriate purposes.[1]

APPENDIX II

1. The withdrawal of the totality of U.S. forces and those of foreign countries in the U.S. camp from South Vietnam and other Indochinese countries should be completed within 1971.

2. The release of all military men and civilians captured in the war should be carried out parallel and completed at the same time with the troop withdrawal mentioned in Point 1.

3. In South Vietnam, the United States should stop supporting Thieu-Ky-Khiem so that there may be set up in Saigon a new administration standing for peace, independence, neutrality and democracy. The Provisional Revolutionary Government of the Republic of South Vietnam will enter into talks with that administration to settle the internal affairs of South Vietnam and to achieve national concord.

4. The U.S. Government must bear full responsibility for the damages caused by the United States to the people of the whole Vietnam. The Government of the Democratic Republic of Vietnam and the Provisional Revolutionary Government of the Republic of South Vietnam demand from the U.S. Government reparations for the damages caused by the United States in the two zones of Vietnam.

5. The United States should respect the 1954 Geneva agreements on Indochina and those of 1962 on Laos. It should stop its aggression and intervention in the Indochinese countries and let their peoples settle by themselves their own affairs.

6. The problems existing among the Indochinese countries should be settled by the Indochinese parties on the basis of mutual respect for independence, sovereignty and territorial integrity, and noninterference in each

other's internal affairs. As far as it is concerned, the Democratic Republic of Vietnam is prepared to join in resolving such problems.

7. All the parties should achieve a cease-fire after the signing of the agreements on the above-mentioned problems.

8. There should be an international supervision.

9. There should be an international guarantee for the fundamental national rights of the Indochinese peoples, the neutrality of South Vietnam, Laos and Cambodia, and lasting peace in this region.

The above points form an integrated whole.[1]

APPENDIX III

1. The U.S. must set a date and unilaterally remove all troops and weapons from South Vietnam, dismantle its bases and halt the Vietnamization program. Release of American POW's will begin and end on the same dates as the American troop pullout begins and ends. A cease-fire with U.S. forces will be declared as soon as agreement is reached on withdrawal.

2. Simultaneously, the U.S. must renounce support for the "puppet" government of South Vietnamese President Nguyen Van Thieu and support formation of a coalition government of "national concord" that will hold power until general elections. A cease-fire with South Vietnam will go into effect after the new government is created.

3. The question of "Vietnamese armed forces" in South Vietnam will be settled by the North and South, with no U.S. interference.

4. North and South Vietnam will negotiate step-by-step reunification of the country. Pending agreement, South Vietnam will be neutralized and must refrain from any foreign military alliances.

5. South Vietnam will establish diplomatic and economic relations with all countries—Communist and non-Communist alike.

6. The U.S. must bear "full responsibility" for war damage in both North and South Vietnam.

7. North and South Vietnam will agree on the kind of international guarantees needed to keep the peace.[1]

NOTES

Chapter One

1. TV interview, Today Show, September 9, 1968.
2. Letter to General Minh, Released January 1, 1964, *Public Papers of the Presidents of the United States,* Lyndon B. Johnson, 1963-1964, I, 106.
3. News Conference February 1, 1964, *ibid.,* I, 257.
4. *Ibid.,* I, 370.
5. Philip L. Geyelin, *Lyndon B. Johnson and the World,* 181.
6. Townsend Hoopes, *The Limits of Intervention: An Inside Account of How the Johnson Policy of Escalation Was Reversed,* 1-2. In January 1965, Hoopes became deputy assistant secretary of defense for international security affairs. From October 1967 to February 1969, he was undersecretary of the air force. His very able study is among the most moderate and careful evaluations of Johnson's war policy. Since it was written by an insider and participant in these events, it becomes almost a primary source for a study of these years. Hereafter cited as Hoopes, *Limits.*
7. *Ibid.,* 7.
8. Geyelin, *Johnson and the World,* 182.
9. Hoopes, *Limits,* 167-168.
10. *New York Times* and *Newsweek* reports cited in Alfred Steinberg, *Sam Johnson's Boy: A Close-Up of the President from Texas,* 752.
11. *Ibid.,* 752-753.
12. *Ibid.,* 753.
13. *Ibid.,* 753-755.
14. Hoopes, *Limits,* 30-31.
15. *Ibid.,* 31.
16. *Ibid.* Hoopes offered no evidence that Humphrey ever believed military victory, whatever that meant, was possible. He never "got on the team" in that sense. Also the president emphatically denied that he ever aimed at a military victory over Hanoi, but asserted our purpose was to protect the people of South Vietnam from Communist conquest. Interview with Walter Cronkite, CBS, February 6, 1970.
*"Erroneously" because the Congress and many others knew the Tonkin Gulf Resolution authorized the strong responses given, and they were not surprised at the action Johnson took. Nor were they really unaware of the military buildup. Hoopes was a dove who was strongly antiwar and unfairly belittled Johnson.

17. *Ibid.*, 31-32.

18. Message from the President of the United States (Kennedy) to the President of the Republic of Viet-Nam (Diem), December 14, 1961, U.S. Department of State, *American Foreign Policy: Current Documents, 1961*, pp. 1056-1057.

19. Statement Read and Replies Made by the Secretary of State (Rusk) to Questions Asked at a News Conference, March 1, 1962 (Excerpts), *ibid., 1962*, pp. 1101-1102.

20. Hoopes, *Limits*, 62.

21. Cited in Steinberg, *Sam Johnson's Boy*, 760.

22. *Ibid.*

23. See able chapter 7 entitled "Americanization of the War," George M. Kahin and John W. Lewis, *The United States in Vietnam*, 151-175.

24. Hoopes, *Limits*, 7.

25. *Ibid.*, 8.

26. *Ibid.*, 9.

27. *Ibid.*, 15.

28. *Ibid.*, 9-10.

29. *Ibid.*, 10.

30. *Ibid.*, 11-12.

31. *Ibid.*, 12.

32. *Ibid.*, 16.

33. *Ibid.*, 16-19.

34. *Ibid.*, 21.

35. *Ibid.*, 59-60.

36. In answer to a question at the Washington session of the annual meeting of the American Historical Association, December 1969, Walt Rostow emphatically declared that the president had been officially requested to send ground forces.

37. General Earle G. Wheeler, "The U.S. Achievements in Viet-Nam," *Department of State Bulletin*, February 6, 1967, p. 187.

38. Theodore Draper, *Abuse of Power*, 84.

39. Steinberg, *Sam Johnson's Boy*, 760-761.

40. *Ibid.*, 761-762.

41. *New York Times*, January 1 and 2, 1964.

42. See memorandum of December 30, 1965, in Hoopes, *Limits*, 44. Antiwar forces, however, could never convince the public that Russia really wished us out of a war that cost us so much and her so little. They failed to explain why our major enemy would help us to extricate ourselves from such a bog. Possibly rising concern with China spurred Russia's desire for better relations with us.

43. *Ibid.*, 44-45.

44. *Ibid.*, 46-48.

45. See the president's statement made before the American Bar Association at New York, August 12, 1964, *Department of State Bulletin*, August 31, 1964, pp. 299-300. See also a list of several versions of this statement in the campaign of 1964, Steinberg, *Sam Johnson's Boy*, 767.

46. Steinberg, *Sam Johnson's Boy*, 763-764.

47. *Ibid.*, 765.

48. *Ibid.*

49. Lyndon B. Johnson, *The Vantage Point: Perspectives of the Presidency, 1963-1969*, 114.

50. *Ibid.*, 115.

51. *Ibid.*

52. *Ibid.*, 115-116.

53. *Ibid.*, 116-117.

54. *Ibid.*, 120.

55. *Ibid.*, 127.

56. See also brief account in Admiral U. S. G. Sharp and General W. C. Westmoreland, *Report on the War in Vietnam* (As of 30 June 1968), 11-13. Hereafter cited as Sharp and Westmoreland, *Report.*

57. Speech made before the American Bar Association, New York, August 12, 1964, *Department of State Bulletin*, August 31, 1964, p. 300.

58. News Conference, September 14, 1964, *ibid.*, October 5, 1964, p. 470.

59. Radio and Television Report to the American People Following Renewed Aggression in the Gulf of Tonkin, August 4, 1964, Johnson, *Public Papers: 1963-1964*, II, 927-928.

60. Ernest Gruening and Herbert W. Beaser, *Vietnam Folly*, 470-471. See full statement of the attacks and Gulf of Tonkin Resolution in Johnson, *Vantage Point*, 112-120.

61. Special Message to the Congress on U.S. Policy in Southeast Asia, August 5, 1964, Johnson, *Public Papers: 1963-1964*, II, 932.

62. Cited in Steinberg, *Sam Johnson's Boy*, 764.

63. Interview with Walter Cronkite on CBS concerning halting the bombing, February 6, 1970. See also Johnson, *Vantage Point*, 118-119.

64. See review by E. W. Kenworthy of Joseph C. Goulden's *Truth is the First Casualty—The Gulf of Tonkin Affair: Illusion and Reality*, in *New York Times*, October 5, 1969. See also *The Pentagon Papers: The Defense Department History of United States Decisionmaking on Vietnam*, III, 183-192.

65. See accounts in *New York Times*, January 21 and 25, and February 4, 1968.

66. See brief account, *ibid.*, February 4, 1968.

67. *Ibid.*, August 9, 1964.

68. Speech to the American Bar Association, August 12, 1964, Johnson, *Public Papers: 1963-1964*, II, 953.

69. *Ibid.*, II, 953-954.

70. Remarks at Syracuse University on the Communist Challenge in Southeast Asia, August 5, 1964, *ibid.*, II, 929-930.

71. Statement of Senator Nelson, *New York Times*, October 6, 1964. Also see account in Gruening and Beaser, *Vietnam Folly*, 280-281.

72. Editorial, *New York Times*, October 8, 1964.

73. Sharp and Westmoreland, *Report*, 84 and 95. See also Johnson, *Vantage Point*, 137-143.

74. Robert Shaplen, *The Lost Revolution: The U.S. in Vietnam, 1946-1966*, 293.

75. *Ibid.*, 303-304.

76. U.S. Congress. Senate Committee on Foreign Relations, 89th Cong., 2d sess., January 6, 1966. *The Vietnam Conflict: The Substance and the Shadow.* Report of Senator Mansfield, et al. Hereafter: Mansfield, *Substance and Shadow.*

77. David Rees, *Korea: A Limited War*, 26.

78. U.S. Department of State. Bureau of Public Affairs. *The Question of a Formal Declaration of War in Viet-Nam*, 1.

79. Jacob K. Javits, "The Congressional Presence in Foreign Relations," *Foreign Affairs*, January 1970, p. 226.

80. *Ibid.*

81. *Question of a Formal Declaration*, 1.

82. *Ibid.*, 1-2.

83. *Ibid.*, 2.

84. *Ibid.*, 2-3.

85. *New York Times*, September 13, 1964. Also Kahin and Lewis, *U.S. in Vietnam*, 161.

86. Kahin and Lewis, *U.S. in Vietnam*, 161-163.

87. *Ibid.*, 163.

88. *Ibid.*

89. Steinberg, *Sam Johnson's Boy*, 769-771.

90. Sharp and Westmoreland, *Report*, 98-99.

91. See the account in Kahin and Lewis, *U.S. in Vietnam*, 181-183.

92. W. W. Rostow, *The Diffusion of Power: An Essay in Recent History*, 448.

93. *Ibid.*

94. *Ibid.*, 449.

95. Johnson, *Vantage Point*, 138.

96. *Ibid.*, 142-147.

97. *Ibid.*, 147.

98. *Ibid.*, 148.

99. *Ibid.*

100. *Ibid.*, 150-151.

101. *Ibid.*, 151-152.

102. James W. Fulbright, "The Fatal Arrogance of Power," *New York Times Magazine*, May 15, 1966.

103. Steinberg, *Sam Johnson's Boy*, 773.

104. *Ibid.*, 772.

105. *Ibid.*, 775.

106. News Conference of June 2, 1964, Johnson, *Public Papers: 1963-1964*, I. 733-734.

107. Steinberg, *Sam Johnson's Boy*, 776.

108. *Ibid.*, 776-777.

109. See biographies of Johnson: Rowland Evans and Robert Novak, *Lyndon B. Johnson: The Exercise of Power*, 541-544, and Steinberg, *Sam Johnson's Boy*, 776-777.

110. Sharp and Westmoreland, *Report*, 76.

111. *Ibid.*, 5.

Chapter Two

1. Rusk's Speech of February 25, 1965, "The Bases of American Policy," Richard P. Stebbins and Elaine P. Adam, eds., *Documents on American Foreign Relations, 1965*, pp. 131-133.

2. *Ibid.*, pp. 133-134.

3. Statement by the President, March 25, 1965, *ibid.*, pp. 135.

4. *Ibid.*, pp. 135-136.

5. Refers to a meeting in Cairo in October 1964 of delegates from Afghanistan, Algeria, Cyprus, Ceylon, Ethiopia, Ghana, Guinea, India, Iraq, Kenya, Nepal, Syria, Tunisia, Uganda, the United Arab Republic, Yugoslavia, Zambia and Uganda, *ibid.*, pp. 136-138.

6. Declaration of the Seventeen Non-aligned Countries, March 15, 1965, presented to the United States April 1, 1965, *ibid.*, pp. 136-138.

7. See United States Reply, April 8, 1965, *ibid.*, pp. 138-139.

8. *Ibid.*, pp. 139-140.

9. *Ibid.*, p. 140.

10. Stephen Pan and Daniel Lyons, *Vietnam Crisis*, 207.

11. Evans and Novak, *Lyndon B. Johnson*, 545.

12. See perceptive article by James Reston, *New York Times*, May 25, 1969.

13. "Statement by the National Liberation Front," March 22, 1965, Kahin and Lewis, *U.S. in Vietnam*, Appendix 12, 415-421.

14. "Pattern for Peace in Southeast Asia": Address by the President at Johns Hopkins University, Baltimore, April 7, 1965, Stebbins and Adam, eds., *Documents: 1965*, pp. 140-141.

15. *Ibid.*, p. 142.

16. *Ibid.*, pp. 142-143.

17. *Ibid.*, pp. 144-146.

18. Kahin and Lewis, *U.S. in Vietnam*, 211.

19. News Conference Statement by the President, June 17, 1965, Stebbins and Adam, eds., *Documents: 1965*, p. 165.

20. Rusk's Press Conference, June 18, 1965, *ibid.*, pp. 166-167.

21. *Ibid.*, p. 167.

22. News Conference Statement by the President, July 28, 1965, *ibid.*

23. "Four Steps to Peace": Address by Secretary Rusk before the American Foreign Service Association, Washington, June 23, 1965, *ibid.*, pp. 167-176.

24. Communist Terms for Negotiation: Statement by Pham Van Dong, Prime Minister of the Democratic Republic of Vietnam, April 8, 1965, *ibid.*, pp. 147-149.

25. See discussion in David Kraslow and Stuart H. Loory, *The Secret Search for Peace in Vietnam*, 37 and note. Also Kahin and Lewis, *U.S. in Vietnam*, 210 and note.

26. Pan and Lyons, *Vietnam Crisis*, 200-202.

27. · *Ibid.* Italics added by Pan and Lyons.

28. *Ibid.*, 202-203.

29. Steinberg, *Sam Johnson's Boy*, 777.

30. Supplemental Appropriation for Vietnam. Message from the President to the Congress, May 4, 1965, Stebbins and Adam, eds., *Documents: 1965*, pp. 158-159.

31. *Ibid.*, pp. 160-161.

32. *Ibid.*, p. 161.

33. *Ibid.*

34. Steinberg, *Sam Johnson's Boy*, 777-778.

35. Gruening and Beaser, *Vietnam Folly*, 297.

36. Rusk's "Four Steps to Peace" Speech of June 23, 1965, to the American Foreign Service Association, Stebbins and Adam, eds., *Documents: 1965*, pp. 170-171.

37. *Ibid.*, p. 174.

38. Presidential News Conference, July 28, 1965, *ibid.*, p. 181.

39. *Ibid.*, pp. 178-179.

40. *Ibid.*, pp. 185-186.

41. *Ibid.*, pp. 191-192.

42. Full Statement by Humphrey, *ibid.: 1966*, pp. 192-195.

43. *Ibid.*, pp. 193-194.

44. Steinberg, *Sam Johnson's Boy*, 779-780.

45. News Conference of July 28, 1965, Johnson, *Public Papers: 1965*, II, 794-803.

46. Steinberg, *Sam Johnson's Boy*, 780.

47. Conversation quoted in *ibid.*, 781.

48. *Ibid.*

49. Hoopes, *Limits*, 48-50. See also Johnson, *Vantage Point*, 240-241.

50. Steinberg, *Sam Johnson's Boy*, 781.

51. *Ibid.*

52. Hoopes, *Limits*, 49.

53. "Initiative for Peace," Statement by Arthur J. Goldberg, United States Representative to the General Assembly of the United Nations, Press Release, September 22, 1966, *Department of State Bulletin*, October 10, 1966, pp. 518-525.

54. *Ibid.*

Chapter Three

1. Shaplen, *Lost Revolution*, 357-358.

2. Steinberg, *Sam Johnson's Boy*, 782.

3. *Ibid.*, 783.

4. *Ibid.*

5. *Ibid.*, 783-784.

6. *Ibid.*, 784.

7. Johnson, *Vantage Point*, 233.

8. *Ibid.*, 250.

9. *Ibid.*, 233.

10. See a brief resume of the story taken from the four volumes of the *Pentagon Papers* first revealed by Jack Anderson, *New York Times*, June 28, 1972.

11. *Ibid.*

12. *Ibid.*

13. *Ibid.*

14. *Ibid.*

15. *Ibid.*

16. *Ibid.*

17. *Ibid.*

18. *Ibid.*

19. *Ibid.*

20. *Ibid.*

21. *Ibid.*

22. *New York Times*, June 28, 1972.

23. Gruening and Beaser, *Vietnam Folly*, 287.

24. *Ibid.*, 287-288.

25. *Ibid.*, 288-289.

26. *Ibid.*, 289-292.

27. Evans and Novak, *Lyndon B. Johnson*, 551.

28. Gruening and Beaser, *Vietnam Folly*, 292.

29. Mansfield, *Substance and Shadow*.

30. Gruening and Beaser, *Vietnam Folly*, 302.

31. Mansfield, *Substance and Shadow*.

32. Gruening and Beaser, *Vietnam Folly*, 302-303.

33. Annual Message to the Congress on the State of the Union, January 12, 1966, Johnson, *Public Papers: 1966*, I, 11.

34. Gruening and Beaser, *Vietnam Folly*, 303.

35. *Ibid.*

36. Letter to the Speaker Transmitting Proposed Supplemental Appropriations in Support of Operations in Southeast Asia, January 19, 1966, Johnson, *Public*

Papers: 1966, I, 32-33.

37. Gruening and Beaser, *Vietnam Folly,* 304.

38. Reply to a Letter from a Group of House Members Relating to the Situation in Vietnam, January 22, 1966, Johnson, *Public Papers: 1966,* I, 44-45.

39. Gruening and Beaser, *Vietnam Folly,* 305-306.

40. Reply to a Letter from a Group of Senators Relating to the Situation in Vietnam, January 28, 1966, Johnson, *Public Papers: 1966,* I, 112.

41. Evans and Novak, *Lyndon B. Johnson,* 563.

42. Gruening and Beaser, *Vietnam Folly,* 307-308.

43. *Ibid.,* 308.

44. *Ibid.,* 308-310.

45. *Ibid.,* 310-311.

46. *Ibid.,* 311.

47. Evans and Novak, *Lyndon B. Johnson,* 566-568.

48. The Declaration of Honolulu, February 8, 1966, Johnson, *Public Papers: 1966,* I, 153-155.

49. Steinberg, *Sam Johnson's Boy,* 786-787.

50. Gruening and Beaser, *Vietnam Folly,* 311.

51. Steinberg, *Sam Johnson's Boy,* 787-788.

52. *Ibid.,* 788.

53. *Ibid.,* 788-789.

54. Gruening and Beaser, *Vietnam Folly,* 312.

55. *Ibid.,* 313.

56. *Ibid.,* 313-314.

57. *Ibid.,* 314-315.

58. *Ibid.,* 316.

59. *Ibid.,* 317.

60. *Ibid.,* 319-320.

61. Ibid., 320.

62. Steinberg, *Sam Johnson's Boy,* 790.

63. *Ibid.*

64. *Ibid.,* 791.

65. *Ibid.*

66. *Ibid.,* 791-792.

67. *Ibid.,* 792-793.

68. Walter Cronkite, interview, CBS, February 6, 1970.

69. Steinberg, *Sam Johnson's Boy,* 793-794.

70. *Ibid.,* 794-795.

71. *Ibid.,* 795-796.

72. *Ibid.,* 796.

73. *Ibid.,* 796-797.

74. *Ibid.,* 797.

75. *Ibid.,* 799.

76. Johnson, *Vantage Point,* 240.

77. *Ibid.,* 240-241.

78. *Ibid.,* 245.

79. Steinberg, *Sam Johnson's Boy,* 800.

80. *Ibid.*

81. *Ibid.,* 801.

82. *Ibid.*

83. Johnson, *Public Papers: 1967*, I, 178.

84. Speech to the Foreign Policy Association, New York, November 14, 1967, Stebbins and Adam eds., *Documents: 1967*, pp. 27-28.

85. *Ibid.*, p. 28.

86. *Ibid.*, p. 29.

87. *Ibid.*, pp. 29-30.

88. Steinberg, *Sam Johnson's Boy*, 804.

89. *Ibid.*, 805-806.

90. *Ibid.*, 806-807.

91. *Ibid.*, 807.

92. *Ibid.*, 808.

93. Johnson, *Vantage Point*, 241-242.

94. Address on U.S. Policy in Vietnam Delivered Before a Joint Session of the Tennessee State Legislature, March 15, 1967, Johnson, *Public Papers: 1967*, I, 348-349.

95. Steinberg, *Sam Johnson's Boy*, 808.

96. Statement by the President on the New Constitution Adopted by the Constituent Assembly of the Republic of Vietnam, March 20, 1967, Johnson, *Public Papers: 1967*, I, 379-380.

97. Steinberg, *Sam Johnson's Boy*, 809.

98. *Ibid.*, 809-810.

99. *Ibid.*, 810.

100. *Ibid.*

101. *Ibid.*, 810-811.

102. *Ibid.*, 811.

103. *New York Times*, September 6, 1968.

104. Steinberg, *Sam Johnson's Boy*, 811.

105. *Ibid.*, 812-814.

106. *Ibid.*, 818-819.

107. *Ibid.*, 819.

108. *Ibid.*, 821-825.

109. *Ibid.*, 828.

110. *Ibid.*

111. See article by Robert F. Drinan, S.J., *Washington Post*, June 21, 1969.

112. Reaffirmation of United States Policy: Address by President Johnson Before the National Legislative Conference, San Antonio, Texas, September 29, 1967, Stebbins and Adam, eds., *Documents: 1967*, p. 242.

113. Johnson, *Vantage Point*, 267-268.

114. *New York Times*, September 22, 1968.

115. See brilliant study by Chester L. Cooper, *The Lost Crusade: America in Vietnam*. 330.

116. Steinberg, *Sam Johnson's Boy*, 830.

117. Hugh Sidey, *A Very Personal Presidency: Lyndon Johnson in the White House*, 218.

118. *New York Times*, January 1, 1969.

Chapter Four

1. See Johnson, "The Making of a Decision, Vietnam 1967-1968," *Vantage Point*, Chap. 17, pp. 365-424.

2. *Ibid.*, 369.

3. *Ibid.*, 369-370.

4. *Pentagon Papers,* IV, 107.

5. Cited in *ibid.,* IV, 116-117.

6. *Ibid.,* IV, 117.

7. *Ibid.,* IV, 126-127.

8. *Ibid.,* IV, 127-129.

9. *Ibid.,* IV, 128-132.

10. Johnson, *Vantage Point,* 372-373.

11. *Ibid.,* 373-374.

12. *Ibid.,* 376.

13. Cited in *ibid.,* 377.

14. *Ibid.,* 377-378.

15. *Ibid.,* 380.

16. See Clark M. Clifford, "A Viet Nam Reappraisal," *Foreign Affairs,* July 1969, p. 618.

17. Johnson, *Vantage Point,* 388-389.

18. Hedrick Smith, et al., "The Vietnam Policy Reversal of 1968," Part I, *New York Times,* March 6, 1969. The first of a two-part article, the second part of which appeared on March 7, 1969

19. Cronkite TV interview with President Johnson, CBS, February 2, 1970.

20. Smith, "Reversal," I, *New York Times,* March 6, 1969.

21. *Ibid.*

22. Johnson disclosed that "he never asked for a declaration of war against North Vietnam because he feared that some secret treaty would then automatically require Communist China or the Soviet Union to fight in defense of North Vietnam," *New York Times,* February 7, 1970.

23. Smith, "Reversal," I, *New York Times,* March 6, 1969.

24. *Ibid.* Within one month Johnson went from a policy of "no retreat" to disengagement (February 27, 1968, to March 31, 1968). See Don Oberdorfer, *Tet,* Chap. 8, "Turnaround," pp. 295-342.

25. Smith, "Reversal," I, *New York Times,* March 6, 1969.

26. On February 2, 1970, Johnson said Rusk, Rostow, and others played the major roles in advising the reversal. Television interview with Walter Cronkite on CBS.

27. Johnson, *Vantage Point,* 393.

28. Smith, "Reversal," I, *New York Times,* March 6, 1969.

29. Clifford, "Reappraisal," p. 609.

30. Smith, "Reversal," I, *New York Times,* March 6, 1969.

31. Clifford, "Reappraisal," pp. 609-610.

32. Rostow, *Diffusion of Power,* 520.

33. Hoopes, *Limits,* 173.

34. *Ibid.,* 174.

35. *Ibid.,* 174-175.

36. The attitude Clifford here stated the president appeared to contradict in his *Vantage Point* account; there he expressed concern that Clifford's review board took a negative approach to possible peace negotiations. See Johnson, *Vantage Point,* 398.

37. Smith, "Reversal," I, *New York Times,* March 6, 1969.

38. *Ibid.*

39. *Ibid.*

40. *Ibid.*

41. *Ibid.*

42. *Ibid.*
43. *Ibid.*
44. Clifford, "Reappraisal," pp. 610-611.
45. *Ibid.*, p. 611.
46. *Ibid.*, pp. 611-612.
47. *Ibid.*, pp. 612-613.
48. *Pentagon Papers,* IV, 568.
49. *Ibid.*, IV, 575-584.
50. *Ibid.*, IV, 586-587.
51. Clifford, "Reappraisal," p. 613.
52. Smith, "Reversal," I, *New York Times,* March 6, 1969.
53. *Ibid.*,
54. *Ibid.*
55. *Ibid.*
56. *Ibid.*
57. Hoopes, *Limits,* 182-183.
58. *Ibid.*, 183-184.
59. Smith, "Reversal," I, *New York Times,* March 6, 1969.
60. *Ibid.*, II, March 7, 1969.
61. *Ibid.*
62. *Ibid.*
63. *Ibid.*
64. *Ibid.*
65. Quotation of Max Lerner in Hoopes, *Limits,* 202-203.
66. *Ibid.*, 203-204.
67. *Ibid.*, 204-205.
68. *Ibid.*, 205.
69. Smith, "Reversal," II, *New York Times,* March 7, 1969.
70. *Ibid.*
71. *Ibid.*
72. *Ibid.*
73. *Ibid.*
74. *Ibid.*
75. *Ibid.*
76. *Ibid.*
77. *Ibid.*
78. The President's Address to the Nation Announcing Steps to Limit the War in Vietnam and Reporting His Decision Not to Seek Reelection," March 31, 1968, Johnson, *Public Papers: 1968,* I, 469-476.
79. Smith, "Reversal," II, *New York Times,* March 7, 1969.
80. Clifford, "Reappraisal," p. 613.
81. *Ibid.*, pp. 617-618.
82. *Ibid.*, pp. 618-619.
83. *Ibid.*, p. 619.
84. *Ibid.*
85. *Ibid.*, pp. 621-622.
86. Cited in Johnson, *Vantage Point,* 399.
87. *Ibid.*, 402-403.
88. *Ibid.*, 406-407.

89. *Ibid.*, 415.
90. *Ibid.*
91. *Ibid.*, 418.
92. *Ibid.*
93. Rostow, *Diffusion of Power*, 522.
94. Cited *ibid.*, 519.
95. *Ibid.*
96. *Ibid.*
97. Cited in *Pentagon Papers*, IV, 592.
98. *Ibid.*, IV, 603.
99. Johnson, *Vantage Point*, 422.
100. *Ibid.*, 422-423.
101. *Ibid.*, 423.
102. Clifford, "Reappraisal," p. 614.
103. Johnson, *Vantage Point*, 426-427.
104. See chap. 18, "A Beginning and an End: March 31, 1968," *ibid.*, 425-437.
105. News Conference, January 3, 1969, *New York Times*, January 4, 1969.
106. Clifford, "Reappraisal," p. 614.
107. *Ibid.*
108. *Ibid.*, p. 615.
109. *Pentagon Papers*, IV, 602-603.
110. Rostow, *Diffusion of Power*, 522-523.
111. *Ibid.*, 523-524.
112. See reports in *New York Times*, October 18, 1968.
113. *Ibid.*, January 10, 1971.
114. *Ibid.*
115. *Ibid.*
116. *Ibid.*, January 6, 1971.
117. *Ibid.*
118. *Ibid.*
119. Clifford, "Reappraisal," p. 615.
120. See reports in *New York Times*, October 18, 1968.
121. Clifford, "Reappraisal," pp. 615-616.
122. *Ibid.*
123. *Ibid.*, pp. 616-617.
124. *Ibid.*, p. 617.
125. *Ibid.*
126. Richard B. Morris and William Greenleaf, *U.S.A.: The History of a Nation*, II, 1132-1133.

Chapter Five

1. *New York Times*, August 3, 1969.
2. Excerpts from Unofficial Account of President Nixon's Meeting with Reporters, *ibid.*, July 26, 1969.
3. *Ibid.*
4. *Ibid.*
5. *Ibid.*, August 3, 1969.
6. *Ibid.*

7. Frank N. Trager, "The Nixon Doctrine and Asian Policy," *Southeast Asian Perspectives*, June 1972, pp. 1-34. "What began as a speech about 'Vietnamization' at Guam in July 1969 has been enlarged into a 'doctrine' set forth in three important documents issued as *Reports to the Congress* under the general title of *U.S. Foreign Policy for the 1970s*. Each has a subtitle: *A New Strategy for Peace* (February 18, 1970); *Building for Peace* (February 25, 1971); and *The Emerging Structure of Peace* (February 9, 1972)." *Ibid.*, pp. 2-3.

8. *New York Times*, July 29, 1969.

9. *Ibid.*

10. *Ibid.*, August 3, 1969.

11. *Ibid.*, January 11, 1970.

12. Address to the Nation on the War in Vietnam, November 3, 1969, *Public Papers of the Presidents of the United States*, Richard Nixon, 1969, pp. 905-906.

13. *New York Times*, January 11, 1970.

14. *Ibid.*

15. *Ibid.* August 3, 1969.

16. *Ibid.*

17. *Ibid.*, June 29, 1970.

18. *Ibid.*

19. Nixon and Thieu statements, *ibid.*, July 31, 1969.

20. *Ibid.*

21. *Ibid.*

22. Editorial, *ibid.*, August 5, 1969.

23. *Ibid.*, August 1, 1969.

24. *Washington Post*, August 18, 1969.

25. *New York Times*, August 5, 1969.

26. *U.S. News & World Report*, September 29, 1969, p. 32.

27. Marvin Kalb and Bernard Kalb, *Kissinger*, 140.

28. *Roanoke Times*, October 13, 1969.

29. *U.S. News & World Report*, October 6, 1969, p. 76.

30. See exchange of letters between the student and the president of October 13, 1969, *New York Times*, October 14, 1969.

31. Nixon's Address to the Nation, *ibid.*, May 15, 1969.

32. *Ibid.*, October 14, 1969.

33. *Ibid.*

34. *Ibid.*

35. Marvin Kalb and Bernard Kalb, *Kissinger*, 367-368.

36. *Ibid.*, 175.

37. *Ibid.*, 299.

38. See statement in *New York Times*, November 1, 1969.

39. *Ibid.*

40. Townsend Hoopes, "Legacy of the Cold War in Indochina," *Foreign Affairs*, July 1970, p. 613.

41. *New York Times*, February 15, 1970.

42. Marvin Kalb and Bernard Kalb, *Kissinger*, 142.

43. *New York Times*, October 29, 1969.

44. Address to the Nation on the War in Vietnam, November 3, 1969, Nixon, *Public Papers: 1969*, p. 901.

45. *Ibid.*, pp. 901-902.

46. *Ibid.*, p. 902.

47. *Ibid.*, pp. 902-903.

48. *Ibid.*, p. 908.

49. *Ibid.*, p. 903.

50. *Ibid.*, pp. 904-905.

51. *Ibid.*, pp. 905-906.

52. *Ibid.*

53. *Ibid.*, p. 906.

54. *Ibid.*, pp. 906-907.

55. *Ibid.*, p. 907.

56. *Ibid.*, p. 909.

57. Address to the Nation on Progress Toward Peace in Vietnam, December 15, 1969, *ibid.*, pp. 1025-1027.

58. *Ibid.*, p. 1026.

59. *Ibid.*, pp. 1026-1027.

60. *Ibid.*

61. *Ibid.*, pp. 1027-1028.

62. Annual Message to the Congress on the State of the Union, January 22, 1970, Nixon, *Public Papers: 1970*, p. 9.

63. First Annual Report to the Congress on United States Foreign Policy for the 1970's, February 18, 1970, *ibid.*, p. 116.

64. *Ibid.*, pp. 116-117.

65. *Ibid.*, p. 117.

66. *Ibid.*, p. 118.

67. *Ibid.*, p. 119.

68. *Ibid.*, pp. 144-145.

69. *Ibid.*, p. 147.

70. *Ibid.*, pp. 147-148.

71. *Ibid.*, pp. 148-149.

72. *Ibid.*, p. 150-151.

73. Marvin Kalb and Bernard Kalb, *Kissinger*, 131-133.

74. *Ibid.*, 172.

75. *Ibid.*, 148.

76. July 2 television interview with John Chancellor, Eric Sevareid and Howard K. Smith, *New York Times*, July 3, 1970.

77. *Ibid.*, November 6, 1970.

78. *Ibid.*, October 8, 1970.

79. Address to the Nation About a New Initiative for Peace in Southeast Asia, October 7, 1970, Nixon, *Public Papers: 1970*, p. 825.

80. *Ibid.*, pp. 825-826.

81. *Ibid.*, p. 826.

82. *Ibid.*, pp. 826-827.

83. *Ibid.*, p. 827.

84. *Ibid.*, p. 828.

85. *New York Times*, October 10, 1970.

86. *Ibid.*, October 8, 1970.

87. *Ibid.*

88. *Ibid.*, October 9, 1970.

89. *Ibid.*

90. *Ibid.*, February 19, 1970.

Chapter Six

1. News Conference, November 12, 1971, Nixon, *Public Papers: 1971*, p. 1103 and p. 1105.
2. News Conference, September 16, 1971, *ibid.*, p. 952.
3. *Ibid.*
4. *Ibid.*, pp. 952-953.
5. *New York Times,* October 16, 1971.
6. *Ibid.*, September 23, 1971.
7. *Ibid.*, January 4, 1972. Also see *ibid.*, January 5, 1972.
8. *Ibid.*, January 9, 1972.
9. *Ibid.*
10. *Ibid.*, January 19, 1972.
11. *Ibid.*, January 21, 1972.
12. *Ibid.*, January 30, 1972.
13. Address to the Nation Making Public a Plan for Peace in Vietnam, January 25, 1972, Nixon, *Public Papers: 1972*, pp. 100-101.
14. *Ibid.*, pp. 101-102.
15. *Ibid.*, p. 102.
16. *Ibid.*, pp. 102-103.
17. *Ibid.*, p. 103.
18. New peace proposal by the governments of the United States and South Vietnam for a negotiated settlement of the Indochina conflict as released by the White House, January 25, 1972, *New York Times,* January 26, 1972. Also in Nixon, *Public Papers: 1972*, pp. 105-106. See Appendix.
19. Address to the Nation, January 25, 1972, Nixon, *Public Papers: 1972*, pp. 103-104.
20. *Ibid.*, p. 104.
21. William Safire, *Before the Fall: An Inside View of the Pre-Watergate White House*, 401.
22. *Ibid.*
23. Hanoi's Nine-Point Plan, *New York Times,* February 1, 1972. See Appendix.
24. Vietcong Seven-Point Plan, *U.S. News & World Report,* February 7, 1972, p. 12. See Appendix.
25. From the Official Transcript of Kissinger's News Conference, January 26, 1972, *ibid.*, February 7, 1972, pp. 62-66.
26. *Ibid.*
27. "Why Does Hanoi Refuse to Make Peace?" *ibid.*, pp. 11-12.
28. *Ibid.*
29. See official statements by the delegations of North Vietnam and the Vietcong at the Paris talks, *New York Times,* Janaury 27, 1972.
30. *Ibid.*
31. *Ibid.*
32. *Ibid.*, February 4, 1972.
33. *Ibid.*, February 6, 1972.
34. *Ibid.*
35. *Ibid.*
36. *Ibid.*
37. See a lengthy discussion of the enemy's case, *ibid.*
38. See discussions in *U.S. News & World Report,* February 7, 1972.

39. See several reports in *New York Times*, February 11, 1972.

40. News Conference, February 10, 1972, Nixon, *Public Papers: 1972*, p. 352.

41. *Ibid.*

42. See accounts in *New York Times*, February 3 and 4, 1972.

43. *Ibid.*

44. *Ibid.*

45. *Ibid.*, February 8, 1972.

46. President Nixon's News Conference, February 10, 1972, *ibid.*, February 11, 1972.

47. *Ibid.*, April 16, 1972.

48. Address to the Nation on Vietnam, April 26, 1972, Nixon, *Public Papers: 1972*, pp. 550-551.

49. Safire, *Before the Fall*, 417. Kent State referred to the great tragedy on that Ohio college campus on May 2, 1970, when the national guard fired upon protesters against the war, killing four students and wounding several others.

50. Address to the Nation on Vietnam, April 26, 1972, Nixon, *Public Papers: 1972*, pp. 551-553.

51. *Ibid.*, pp. 553-554.

52. Testimony by Secretary of State William P. Rogers at the Senate Foreign Relations Committee Hearings, April 17, 1972, cited in *New York Times*, April 18, 1972.

53. *Ibid.*

54. Laird's position, *ibid.*

55. *Ibid.*, April 19, 1972.

56. Text of Statement by North Vietnam on 1968 Talks That Led to U.S. Bombing Halt, *ibid.*, April 21, 1972. See also *ibid.*, April 20, 1972.

57. *Ibid.*, April 22, 1972. See also Johnson, *Vantage Point*, 514-520.

58. Mark W. Clark, "Turning on the Heat in Vietnam," *ibid.*, September 1, 1972.

59. *Ibid.*

60. Marvin Kalb and Bernard Kalb, *Kissinger*, 346.

61. *Ibid.*, 310.

62. *New York Times*, April 19, 1972. See also Marvin Kalb and Bernard Kalb, *Kissinger*, 287-308.

63. *New York Times*, April 17, 1972.

64. *Ibid.*, April 19, 1972.

65. Steve Young, Letter to the Editor, April 4, 1972, *ibid.*, April 16, 1972.

66. *Ibid.*, May 2, 1972.

67. Nixon, *Public Papers: 1972*, pp. 559-560.

68. *New York Times*, May 7, 1972.

69. *Ibid.*

70. Address to the Nation on the Situation in Southeast Asia, May 8, 1972, Nixon, *Public Papers: 1972*, pp. 583-584.

71. *Ibid.*, pp. 584-585.

72. *Ibid.*, p. 585.

73. *Ibid.*, pp. 585-586.

74. *Ibid.*, 586.

75. Excerpts from Henry A. Kissinger's News Conference, May 9, 1972, on U.S.-North Vietnamese Exchanges, *New York Times*, May 10, 1972.

76. *Ibid.*

77. *Ibid.*

78. *Ibid.*

79. For additional evidence that the enemy could absorb our bombing damage and escalate his war effort, see Jason Summer Study, *Pentagon Papers*, IV, 115-120.

80. *U.S. News & World Report*, May 22, 1972, p. 29.

81. *New York Times*, May 10, 1972.

82. Kissinger's News Conference on U.S.-North Vietnamese Exchanges, May 9, 1972, *ibid.*

83. *Ibid.*

84. *Ibid.*

85. See a very perceptive article by Max Frankel, "New Nixon Strategy: Pressure on Moscow," *ibid.*

86. *Ibid.*

87. *Ibid.*

88. Kissinger's News Conference, May 9, 1972, *ibid.*, May 10, 1972.

89. See brilliant summary by Theodore C. Sorensen, aide to President Kennedy, "It Isn't the Cuban Missile Crisis," *ibid.*, May 12, 1972.

90. *Ibid.*

91. *Ibid.*, May 13, 1972.

92. Excerpts from a statement by Tho at a News Conference in Paris, May 12, 1972, *ibid.*

93. *Ibid.*, May 10, 1972.

94. *Ibid.*, May 13, 1972.

95. *Ibid.*

96. News Conference, June 29, 1972, Nixon, *Public Papers: 1972*, p. 707.

97. *Ibid.*, p. 716.

98. News Conference, July 27, 1972, *ibid.*, p. 746.

99. *Ibid.*, p. 748.

100. *Ibid.*, pp. 748-749.

101. *New York Times*, June 20, 1972.

Chapter Seven

1. See special section, "The Shape of Peace," *Time*, November 6, 1972, pp. 14-40.

2. *New York Times*, October 28, 1972.

3. *Ibid.*, September 12, 1972.

4. News Conference, October 5, 1972, Nixon, *Public Papers: 1972*, pp. 953-954.

5. *Ibid.*, p. 954.

6. *New York Times*, October 22, 1972.

7. *Ibid.*, November 5, 1972.

8. *Ibid.*

9. *Ibid.*, November 24, 1972.

10. Marvin Kalb and Bernard Kalb, *Kissinger*, 351-352.

11. *Ibid.*, 353.

12. See the October 26, 1972, announced Text of the North Vietnamese Statement on the Secret Negotiations with the U.S., *New York Times*, October 27, 1972.

13. *Ibid.*

14. *Ibid.*

15. Main points of the October 8, 1972, agreement summarized, *ibid.*

16. *Ibid.*

17. Transcript of Kissinger's News Conference on the Status of the Cease-Fire Talks," *ibid.*

18. *Ibid.*

19. *Ibid.*

20. *Ibid.*

21. *Ibid.*

22. *Ibid.*

23. *Ibid.*

24. "A Deal with Hanoi, a Duel with Thieu," *Newsweek,* October 30, 1972, pp. 24-25.

25. Text of the North Vietnamese Statement on the Secret Negotiations with the U.S., *New York Times,* October 27, 1972.

26. Marvin Kalb and Bernard Kalb, *Kissinger,* 369.

27. *Ibid.*

28. *New York Times,* October 27, 1972.

29. Text of the South Vietnamese Declaration at the Paris Peace Talks, *ibid.*

30. *Ibid.,* September 10, 1972.

31. *Ibid.,* October 29, 1972.

32. "A Deal with Hanoi, a Duel with Thieu," *Newsweek,* October 30, 1972, pp. 24-25.

33. *Ibid.*

34. President Nixon, talking informally with newsmen at the White House, February 15, 1973, *U.S. News & World Report,* February 26, 1973, p. 23.

35. "Could It Have Been Settled Sooner?" *Time,* November 6, 1972, p. 18.

36. Kissinger's News Conference, December 16, 1972, *New York Times,* December 17, 1972.

37. *Ibid.*

38. *Ibid.*

39. *Ibid.*

40. *Ibid.*

41. *Ibid.*

42. See text, *ibid.,* October 27, 1972.

43. Marvin Kalb and Bernard Kalb, *Kissinger,* 403-404.

44. *New York Times,* December 24, 1972.

45. "Why Vietnam War Drags On," *U.S. News & World Report,* January 1, 1973, pp. 9-12.

46. *Ibid.*

47. Safire, *Before the Fall,* 668.

48. *Ibid.,* 668-669.

49. *Ibid.,* 431.

50. "Why Vietnam War Drags On," *U.S. News & World Report,* January 1, 1973, p. 11.

51. Kissinger's News Conference, December 16, 1972, *New York Times,* December 17, 1972.

52. *Ibid.,* December 20, 1972.

53. *Ibid.,* December 31, 1972.

Chapter Eight

1. *New York Times,* January 6, 1973.
2. Kissinger's News Conference, January 24, 1973, *ibid.,* January 25, 1973.
3. "What Christmas Bombing Did to North Vietnam," *U.S. News & World Report,* February 5, 1973, p. 18.
4. *New York Times,* January 24, 1973.
5. *Ibid.,* January 18 and 19, 1973.
6. *Ibid.,* January 19, 1973.
7. Full published version of The Vietnam Agreement and Protocols, *ibid.,* January 25, 1973.
8. President's Proclamation, *ibid.,* January 27, 1973.
9. President Nixon's Address, January 23, 1973, *ibid.,* January 25, 1973.
10. Kissinger's News Conference, January 24, 1973, *ibid.*
11. *Ibid.*
12. *Ibid.*
13. Kissinger's News Conference, March 26, 1973, *ibid.,* March 27, 1975.
14. *Ibid.*
15. *Ibid.*
16. *Ibid.*
17. *Ibid.*
18. President Nixon's News Conference, March 15, 1973, *Ibid.,* March 16, 1973.
19. Kissinger's News Conference, February 22, *ibid.,* February 23, 1973.
20. Nixon's News Conference, March 2, 1973, *ibid.,* March 3, 1973.
21. *U.S. News & World Report,* April 9, 1973, p. 86.
22. See his statement in *Roanoke Times,* April 3, 1975.

Chapter Nine

1. See Mohandas K. Gandhi, *An Autobiography: The Story of My Experiment with Truth,* 318-319.
2. Quotation taken from notes transcribed by C. L. Sulzberger of his interview with President Nixon on March 8, 1971, *New York Times,* March 10, 1971.
3. Cooper, *Lost Crusade,* 425-427.
4. Bernard B. Fall, "Viet Nam in the Balance," *Foreign Affairs,* October 1966, pp. 15-16.
5. Sir Robert Thompson, *No Exit from Vietnam,* 62-63.
6. *Ibid.,* 60.
7. *Ibid.,* 59-61.
8. Arthur Schlesinger, Jr., "Vietnam and the End of the Age of Superpowers," *Harper's,* March 1969, p. 48.
9. *New York Times,* March 17, 1975.
10. Schlesinger, "Vietnam and the End of the Age of Superpowers," p. 46.
11. Cooper, *Lost Crusade,* 427-430.
12. C. L. Sulzberger's column, *New York Times,* March 3, 1971.
13. *Ibid.*
14. Cooper, *Lost Crusade,* pp. 264-266.
15. *Ibid.,* 437.
16. Charles W. Yost, "The United Nations: Crisis of Confidence and Will," *Foreign Affairs,* October 1966, pp. 19-26.

Chapter Ten

1. President's Proclamation, *New York Times,* May 8, 1975.
2. *Ibid.,* March 31, 1975.
3. *Ibid.*
4. *Roanoke Times,* April 27, 1975.
5. *Ibid.*
6. See resume of these events by Malcolm W. Browne, *New York Times,* March 31, 1975.
7. *New York Times,* April 3 and 16, 1975.
8. *Ibid.,* April 12, 1975.
9. *Ibid.,* April 6 and 9, 1975.
10. President Ford's News Conference, *ibid.,* April 4, 1975.
11. *Ibid.*
12. *Ibid.*
13. *Ibid.*
14. *Ibid.,* April 24, 1975.
15. See speech of April 21, 1975, and account in *ibid.,* April 22, 1975.
16. *Ibid.,* April 12, 1975.
17. The letters were made public April 30 by Nguyen Tien Hung, former aide to President Thieu, *ibid.,* May 1, 1975.
18. *Ibid.,* May 21, 1975.
19. *Ibid.,* May 2, 1975.
20. *Ibid.*
21. *Ibid.*
22. *Ibid.,* April 11, 1975.
23. The following perceptive account is by David K. Shipler, *New York Times* Saigon correspondent for nineteen months, *New York Times,* April 27, 1975.
24. *Ibid.*
25. *Ibid.*
26. *Ibid.,* February 10, 1975.
27. *Ibid.*
28. Shipler, *ibid.,* April 27, 1975.
29. *Ibid.,* April 18, 1975.
30. *Ibid.,* April 22, 1975.
31. See excerpts of President Ford's New Orleans speech, *ibid.,* April 24, 1975.
32. *Ibid.*
33. *Ibid.*
34. Fox Butterfield, "How South Vietnam Died—by the Stab in the Front," *New York Times Magazine,* May 25, 1975.
35. *New York Times,* April 26, 1975.
36. *Ibid.,* April 18, 1975.
37. *Ibid.,* April 30, 1975.
38. *Ibid.,* May 19, 1975.
39. *Ibid.,* April 30, 1975.
40. *Ibid.,* May 12, 1975.
41. *Ibid.,* March 29, 1975.
42. *Ibid.*
43. *Ibid.,* May 17, 1975.

44. *Ibid.*, April 7, 1975.
45. *Ibid.*, April 8, 1975.
46. *Ibid.*, April 6, 1975.
47. *Ibid.*, March 31, 1975.
48. James Thompson, *ibid.*, April 10, 1975.
49. *Ibid.*, April 24, 1975.
50. Howard Wriggins, Letter to the Editor, *ibid.*, May 6, 1975.
51. See very perceptive article by Malcolm W. Browne, "How Did It Happen? Some Replies," *ibid.*, April 24, 1975.
52. *Ibid.*
53. *Ibid.*
54. *Ibid.*
55. Maxwell Taylor, "The 'Vietnam Disaster' and U.S. Security," *ibid.*, May 9, 1975.
56. *Ibid.*, May 14, 1975.

Appendix I
Nixon's Peace Proposal, January 25, 1972

1. *New York Times,* January 26, 1972.

Appendix II
Hanoi's Secret Nine-Point Plan, June 6, 1971

1. *New York Times,* February 1, 1972.

Appendix III
Vietcong Seven-Point Plan, July 1, 1971

1. *U.S. News & World Report,* February 7, 1972, p. 12.

BIBLIOGRAPHY

Books

American Policy Vis-A-Vis Vietnam: In Light of Our Constitution, the United Nations Charter, the 1954 Geneva Accords, and the Southeast Asia Collective Defense Treaty. Memorandum of Law prepared by Lawyers Committee on American Policy Towards Vietnam, 38 Park Row, New York, 1965.

Boettiger, John R., ed. *Vietnam and American Foreign Policy.* Boston: D. C. Heath and Company, 1968.

Brandon, Henry. *The Retreat of American Power.* New York: Delta, 1974.

Brelis, Dean. *The Face of South Vietnam.* Boston: Houghton Mifflin, 1968.

Browne, Malcolm W. *The New Face of War.* New rev. ed. Indianapolis: Bobbs-Merrill, 1968.

Cooper, Chester L. *The Lost Crusade: America in Vietnam.* New York: Dodd, Mead & Co., 1970.

Council on Foreign Relations. *The United States in World Affairs.* New York: Harper & Row, 1956-1967.

Draper, Theodore. *Abuse of Power.* New York: The Viking Press, 1967.

Eden, Sir Anthony. *Toward Peace in Indochina.* Boston: Houghton Mifflin, 1966.

Evans, Rowland, and Robert Novak. *Lyndon B. Johnson: The Exercise of Power.* New York: New American Library, 1966.

Fulbright, James W. *The Arrogance of Power.* New York: Random House, 1966.

____. *The Vietnam Hearings.* New York: Vintage, 1966.

Galula, David. *Counter-Insurgency Warfare: Theory and Practice.* New York: Frederick A. Praeger, 1964.

Gandhi, Mohandas K. *An Autobiography: The Story of My Experiments with Truth.* Boston: Beacon Press, 1959.

Gettleman, Marvin E., ed. *Vietnam: History, Documents, and Opinions on a Major World Crisis.* New York: Fawcett, 1965.

Geyelin, Philip L. *Lyndon B. Johnson and the World.* New York: Frederick A. Praeger, 1966.

Giap, Vo Nguyen. *People's War People's Army, The Viet Cong Insurrection Manual for Underdeveloped Countries.* New York: Frederick A. Praeger, 1965.

Goulden, Joseph C. *Truth Is the First Casualty—The Gulf of Tonkin Affair, Illusion and Reality.* Chicago: Rand McNally & Company, 1969.

Gruening, Ernest, and Herbert W. Beaser. *Vietnam Folly*. Washington, D.C.: The National Press, 1968.

Gurtov, Melvin. *Southeast Asia Tomorrow: Problems and Prospects for U.S. Policy*. Baltimore: The Johns Hopkins Press, 1970.

Halberstam, David. *The Best and the Brightest*. Greenwich, Conn.: Fawcett, 1973.

Hammer, Richard. *The Court-Martial of Lt. Calley*. New York: Coward, McCann & Geoghegan, 1971.

Hersh, Seymour M. *My Lai 4*. New York: Random House, 1970.

Higgins, Marguerite. *Our Vietnam Nightmare*. New York: Harper & Row, 1965.

Hoopes, Townsend. *The Limits of Intervention: An Inside Account of How the Johnson Policy of Escalation Was Reversed*. New York: The McKay Company, 1969.

Johnson, Lyndon Baines. *The Vantage Point: Perspectives of the Presidency, 1963-1969*. New York: Holt, Rinehart and Winston, 1971.

Kahin, George McTurnan, and John W. Lewis. *The United States in Vietnam*. New York: Delta Books, 1967.

Kalb, Marvin, and Bernard Kalb. *Kissinger*. Boston: Little, Brown and Company, 1974.

Kraslow, David and Stuart H. Loory. *The Secret Search for Peace in Vietnam*. New York: Vintage, 1968.

McCarthy, Mary. *Vietnam*. New York: Harcourt, Brace & World, 1967.

Mecklin, John. *Mission in Torment*. New York: Doubleday & Company, 1965.

Morris, Richard B., and William Greenleaf. *U.S.A.: The History of a Nation*. 2 vols. Chicago: Rand McNally & Company, 1969.

Nighswonger, William A. *Rural Pacification in Vietnam*. Praeger Special Studies in International Politics and Public Affairs. New York, 1966.

Oberdorfer, Don. *Tet*. New York: Avon, 1972.

Osborne, Milton E. *Strategic Hamlets in South Viet-Nam: A Survey and a Comparison*. Data Paper 55. Ithaca, N.Y.: Cornell Southeast Asia Program, 1965.

Pan, Stephen, and Daniel Lyons, *Vietnam Crisis*. New York: Twin Circle Publishing Company, 1967.

Paret, Peter, and John W. Shy. *Guerrillas in the 1960's*. New York: Frederick A. Praeger, 1966.

Pfeffer, Richard, ed. *No More Vietnams? The War and the Future of American Foreign Policy*. New York: Harper & Row, 1968.

Pike, Douglas. *Viet Cong, The Organization and Techniques of the National Liberation Front of South Vietnam*. Cambridge, Mass.: The M.I.T. Press, 1966.

Rees, David. *Korea: The Limited War*. New York: The Macmillan Company, 1964.

Reischauer, Edwin O. *Beyond Vietnam: The United States and Asia*. New York: Vintage, 1967.

Rostow, W. W. *The Diffusion of Power: An Essay in Recent History*. New York: The Macmillan Company, 1972.

Safire, William. *Before the Fall: An Inside View of the Pre-Watergate White House*. New York: Doubleday & Company, 1975.

Schlesinger, Arthur M., Jr. *The Bitter Heritage: Vietnam and American Democracy, 1941-1966*. Boston: Houghton Mifflin, 1967.

Schurmann, Franz, et al. *The Politics of Escalation in Vietnam*. Greenwich, Conn.: Fawcett, 1966.

Scigliano, Robert, and Guy H. Fox. *Technical Assistance in Vietnam: The Michigan State University Experience*. New York: Frederick A. Praeger, 1965.

Shaplen, Robert. *The Lost Revolution, The U.S. in Vietnam 1946-1966.* First Harper Colophon ed. New York: Harper & Row, 1966.

Sidey, Hugh. *A Very Personal Presidency: Lyndon Johnson in the White House.* New York: Atheneum, 1968.

Sorensen, Theodore C. *The Kennedy Legacy.* New York: The Macmillan Company, 1969.

Stebbins, Richard P. *The United States in World Affairs, 1967.* New York: Simon and Schuster, 1968.

Steinberg, Alfred. *Sam Johnson's Boy, A Close-Up of the President from Texas.* New York: The Macmillan Company, 1968.

Stone, I. F. *In a Time of Torment.* New York: Random House, 1967.

Taylor, Telford. *Nuremberg and Viet-Nam: An American Tragedy.* Chicago: Quadrangle, 1970.

Thompson, Sir Robert. *Defeating Communist Insurgency, The Lessons of Malaya and Vietnam.* New York: Frederick A. Praeger, 1966.

_____. *No Exit from Vietnam.* New York: The David McKay Company, 1969.

Zagoria, Donald S. *Vietnam Triangle, Moscow, Peking, Hanoi.* New York: Pegasus, 1967.

Articles

Clifford, Clark. "Viet Nam Reappraisal," *Foreign Affairs,* July 1969.

Cooper, Chester L. "Vietnam: The Complexities of Negotiation," *Foreign Affairs,* April 1968.

Fall, Bernard B. "Viet Nam in the Balance," *Foreign Affairs,* October 1966.

Fulbright, James W. "The Fatal Arrogance of Power," *New York Times Magazine,* May 15, 1966.

Halberstam, David. "Return to Vietnam," *Harper's Magazine,* December, 1967.

Hoopes, Townsend. "Legacy of the Cold War in Indochina," *Foreign Affairs,* July 1970.

_____. "The Fight for the President's Mind," *Atlantic,* October 1969.

Javits, Jacob K. "The Congressional Presence in Foreign Relations," *Foreign Affairs,* January 1970.

Kissinger, Henry A. "The Viet Nam Negotiations," *Foreign Affairs,* January 1969.

Kristol, Irving. "We Can't Resign as 'Policeman of the World,' " *New York Times Magazine,* May 12, 1968.

Nixon, Richard M. "Asia after Viet Nam," *Foreign Affairs,* October 1967.

Scheer, Robert, and Warren Hinckle, "The Vietnam Lobby," *Ramparts,* July 1965.

Schlesinger, Arthur M., Jr. "Vietnam and the End of the Age of Superpowers," *Harper's Magazine,* March 1969.

Trager, Frank N. "The Nixon Doctrine and Asian Policy," *Southeast Asian Perspectives,* June 1972.

Yost, Charles W. "The United Nations: Crisis of Confidence and Will," *Foreign Affairs,* October 1966.

Documents

Public Papers of the Presidents of the United States. Lyndon B. Johnson. 1963-1969. 10 vols., Washington, D.C.: Government Printing Office, 1965-1970.

Public Papers of the Presidents of the United States. Richard Nixon. 1969-1972. 4 vols. Washington, D.C.: Government Printing Office, 1971-74.

Sharp, U. S. G., and W. C. Westmoreland. *Report on the War in Vietnam* (As of 30 June 1968). Washington, D.C.: Government Printing Office, 1968.

Stebbins, Richard P., and Elaine P. Adam, eds., *Documents on American Foreign Relations, 1965-1966.* 2 vols. New York: Harper & Row, 1966-67.

_____. *Documents on American Foreign Relations, 1967,* New York: Simon and Schuster, 1968.

The Pentagon Papers: The Defense Department History of United States Decisionmaking on Vietnam. 4 vols. The Senator Gravel Edition. Boston: Beacon Press, 1971.

U.S. Congress. Senate. Committee on Foreign Relations, 89th Cong. 1st sess. January 14, 1965. *Background Information Relating to Southeast Asia and Vietnam.* Washington, D.C.: Government Printing Office, 1965.

_____. Hearings, 90th Cong., 1st sess. February 21, 1967. *Conflicts between United States Capabilities and Foreign Commitments,* Lt. Gen. James M. Gavin (U.S. Army Retired). Washington, D.C.: Government Printing Office, 1967.

_____. Hearings, 90th Cong. 1st sess. February 2, 1967. *Harrison Salisbury's Trip to North Vietnam.* Washington, D.C.: Government Printing Office, 1967.

_____. Hearings, 90th Cong. 2d sess. February 20, 1968. *The Gulf of Tonkin, The 1964 Incidents.* Washington, D.C.: Government Printing Office, 1968.

_____. 90th Cong. 2d sess. 1968. *The Gulf of Tonkin, The 1964 Incidents,* Part II, Supplementary Documents. Washington, D.C.: Government Printing Office, 1968.

_____. *The Heart of the Problem.* Statements by Secretary Rusk and Gen. Maxwell D. Taylor before the Senate Committee on Foreign Relations, Department of State Publication 8054, Far Eastern Series 146. Washington, D.C.: Government Printing Office, March 1966.

_____. *The Legality of United States Participation in the Defense of Viet-Nam.* Legal memorandum submitted by Leonard D. Meeker. Washington, D.C.: Government Printing Office, 1966.

_____. Hearings, 88th Cong., 2d sess., August 6, 1964. *The Southeast Asia Resolution.* Washington, D.C.: Government Printing Office, 1966.

_____. 89th Cong., 2d sess., January 6, 1966. *The Vietnam Conflict: The Substance and the Shadow.* Report of Senator Mansfield et al. Washington, D.C.: Government Printing Office, 1966.

U.S. Department of State. *Aggression from the North: The Record of North Viet-Nam's Campaign to Conquer South Viet-Nam.* Washington, D.C.: Government Printing Office, February, 1965.

_____. Bureau of Public Affairs. Historical Division. *American Foreign Policy: Current Documents, 1961.* Washington, D.C.: Government Printing Office, 1965.

_____. *Bulletin,* Washington, D.C.: Government Printing Office, 1964-1967.

_____. *Initiative for Peace,* Washington, D.C.: Government Printing Office, October 1966.

_____. *The Issue in Viet-Nam.* George W. Ball. Washington, D.C.: Government Printing Office, March 1966.

_____. *The Pledge of Honolulu.* Washington, D.C.: Government Printing Office, March 1966.

_____. *The Question of a Formal Declaration of War in Viet-Nam.* Public Information Series. n.d.

_____. *United States Policy in Viet-Nam.* Robert S. McNamara. Washington, D.C.: Government Printing Office, May 1964.

Periodicals and Newspapers

Atlantic
Foreign Affairs
Harper's Magazine
Newsweek
New York Times
Ramparts
Roanoke Times
Southeast Asian Perspectives
Time
U.S. News & World Report
Washington Post

INDEX